PENGUIN BOOKS

THE GOOD BOATMAN

Born in 1935, Rajmohan Gandhi, biographer, commentator and a former Member of Parliament, is currently Research Professor with the Centre for Policy Research, New Delhi. He has written the lives of Chakravarti Rajagopalachari (1878–1972), India's first Indian Governor-General, Vallabhbhai Patel (1875–1950), Gandhi's colleague in the freedom movement and Deputy Prime Minister of India, 1947–50, and a study of the Hindu-Muslim relationship, *Understanding the Muslim Mind*.

PENGUIN BOOKS
THE GOOD BOATMAN

Born in 1935, Rajmohan Gandhi, biographer, columnist and a former Member of Parliament, is currently Research Professor with the Centre for Policy Research, New Delhi. He has written the lives of Chakravarti Rajagopalachari (1878–1972), India's first Indian Governor-General, Vallabhbhai Patel (1875–1950), Gandhi's colleague in the freedom movement and Deputy Prime Minister of India 1947–50, and a study of the Hindu-Muslim relationship, Understanding the Muslim Mind.

RAJMOHAN GANDHI

The Good Boatman

A Portrait of Gandhi

PENGUIN BOOKS

Penguin Books India (P) Ltd., 210 Chiranjiv Tower, 43 Nehru Place,
New Delhi 110 019 India
Penguin Books Ltd., 27 Wrights Lane, London W8 5TZ, UK
Penguin Books USA Inc., 375 Hudson Street, New York, New York 10014, USA
Penguin Books Australia Ltd., Ringwood, Victoria, Australia
Penguin Books Canada Ltd., 10 Alcorn Avenue, Suite 300, Toronto,
Ontario, MAV 3B2, Canada
Penguin Books (NZ) Ltd., 182-190 Wairau Road, Auckland, 10, New Zealand

First published in VIKING by Penguin Books India 1995
First published in Penguin by Penguin Books India 1997

Copyright © Rajmohan Gandhi 1995

All rights reserved

10 9 8 7 6 5 4 3 2 1

Published under the auspices of the Centre for Policy Research, New Delhi

Typeset in *Times Roman* by R. Ajith Kumar

This book is sold subject to the condition that it shall not, by way of trade
or otherwise, be lent, resold, hired out, or otherwise circulated without the
publisher's prior written consent in any form of binding or cover other than
that in which it is published and without a similar condition including this
condition being imposed on the subsequent purchaser and without limiting
the rights under copyright reserved above, no part of this publication may
be reproduced, stored in or introduced into a retrieval system, or transmitted
in any form or by any means (electronic, mechanical, photocopying,
recording or otherwise), without the prior written permission of both the
copyright owner and the above-mentioned publisher of this book.

To all who prize freedom without hate,
including Nelson R. Mandela, the Dalai Lama, and
Aung San Suu Kyi

Contents

Contents

Preface

GANDHI'S REPUTED ELUSIVENESS, frequently expressed in the question, "Was he a saint or a politician?" and embodied in extreme form in the observation, 'The man of insight to lay bare Gandhi's soul has not yet arisen,'[1] is one reason for this attempt. Several biographers of Gandhi have concurred with the view of some of the Raj's Viceroys that Gandhi's was a difficult personality to get a hold on. And they have done so even though few persons in this century were so closely watched and scrutinized as Gandhi was. This study seeks, in all humility, to comprehend Gandhi — to understand him in his heart.

There was also a personal need for clarity. For years, ever since my childhood, he has been both a wonder and a weight. When, as a twelve-year-old grandson, I saw his body in Birla House, I half expected him to stand up and start walking. Even on the train from Delhi that was taking to Triveni in Allahabad his ashes that I had assisted in collecting, I thought he might break out whole and alive from the pot containing the ashes. It was only when the vessel was emptied into the river waters that I accepted the end.

His effect is not dead. In India and in other lands, Gandhi means much to people, and numerous have been the efforts and struggles influenced by him. In 1975-7, almost thirty years after his death, Gandhi was a rallying point for the movement against the Emergency in India. Most Indian political parties, from the Left to the Right, secular parties as well as 'religious' ones, invoke his name from time to time. He is a metaphor and a standard. When the Babri Masjid was razed in December 1992, the unhappiness of many was expressed in likening the shock to the killing of Gandhi forty-five years earlier.

---

[1] Quoted by C.S. Venkatachar in Philips and Wainwright (ed.), *The Partition of India*, Allen & Unwin, London, 1970, p.473.

President Corazon Aquino of the Philippines told me in 1988 of what Gandhi had meant to her late husband. In 1993, a Russian novelist spoke to me of the decisive difference between a Lenin who, at the start of his revolution, dismissed as inconsequential the murder of two political opponents, and a Gandhi who stopped a nationwide campaign when the Raj's policemen were killed in Chauri Chaura.

In Warsaw in 1991, a Polish senator described to me the pro-democracy impact of Attenborough's film on Gandhi when his country was under dictatorship. In Pietermaritzburg in South Africa, I saw, in 1993, Blacks, Whites and Indians gathering for encouragement at a Gandhi statue. An academic from Georgia said to me in May this year that Gandhi is an inspiration to people struggling for peace and democracy in their land in the Caucasus. And so on; the list, as they say, is only illustrative.

Institutes for the study and application of nonviolence and for conflict-resolution have multiplied across the world; many of them draw some or much inspiration from Gandhi.

I have marvelled, but I have also been troubled. Gandhi wanted us to turn the searchlight inwards, and that is seldom wholly pleasant, for most of us hide unattractive corners. He disturbed in other ways too. The lifestyle he prescribed seemed too severe, and some of his practices seemed strange. If I wanted to understand him fully, I also needed to face him fully.

Again, Gandhi was a key figure in the biographies I had done. Two of my subjects, Vallabhbhai Patel and C. Rajagopalachari, took him as their master for much of their lives, and a third, M.A. Jinnah, saw him as a rival and a foe. Coming across Gandhi so often and in so many interesting situations, I felt I had to study him for himself.

More important, however, were the questions on several minds, including my own. A crucial one was linked to Gandhi's failure to free India in unity, a goal that seemed to mean so much to him. Then there was the great violence in the subcontinent towards the end of Gandhi's life, a life which had been dedicated to nonviolence. Why the violence occurred and why Gandhi was unable to prevent it were questions I wanted to go into.

The nature of Gandhi's God and of his ethics, just where he stood on caste and untouchability, the individuals and incidents that linked him to African-American leaders and, after his death, to Martin Luther King Jr., the meaning and significance of *Hind Swaraj,* why he preferred Nehru over Patel and other candidates for the political succession in India — these are among the questions this study examines. It focuses, too, on the last years of his life, which saw fulfilment and tragedy both.

This study is a product of my association, begun in July 1992, with the Centre for Policy Research (CPR), New Delhi. It would not have come about but for CPR's role. My sincerest thanks go to V.A. Pai Panandiker, its Director. Of course, I alone am responsible for the opinions expressed in this work, and for any errors that might have entered it.

Part of this work was also done at the Institute for Conflict Analysis and Resolution (ICAR) in George Mason University, Fairfax, Virginia, where I was the Bryant Wedge Visiting Professor for Spring 1995. Christopher Mitchell, ICAR's Director when I was offered the visiting professorship, and his successor, Kevin Clements, were considerate in letting me devote much of my time to completing this study.

Help also came from the Jayaprakash Institute of Human Freedoms, Bombay, headed by Nani Palkhivala. I acknowledge it with appreciation and gratitude.

For permission to quote Gandhi's writings, I thank the Navajivan Trust, Ahmedabad.

Multiplying my indebtedness to her, my wife Usha once more backed me — secretarially, with research, by obtaining, preserving and retrieving information, and in other ways.

The material available in the Nehru Memorial Library and the Gandhi Sangrahalaya, both in New Delhi, was of immense assistance, and Haridev Sharma, the Nehru Library's Deputy Director, provided valuable leads and support.

I pray that this study contributes to a truer understanding of Gandhi and the great issues he wrestled with, and with which we and our children too must wrestle.

8 June 1995
New Delhi

R.G.

Introduction

CONCEIVED AS AN inquiry for students of Gandhi, this work seemed also to produce a portrait to interest the general reader. Since most people think they know him but in fact do not, it is perhaps desirable that they should find here the Gandhi with his clarities and confusions, strengths and weaknesses, triumphs and failures — in short, the real, complex Gandhi — rather than the simplified Father of the Nation and apostle of nonviolence frozen in statues or reduced to a few predictable strokes of an artist's pen.

It may be useful to provide here a brief sketch of Gandhi's life. Born in 1869 in the coastal town of Porbandar, the last offspring of Karamchand ('Kaba') and Putlibai (or Putliba) Gandhi, Mohandas was married at the age of thirteen to Kasturbai (or Kasturba), a girl his age and of the same caste of Modh Vanias (Banias). A shy and in some ways fearful lad with a precocious conscience and a strong will, Mohan was more of a leader among his classmates and friends than he reveals in his autobiography, and seemed to have a remote sense that life would demand much of him.

Like his father Uttamchand, Karamchand was 'Prime Minister' or chief administrator of the princely state of Porbandar, and served also as the Prime Minister of Rajkot state. The fact that Mohandas, a diligent nurse to his father, was in bed with his young wife at the moment of Kaba Gandhi's death was a shame he could never forget. Another significant event in his youth was his departure for England to study law in the teeth of strong opposition from his caste and family, which melted a little when Mohandas swore solemnly that he would abjure meat, liquor and women in England.

He was nineteen, the father of a boy and had little practice of speaking or writing English when he sailed for London. Three years later he returned a Barrister, speaking of 'dear London' and the friends he had left behind, and glad at having kept his vows. In his autobiography he writes of a spiritual interest quickened in London, but there is evidence that Indian self-respect too was tugging at him.

On returning to India in the summer of 1891 he heard that his mother was no more. Lack of success in Bombay's courtrooms was a second shock. Some months later came a third: Gandhi was forcibly removed from the Rajkot office of the British political agent in Kathiawad. In the circumstances, Gandhi was only too glad to accept an offer of legal work in South Africa from a Porbandar firm doing business in that land.

South Africa, where he finally spent twenty-one years (1893-1914) instead of the twelve months to which he had first committed himself, seemed to change him. There the young Gandhi spoke out, in the courtroom and outside, against the discrimination faced by the multilingual, multi-religious Indian community of indentured workers, traders and clerks, organized the community, initiated the Natal Indian Congress, started *Indian Opinion*, founded his earliest Ashrams, first in Natal and then in the Transvaal, embraced (with help from Leo Tolstoy and John Ruskin) the idea of bread labour, and discovered a way of fighting, named satyagraha by him, in which the fighter preferred accepting suffering to inflicting it.

A positive result of the mistreatment meted out to him and other Indians in South Africa was that it sharpened Gandhi's understanding of the misery of India's untouchables. In 1906, in the hills and valleys of the Zulu country, Gandhi resolved in favour of poverty and brahmacharya or chastity, and also to widen, almost indefinitely, the meaning of family — to include, if possible, all of India in it.

During visits to India in 1896 and 1901-2, he travelled extensively, acquainted leading personalities with the plight and struggles of their compatriots in South Africa, and attended, in Calcutta, a session of the Indian National Congress, which had been founded in 1885. By 1909-10 many in India had heard of Gandhi; Joseph Doke's biography of an under-forty Gandhi was published in 1909; at the Lahore Congress the same year, one of the body's most eminent figures, Gopal Krishna Gokhale, who had received Gandhi in 1896 and hosted him in 1901-2, spoke of him in extraordinary terms; and in 1910 there was talk of making Gandhi President of Congress in India.

Hind Swaraj, Gandhi's manifesto in defence of the civilization, unity and liberty of India, presenting nonviolent struggle as the way suited to India's genius and censuring the West's civilization as violent and materialistic, was published in 1909-10. The years between 1908 and 1914 saw satyagraha campaigns in South Africa in which virtually every section of the Indian community took part, women as well as men, and which resulted in prison terms for Gandhi and hundreds of his colleagues. They also saw encounters between Gandhi and the South African leader, Jan Smuts, and significant if partial victories for the Indian community.

The India to which Gandhi returned in January 1915 was one from which Britain was seeking recruits for the world war that was on. It was also an India disliking alien rule. But the great reality facing Gandhi was that distrust of fellow-Indians was a sentiment equally strong and pervasive. India seemed crippled by untouchability and divided by religion, caste and class, with each section soliciting the Raj's intervention in its favour and against a rival section.

Until 1919-20, Gandhi sought Indian freedom within the British Empire. In his autobiography he claimed that he hardly knew 'anybody to cherish such loyalty as I did' to the Empire. With 'careful perseverance' he learnt the tune of 'God Save the Queen,' 'always joined in the singing whenever it was sung,' and taught it to his children. By the summer of 1920 he was the Empire's most resolute rebel.

Rulers of princely states, landlords with large holdings and Untouchable and Muslim leaders were, however, wary of Indian independence; they feared it would be rule by classes, castes or communities inimical to their interests. If they combined their resources and numbers, the groups susceptible to such fears were capable of blocking a freedom movement. Gandhi prevented such a coming together by allaying the fears of rulers and landlords, persuading the Untouchables that Hindu society was changing, and assuring some Muslims for all time and many Muslims for some time that Indian freedom would not mean Hindu Raj.

He was aided in his efforts by his ascetic life style, identification with all Indians, systematic condemnation of untouchability and all notions of high-and-low, and a stress on nonviolence joined with a readiness to say 'No' to the Raj. Also at work was the conviction that India could demonstrate nonviolence to the world, and a self-confidence revealed in a 1931 statement he made in London: 'We have problems that would baffle any statesman. We have problems that other nations have not to tackle. But they do not baffle me.'[1]

Gandhi's persistence in identifying and tackling Indian (and not just British) weaknesses and his championing of the needs of the underdog won the world's attention. Satyagrahas he conducted in 1917 in North Bihar (in defence of indigo-growing peasants), in 1918 in Ahmedabad (on behalf of textile workers) and Gujarat's Kheda district (over the land tax on peasants), and in 1919 against all-India curbs on expression embodied in the Rowlatt Act of that year, brought Gandhi centre-stage in Indian politics.

In 1920 Muslim resentment at what was seen as the betrayal of a British promise in relation to Turkey flared up just when, to the outrage of many, the Raj seemed to be whitewashing offences that were related to the Jallianwala killings of the previous year. Gandhi took the opportunity to launch a nationwide struggle against the Raj in which, in unprecedented numbers, Indians of all backgrounds and regions took part.

From 1920 Gandhi was Congress's, and in some ways India's, virtually unquestioned leader. The Salt March of 1930 — an all-India defiance of the salt tax by the simple yet illegal expedient of picking up, selling or buying the salt offered up by the sea — was another milepost; it resulted in a pact between the Viceroy, Lord Irwin, and Gandhi, which underscored the right Gandhi had earned to speak for India.

Objections to this right voiced by leaders of Muslim bodies and by Dr Ambedkar, who led large sections of the Untouchables, revealed Indian cracks and complexities. But prospects of a transfer of power to Congress seemed fair in 1937, when, following elections to provincial legislatures, most provincial governments came under its control.

Hitler's war killed those prospects by making the Raj more cautious, while Congress and the Indian people became more impatient for self-government. Led by Mohamed Ali Jinnah, the Muslim League demanded and obtained assurances from Britain that power would not be transferred in India without the League's agreement. In March 1940 the League made it clear that it would agree to independence only if preceded by the creation of a homeland or homelands for Muslims.

To this apparent deadlock Gandhi responded with the Quit India movement of 1942, his last and in some ways most dramatic campaign. The campaign sent him, his wife Kasturba, and tens of thousands of Indians, including all Congress leaders and activists, to prison. Following Kasturba's death in detention and an illness interpreted as terminal by the Raj, Gandhi was released in the summer of 1944; and the Congress Working Committee a year later.

Two years later, after prolonged negotiations, Britain, Congress and the League agreed on a plan to divide and free India, which was implemented in August 1947. Yet from October 1946 communal violence destroyed peace, lives and trust in different parts of the subcontinent, and Gandhi, unhappy with Partition but unable to prevent it, spent the last eighteen months of his life amidst Hindu, Muslim and Sikh victims of violence, healing wounds and restoring relations.

Some of his endeavours appeared pro-Muslim to many Hindus and Sikhs angered by Partition and the violence surrounding it. On 30 January 1948, while walking to his evening prayers, a 78-year-old Gandhi was killed by Nathuram Godse, a Hindu extremist.

As we have noted, he had critics among Muslims too, and among the Untouchables. Some accused him of harbouring a hidden agenda for caste Hindu domination. Others decried him as a foe of material progress. However, Nehru said when Gandhi died that his was a light of the living truth that would continue to shine, and Einstein observed that future generations would not easily believe that one like Gandhi had ever lived in flesh and blood.

He was seen as illwill's antithesis. Mian Iftikharuddin, president of the West Punjab Muslim League, said after the assassination: 'Each one of us who has raised his hand against innocent men, women and children during the past months, who has publicly or secretly entertained sympathy for such acts, is a collaborator in the murder of Mahatma Gandhi.'[2]

Much earlier, in 1910, Leo Tolstoy had described Gandhi's work in the Transvaal as 'most fundamental and important,' and in 1909 Gopal Krishna Gokhale had declared before a Congress session in Lahore that in the forty-year-old Gandhi 'Indian humanity' had 'reached its high watermark.'[3]

Awarded the Nobel Prize for Peace in 1989, the Dalai Lama accepted it not only on behalf of 'the oppressed everywhere' and 'the six million Tibetan people' but also 'as a tribute to the man who founded the modern tradition of nonviolent action for change, Mahatma Gandhi, whose life taught and inspired me.'[4] In 1995, felicitating the Dalai Lama on his sixtieth birthday, Vaclav Havel, President of the Czech Republic, recalled Gandhi as well.[5]

Thus for close to a century gifted individuals have continued to admire Gandhi. Again, if in earlier decades he was a father figure for colonies striving for freedom, today Gandhi commands prestige in the Green movement because he espoused the simple life and the rights of the earth; and he remains a symbol for nonviolent struggle.

❋

Such then is the man whose heart and mind this study seeks to probe through a series of inquiries. The driving force or forces at different stages in Gandhi's life, including his boyhood and youth, the nature of his nonviolence and its relationship with the violence that India saw, his encounter with the West and the British Empire — these are the subjects of the first four chapters. *Hind Swaraj* is examined in the fifth chapter.

The sixth deals with Gandhi's God, character and personality, and among other things looks at the controversial experiments that he said were undertaken to test his purity, and also at Gandhi's relationship with Kasturba and their sons. How he related, or did not relate, to the Africans in South Africa is studied in Chapter 7, which also looks at his contacts with Black America.

Chapter 8 deals with his position on untouchability and caste and the disputes Ambedkar had with him on those subjects. The path to Partition is traced, and his role in relation to it studied, in Chapter 9, this book's longest section. Gandhi's selection of heirs or an heir is the subject of Chapter 10, and in the chapter that follows we walk with Gandhi during the months between independence and his death. Chapter 12, concluding the study, tries to assess the meaning of his life for the present and the future.

A word on references. Many are provided along with the text. Because Gandhi's autobiography, *My Experiments with Truth*, and *Satyagraha in South Africa* have appeared in several editions, page numbers for quotations from them have not been supplied. For the same reason, only chapter numbers have been given for quotes from *Hind Swaraj*. The principal source, *The Collected Works of Mahatma Gandhi*, is assumed rather than named: thus (12:325) means p.325 of vol.12 of *The Collected Works*. Again (45) would mean p.45 of the work, any work, last mentioned. Page numbers cited against *Understanding the Muslim Mind (UMM)*, *Rajaji* or *Patel* belong to the author's works bearing those titles — the Bibliography provides details of these and other works to which the text refers.

Chapter 1

Nonviolence

ONE OF SEVERAL ways of attempting to unveil Gandhi's heart is to examine his nonviolence, which, as every student of Gandhi knows, was much more than an abhorrence of war or bloodshed; and one way of understanding Gandhi's nonviolence is to start with his reaction to the 1946 mutiny in the Royal Indian Navy (RIN). We will preface that, however, with a look at Gandhi's attitude to ships.

Everyone knows that his *Hind Swaraj*, written in 1909, excoriates modern civilization. Hospitals, law courts and railways are attacked in it, and planes and fast cars mocked. Later we will dwell at some length on *Hind Swaraj*, but here let us note that it does not condemn ships. This partiality for ships may have something to do with Gandhi's birth in and fondness for Porbandar, which lies on the Arabian Sea.

In 1907 Gandhi informed his first biographer, Joseph Doke, that 'the sea was almost within a stone's throw' from Porbandar's walls. 'It swept around the city so closely that at times it made almost an island of Porbandar' (Doke: 17). From Gandhi, Doke learnt that vessels made in Porbandar 'might be met with from Zanzibar to Aden' and that 'doing business in the great waters' had been the city's chief occupation from remote antiquity, giving its people a 'wide knowledge of men and things in other lands.' In 1925 Gandhi said that 'the sea was an epitome of adventures' and added that Indians 'needed the spirit of adventure in their national life' (26:257).

From 1888 to 1931 Gandhi made fifteen voyages — between

India and England, and India and South Africa, and South Africa and England. Whether travelling first-class or on deck, he was always a good sailor. During storms 'his feet were steady on the swaying deck' and he 'liked the stormy surge and the splash of the waves.'[1] On a calmer journey he was captivated by the moon and the stars dancing in the waves (1:13).

This first voyage was on the P & O liner *Clyde,* which took him from Bombay to Tilbury in 1888. Gandhi, who turned nineteen after arriving in England, 'appreciated the social organization of the ship and the efficiency with which passengers were served' and marvelled at the engineering behind the Suez Canal, built in 1869, the year of his birth (1:15).

In 1896-7, the steamer *Courland* bringing Gandhi, his wife Kasturba and their children from Bombay to Durban was lashed by a tempest near Madagascar. The boat pitched and rolled alarmingly, and its passengers were thoroughly frightened. Gandhi, who along with the *Courland's* skipper, Milne, worked to calm them, noticed that during moments of seeming danger Hindus, Muslims and Christians all spontaneously cried out to God. The sounds and names differed but the cry was the same, triggering in Gandhi a thought process that would lead to the multifaith prayers in his ashrams.

It was on the *Kildonan Castle,* which took him from London to Durban in 1909, that Gandhi produced *Hind Swaraj.* 'I wrote,' he says, 'only when I could hold myself no longer.' He wrote as one compelled, covering 275 sheets of the ship's notepaper with about 30,000 Gujarati words in ten days. Only three lines were scratched out and very few words corrected. We will consider *Hind Swaraj* in due course. Gandhi and the sea is still our subject. In his *Satyagraha in South Africa,* written in the early 1920s, Gandhi speaks of the sea while acknowledging the racial tolerance existing in the Cape province. Referring to the centrality in Cape Town of Table Mountain, he says: 'And as it (Table Mountain) is just on the seashore, the sea always washed its foot with its clear waters.'

Let us recall, too, that it was to the sea at Dandi (and the salt in the sea) that Gandhi marched in his 1930 freedom bid. His disciple Madeleine Slade, or Mira Behn, who from time to time served as his emissary to the Raj and also to the Congress High Command, was the daughter of an English admiral. Accompanying Gandhi on his 1931 voyage to London on the *Rajputana,* she noted that as a sailor Gandhi 'was out and away the best' among his party (*Pilgrimage*: 131). The last Viceroy Gandhi faced, a kin of the British royal family, was a famed sea lord. In a May 1947 letter in which Gandhi asked Mountbatten to shelve his plans for dividing India and to focus on British withdrawal, leaving Indians free to decide afterwards on partition, he also wrote: 'Your task as undisputed master of naval warfare, great as it was, was nothing compared to what you are called to do now. The singlemindedness and clarity that gave you success are much more required in this work' (8.5.47; 87:435). Almost four decades earlier, in *Hind Swaraj,* Gandhi prefaced a challenge to British power by addressing the British in the following terms: 'You have great military resources. Your naval power is matchless.' Four years before *Hind Swaraj* was written, the Japanese navy inflicted a defeat on the Russians. Below is a contemporary account of the battle:

> [Japan] stormed the Fort of Port Arthur, captured Mukden and has done other deeds of valour . . . Not only did she defeat the great Russian fleet, but wounded its great Admiral and did not leave intact a single Russian man-of-war . . . Many had thought that Japan would find herself in a difficult situation once the Russian fleet reached Singapore. It was also known that the Japanese navy . . . had fewer battleships than Russia. But in scouting and watchfulness, Japan surpassed all the others. Admiral Togo's spies were very accurate in their intelligence, and he pounced upon the Russian fleet when it was most vulnerable . . .
>
> England won a great [naval] victory in the sixteenth century. The 'invincible' Spanish Armada was then destroyed in the English channel . . . but the heavens then came to the succour of England . . . In the nineteenth century Nelson scored a great victory off the Cape of

> Trafalgar and the British Navy won for itself a pre-
> eminent position. Japan did not receive any unexpected
> help. She had only the firm determination to win . . . The
> secret of this epic heroism . . . is: unity, patriotism and the
> resolve to do or die.

The article in which these lines appeared was in the Gujarati
language. It was published in *Indian Opinion* on 10 June 1905. Its
author was M.K. Gandhi (3:466). These facts are cited as
background and for their intrinsic interest, not to claim any direct
connection between them and Gandhi's response to the 1946 naval
mutiny, which occurred eighteen months before independence.

❄

The Royal Indian Navy mutiny took place in the third week of February 1946. Its story has been related by one of its protagonists, B.C.
Dutt, in his *Mutiny of the Innocents*. The initiators were young
ratings thrilled by the exploits of the Indian National Army (INA)
and by the release in January 1946 of three INA officers, a Hindu, a
Muslim and a Sikh, whom the Raj had tried to convict for 'waging
war against the King.' Highlighting the discriminatory attitudes of
some of RIN's white officers and making an issue of the food given
to ratings, the initiators enlisted their less radical mates. However,
none among the large number of RIN's Indian officers joined the
defiance. Its first stage was the capture on 19 February of the
shore-based signal school in Bombay, HMIS Talwar, where the Union
Jack was hauled down. A Naval Central Strike Committee (NCSC)
was formed, shore-to-ship and ship-to-ship communications were
installed and a number of ships taken over. Flags of the Congress
and the Muslim League were flown over the seized ships. The
mutiny's young leaders thought that they were in a position to 'offer
the Royal Indian Navy on a platter' to any Indian leaders willing to
take it. (After spending much of the war period in detention, Gandhi
and the Congress High Command were now free.)

The mutiny leaders first went to Aruna Asaf Ali, who was in

Bombay. Accounts of her underground role in the 1942 movement had impressed them. She proved disappointing. According to Dutt, 'she merely advised us to remain calm . . . and to take up [our] service demands with the Naval authorities.' Aruna 'directed' the mutiny leaders to Vallabhbhai Patel, who was also in Bombay, and Jinnah, the Muslim League chief. Dispirited by Aruna's response, the mutineers sent negotiators on 20 February to Vice Admiral J.H. Godfrey, the Flag Officer commanding the RIN, who suggested that 'all ratings should return to their ships and establishments.'

This the ratings were unwilling to do. The next day saw a lengthy exchange of fire between shore-based mutineers and loyal troops attempting to confine them to barracks. Many ratings were killed. Aruna's response was to urge Bombay's workers and students to strike in sympathy with the ratings. Achyut Patwardhan, the socialist leader, and some Communist leaders backed Aruna's call. Patel opposed it. On 22 February a number of millhands and students took to the streets and there was widespread destruction. Public buildings and railway stations were burnt down, shops were looted. That day the mutineers met Patel, who frankly told them that he agreed with the RIN chief that 'there ought to be discipline in the navy' and advised a surrender. Patel added that he would do his best to prevent victimization and obtain acceptance of the ratings' legitimate demands. An exhausted NCSC accepted the advice. Instructions to surrender were signalled to all ships, accompanied by a reference to Patel's advice and assurance. Some Muslim ratings sought Jinnah's views, which were the same as Patel's. On 23 February the mutiny was over. The exercise and related disturbances in Bombay took 236 lives and saw 1156 injured.

Gandhi received an account of the mutiny and the violence from Patel, who wrote to him: 'We are done for, finished, if we don't stand up to this.' Afterwards Dutt felt that he and his co-rebels had been 'immature' and that the mutiny was 'a great futility.' Others, true, have suggested that the three-member Cabinet Mission that spent three months in 1946 in India was sent because of the mutiny. 'It seems more than a mere coincidence,' Brecher writes in his biography of Nehru, 'that the announcement about the British Cabinet Mission was made on 19 February, 1946, one day after the outbreak of the mutiny' (308-9). 'The Bombay mutiny undoubtedly had its effect on London,' writes Michael Edwardes in his study of Nehru, 'for a day after the outbreak Clement Attlee announced that a delegation of senior cabinet ministers would go to India' (166). The erroneous notion gained currency because London's announcement of the visit coincided with the RIN mutiny. In fact the Mission had been decided upon four weeks earlier; Wavell, the Viceroy, was informed of it on 24 January.

Gandhi's first response to the mutiny came in a press statement that he issued on 23 February, before word of its end had reached him. He noted, firstly, that 'this mutiny in the navy and what is following is not, in any sense of the term, nonviolent action.' He said next that 'inasmuch as a single person is compelled to shout Jai Hind or any popular slogan, a nail is driven into the coffin of swaraj in terms of the dumb millions of India.' Terming the mutiny 'unbecoming', he said that a 'dignified' and 'manly' way of 'nonviolent resistance' was open to the aggrieved ratings — they could discontinue their service. He asked the 'known and unknown leaders of this thoughtless orgy of violence' to 'know what they are doing and then follow their bend.' Then came these words: 'I have deliberately used the adjective "thoughtless". For there is such a thing as thoughtful violent action. What I see happening just now is not thoughtful' (83:170-71).

A prescient statement followed. Said Gandhi: 'A combination between Hindus and Muslims and others for the purpose of violent action is unholy and will lead to and probably is a preparation for mutual violence — bad for India and the world.'

Aruna Asaf Ali criticized Gandhi's statement. Claiming that people 'are not interested in the ethics of violence or nonviolence,' she said that people's violence had helped the 1942 movement. As for the communal question, she would 'rather,' she said, 'unite Hindus and Muslims at the barricade than on the constitutional front.'

On 26 February, Gandhi made points that included answers to Aruna's. Stating that he 'admired her bravery, resourcefulness and burning love for the country,' he added that he had not liked 'her being underground' during the 1942 movement. Underground activity by 'a select few' excluded the bulk of the population. 'Only open challenge and open activity is for all to follow' and 'real swaraj must be felt by all, man, woman and child.'

India, he claimed, 'has become a pattern for all exploited races on earth because India's has been an open, unarmed effort which demands sacrifice from all without inflicting injury on the usurper.' His reading of 1942, he added, was different from that of 'the brave lady.' 'It was good that the people rose spontaneously. It was bad that some or many resorted to violence.'

He answered Aruna's remark on Hindu-Muslim unity at the barricade by saying that 'fighters do not always live at the barricade . . . The barricade life has always to be followed by the constitutional. That front is not taboo for ever.' As for the people not being interested in the ethics of violence, Gandhi argued that 'they are very much interested in knowing the way which will bring freedom to the masses — violence or nonviolence.'

By this time the surrender of the ratings was public knowledge. Gandhi said the mutineers were 'foolhardy' and added: 'It is a matter of great relief that the ratings have listened to Sardar Patel's advice to surrender. They have not surrendered their honour. So far as I can see, in resorting to mutiny they were badly advised. If it was for grievance, fancied or real, they should have waited for the guidance and intervention of political leaders of their choice.'

This was followed by a clinical remark. 'If they mutinied for the freedom of India,' said Gandhi, 'they were doubly wrong. *They could not do so without a call from a prepared revolutionary party.* They were thoughtless and ignorant, if they believed that by their might they would deliver India from foreign domination.'

'They could not do so without a call from a prepared revolutionary party.' Arguing for nonviolence, indicating a nonviolent alternative, dissenting from the 1942 violence and upholding an 'open challenge and activity' in which everyone can have a part, Gandhi is nonetheless willing to test violence and nonviolence on the ground of effectiveness, and also to distinguish, in his mind and publicly, between thoughtless and thoughtful violence, between foolhardiness and a mutiny that answered 'a call from a prepared revolutionary party' (83:182-4).

❋

The question of violence confronted Gandhi during virtually every day of his long life. The issues involved included whether or not to eat meat, how to respond to a physical attack on his person or loved ones or to a physical and cultural hold over his people, how to react to assaults on the dignity of Indians in South Africa, whether or not to assist the British Empire when it seemed threatened (by the Boers in South Africa at the turn of the century, by the 1906 Zulu rebellion and during the first and second world wars), the character of his freedom campaigns in India, the use of lethal weapons by Indians against the British or against one another, and how to respond to the conflict in Kashmir within months of freedom, or to the bomb thrown at him ten days before his death.

It is neither possible nor necessary to go into all these and other ways in which the question of violence faced Gandhi. Entering the subject by way of the 1946 mutiny, we have seen that a smell of violence was not the only thing Gandhi was vigilant against.

We may also note an early inclination in favour of nonviolence. In 1907 he told Joseph Doke, his first biographer, that a Gujarati verse he learned at school had 'clung to me.' The substance of this verse was that it was all right to give a man a drink in return for one but 'real beauty consists in doing good against evil.' Then, Gandhi added, 'came the Sermon on the Mount,' (in London, 1888-91, and Pretoria, 1893-94) with which 'I was simply overjoyed' (Doke: 100). We are entitled, I think, to see this inclination also in his lifelong concern with nursing, which began with a three-year stint between the ages of twelve and fifteen when he served his ailing father, and remained with him until the end, and in his desire as a boy to be a doctor, which briefly resurfaced in South Africa. That early duty might have turned another person against nursing and the tendencies that go with it; it is a clue that in Gandhi's case it launched a habit.

We started by noting that Gandhi's nonviolence was more than an abhorrence of war, yet it seems clear that violence horrified him. We can look at a string of quotes:

'India's acceptance of the doctrine of the sword will be the hour of my trial. I hope I shall not be found wanting' (*Young India,* 11.8.20). 'If I am in the minority of one, I must try to make converts. Whether one or many, I must declare my faith that it is better for India to discard violence altogether even for defending her borders . . . With the loss of India to nonviolence the last hope of the world will be gone' (*Harijan,* 14.10.39).

'My mission is to convert every Indian, whether he is a Hindu, Muslim or any other, even Englishmen and finally the world, to nonviolence for regulating mutual relations whether political, economic, social or religious. If I am accused of being too ambitious, I should plead guilty' (*Harijan,* 13.1.40).

'Moral [independence] means freedom from armed defence forces. My conception of Ramrajya excludes replacement of the British army by a national army of occupation. A country that is governed by even its national army can never be morally free and therefore, its so-called weakest member can never rise to his full moral height . . .' (New Delhi, 29.4.46; 84:80).

'I do not know how many swear by nonviolence...I know on the contrary that many would have India become a first-class military power...I know that if India is to be the leader in clean action based on clean thought, God will confound the wisdom of these big men' (21.7.46; 85:34).

'Militarization of India would mean her own destruction as well as of the whole world' (*Harijan,* 14.12.47).

These quotes can be fully understood only in their context, and several of them suggest, or were accompanied by, a reasoning (apart from any predisposition) in favour of his position. Yet taken together they breathe a personal loyalty to nonviolence.

Despite this predisposition, and despite a brave effort to extract nonviolence from the Gita, Gandhi raised and led an Indian Ambulance Corps in the Boer and Zulu wars and raised a similar corps out of Indian students in London at the start of the first world war. This was only partly because his nonviolence was yet to mature. By the time he left South Africa for good in 1914, this nonviolence had, in essence, found its eventual character. He associated himself in one way or another with the wars because he felt that he had to respond to considerations besides nonviolence or violence.

He had claimed and fought for Indian rights in South Africa as a citizen of the Empire and on the basis of a series of pronouncements on the Empire's behalf, starting with Queen Victoria's words in 1858. In a proclamation addressed to the princes, chiefs and people of India, she had declared that the British government was 'bound to the natives of our Indian territories by the same obligations of duty which binds us to all our other subjects,' and that 'all shall alike enjoy the equal and impartial protection of the law.' And he felt that obligations to support the Empire in its difficulties flowed inescapably from this claim of rights. This was to be his reasoning over all the three wars, the Boer, the Zulu and the First World War.

Not that the decisions were easy or simple ones. On the first occasion he was conscious that the Boers (against whom the Empire's forces, including his unit, were ranged) were resisting England with a cultural autonomy and bravery that he wanted Indians to have vis-a-vis the British. Yet he felt that he could not stay aloof from the conflict and still fight for Indian rights; and he wanted to refute the sneer common among the British in South Africa that 'if danger is threatened, the Indians would run away' (Doke: 63). Gandhi offered the Indians' help 'in whatever capacity,' including as soldiers, but only an ambulance corps was accepted. The terms included exemption from the firing line but Gandhi and his men entered it when their help was requested at Spion Kop and Vaal Krantz.

In March 1904 in Johannesburg, Gandhi and a handful of colleagues and volunteer nurses were engaged in what Doke called a 'hand-to-hand fight with death,' the isolation and nursing of Indians stricken with plague. The exercise saved a few of the infected ones (though 113 including 55 Indians died in the month-long epidemic) and saved many more of all races from infection. It raised no issue of violence (Doke: 76).

The decision to offer assistance to the forces suppressing the 1906 Zulu or Bambata rebellion was harder to arrive at than Gandhi's decision over the Boer war, for it meant aligning with a white Empire against the defying Zulus, and even harder to sustain because of the harshness employed by the British in subduing the rebels. Yet, withholding help could have destroyed the Indians' credentials in British-ruled South Africa.

For more than one reason the Zulu episode merits a closer look but first we should note that the 1904-5 war between Japan and Russia was the subject of several comments by Gandhi in *Indian Opinion*, the weekly journal serving as his organ in South Africa. We have already seen something of his description of a naval clash in that war. Here we should mark that Gandhi's comments did not touch on the ethics of going to war. He shared the joy of the East in an Asian land defeating a European power, but a racial element was but rarely seen in his reactions, whereas that element dominated responses in India. His focus was on the discipline, unity and bravery of the Japanese forces, which he urged Indians in South Africa and at home to emulate.

The genesis of the Zulu episode and Gandhi's thinking on it can be found in editions of *Indian Opinion* in April 1905:

> Important events, the effects of which will not be forgotten for many years, took place in Natal last week . . . The Kaffirs (*at the time a common South African phrase, derogatory as it was, for Africans*) in Natal rose against the poll-tax. Sergeants Hunt and Armstrong were killed in the revolt. Martial law was declared in Natal . . . Some Kaffirs were prosecuted under the martial law, and twelve of them were condemned to death . . . The Kaffirs from neighbouring areas and their chiefs were invited to witness the execution . . . Twelve lives have been taken for two. The twelve Kaffirs were blown to death at the mouth of a cannon on Monday.

Noting the Natal colony's success in ignoring London's reservations about the execution and the colony's increased leverage, Gandhi added:

> It is only the Blacks who stand to lose by this. They have no vote. Where they have it, they cannot use it effectively . . . The colonial authority will place greater restrictions on them, and they alone will get justice who ingratiate themselves with it. Great changes are likely to take place in South Africa during the coming years. The Indians and other Blacks have much to ponder and they must act with circumspection (*Indian Opinion*, [Guj.], 7.4.06; 5:266-7).

Let us mark that here Gandhi speaks of Indians as a section of the Blacks. (The English version of *Collected Works* says 'coloured' but Gandhi wrote 'kala' or 'kalo' in his Gujarati article.) A week later Gandhi wrote:

> Though the 12 Kaffirs were put to death, the rebellion instead of being quelled has gathered strength . . . The dead (*in a clash with Chief Bambata, who had been deposed and was leading the rebellion*) included those who had shot the 12 Kaffirs. Such is the law of God . . . Bambata is still at large. There is no knowing how all this will end.
>
> What is our duty during these calamitous times in the colony? It is not for us to say whether the revolt of the Kaffirs is justified or not. We are in Natal by virtue of the British power. Our very existence depends upon it. It is therefore our duty to render whatever help we can (*Indian Opinion* [Guj.], 14.4.06; 5:281-2).

The Indian offer was made and accepted, and two dozen or so of the Natal Indians served in March-April 1906 in the stretcher-bearing corps, with Gandhi, invested with the rank of sergeant-major, at their head. Details of this exercise of about six weeks can be pieced together from relevant *Indian Opinion* numbers, Doke's biography of Gandhi (published in 1909 but written in 1907-8), and Gandhi's accounts in his *Satyagraha in South Africa* and *Experiments with Truth*, both written in the 1920s. The *Indian Opinion* numbers show that associating with a violent operation was not an issue for him at the time. But the experience influenced Gandhi's subsequent attitude to violence.

The exercise involved carrying the wounded behind an infantry column to a base hospital. Sometimes it meant twenty to twenty-five mile marches up and down hills. Often the wounded were Zulu 'friendlies' mistakenly shot by the colony's soldiers. There was additional work. In *Satyagraha* Gandhi writes:

> It was no part of our duty to nurse the wounded after we had taken them to the hospital . . . [But] the good Doctor (Dr Savage, in charge of the ambulance) told us that he could not induce the Europeans to nurse the Zulus, . . . and that he would feel obliged if we undertook this mission of mercy. We were only too glad to do this. We had to cleanse the wounds of several Zulus which had not been attended to for as many as five or six days and were therefore stinking horribly. We liked our work. The Zulus could not talk to us, but from their gestures and the expression of their eyes, they seemed to feel as if God had sent us to their succour.

Finding that Gandhi spoke 'with great reserve' of what he saw during the exercise, Doke concluded that 'it was not always creditable to British humanity.' According to Doke, 'as a man of peace, hating the very thought of war, it was almost intolerable for [Gandhi] to be so closely in touch with this expedition.' Also writing in 1909, Polak thought that Gandhi 'must have had searchings of conscience as to the propriety of allying himself, even in that merciful capacity, with those capable of such acts of revolting and unexcusable brutality.'[2] In his study of Gandhi, the psychoanalyst Erikson suggests (194) that the exercise of cleansing the gunshot wounds and binding rents made by the lash — of 'witnessing the outrages perpetrated on black bodies by white he-men' — aroused in Gandhi 'both a deeper identification with the maltreated and a stronger aversion against all male sadism.'

Recalling, in the 1920s, 'a very important epoch in my life,' Gandhi wrote in the Autobiography: 'On reaching the scene of the "rebellion" I saw that there was nothing to justify the name of "rebellion." The Boer war had not brought home to me the horrors of war with anything like the vividness that the "rebellion" did. This was no war but a manhunt . . . To hear every morning the reports of the soldiers' rifles exploding like crackers in innocent hamlets, and to live in the midst of them was a trial. But I swallowed the bitter draught, especially since the work of my corps consisted only in nursing the Zulus.'

It was, Gandhi says, 'a sparsely populated part of the country. Few and far between in the hills and dales were the scattered Kraals of the simple and so-called uncivilized Zulus.' In his treks across this Zululand terrain, with or without the wounded, he 'often fell into deep thought.'

As a result of the episode, Gandhi has written, 'two ideas which had long been floating in my mind became firmly fixed.' He took the vows of brahmacharya, 'so full of wonderful potency' and poverty. 'In a word, I could not live both after the flesh and the spirit.' His decision or decisions 'brought a certain kind of exultation. Imagination also found free play and opened out limitless vistas of service.' He also spoke of living no more for 'children and wealth,' a decision that went beyond the 1893 decision on the Maritzburg platform to defend the Indian community's rights and, as P. Mani puts it, seemed to override the survival instinct.

Erikson, Martin Green and Mani, among others, agree that this episode is as significant as Gandhi himself hints at (which is more than what Gandhi says). According to Green, the vow of brahmacharya was to Gandhi 'a way to promote the triumph of caritas over eros' (160). Erikson I have already quoted. Mani cites Gandhi — 'Perfect brahmacharis are perfectly sinless. They are, therefore, near to God. They are like God.' He suggests that in making the brahmacharya decision Gandhi felt a sense of great power, an inference confirmed by Gandhi's remarks about 'exultation' and 'limitless' vistas of service.

In Gandhi's intriguing, somewhat cryptic, but not, we may be sure, careless phrases, we may also detect, given the setting of the exercise, a widening of Gandhi's horizons beyond race and country. Mani's surmise that creativity was triggered in Gandhi by the contrast between the might and cruelties of the whites (whose campaign Gandhi had gone to assist) and the 'innocence and legitimacy of the natives' (whom he ended up carrying and nursing), seems also supported by what we have quoted from Gandhi, and 'proved' by the satyagraha, Gandhi's first, that was launched on the heels of the Zulu episode. If the ejection from the train at Maritzburg evoked from a shivering Gandhi a crucial decision not to run from the field of battle, his experiences and reflections in the Zululand battlefields seemed to tell Gandhi, with irresistible force and clarity, that his battles, his weapons and he himself had to be clean, and also that he, with all his limitations, could battle well and on a large scale, even on a wide, borderless canvas.

The Zulu episode was immediately followed by Gandhi's, and South Africa's Indian community's, first satyagraha. We will not linger on that oft-told story, but it is worth noting that word of the Transvaal Act that drew forth the satyagraha had reached Gandhi during his treks in the Zulu country. If we set this fact alongside Gandhi's remark (in a preface to a 1938 reprint of *Hind Swaraj*) that the first satyagraha preempted the violence that some angry elements in the Indian community were inclined to perpetrate, then we find a link in Gandhi's mind between the vow of brahmacharya that preceded and, as sensed by him, engendered satyagraha, and a victory over violence.

Arriving in England in 1906 on a mission linked to the first satyagraha, the first thing that Gandhi did was to call on a group of Indian revolutionaries in London, living in a place called India House. Gandhi spent two nights at India House and returned to it on three Sunday evenings for discussions with Shyamji Krishnavarma and others. Satyagraha was Gandhi's answer to violence, and he presented it to the violence-inclined as a better alternative.

Gandhi's lone trek in Noakhali in 1946-7 resembled his Zululand marches. Both terrains were physically striking, one with its hills and glens, and the other with its leafy soil across a web of rivers. The thirty-seven-year-old sergeant-major in boots, carrying one end of a stretcher in the Zulu country, walked barefoot in Noakhali, holding a staff, and was seventy-seven. As before, he carried a weight, this time a load of anxiety, rejection and sorrow — a result of the looming division of the country, the attitude of Congress's leaders, and the Hindu-Muslim killings. Coping with others' wounds was again his mission; this time the wounds included memories of terrible sights, cries and experiences. As in the Zulu country, people in Noakhali, men and more often women, looked at him with appealing eyes. Declaring that courage rather than solace was what he had to offer, he described himself as a soldier in Noakhali, which is what he had been in Zululand. The exultation of the Zulu experience was not repeated in Noakhali, but he summoned all his reserves of body and soul and pitted them against the subcontinent's follies. Finally, in Noakhali Gandhi daringly tested that link between brahmacharya and power of which he had had a vision in the Zulu country. If the first satyagraha followed Gandhi's Zululand experience, his last satyagrahas, the peace-bringing fasts in Calcutta and Delhi, were the consequences of Noakhali.

❈

Between the Zulu war and the 1914-18 world war lay a series of satyagraha campaigns by Indians in South Africa involving marches, pledges and acts of nonviolent disobedience of laws identified as unjust, prison terms and other hardships, leading in some cases to death, and a refusal to hit back. For Gandhi personally this meant, among other things, that he pardoned fellow-Indians who had struck him down (in 1908) with kicks, sticks and an iron pipe, objecting to a settlement that Gandhi had accepted. By January 1914, when Gandhi and Smuts reached an agreement on the Indians' demands, Gandhi was identified with a rejection of modern civilization (*Hind*

Swaraj had been written in 1909), a refusal to kill and an opposition to violence, and seems to have concluded within himself that it was improper to offer any support, even that of a nurse, to a war.

The first world war commenced after he and Kasturba had sailed from South Africa for the last time, and before they had landed in England, where he had planned to meet Gokhale before finally returning to India. To a real war Gandhi did not react in the way he had thought he would to an imagined war. Since (he said) he had not yet renounced either modern civilization or the protection of the Empire's armed forces, he again decided, while in London, to raise an ambulance corps. Some of his key supporters were shocked. The South African novelist Olive Schreiner, who with her husband had backed Gandhi's struggles, could not understand how he could offer to serve the English government in 'this evil war.'[3]

But as before Gandhi was weighing several factors, and one of them, this time, was the attitude most likely to advance the cause of Indian freedom. Concluding that staying aloof would hinder that cause, he threw himself, despite having fallen ill, into raising a corps from among the Indians in England. He had wished to lead the corps (without carrying a weapon) but his illness came in the way. The war prevented Gokhale's visit to England, and after an unhappy stay of more than four months Gandhi and Kasturba left for India. The unhappiness was not due to his lengthy illness (which he saw as a personal failing) or the related frustration of his hope of leading a nursing corps again; he seemed to hate the speed, noise and excitement of wartime England. 'Dear London' had been his verdict after his three-year sojourn there as a student, and he had been happy enough on a 1906 visit (in the cause of Indians in South Africa) to the metropolis, but on the two journeys that followed, in 1909 and 1914, he seemed to find himself increasingly a stranger. Despite the unease, and despite a previous resolve not to do so, he presented the Empire with a hundred-strong ambulance corps.

Arriving in India in January 1915, Gandhi toured and studied the country for a year. He set up his ashrams, recruited members for them, found allies for his politics, sought strategies to deal with the Hindu-Muslim issue, untouchability and caste, and won a satyagraha for poor Biharis working on indigo plantations, and another for pea- sants in Gujarat's Kheda district. But violence and nonviolence remained central issues for him. The world war was still on, and his arrival had sparked a debate on the place of violence in India's effort for freedom. On the latter question he was unequivocal. In October 1916 he presented ahimsa as the essence of Hinduism and said that a man like Lala Lajpat Rai 'need not fear the ahimsa of his father's faith.' He added that his own commitment to ahimsa would remain unaffected even 'if I suddenly discovered that the religious books . . . bore a different interpretation.' He accepted the prevalence of weakness in India but said: 'If we are unmanly today, we are so not because we do not know how to strike but because we fear to die' (13:294-7).

BUt the question of his role in the war continued to agitate him, ans his eventual response was to spend 1918's summer in Kheda's scorching countryside seeking recruits for the Empire's army. Defending the exercise, he argued, in a letter to his English friend C.F.Andrews, that 'you cannot teach ahimsa to a man who cannot kill.' He also said that the kshatriya rather than the bania spirit, soldierly virtues and indeed military training were needed for India's regeneration. There was politics in this, of course. Gandhi frankly argued with politicians and others that support to the war effort with recruits would help India acquire the status of a Dominion. But there was soul-searching as well, linked to his awareness of Indian cowardice. To another English friend, Florence Winterbottom, he wrote in June 1918:

I am going through perhaps the severest trials of my life. I had hoped . . . to be able in India to retire from the War. Now I find I am in the thick of it . . . I want to raise men to fight, to deal death to men who, for all they know, are as innocent as they. And I fancy that through this sea of blood I shall find my haven . . . I find men are incapable through cowardice of killing. How shall I preach to them the virtue of non-killing? And so I want them to learn the art of killing! This is all awful. But such is the situation before me. Sometimes my heart sinks within me...[4]

Rajendra Prasad, a close colleague from the previous year, observed that not knowing God's will agonized Gandhi, who often wept.[5] His exertions in Gujarat were largely fruitless. Risking their lives for the Empire was about the last thing that the Kheda peasants wanted to do. Soldiering was not their line, and the fate of Britain not their concern. The hundred or so enlisting in response to Gandhi's call came mostly from his ashramite circle. Internal conflict produced a breakdown in Gandhi's health. Thinking he was near his end, he told colleagues what they should do after his death. But he did not die. What ended was the War itself, and the sepoys Gandhi had raised were not called upon to serve or shoot.

Some of Gandhi's major satyagrahas took place between the first and second world wars. Gandhi saw them as proving the superiority of nonviolence over violence. His suspension of mass civil disobedience following the brutal killing of policemen in Chauri Chaura in 1922 symbolized what he stood for, and what he stood against. 'I never performed a greater service to my country,' he said in 1926, referring to the suspension.[6] Earlier, after the Jallianwala Bagh massacre, he had insisted, in the teeth of fierce opposition, that Congress should condemn Indian violence even as it excoriated the Raj's. But he admitted that there would be armies in the swaraj he was fighting for. 'Alas, in my swaraj of today there is room for soldiers,' he said in 1925 (26:114), and in 1927 he was more precise. In a letter urging Dr Mukhtar Ahmed Ansari to accept Congress's presidency, he said that when Congress comes to power, 'the law, diplomacy, military and the rest, we shall leave to Motilalji and company,' adding, 'If Panditji (Motilal Nehru) thinks that Shaukat Ali would be good company, he may throw at him the military departments' (34:304-5).

There were other compromises with doctrinaire ahimsa. It was not against nonviolence for the Ashram to destroy diseased dogs, he said. And when a young heifer in Sabarmati was sick beyond treatment, Gandhi 'stooped down and took the heifer's front . . . leg' while 'the doctor put the injection through the ribs, and there was a spasm, and it died.' Mira Behn saw that 'Bapu didn't say a word, except he took a cloth and covered the heifer's face with it, and then in complete silence he walked back to the ashram.'[7] A Jain friend wrote to him, 'Gandhi, you killed that cow, and if I do not kill you in return, I am no Jain.'[8] Gandhi did not concede that he had betrayed nonviolence.

When he met Mussolini in Rome in 1931, another facet of his nonviolence was revealed. He disliked the Italian dictator's trophies of war and suspected his 'catlike eyes.' He thought Mussolini was 'a cruel man.'[9]

Congress was in a phase of careful cooperation with the Raj when the clouds of the second world war began to gather. Congress ministries were in office in eight provinces. But the Muslim League was persuading the Muslims that Congress rule was Hindu raj; and there were others, including the princes and men like Ambedkar and Savarkar, who claimed that Gandhi and Congress did not speak for all the non-Muslims either. Among the people at large, Britain's refusal to concede freedom was giving birth to anti-British and pro-Axis feelings. As always, Gandhi's attitude to the war was influenced both by his views on nonviolence and by the state of politics.

A year before the war, Gandhi had made plain what he thought of Hitler: 'If there ever could be a justifiable war in the name of and for humanity, a war against Germany, to prevent the wanton persecution of a whole race, would be completely justified. But I do not believe in any war' (*Harijan*, 26.11.38). When war broke out, Gandhi met the Viceroy, Linlithgow, and told him he viewed it 'with an English heart.' He could not commit Congress, he added, but personally he was for Congress giving unconditional though nonviolent support to Britain.

However, Nehru was in 'a combative mood' against the British and Subhas Bose, president of Congress until April 1939, advocated a militant line: no 'Indian men, money and resources' should go into this 'imperialist war.'[10] Public opinion seemed receptive to the Bose-Nehru line; but a refusal to cooperate with Britain also meant Congress's exit from provincial office. In the event, Gandhi's suggestion that the Congress Working Committee should offer unconditional nonviolent support to Britain was rejected; and Britain was taken to task for refusing to state that her war aims included India's freedom, and for drafting India into the war without her consent. The Congress ministries went out — and Congress's opponents celebrated 'deliverance' from its rule.

After the fall of France, Congress wanted to offer full cooperation in the war to England in return for a Congress-led government at the centre and a promise of independence at the end of the war. Gandhi disagreed. His nonviolence came in the way, he said. Also, he did not think Britain would accept the offer. His view was rejected and Congress made its offer in July 1940. Gandhi, the Working Committee said, would have 'complete liberty to pursue his great ideal of nonviolence.' The words concealed a rejection that was a precursor of 1946 and 1947, but Britain turned down Congress's offer. The Raj was beginning to enjoy, when it did not foster, the ascendancy of non-Congress elements, and it did not wish to see rebels in office again.

Congress returned to Gandhi, who now advised a campaign of individual disobedience. Mass disobedience would hurt 'the British people when their very existence hangs in the balance' but to do nothing would 'kill Congress.' Individual disobedience meant the recitation by each carefully selected satyagrahi of a single sentence: 'It is wrong to help the British war effort with men or money.' A few subscribed to the sentence because of their nonviolence, many more because of the way Britain had treated India. Its recital sent hundreds of Congress leaders to prison. By the time they were released in the latter part of 1941, Germany had attacked Russia and Subhas Bose had slipped out of India to seek help from Germany for Indian independence. In December, Japan attacked Pearl Harbor and drew America into the war.

Once more Congress leaders attempted a settlement with Britain. Suspending satyagraha, the Working Committee offered cooperation in the Allies' war if India's freedom was declared. Once more

Gandhi demurred. But he did not disown the Working Committee and in fact asked the All India Congress Committee (AICC) to ratify the proposal, his own views notwithstanding. Indirectly, therefore, he was prepared, in January 1942, to associate himself with the war.

After Singapore fell to the Japanese in February and Rangoon in March, Churchill sent his cabinet colleague and leader of the House of Commons, Stafford Cripps, to negotiate with Indian leaders. Cripps offered full dominion status to India after the war and a national government right away but he also offered every province a right of secession at the end of the war, and he was unable to assure Congress that the wartime national government would have sufficient powers vis-a-vis the Viceroy. The offer of independence to the provinces was Cripps's response to the Muslim League's Pakistan demand, articulated first in March 1940. The Congress Working Committee rejected the Cripps offer largely because of the limitations on the proposed national government. Gandhi's dislike was focussed on the balkanisation of India that Cripps and Churchill seemed prepared to contemplate.

Japan was at India's gate. Subhas Bose, backed by Japan and symbolizing a culture of militarism — the gun and the boot as against Gandhi's charkha and wooden sandals — was increasingly popular. Jinnah demanded India's break-up and Churchill seemed ready to support him. India's integrity, satyagraha and nonviolence all seemed threatened, and Gandhi responded with Quit India. He had said in 1940 that he did not wish to embarrass the British. He had also said that a mass campaign could spark off Hindu-Muslim riots. Now, with Britain in greater danger than in 1940 and Hindu-Muslim relations at least as tense as in 1940, he felt he had to declare a rebellion.

We will not go here into the pains and glories of that movement — its killings, imprisonments and heroisms. What we should observe is that Gandhi urged Indians to defy the Raj nonviolently — and he indicated that violence by those disagreeing with his methods would not, this time, halt his movement. We should note too that to obtain the agreement of Nehru and Azad to Quit India (Jawaharlal was fearful that it would impede the defence of China and Russia), Gandhi had agreed that Allied troops could remain in India after British rule ended. Gandhi wanted freedom and India's unity; he also wanted nonviolence in India's fight for freedom and in her attitude to the war. The four goals were not fully consistent with one another and Gandhi had to compromise.

After some months of alarm, the Raj crushed the Quit India movement. Its prisons were full but Britain had not left India. Shortly after his release in the summer of 1944 (the Raj thought he was dying and did not want the onus), Gandhi told the new Viceroy, Wavell, that he was prepared to advise the Working Committee that disobedience could no longer be offered and that Congress should cooperate fully with the war effort if a responsible national government was formed. Again he was willing to compromise on nonviolence.

When communal violence broke out in 1946 and 1947, coinciding with the onset of independence and partition, Gandhi's primary prescription was courage, the essence of which, in his view, was defiance of death. He preferred, he always said, nonviolent defiance to violent forms, but violent defiance to flight or submission. Looters, rapists and those demanding a change of religion at knifepoint had to be resisted by Hindus, Muslims and Sikhs, nonviolently if possible and violently if necessary. Each side should admit its own follies and not focus solely on the wickedness of the other side, and it was the duty of majority communities and security forces to protect weak minorities. He would continue to work for a nonviolent world; meanwhile, security forces in both India and Pakistan had their role, and it was necessary that they should be guided by bias-free men. Gandhi spelt out his attitude in utterances that followed the multifaith public prayers conducted by him every evening, and through two fasts against communal violence, one in Calcutta in September 1947 and another in Delhi in January 1948. The utterances and the fasts suggest that Hindu-Muslim trust was his primary goal and represented nonviolence to him.

He worried about the refugees streaming into Delhi's makeshift camps, Hindus and Sikhs who had fled from West Punjab, the Frontier and Sind, as well as Muslims fleeing from U.P., other parts of North India and some Delhi localities as well. For both lots of refugees he collected gifts of blankets for the winter that was approaching. Daily, in large numbers sometimes, the aggrieved of all communities met him — where he lived, in Birla House, or in the refugee camps he visited. He told each side of what the other had also gone through. In his post-prayer remarks, which the radio as well as the press carried, he relayed, from accounts reaching him, items that might shame or stir: a man on a train pounced upon and killed before scores of approving or silent fellow-passengers, because his appearance had betrayed him; a conversion at knifepoint; members of one community sheltering hunted members of another; and so on. Such strivings for humanity and Hindu-Muslim trust were the positive facets of Gandhi's nonviolence in 1947.

When Pakistani tribesmen attacked Kashmir in October 1947, the ruler, Hari Singh, acceded to India, ending the hesitation he had shown until then. Hari Singh also gave a free hand to Sheikh Abdullah, his prisoner until the previous month and the leader with the largest following in the state. The Indian Cabinet flew troops into Srinagar to defend Kashmir. Gandhi did not oppose the action. In his post-prayer speech on 29 October he said:

> How many soldiers could be sent by plane? Only a few could be sent. Then they have to carry their arms, food supplies and clothes. And their clothes have got to be thick and heavy. Even an excess of one pound of weight becomes an extra burden . . .
>
> What can you or I think about it? After all, I have spent my life thinking over these things. I do not believe in armed fighting but I must know what it is. On the one hand are 1,500 Indian soldiers and on the other all those Afridis and others. And there is Sheikh Abdullah. He is called the lion of Kashmir . . . He has decided to do his utmost. Pandit Nehru and his cabinet came to the conclusion that something should be done and those soldiers were sent. What should they do? Let them fight to the end and

NONVIOLENCE • 25

die fighting. The job of armed soldiers is to march ahead and repel the attacking army.

The soldiers will have really done their duty when all of them lay down their lives in saving Srinagar. And with Srinagar the whole of Kashmir would be saved. What would happen after that? All that would happen would be that Kashmir would belong to the Kashmiris.

After all, Kashmir cannot be saved by the Maharaja. If anyone can save Kashmir, it is only the Muslims, the Kashmiri Pandits, the Rajputs and the Sikhs who can do so. Sheikh Abdullah has affectionate and friendly relations with all of them ... He would not let the Hindus and Sikhs there die before the Muslims. If this is the attitude of the Sheikh and if he has influence on the Muslims, all is well with us ... Through Kashmir that poison might be removed from us (89:432-4).

The context makes it clear that he means Hindu-Muslim mistrust by 'that poison.' The Hindu-Muslim link is what absorbs him. The use of arms is not the issue. Moreover, he claims the right to watch the armed fighting and to think about it though he does not believe in it. And he is not a disinterested spectator.

On 5 November he replied to criticism that though he had advised Churchill, the Jews and others in Europe threatened by Nazism during the Second World War 'to give up arms and become nonviolent,' he had not asked the government of India to defend Kashmir nonviolently. His was a three-point answer. Firstly, the government was not his. 'If I could have my way of nonviolence and everybody listened to me, we would not send our army as we are doing now. And if we did send, it would be a nonviolent army.' But 'I am nobody and no one listens to me.' Nonviolence was 'acceptable till we attained independence.' 'Now they (Nehru, Patel and others in the cabinet) wonder how they can rule with nonviolence.' Secondly, 'in Kashmir, Sheikh Abdullah is giving a brave fight — I have always admired bravery. When I see something good and fail to give it true credit, I cannot be truly nonviolent.'

Thirdly, when he urged Churchill to try nonviolence he had the example of successful nonviolence in India behind him. Now Hindus and Muslims seemed to be at one another's throats. 'In his time Mr Churchill could not say but today Sheikh Abdullah and the army which has gone there can tell me that my nonviolence has failed in Delhi where acts of barbarism are being committed' (89:480-2).

He would not press for nonviolence but rather see aspects of it in courage and Hindu-Muslim trust, which he thought Kashmir was exemplifying. His hope was that Kashmir would disprove the two-nation theory that had partitioned India and now threatened to force all Hindus and Sikhs out of Pakistan and all Muslims out of India. On 4 November he said that 'the world does not expect from Hindustan, whether as Indian Union or Pakistan, meanness and fanaticism. It expects greatness, goodness and generosity' (89:474). He did not say it expected nonviolence, and he did not expect it either.

Yet he took to task Cariappa, the seniormost Indian officer of the army, for saying that 'nonviolence is of no use under the present circumstances in India and only a strong army can make India one of the greatest nations in the world.' Ahimsa, Gandhi wrote in *Harijan*, was 'outside' Cariappa's 'field,' and more relevant than ever 'in this age of the atom bomb' (16.11.47; 89:492-3). When he called on Gandhi to clarify what he had said, Cariappa was told: 'I hope you will succeed in solving the Kashmir problem nonviolently' (on 18.1.48; 90:450). But this was no more than remembering an ideal. Gandhi also informed Cariappa that he had asked his followers to learn 'discipline and sanitation' from the army, and added that it was the duty of the security forces 'not to show caste and community bias.' He recalled Subhas Bose's success on this score in the Indian National Army (on 3.12.47; 90:165-7).

His clarity that in a clash between his nonviolence and the government's duty the latter should prevail was also evident when Khan Abdul Ghaffar Khan asked him (in June 1947) what India would do if the Pakistan government that was being set up oppressed the people of the N.W.F.P. According to Ghaffar Khan, Gandhi replied that India would be 'in honour bound to come to their aid' and that he for one would advise the Indian government to treat it as *casus belli*. Later when Ghaffar Khan's son Ghani asked Gandhi 'what would happen to his nonviolence in that event,' Gandhi (as related by Ghaffar Khan) said: 'I am nonviolent, the government is not.'[11]

Light on Gandhi's nonviolence had also been thrown twenty-five years earlier by his statement when, for the first and last time, he was tried by the Raj for sedition. (His subsequent arrests were without trial.) Present at the March 1922 trial, N.C. Kelkar, a loyal Tilakite and Gandhi's political critic, saw that Gandhi was 'supremely serene,' 'with submission to none and yet with goodwill to all,' and that 'for once in his official life a Civilian English Sessions Judge nodded respectful salutation to a native in the dock before he himself took his seat on a Bench.'[12] Gandhi pleaded guilty, asked for the severest penalty, and was sentenced for six years. In his statement he said: 'Nonviolence is the first article of my faith. It is also the last article of my creed.' But he did not stop there.

Listing the injuries to India from 'the British connection,' Gandhi began with the Raj's refusal to allow Indians to bear arms. 'A disarmed India has no power of resistance against any aggressor if she wants to engage in an armed conflict with him,' said Gandhi.[13] He was asserting India's right to offer armed resistance. Whether she offered resistance of another sort was for her to decide.

The last two Viceroys of India, Wavell and Mountbatten, were commanders of renown. Wavell did not like Gandhi — it had fallen to him, as Commander-in-Chief of the British forces in the region, to cope with Quit India before he became Viceroy. At his first meeting with Gandhi, which took place in Simla in June 1945, Wavell heard, evidently without interest, Gandhi recalling 'his carrying down the wounded General Woodgate from Spion Kop in 1899,' a reference to Gandhi's role with the stretcher in the Boer War (*Journal*: 146). Though it failed, Gandhi's gambit of a 'war' story is worth noting.

Gandhi and Wavell had a fiery clash in August 1946, shortly after Congress members had been asked by the Viceroy to join his Executive Council as part of what was to be an interim government pending a transfer of power. A similar offer to the Muslim League had been turned down by Jinnah on the grounds that Congress was insincere in its interpretation and acceptance of the British package which linked the interim government to an ingenious formula designed to appease the League's demand for a homeland or homelands for Muslims as well as Congress's demand for an undivided India. The divergence in interpretation had triggered bitter charges and counter-charges — and large-scale rioting in Calcutta.

Wavell called Gandhi and Nehru over, showed them a statement he had prepared saying that Congress accepted the League's interpretation, which the Viceroy said was also his and the British government's, and asked them to sign it. If they were unwilling to do so, he would not (Wavell said) convene the Constituent Assembly that had been created by the package. Expressing their unwillingness, Gandhi and Nehru claimed support for their interpretation in the text of the British formula. Disagreeing, Wavell warned of an escalation in rioting. 'The argument,' in Wavell's words, 'went on for some time, and Nehru got very heated. Gandhi said that if a bloodbath was necessary it would come about in spite of nonviolence.' A footnote in Wavell's *Journal* written by Penderel Moon, the editor, reads: 'Lord Wavell always used to say that on this occasion Gandhi thumped the table and said, "If India wants her bloodbath, she shall have it." ' In the *Journal* Wavell writes: 'I said I was very shocked to hear such words from him.'

Later that evening Wavell received a letter from Gandhi in which Gandhi asked him to withdraw his offer to Congress if he held to the views he had conveyed at the interview, and also to obtain for himself a legal aide. (This related to Wavell's oft-repeated remark at the interview that he was 'a plain man and a soldier' and not a lawyer.) If riots multiply, Gandhi added, that 'will be chiefly due to the continued presence in India of a foreign power strong and proud of its arms.' The letter concluded with this sentence: 'You will please convey the whole of this letter to the British cabinet.'

The typed statement ready for signature, the insinuation that Indians twisted the meaning of 'plain' words, the tilt (as Gandhi saw it) towards the League, and the threat of not convening the Assembly had offended Gandhi; but even a cool Gandhi would have told Wavell that nonviolence or violence was an Indian decision. In his clash with the British General and Viceroy, he pitted India's will (as he saw it) against Britain's, rather than nonviolence against violence. In the event, the Assembly was convened and Congress ministers, led by Nehru, were inducted. But moves less congenial to Gandhi were also made; we will look later at some of them (341-3).

Gandhi's pride as an Indian was again stung in the last week of June 1947, by when the date of independence had been fixed and the AICC had endorsed its leaders' acceptance of Partition. In an interview he had with Mountbatten, the latter seemed to say that 'if Congress members did not adopt a helpful attitude,' the British might not quit by 15 August. Mountbatten also seems to have told Gandhi that 'if partition had not been made during British occupation, the Hindus being the majority party would have never allowed partition and held the Muslims by force under subjection' (88:226). This second remark was an attack on Gandhi's stand (not supported by Nehru and Patel) that partition was an issue for decision by Indians after British withdrawal.

After the interview Gandhi wrote to Mountbatten that the two comments had 'startled' him. He reminded the Viceroy that 'Congress has solemnly declared' that it would not 'hold by force' any Muslim areas that might wish to separate. In any case, added Gandhi, 'it is physically impossible for millions of caste-ridden Hindus to hold well-knit though fewer millions of Muslims under subjection by force.' But it is the last sentence of the unarmed old man's letter to a young Viceroy conscious of his naval career that reveals Gandhi's passion: 'Even if I stand alone, I swear by nonviolence and truth, together standing for the highest order of courage, before which the atom bomb pales into insignificance, what to say of a fleet of Dreadnoughts' (88:226). He swears by nonviolence and truth, equates them with courage, and defies fleets and the Bomb.

General Jan Smuts was perhaps his favourite military adversary. Smuts sent him books, Gandhi presented him with sandals. Gandhi also, of course, broke Smuts's laws and got thousands of Indians in South Africa to do likewise. Smuts sent him to prison and was glad when Gandhi departed from South Africa in 1914. 'The saint has left our shores,' Smuts wrote to a friend, 'I sincerely hope for ever.'[14] Yet Smuts tried to help Gandhi during the 1931 talks in London.

A peaceful law-defying march by thousands of poor Indians in 1913 was the peak of Gandhi's satyagraha in South Africa. Two accounts left by Gandhi of his arrest during this march reveal additional hues of his nonviolence. In *Satyagraha*, Gandhi describes an incident occurring at three in the afternoon of 9 November 1913, in a Transvaal veldt near Tekworth, between Standerton and Greylingstad. Gandhi was conversing with a few colleagues. Nearby stood two thousand unarmed soldiers of his 'army.' Suddenly a Cape Cart drove up. From it alighted Chamney, chief of immigration in the Transvaal, and a police officer. 'I arrest you,' the police officer told Gandhi. Indicating to the officer that he was not resisting arrest, Gandhi turned to the marchers and was asking them to keep the peace when the police officer interrupted him: 'You are now a prisoner and cannot make any speeches.' Gandhi was taken into the police vehicle, and the officer told the driver 'to drive away at full speed.' Gandhi's army remained calm and did not intervene.

In August 1921, when Gandhi was preparing India for a nation-wide campaign of disobedience, he recalled the Transvaal incident:

> It was in a practically uninhabited tract of country that I was arrested in South Africa when I was marching into a prohibited area with over two to three thousand men and some women ... It was the greatest testimony of merit the government of South Africa gave to the movement. They knew that we were as harmless as we were determined. It was easy enough for that body of men to cut to pieces those who arrested me. It would have not only been a most cowardly thing to do, but it would have been a treacherous breach of their own pledge ... But the men were ... disciplined soldiers (20:465).

Proud as Gandhi was of his army's discipline, and keen to stress discipline's value, he had hated the officer's interruption. In

Satyagraha, written in prison following his 1922 arrest, he writes:

> The officer knew that for the time being I was master of
> the situation, for trusting to our nonviolence he was alone
> in this desolate veldt confronted by two thousand Indians.
> He also knew that I would have surrendered to him even if
> he sent mere summons in writing. Such being the case it
> was hardly necessary to remind me that I was a
> prisoner...But how could an officer forgo an opportunity
> of exercising his brief authority?

Personal dignity, then, and anger at injury to it, could also enter
Gandhi's nonviolence. Ten years after the event he remembers, with
no feeling of gladness, the curb ordered when he was 'master of the
situation,' the insolence of a junior officer towards an adversary
General in the latter's camp. What is also of interest, and a subject
we will later look at closely, is how Gandhi overcame his anger. A
Gandhi nursing his anger could not have been as courteous as he
was with the sequence of officers arresting him in the decades that
followed.

❈

Presenting nonviolence as a weapon, or the best weapon, in the battle
for justice, and seeing the demonstration of its effectiveness as his,
and India's, mission, Gandhi was yet careful to enunciate the plain
political character of Congress's demand for freedom. At a meeting
in London in 1931 he said:

> The object of our nonviolent movement is complete inde-
> pendence for India, not in any mystic sense but in the
> English sense of the term, without any mental reserva-
> tion. I feel that every country is entitled to it without any
> question of its fitness or otherwise. As every country is
> fit to eat, to drink and to breathe, even so is every nation
> fit to manage its own affairs, no matter how badly . . . The

doctrine of fitness to govern is mere eyewash. Independence means nothing more or less than getting out of alien control.[15]

It was to ask for India's right that he went to London in 1931, and his encounters with Wavell and Mountbatten had the same end. These exercises were not primarily for spreading nonviolence. During other encounters he consciously promoted nonviolence. When a pro-Nazi journalist called Captain Strunk called on him in Sevagram in 1937, Gandhi told him: 'Man's dignity is to replace the law of the jungle with the law of conscious love.' 'I have reasoned out the doctrine of the sword,' Gandhi went on. 'And rejected it,' he could have added.[16]

Frequently he spoke of himself as a general. 'I do claim to be a humble soldier. If the reader will not laugh at me, I do not mind telling him that I can become also an efficient general on the usual terms. I must have soldiers who will obey . . .' (*Young India*, 19.6.24). 'I know that I am not a bad general' (*Harijan*, 23.7.38). 'The conditions prescribed by me are not physically impossible . . . But supposing [they] are not fulfilled, I shall cheerfully become the laughing stock of India and descend from the pedestal of generalship' (*Harijan*, 6.1.40).

But he would not act as a general unless appointed by the people or the Congress. 'I am no dictator though I have been given that nickname by unkind friends. I have no sanction for imposing my will on any person' (*Harijan*, 13.1.40).

Snapshots of violence featured in his remarks. 'I have had in my life many an opportunity of shooting down my opponents and earning the crown of martyrdom, but I had not the heart to shoot them. For I did not want them to shoot me.' This he said in 1925 (*Young India*, 7.5.25). And in 1931: 'Having flung aside the sword, there is nothing except the cup of love which I can offer to those who oppose me' (*Young India*, 2.4.31). Yet swinging a sword or firing a gun, whether done by others or himself, were actions he had seen in his mind, if only to be firmly rejected. (We can also recall his picture of his captors being 'cut to pieces.')

Let us look at the candour behind a playful 1924 remark: 'As a rule, I do not read writings in the Indian Press about me whether they are laudatory or condemnatory. Praise I do not need, as I am sufficiently proud of myself without outside help. Condemnation I refrain from reading, lest the Hyde in me get the better of the Jekyll and do violence to my nonviolence' (*Young India*, 8.5.24). He is conscious of a Hyde in him.

Even when he silences his Hyde, Gandhi's nonviolence need not be soothing. It can be hot: 'The hardest metal yields to heat. Even so must the hardest heart melt before a sufficiency of the heat of nonviolence. And there is no limit to the capacity of nonviolence to generate heat' (*Harijan*, 7.1.39).

We have seen that he did soothe and was tender, and later we will recall more of those scenes. But often, and certainly during his battles against the Empire or the government of South Africa, he would select from the Buddha his fight against priestcraft, and from Christ his thrust against moneychangers. Jesus and the Buddha were capable, Gandhi pointed out, of 'intensely direct action.' Christ 'defied the might of a whole empire,' and Gautama 'brought down on its knees an arrogant priesthood' (*Young India*, 12.5.20).

❋

Now that we have looked at the different weaves in Gandhi's non-violent cloth, let us quickly see how he tried to drape India in it. He knew it was new. 'It is good to swim the waters of tradition, but to sink in them is suicide,' he said (37:167). He had taken over ahimsa from Hindu, Jain and Buddhist traditions and coaxed active love and active nonviolence out of it. In 1925 he observed: 'Yours should not be a passive spirituality that spends itself in idle meditation, but it should be an active thing which will carry war into the enemy's camp' (*Young India*, 9.9.25). Ahimsa thus was nonviolent war, a satyagraha against the Raj or the South African government, and if necessary, against untouchability, an Indian prince and millowners; it was also active love towards the weak, the suppressed, the maimed and the sick.

Though he had redefined it, Gandhi claimed that ahimsa was integral to Hinduism and the Indian soil. Thus he argued that the *Mahabharata,* ending with a handful of survivors, showed that violence was 'a delusion and a folly.'[17] In Gandhi's perspective, 'the most distinctive and the largest contribution of Hinduism to India's culture is the doctrine of ahimsa. It has given a definite bias to the history of the country for the last three thousand years and over . . . Its teaching has so far permeated our people that an armed revolution has almost become an impossibility in India, not because, as some would have it, we as a race are physically weak, for it does not require much physical strength so much as a devilish will to press a trigger to shoot a person, but because the tradition of ahimsa has struck deep roots among the people.'[18]

Buddhist and Jain influences were covered under the reference to 'three thousand years and over'. Gandhi claimed that Muslim and Sikh traditions also kept a place for nonviolence. Its consonance with Christianity was not hard for Gandhi to draw. After gazing for long at a lifesize crucifix at the Vatican in 1931, he wrote: 'I saw there at once that nations like individuals could only be made through the agony of the Cross and in no other way. Joy comes not out of infliction of pain on others, but out of pain voluntarily borne by oneself' (*Young India*, 31.12.31).

Appealing to reason as well, Gandhi argued that since life was sacred and all life was one, violence was unholy and also partly suicidal: a bit of himself was killed when a man killed another. Also, violence brutalized the user as well as the victim, reproducing itself in the user through familiarity and in the victim as retaliation.

'The means may be likened to a seed,' said Gandhi, 'the end to a tree; and there is just the same inviolable connection between the means and the end as there is between the seed and the tree' (*Hind Swaraj*, Ch.16). Violence would beget more of itself; nonviolence or love, likewise. Also, Muslims killing Hindus or Sikhs today would tomorrow kill fellow-Muslims; Hindus killing whites or Muslims would in future destroy other Hindus. Again, a killer assumes the status of God rather than man, ascribing to his stand a perfection no human can claim and to his victim an irredeemability that no human can pronounce, for no human can see everything about another. In practice, violence by Indian revolutionaries stood no chance against the apparatus of the Raj. If unexpectedly it did succeed, it would produce not democracy but rule by those with arms.

On the other hand, India winning swaraj through nonviolence would inspire the world. 'I believe absolutely that she has a message for the world,' Gandhi said in 1920 (*Young India*, 11.8.20). And in 1931 he said: 'I feel in the inmost recesses of my heart that the world is sick unto death of bloodspilling. The world is seeking a way out, and I flatter myself with the belief that perhaps it will be the privilege of the ancient land of India to show that way out to the hungering world' (48:8-9).

Yet Gandhi was not without doubts. In 1918, when his friend C.F. Andrews said encouragingly that Indians had rejected 'bloodlust' in times past and nonviolence had become an unconscious instinct with them, Gandhi reminded Andrews that 'incarnations' in Indian legends were 'bloodthirsty, revengeful and merciless to the enemy.' As for the Indians of his time, they might 'have a superstitious horror of blood, but they have as little regard for the life of the enemy as an European' (14:474-5).

The context for this doubt should be remembered: Gandhi was striving at the time to recruit soldiers for the Empire. But his uncertainty also surfaced in other contexts, during communal clashes or when disobedience campaigns turned violent. After Chauri Chaura he said: 'I am a sadder and I hope a wiser man today. I see that our nonviolence is skin-deep' (*Young India*, 2.3.22). When attacked over a calf put to death in his Ashram, Gandhi replied that there was 'far more violence' in actions the critics were silent about — 'in the slow torture of men' and in the 'wanton humiliation and oppression of the weak and the killing of their self-respect.'[19]

In 1946 Gandhi said: 'When I was in detention in the Aga Khan's palace, I once sat down to write a thesis on India as a protagonist of nonviolence. But as I proceeded with my writing, I could not go on. I had to stop.' He had to stop because when he looked at India's past he found not merely 'ahimsa, which to me is the chief glory of Hinduism,' but also 'untouchability, superstitious worship of sticks and stones, animal sacrifice and so on' (86:134). He surely also saw mutual bloodletting in the Indians' history, even as he was seeing it around him, and not just in communal riots. In a letter to Vallabhbhai Patel on 1 August 1946, he said: 'Who are the people who beat up Harijans, murder them, prevent them from using public wells, drive them out of schools and refuse them entry into their homes? They are Congressmen. Aren't they? It is very necessary to have a clear picture of this' (85:102). Doubts about Indian nonviolence seemed to stalk Gandhi's oft-articulated faith in the role of a nonviolent India.

Chapter 2

Two Inner Voices

THE TRANSFORMATION OF the timid Mohan into a victor over an empire and the father of satyagraha is an oft-probed mystery generally resolved with a spotlight on the 1893 ejection at the Maritzburg railway station. Some of those closest to Gandhi have resorted to this explanation, and selective and incomplete quotes from Gandhi himself can lend credence to it. C.F. Andrews, for instance, summarized the Maritzburg incident as follows:

> Gandhi, like Paul, comes clearly under the category of the twice-born among men of religion. He experienced at a special moment in his life that tremendous convulsion of the human spirit which we call 'conversion.' In his early days . . . success had been a main ambition — success in his profession, success in life as a man; and deeper down in his heart, success as a national leader.
>
> He had gone out to South Africa on a business visit to act as a lawyer in an important trial, wherein two Indian merchants were engaged in litigation . . . As he journeyed from Durban and reached Maritzburg this dreadful experience came to him suddenly in its cruel nakedness. He was thrown out of his compartment by the railway official, though he carried a first-class ticket; and the mail train went on without him.
>
> It was late at night and he was in an utterly strange

railway station, knowing no one. There all night long as he sat shivering with cold, after enduring this insult, he wrestled within himself whether to take the next steamer back to India, or to go through to the bitter end, suffering what his own people had to suffer. Before the morning the light came to his soul. He determined by God's grace to play the man . . . This was the turning point from which his new life would begin.[1]

About ten years before his death, Gandhi was asked by the American evangelist John R. Mott to recall 'the most creative experiences' of his life. In his response Gandhi spoke of the Maritzburg incident and said : 'My active nonviolence began from that date.' However, he prefaced the reply with the remark that he could think of 'a multitude' of creative experiences (*Harijan*, 10.12.38).

Six years earlier, Premabehn Kantak, who belonged to Gandhi's Ashramite circle, had asked him to identify his earliest experience of the inner voice. The reply Gandhi gave has a bearing on the 'mystery' of his transformation:

The inner voice is something which cannot be described in words. But sometimes we have a positive feeling that something in us prompts us to do a certain thing. The time when I learnt to recognize the voice was, I may say, the time when I started praying regularly. That is, it was about 1906. I searched my memory and tell you because you asked the question. In fact, however, there was no moment when I suddenly felt that I had some new experience. *I think my spiritual life has grown without my being conscious of the fact, in the same way as hair grows on our body* (3.8.32; 50:326).

He seems to be saying that not revolution but evolution is what happened to him, and that it happened quietly and steadily, without jerks or convulsions, as his free will negotiated with circumstances or 'fate.' In his autobiography, begun in 1925, Gandhi speaks of the struggle in his soul shortly after arriving in England for his legal studies in 1888:

> I would continually think of my home and country. My mother's love always haunted me. At night the tears would stream down my cheeks . . . Everything was strange — the people, their ways, even their dwellings. I was a complete novice in the matter of English etiquette . . . There was the additional inconvenience of the vegetarian vow. Even the dishes that I could eat were tasteless and insipid. I thus found myself between Scylla and Charybdis. England I could not bear, but to return to India was not to be thought of. Now that I had come, I must finish the three years, said the inner voice.

If he was accurate in what he told Premabehn, he probably did not in 1888 ascribe his decision to complete the three years to 'the inner voice.' But the decision was a step in his growth. This London decision, and the conflict preceding it, bear a clear resemblance to the choice five years later in Maritzburg. In considering the place of Maritzburg in Gandhi's life, it is instructive also to look at an episode occuring in Durban on 25 May 1893, within three days or so of his arrival in Durban, and before he took the train for Maritzburg. Dada Abdullah, the man hiring Gandhi's services, had taken the twenty-three-year-old Gandhi to the Magistrate's court and seated him, next to Abdullah's white attorney, at the 'horseshoe' facing the judge. Gandhi was unaware that he was required to remove his turban in the Magistrate's presence. The Magistrate stared at the turban and finally, it would seem, admonished Gandhi indirectly, whereupon Gandhi left the court. The *Natal Advertiser* carried a report the next day.

An Unwelcome Visitor

An Indian entered the Court House yesterday afternoon and took a seat at the horseshoe. He was well-dressed, and it was understood that he was an English barrister, on his way to Pretoria, where he is reported to be engaged in an Indian case. He entered the Court without removing his head-covering or salaaming, and the Magistrate looked at him with disapproval. The new arrival . . . did not attempt to present his credentials, and on returning to the horseshoe was quietly told that the proper course for him to pursue, before taking up his position at the Bar, was to gain admission to the Supreme Court.

At once Gandhi wrote out a letter to the *Advertiser*:

I was startled to read a paragraph in your today's issue referring to myself. I am very sorry if His Worship the Magistrate looked at me with disapproval. It is true that on entering the Court I neither removed my head-dress nor salaamed, but. . . I had not the slightest idea that I was offending His Worship, or meaning any disrespect to the Court. Just as it is a mark of respect amongst the Europeans to take off their hats, in like manner it is in Indians to retain one's head-dress . . . In High Courts in India those Indian advocates who have not discarded their native head-dress invariably keep it on.

As to the bowing, or salaaming as you would call it, I again followed the rule observed in the Bombay High Court . . . The paragraph seems to convey also that though I was told privately not to keep my seat at the horseshoe, I nevertheless 'returned to the horseshoe.' The truth is that I was taken by the chief clerk to the interpreters' room and was asked not to take my seat at the horseshoe the next time I came unless I produced my credentials.

To make assurance doubly sure I asked the chief clerk if I could retain my seat for the day, and he very kindly said 'yes.' I was therefore really surprised to be told again in open court that in order to be entitled to the seat I had to produce credentials etc.

Lastly, I beg His Worship's pardon if he was offended at what he considered to be my rudeness, which was the result of ignorance and quite unintentional (*Natal Advertiser*, 29.5.93; 1:57-8).

Educating whites about Indian customs, saying in print that the judge's remark had 'really surprised' him and apologizing wholeheartedly if, despite his intention, offence had been taken, this pre-Maritzburg Gandhi does not seem very different, in his mix of cultural pride, unafraid self-respect and honest admission, from the later Gandhi we know.

❀

It is a mix also to be found in an earlier Gandhi, the twenty-one-year-old Mohandas about to complete his Inner Temple terms and dinners in London. This Mohandas did not express himself in memorable essays or in debating halls or well-sold journals. Except for one instance, his medium was the curious and humble organ of the London Vegetarian Society, *The Vegetarian*. The exception was a talk by him on, of all subjects, "The Foods of India" which was published in *The Vegetarian Messenger*. But perhaps we should remind ourselves that a young Indian in London in 1891 was not necessarily in a position to choose his platform, audience or theme; and when we look at what Mohandas was saying we are, at the very least, intrigued.

For one thing we find that he was no believer in ahimsa. 'An Indian shepherd,' he says in *The Vegetarian* of 28 February 1891, 'is a finely built man of Herculean constitution. He, with his thick, strong cudgel, would be a match for any ordinary European with his sword.' He speaks of 'the Kshatriyas, the so-called warlike race of India,' concedes the 'sad fact that they have degenerated,' but adds that 'so long as Prithviraj and Bhim and all of their type — not to go to the olden times — are remembered, he will be a fool who would have it believed that they are a weak race.' Meanwhile, 'the truly warlike people, among others, are the people of the North-Western provinces . . . They subsist on wheat, pulse and greens. They are the guardians of peace, largely employed in the native armies.' The reference is not to the Frontier province adjoining Afghanistan but to U.P. and its peasantry.

Mohandas has no consciousness of irony in extolling, in the same breath, warlike races on the one hand and pulses and greens on the other. And by 'shepherd' he seems to mean any rural Indian who by the sweat of his brow wins for himself and his family a living from the Indian soil. But is he merely innocent and quaint? His subject, in a series of articles, is 'Indian Vegetarians,' and this is what he writes:

> Now a question may be asked, 'Has not the British rule effected any change in the habits of the Indian people?' So far as food and drink are concerned, 'yes,' and 'no.' No, because ordinary men and women have stuck to their original food . . . Yes, because those who have learnt a little bit of English have picked up English ideas here and there . . . whether this is for the worse or the better must be left to the reader to judge . . .
>
> The last mentioned class have begun to believe in breakfast, which usually consists of a cup or two of tea . . . The drinking of tea and coffee by the so-called educated Indians, chiefly due to the British rule, may be passed over with the briefest notice. The most that tea and coffee do is to cause a little extra expense, and general debility of health when indulged in to excess, but one of the most greatly-felt evils of the British rule is the importation of alcohol — that enemy of mankind, that curse of civilization . . .
>
> The enemy has spread throughout the length and breadth of India, in spite of the religious prohibition; for even the touch of a bottle containing alcohol pollutes the Mahommedan, according to his religion, and the religion of the Hindu strictly prohibits the use of alcohol in any form whatever and yet, alas! the Government, it seems, instead of stopping, are aiding and abetting the spread of

alcohol. The poor there, as everywhere, are the greatest sufferers.

Here Mohandas speaks of a former Member of Parliament, a Mr Caine, who, 'undaunted,' continues with a crusade against the import of alcohol into India and concludes the instalment by asking: 'But what can the energy of one man, however powerful, do against the inaction of an apathetic and dormant government?' This 'one man' is no doubt Mr Caine, but we wonder whether, while framing the question, Mohandas sensed an 'inner voice' warning him that his own energy, even as 'one man,' might have to be pitted one day against an 'apathetic' government and against all the 'evils of the British rule.'

The reference to the poor, the adjective 'so-called' before 'educated Indians,' the joint Hindu-Muslim stand presented and the question marks against British rule were to be some of the core ingredients in the discourse of the Mahatma that Mohandas became.

For those wanting more evidence, more is available. The 'scavenger' that Gandhi sought in later years to emulate, popularize and assist is brought into the piece (though only with reference to his physical strength). In praise of the figure of his noble 'shepherd,' Mohandas says, 'Without being fierce like a tiger, he is yet strong and brave and docile as a lamb' — very much his future picture of the ideal personality (*The Vegetarian*, 14.3.91).

The following week, too, Mohandas appears in *The Vegetarian*, this time writing, or perhaps asked to write, on 'Some Indian Festivals.' He takes up the Hindu month Ashwin, describes 'Nava Ratri,' proceeds to 'Dashara,' the tenth day of the first fortnight, and then to 'Dhanterash,' 'the thirteenth day of the dark half of the month,' which he says is 'set apart for the worship of "Lakshmi," the goddess of wealth,' and adds:

> Rich people collect different kinds of jewels, precious stones, coins, etc., and put them carefully into a box. These they never use for any other purpose than that of worship. Each year an addition is made to this collection. The worship, i.e., the external worship — *for who, save a*

*select few, is there who does not at heart covet, or in
other words, worship money?* — consists in washing the
money with water and milk, and then decorating it with
flowers and kumkum, i.e., red ochre (*The Vegetarian*,
28.3.91).

Like the future Gandhi, Mohandas is here quick to anticipate and
answer the charge of Mammon-worship by Indians. This Mohandas
is loyal to his Hindu culture and vigilant to defend it; and his weapon
of defence is counter-attack. All who covet money worship it, he
says.

Divali and Holi are enthusiastically described in two succeeding
instalments, but once more Mohandas uses the stage to which he
has found access to make a point. In the holiday season, he says:

Even old family quarrels are patched up. At any rate a
serious attempt is made to do so. Houses are repaired and
whitewashed . . . Old debts, if any, are paid up whenever
possible . . . Alms are freely given . . . On holidays no one
is to quarrel with or swear at any other — a pernicious
habit very much in the vogue, particularly among the lower
classes . . . In a word, everything is quiet and joyful. It
will be easily seen that good and far-reaching consequences
cannot fail to flow from such holidays, which some cry
down as a relic of superstition and tomfoolery, though in
reality they are a boon to mankind, and tend to relieve a
great deal the dull monotony of life among the toiling millions (*The Vegetarian*, 4.4.91).

While repelling the charge of superstition he reveals his snobbery.
Our Mohandas, unwilling as yet to identify with 'the lower classes,'
is nonetheless willing to judge them. Significantly, however, 'the
toiling millions' are already in his gaze. A week later he literally
stands on a stage. If some earlier and later occasions are a guide, he
probably shakes a little and has difficulty summoning his voice. Yet
here he is on 2 May 1891, at Bloomsbury Hall, Hart Street,
Bloomsbury, London. *The Vegetarian* reported: 'After congratu-

lating the previous speaker (a Mrs Harrison) and apologizing for his paper, which was entitled "The Foods of India," [Mr M.K. Gandhi] began to read it. He was rather nervous in the beginning' (1:35).

What he said includes this paragraph: 'It is quite true to say that the great majority of the inhabitants of India are vegetarians. Some of them are so because of their religion, while others are compelled to live on vegetable foods because they cannot afford to pay for meat . . . There are millions in India who live upon one pice — i.e., one-third of a penny — a day . . . These people have only one meal per day, and that consists of stale bread and salt, a heavily taxed article.'

Mohandas's English vegetarian friends, all of them belonging to Britain's respectable classes, had saved him from desolation. They gave him company, a chance to serve a cause (vegetarianism), training in selling a cause (he helped organize meetings and cooked and displayed sample vegetarian meals) and in writing, and friends. With one of them, Josiah Oldfield, he shared lodgings during his final London months. He owed them much. But he would not omit to let them know that while their vegetarianism was a matter of choice, that of the Indian poor was a result of compulsion. And he would remind them of the semi-starvation of the Indian poor. As for 'salt, a heavily taxed article,' this was not the first time he had used the phrase. It occurs in the first instalment of his 'Indian Vegetarians' (7.2.91, 1:19), and in one form or another surfaced several times in his discourse before the world heard of it in 1930.

Mohandas's acquisition of some of the elements of the future Gandhi is also suggested by the care taken in 'The Foods of India' to include the peoples and foods of the country's different parts. Apart from his own western region, he is keen to say something about Bengal and about 'the southern and the northern provinces.' When in his life was our Gandhi willing to present, or represent, anything except the whole of India? The final lines of the paper refer to a goal of unity between India and England, but differences are not cloaked and the reference to the goal is injected with that unmistakable flavour of realism and honour which was to stamp the older Gandhi's discourse:

> In conclusion, I further hope that the time will come when the great difference now existing between the food habits of meat-eating in England and grain-eating in India will disappear, *and with it some other differences which, in some quarters, mar the unity of sympathy that ought to exist between the two countries*. In the future, I hope we shall tend towards unity of customs, and also unity of hearts.

Also worth marking is Mohandas's smile, which is of two kinds, the smile of honesty about himself and the smile of wisdom (often a superior smile) about the world's foolishness. In his talk on 'The Foods of India,' after drawing a distinction between an Indian vegetarian who does not take eggs — 'he thinks that in taking eggs he would kill a would-be life' — but 'does not hesitate to use milk and butter,' one kind of Englishman who might eat eggs, and another who would reject all 'animal products, as they are called here,' including milk, hoping to survive 'on fruits and nuts,' Mohandas adds parenthetically, 'I am sorry to say I have been taking eggs for about a month and a half.'

This is a typical Gandhian confession. I bring it here under his smile of honesty but of course tears too were apt to accompany his truthfulness, and solemnity as well. Towards the close of his time in London, Mohandas was interviewed by a representative of *The Vegetarian* on the circumstances that brought him to London. Mohandas described the obstacles that he had to overcome and the permissions he had to obtain from a variety of relatives. The 'acquiescence' of some, he said, he had 'exacted' — the exercise 'was nothing else'. As for his mother, of whom he was 'the pet,' 'I got her to accede, with much reluctance, to my request' by 'showing the exaggerated advantages of coming to England' (1:44).

'You will, perhaps, be astonished to hear,' Mohandas tells the interviewer, 'that I am married.' He added, 'The marriage took place at the age of twelve.' Not an easy confession to make to the journal's emancipated and sophisticated readers, especially when the confessor has for some time presumed to educate them through its columns. But Mohandas cannot hide facts. His conscience will not let him.

The interviewer is informed that 'an old friend of my father saw and advised me to go to England and take the robe; he, as it were, fanned the fire that was burning within me. I thought to myself, "If I go to England not only shall I become a barrister (*of whom I used to think a great deal*), but I shall be able to see England, the land of philosophers and poets, the very centre of civilization." ' The shot at barristers is an advance warning of *Hind Swaraj*, which was to come eighteen years later; it is also a smile at mankind's, and his own, ambitions (1:42).

Both smiles can be seen in the description of his arrival in England, which forms part of the diary he wrote in November 1888, almost three years before the *Vegetarian* interview:

[At 4 p.m.] Mr Mazumdar, Mr Abdul Majid and I reached the Victoria Hotel (from the docking ship — the three had been together on the *Clyde*.) Mr Abdul Majid told in a dignified air to the porter of the Victoria Hotel to give our cabman the proper fare. Mr Abdul Majid thought very highly of himself but let me write here that the dress which he had put on was perhaps worse than that of the porter. He did not take care of the luggage too, and as if he had been in London for a long time stepped into the hotel. I was quite dazzled by the splendour of the hotel. *I had never in my life seen such pomp.* My business was simply to follow the two friends in silence. There were electric lights all over. There Mr Abdul Majid at once went. The manager at once asked him whether he would choose second floor or not. Mr Majid thinking it below his dignity to inquire about the daily rent said yes. The manager at once gave us a bill of 6 s. each per day and a boy was sent with us. *I was all the while smiling within myself.*

Then we were to go to the second floor by a lift. I did

not know what it was. The boy at once touched something which I thought was lock of the door. But, as I
afterwards came to know, it was the bell and he rang in
order to tell the waiter to bring the lift. The doors were
opened and I thought that was a room in which we were to
sit for some time. But to my great surprise we were brought
to the second floor.

The extract has four 'at onces' and is in the English of an Indian
youth in his nineteenth year who, though 'studying' English as a
subject to 'clear' in his Kathiawad school exams, has hardly spoken
it. Here we have met the Bania Mohandas, and seen the two smiles.
He is frank about his ignorance and surprise, and though writing
only in his diary, can be seen as being quite willing to be laughed at
But he also smiles at vanity and its price. That the price hurt him is
apparent and was in any case stated in the autobiography. The
ability to turn hurt into a smile, a key trait of the later Mahatma,
seems to have existed in the Mohandas of 1888.

In the two short pieces that appeared in *The Vegetarian* in April
1892, nine months after he left England, Mohandas can be seen for
the first and last time in his life as a breezy writer and as almost
nothing else. The subject was his voyage back to India; it is likely
that Oldfield, the editor, had asked Mohandas to 'continue writing
for us' and mentioned the voyage as a topic. It is likely too that the
pieces were largely written on the journey. The snob in Mohandas
again shows his face. In Malta travellers are 'pestered' by 'a crowd
of dirty-looking beggars' and Port Said is 'full of rogues and ras-
cals.' The Portuguese waiters on the *Assam*, into which Bombay-
bound passengers move in Aden from the *Oceana*, 'murder the
Queen's English' and 'are the reverse of clean.'

Mohandas describes the meals in a day of 'an average passenger': the pre-breakfast tea and biscuits, a huge breakfast, its elements detailed, an 'easily digestible' lunch ('dinner') with 'plenty
of mutton and vegetables, rice and curry, pastry and what not . . .
fruit and nuts,' followed by 'a "refreshing" cup of tea and biscuits
at 4 p.m.' and 'a "high tea" at 6.30 p.m. — bread and butter, jam

or marmalade, or both, salad, chops, tea, coffee, etc.' Thereafter, since the sea air was 'so very salubrious,' 'the passengers could not retire to bed before taking a few, a very few — only eight or ten, fifteen at the most — biscuits, a little cheese and some wine or beer.'

'Some very nice ladies and gentlemen [travelled] in the first saloon. But it would not do to have all play and no quarrel, so some of the passengers thought fit to get drunk almost every evening (beg your pardon, Mr Editor, they got drunk almost every evening, but this particular evening they got drunk and disorderly).' And so forth, including remarks about a speech on board that he was all set to make (on vegetarianism, of course) but did not because the evening to be 'devoted to speeches and concerts' never came off: 'The secretary of the committee who [was to] manage these things . . . had asked me to be humorous. I told him that I might be nervous but humorous I could not be.'

Yet, as the remark showed, Mohandas did try to be humorous in these pieces published in April 1892. Was he testing himself for a possible literary career? In a letter he wrote to an Indian friend in September 1892 he refers to the implications of his 'accepting a literary post' and goes on to ask, 'But where is the post? Not an easy thing to get one.' (to R. Patwari, 5.9.22; 1:56) In the autobiography he speaks of an unsuccessful application by him at about this time for a position which involved teaching English for 'one hour daily' in 'a famous high school' in Bombay, and also of his lack of confidence, even before leaving England, in his ability to succeed in law.

Be all that as it may. In the pieces he wrote on his way back to India, Mohandas seems free, for whatever reason, from that consciousness of a cultural divide between India and England which he almost always carried with him, before and after his London studies. It was at the start of this article that Mohandas recorded his warmth about London:

> I could not make myself believe that I was going to India until I stepped into the steamship *Oceana*, of the P. & O.

Company. So much attached was I to London and its environments; for who would not be? London with its teaching institutions, public galleries, vegetarian restaurants, is a fit place for a student and a traveller, a trader and a 'faddist' — as a vegetarian would be called by his opponents. Thus it was not without regret that I left dear London (1:50-51).

The entertaining article ended, as it had begun, on a serious note:

What a human cargo was on the *Oceana* and the *Assam!* Some were going to make fortunes in Australia . . .; some, having finished their studies in England, were going to India in order to earn a decent living. Some were called away by a sense of duty, some were going to meet their husbands in Australia or India, as the case may be, and some were adventurers who, being disappointed at home, were going to pursue their adventures, God knows where (1:50-56).

The Mohandas returning to India in the monsoon of 1891 thus appears to be a dogged young man with an unclear future and also with a sparkle, capable of looking at life's funny side but yielding to his inner voices. For there seem to be two of these: one insisting purely on facts, on the truth about matters such as his childwife, the eggs he has consumed and other such awkward realities about himself as well as about others, and the other demanding that he should not let his side down. This side is his Hindu culture and religion, his people and their past, but it is also the culture, religion, community and past of non-Hindu Indians. No short word or phrase quite describes what he wishes to defend or identify with, it is emotional, political and national — but 'India' or Indian honour' comes close.

He seems unable to defy his moral conscience, and 'India' or 'Indian honour,' insofar as he can interpret or sense its pull, also seems to stir him. If both voices say the same thing or consistent things, he will be whole and at peace, and he may also lead a people, for which people can fail to follow one doggedly loyal to God and country? But conflict and sorrow may be his fate if the two tug at him in different directions. Unlike some Indian patriots, he does not see India as his God or Goddess. Yet India (as he conceives her) is a second pull or passion with him, rooted next to the first, and capable of harmonizing or clashing with it.

If, then, there are reasonable indications to suggest that the young Gandhi of 1891 is one sharply and unusually aware of the two inner voices of truth and nation, we have to ask how he came to be this person, and take a brief look not only at his childhood and boyhood in India but also at aspects of his encounter with England left out of our examination of the Mohandas of 1891.

❋

We need not dwell on some well-known incidents: the boy Mohan, unable and unwilling to understand his teacher's advice to copy the spelling of 'kettle', or crying because his headmaster in Rajkot wrongly accused him of lying, or moved by a song about Shravana, a play about Harishchandra and stories from the Ramayana. Their significance is obvious, and we can usefully reflect on the nature of a boy who 'acted Harishchandra to [himself] times without number' and 'often wept' thinking of the story. We will take for granted, also, the equally well-known and well-understood trauma of the fifteen-year-old Mohan learning, while in an embrace with his equally young wife, of his father's death, and the consequences, in the young man's future attitudes towards sex, of that trauma. But it may be helpful not to rush past two other features of Mohan's boyhood, his apology to his father and his nursing him.

Our familiarity with the apology can prevent an appreciation of the act of the fifteen-year-old apologizer. He had clipped out a bit of precious metal from his brother's golden amulet in order to help the brother clear a debt. His conscience gnawing him, Mohan wrote out a confession (he did not have the courage to make it orally) and trembled as he handed it to the former Prime Minister of Porbandar, Rajkot and Wankaner. The father 'read it through,' and tears 'trickled down his cheeks, wetting the paper. For a moment he closed his eyes in thought and then tore up the note. He had sat up to read it. (Karamchand Gandhi was ill and not far from death.) He again lay down. I also cried . . . Those pearl-drops of love cleansed my heart, and washed my sin away.'

The confession said that Father would now know that his son was but a common thief; it added that he would steal no more. Mohan's sister Raliatben remembered the confession all her life — an interesting fact, considering that she was critical of her younger brother on several scores. (She remembered also, while discussing the incident with Pyarelal, that Mohan had first gone to his mother with the confession; Putlibai asked him to speak to his father.) We are entitled to see in the act a mix of conscience and courage, and we should see it in the context of the deep attachment between the boy and his parents. (He would contest any claim of a deeper relationship with one's parents, Gandhi told Mahadev Desai in 1918.[2])

Erikson links the boy's nursing of his ailing father over a period of almost three years to Gandhi's involvement later in his life with the untouchables, the sick and the lepers, and also to the occasions when Gandhi offered to nurse political foes, rivals and allies. According to Erikson, Gandhi nursed to conquer. I want to stress that the three-year-experience did not turn the lad against the chores of nursing. It revealed an early ability to enjoy a burden — to turn pain into a smile, as we saw.

References to his youth in Rajkot are rare in the older Gandhi's recorded discourse. However, he once said: 'When I recall my school days, I have a vivid recollection of boys who put on an air, because they were considered to be clever . . . [or] because they had athletic skill and had physical power . . . But . . . their pride went before destruction, for the weaker ones, realizing their haughtiness, segregated them . . . and so they really dug their own graves . . .' (34:505-6). In the Autobiography he tells of Sheikh Mehtab, who dazzled Mohan with his speed and leaps as an athlete, persuaded him to eat meat in order, among other things, 'to drive the English out of India,' took him to a Rajkot brothel, where Mohan sat paralyzed on the bed of a prostitute (whose fee had been paid by Mehtab), until, 'with abuses and insults,' he was shown the door. Yet Mohan hoped to reform Mehtab.

The boy's friendship with Mehtab was part of an early and life-long interest in Hindu-Muslim companionship. The diary he wrote soon after arriving in London, mentioning the names of friends bidding him farewell in Rajkot and at railway stations between Rajkot and Bombay, refers to 'Latib' (Latif?) and 'Usmanbhai.'

In 1947, Gandhi claimed that his belief in 'complete brotherhood' among Hindus, Muslims and Parsis dated back to 'before 1885,' before 'the Congress was born.' 'At the time that communal unity possessed me, I was a lad twelve years old,' he added (89:144-5). We do not know whether the dream of Hindu-Muslim friendship started with his association with Mehtab, or whether he had Muslim friends before then.

In building friendships with Muslim (and Parsi) boys, Mohan was evidently encouraged by the example of his father, who at times received Muslim and Parsi friends in his home and listened, along with his nursing boy, to their talk 'about their own faiths.' Mohan also knew that his father's father Uttamchand Gandhi, the ablest in a line of Gandhis serving as Prime Ministers to rulers in Kathiawad, had been defended by an Arab bodyguard. This was when a cannon bombarded the house of the Gandhis under the orders of Rani Rupaliba, then the regent of Porbandar, who had been incensed by Uttamchand's protection of a state treasurer she disliked.

The background of Mohan's mother Putlibai too may have played a role. A devout Hindu with a regard for some learned Jains, she belonged to the Pranami sect which had incorporated some Islamic features and did not worship idols. Yet Mohan seems to have questioned some of his mother's views. In 1921 he told Andrews that he 'used to laugh at my dear mother for making us bathe if we brothers touched any pariah' (19:288-90). He amplified the remark in a speech the same year to a gathering of untouchables in Ahmedabad:

> I was hardly yet twelve ... A scavenger named Uka, an untouchable, used to attend our house for cleaning latrines. Often I would ask my mother why it was wrong to touch

him and why I was forbidden to do so. If I accidentally touched Uka I was asked to perform the ablutions. . . . I was a dutiful and obedient child but . . . I often had tussles with [my parents] on this matter. I told my mother that she was entirely wrong in considering physical contact with Uka as sinful.

While at school I would often happen to touch the 'untouchables'; and, as I never would conceal the fact from my parents, my mother would tell me that the shortest cut to purification, after my unholy touch, was to cancel it by touching any Muslim passing by.'

This, Gandhi admitted, he 'often did' as a boy, but only, he said, 'out of reverence for my mother,' 'never' believing it to be proper (19:569-75). The boyhood disputation was remembered by Gandhi more than once. In 1939 he recalled: 'My mother said, "You must not touch this boy, he is an untouchable." "Why not?" I questioned back' (69:201).

British rule was a resented reality in Mohan's world. At times, though, it was praised: Mohan would never forget a verse from his childhood about the peace the English had brought (89:288). But he would also remember that a British officer, an assistant political agent, had detained his father for some hours. The officer having spoken discourteously of the Rajkot ruler, Kaba Gandhi objected, and the officer asked him to apologize. On refusing to do so, Kaba Gandhi was detained under a tree.

Mohan would also remember the 'disgust and torture' on his father's 'face as he was putting his legs into his stockings and his feet into ill-fitting and inflexible boots' prescribed for his attendance at a Rajkot durbar in honour of the visiting Governor of Bombay. 'He had to do this,' Gandhi would recall (*Early Phase*: 188). British rule was an imposition. And it was alien.

Taking umbrage at it was a key factor in the reaction against Christian missionaries from Britain in the Rajkot of Gandhi's childhood and boyhood to which the autobiography refers. Mohan heard that a convert to Christianity 'had to eat beef and drink liquor and change his clothes and go about in European costume including a hat.' Gandhi recalled that such talk 'got on my nerves.' On one occasion he had himself heard Hindu gods slighted from 'a corner near the high school.' 'I could not endure this,' Gandhi remembered.

This is strong language, and indicative of the depth of the lad Mohan's feeling against slights to his culture, of his nationalism. When the autobiography appeared, the Rev. H.R. Scott, an Irish Presbyterian, protested. Scott said he was the only Rajkot-based missionary at the time and had never slandered Hindus or their gods or persuaded converts to eat beef or drink liquor. Gandhi accepted the repudiation but added that 'the painful memory' of the preaching he had heard was 'still vivid before me.' Perhaps he had heard a visiting missionary. Be that as it may, Mohan's world took a poor view of the white man's culture and a worse one of an Indian exchanging his inherited culture for it.

This perception, or prejudice, is clearly seen, after Kaba Gandhi's death, in the reaction to the advice of Mavji Dave, an old family friend, that Mohan should go to London and become a barrister. Even before this, Mohandas says in his London Diary, 'I had a secret design in my mind of coming here to satisfy my curiosity of knowing what London was.' Earlier still, Kaba Gandhi had apparently expressed a desire to send Mohan, his third son, to England. However, Dave's suggestion was attacked by Mohan's relatives and caste elders. The idea was 'disgraceful' (1:6) and 'unholy' (1:44). The autobiography records what an uncle told Mohan: 'I am not sure whether it is possible for one to stay in England without prejudice to one's own religion . . . When I meet these big barristers, I see no difference between their life and that of Europeans. They know no scruples regarding food. Cigars are never out of their mouths. They dress as shamelessly as Englishmen . . . I am shortly going on a pilgrimage and have not many years to live. At the threshold of death, how dare I give you permission to go to England, to cross the seas?'

We will not go into the details, fascinating as they are, of how Mohan overcame objections and obstacles and made it to England.

But we have to note his determination. In the London Diary he says: 'I must write that had it been some other man in the same position which I was in, I dare say he would not have been able to see England' (1:9).

And his keenness. In the interview to *The Vegetarian*, shortly before leaving England, he said: 'Sleeping, waking, drinking, eating, walking, running, reading, I was dreaming and thinking of England.' And, finally, the vows he took before his mother, in the presence of Becharji Swami, 'originally a Modh Bania (Gandhi's caste)' who had 'now become a Jain monk.' The Swami 'administered the oath and I vowed not to touch wine, woman and meat. This done, my mother gave her permission.'

Mohandas asked Frederick Lely, the British Agent in Porbandar, for a grant for the London exercise. To meet him Mohan had made a five-day journey by bullock-cart and camel from Rajkot. He sent in a letter and secured an appointment. What happened is related in the 1888 Diary: 'For the first time in my life I had an interview with an English gentleman. Formerly I never dared to front them. But thoughts of London made me bold. I had small talk with him in Gujarati. He was quite in a hurry. He saw me when he was ascending the ladder of the upper storey of his bungalow. He said the Porbandar state was very poor and could not give me any pecuniary help. However, he said I should first graduate in India and then he would see if he could render me any help. I did not expect such a reply from him.'

'Small talk' no doubt means 'a short talk,' and 'ladder' refers to a flight of steps. In the autobiography Gandhi says: 'I had made elaborate preparations to meet [Lely]. I had carefully learnt up a few sentences and had bowed low and saluted him with both hands. But all to no purpose!'

Mohandas also called on the ruler of Rajkot, who presented a photo of himself, and on Colonel J.W. Watson, the Raj's Political Agent in Kathiawad, who gave, in Mohandas's words in the diary, 'a trivial note of introduction which he said . . . was worth one lac of rupees.' 'Now really it makes me laugh,' writes Mohandas in the diary. He adds: 'Here I must write that the fulsome flattery which I had to practise about this time had made me quite angry' (1:8).

When a youth who has just turned nineteen records that he is angry at himself for having flattered men in power, and decides that the memory of a bitter disappointment will only 'make me laugh,' we are entitled to see some steel in his will.

Mohan had more 'leadership' than the Mahatma discloses in the autobiography. He is depicted there as being a coward, afraid of serpents, thieves, ghosts and the dark. Kasturba, on the other hand, was fearless, Gandhi recalls. But we know that the boy Mohan often acted as an umpire in games, sent violators out of the pitch and sorted out quarrels. 'Sure, I was the leader of the boys in my class,' he said to Kalelkar, when the latter once asked for more information about his boyhood than Gandhi had given in the autobiography.[3]

We know also that friends at Alfred High School, Rajkot, presented him an address before he left for England. Gandhi recalled that he was shaking when he 'stammered out' a Gujarati speech in reply, but we may note that *The Kathiawar Times* published an English translation of what he said: 'I hope that some of you will follow in my footsteps, and after your return from England you will work wholeheartedly for big reforms in India' (1:1).

We are not taking hindsight's aid if we read into this simple sentence an interest in something more than himself. The autobiography conceals what the London Diary, articles and interviews reveal — Mohan's curiosity. He soaks himself in the world around him, whether it is 'a day in the life' of the person he calls 'the Indian shepherd,' or, as in the idyllic paragraph below, a scene on a festival day:

> You are standing near the corner of a public road. Mark the shepherd trotting onward in his milk-white suit, worn for the first time, with his long beard turned up beside his face and fastened under his turban, singing some broken verses. A herd of cows, with their horns painted red and green and mounted with silver, follow him. Soon after you see a crowd of little maids, with small earthen vessels

resting on cushions placed on their heads. You wonder
what those vessels contain. Your doubt is soon resolved
by that careless maid spilling some milk from her vessel.
Then observe that big man with white whiskers and a big
white turban, with a long reed pen thrust into his turban.
He has a long scarf wound round his waist with a silver
inkstand adjusted in the scarf. He, you must know, is a
great banker (*The Vegetarian*, 4.4.91; 1:31).

Also, no matter how inclined to tremble, he was, as already mentioned, resolute. There is no need to give here an account of the
firmness with which he stood up to caste leaders who continued to
denounce, until and even after his departure from Bombay, his London plan. However an additional sentence from the Diary may be in
order: 'But I am not a man who would, after having formed any
intention, leave it easily.'

We also get the impression that he was thought resolute by his
peers. Certainly he must have been regarded as something of a
leader, for he says in the Diary:

Many had come to bid me farewell on the night (of leaving Rajkot for Bombay). Messrs. Kevalram, Chhaganlal
(Patwari), Vrajlal, Harishankar, Amolakh, Manekchand,
Latib, Popat, Bhanji, Khimji, Ramji, Damodar, Meghji,
Ramji Kalidas, Naranji, Ranchhoddass, Manilal were
among those who came. Jatashankar, Vishvanath *and
others may be added*.

The sentence in the Diary that most clearly reveals Mohandas's
awareness of his prestige occurs in the following paragraph. (The
Meghjibhai mentioned is a relative who had promised money for the
London exercise, but Putlibai had told her son that he 'would never
get any money from him.'):

Now here is what took place at Rajkot during my absence
(*he was in Porbandar to meet Lely*). My friend Sheikh

Mehtab who, I should say, is very full of tricks, reminded Meghjibhai of his promise and forged a letter with my signature in which he wrote that I stood in need of Rs 5,000 and so on. The letter was shown to him and it actually passed for a letter written by me. Then, *of course, he was quite puffed up* and made a solemn promise of giving me Rs 5,000 (1:6).

If Mohandas assumes that as a matter of course a relative like Meghjibhai would be 'quite puffed up' by a request with his signature, then he is aware of being more than a nobody. Brilliant in neither studies nor games, trembling before a crowd, and unable, despite rough as well as patient efforts, to dominate or educate his spirited, beautiful but illiterate wife, the Mohandas who sailed out of Bombay in September 1888, a month before his nineteenth birthday, was yet a leader in the limited world to which he belonged. And if the trembling he then displayed, and later recalled, owed something to timidity, perhaps it owed more to a sense of demands on his will larger than he could calmly face — or resist. And though the autobiography makes no such claim, the records of his youth and his references to his youth in later life hint at an early acceptance, even if mostly in the subconscious, of an awesome responsibility on behalf of an injured India.

❋

Arriving in London, Mohandas found he enjoyed reading the newspapers. 'In India [he] had never read a newspaper,' but in London he spent an hour a day reading *The Daily News, The Daily Telegraph* and *The Pall Mall Gazette*. The axe he employed on his expenses never touched the papers. Also, as Pyarelal was to find out, it was in 1888, the year of his arrival in London, that Mohandas started a lifelong practice of cutting out and preserving items from the papers. If this suggests an early inclination towards public affairs, the fact that he soon composed his London Diary suggests, at the very least, that he also took himself seriously.

He has not himself left reasons for the Diary. I would guess they were three. Firstly, to record what was clearly a feat, his success in getting to England. Secondly, to confront himself and the choice between returning, defeated, to India and battling it out in a London that seemed cruelly inhospitable to one who had bound himself against touching meat. Thirdly, to practise writing English. I suspect that he was beginning to enjoy what he read — the newspapers and a range of books, not necessarily all connected with his studies — and was tempted to write himself. The Diary's second sentence — 'The scene opens about the end of April' — could have been the beginning of anyone's writing career. Yet even in this inauguration the writer is second to the man examining himself, his strength, his integrity. This is shown, I think, by what was quoted earlier from the Diary.

The autobiography is full of Mohandas's struggles with diet, lodgings, budget and identity. He tried, he tells us, to 'ape the English gentleman' — to dance, play the violin, speak French, be eloquent in English, devoting 'ten minutes every day before a huge mirror, watching myself, arranging my tie and parting my hair in the correct fashion,' and so forth — but gave up the attempt. It is only incidentally that he mentions the people he met in London — people like Cardinal Manning, the divine who led a dock strike; the leaders of Theosophy, Mme Blavatsky and Annie Besant; Dadabhai Naoroji, who had presided in 1886 at the second session of the Indian National Congress, founded a year earlier, and who would be elected in 1892 to the House of Commons, and Ranjitsinhji, prince and cricketer. When Charles Bradlaugh, the MP who was sometimes called 'the Member for India,' died, Mohandas attended the funeral. He often saw, and worked with, the prominent writers and doctors linked to the vegetarian movement, the discovery of which had thrilled Mohandas; and he heard sermons by some of the famous preachers of Britain of the time, including Charles Spurgeon, Joseph Parker and Dean Farrar.

I mention the names because it is easy to conclude from the autobiography's stress on the shyness of Gandhi's youth that he mostly kept to himself in London. The truth is that he met several influential persons, many of them involved with India. Mohandas, the diffident law student, kept himself abreast of political and social currents. He also 'studiously followed from day to day' court proceedings that touched on the Irish struggle for home rule (*Early Phase* 1:232).

A request by a pair of English friends involved in Theosophy that he should explain the Gita to them embarrassed Gandhi: he did not know it. But he read Edwin Arnold's version, *The Song Celestial*, along with them and was stirred. Arnold's *Light of Asia* had a similar effect and taught him about the Buddha. The Sermon on the Mount, which followed in his reading, 'went straight to [his] heart;' and he read Carlyle on the Prophet of Islam. Also a pointer was his joining the Anjuman-e-Islamia, an association of Muslim students in London.

When a young Hindu anxious to preserve his vegetarianism joins the Islamia, he bares a concern for an India beyond Hinduism. Also revealing about his London time is a remark he made on Pan-Islamism during a talk with Bengal's Muslim leaders in May 1947: 'I had evidence of it even while I was a student in England many years ago' (87:442-3). This would mean that London's young Mohandas was alert to the tenor of the Islam of his Muslim acquaintances.

Some friendships he formed in London lasted a lifetime. One was with Pranjivan Mehta, a Kathiawad doctor older than Mohandas who was pursuing higher studies in medicine. Mehta backed Gandhi's struggles in South Africa and India with money and in 1912 became the first Indian to author a book on Gandhi.

We should reflect on the intensity of Gandhi's concern about the vows. To the horror of an Indian companion, Dalpatram Shukla, he hailed a waiter at a posh restaurant to ask if the soup contained meat. A normal query of 1995 was in 1888 or 1889 an unthinkable breach of etiquette. The companion could save his dignity only by asking Mohandas to leave the restaurant, which the meek Gandhi did. But this meek youth also told Shukla and others who raised the subject with him that he would rather die than break his vow (1:48). Such an affirmation was necessary because a series of white and brown men had told him that it was impossible to survive in England without meat and liquor.

Josiah Oldfield, editor of *The Vegetarian,* with whom young Gandhi shared lodgings for some months in 1891, survived Gandhi. After Gandhi's death he recalled his integrity: 'I have always felt since that the Indians coming to England have to face the same great testing examination. If they fail, they prove that they have commonplace minds and they drop into the ordinary run of English diet, English habits, and general mediocrity. If, on the other hand, they can stand firm in their faith and be prepared to die for it, they prove themselves men indeed. Upon this class of men does the mantle of Gandhi still fall . . .'[4]

Asked by *The Vegetarian* about his time in England, Gandhi ended his response as follows: 'In conclusion, I am bound to say that during my nearly three years' stay in England, I have left many things undone, and have done many things which I perhaps might better have left undone, yet I carry one great consolation with me, that I shall go back without having taken meat or wine, and that I know from personal experience that there are so many vegetarians in England' (*The Vegetarian,* 20.6.91).

It would have been indelicate to say so in a newspaper interview, but he had also managed to keep the vow about women, though not without some teetering on the brink recalled in the autobiography. (Visiting Portsmouth, along with Mazumdar, for a Vegetarian conference, he took part with his friends and their landlady in a round of bridge. Jokes flowed, including 'indecent' ones. Mohandas was 'captured.' He 'joined in,' and was 'about to go beyond the limit, leaving the cards and the games to themselves,' when Mazumdar rebuked him. 'Whence this devil in you, my boy?' he asked. Mohandas fled from the scene and went 'quaking, trembling and with beating heart' to his room. Next day, cutting his stay short, he left Portsmouth.)

❈

We should mark the significance he gave to returning unscathed. At first sight the final phrase about the existence of 'so many vegetarians in England' seems a fall from the solemn to the trite and at the most a gesture to *The Vegetarian's* clientele, but it holds a deeper meaning. Until he had met the British vegetarians, he had refrained from meat because of the vow but, as he himself states, was pro-meat in his mind. English circumstances had been overcome not by free will but by a will bound by a vow. His new friends, and books like *Plea for Vegetarianism* by Henry Salt (whom, too, he met), made him a vegetarian by choice. They did more. Endorsing and respecting his vows — Oldfield's remark reflected their thinking — these friends acknowledged the worth of the culture to which Mohandas had stayed loyal.

He was drawn to these men and women; their character and courage evoked his respect, and they seemed to enjoy a standing in British society. The coincidence between their views and his mother's was not a small discovery for Mohandas. It gave a vital legitimacy to his Indian inner voice. In the autobiography he writes that his London experiences 'harmonized my inward and outward life' and that 'my soul knew no bounds of joy.' The context for these words was the frugality he had embraced but they also apply, I think, to the concord he felt in London between the universal and the Indian, between pure truth and his vows.

We should note, too, that his 'acquaintance with religions' (his title for the relevant chapter in the autobiography) was a spinoff of his encounters with these men and women. Some of them urged him to consider Christianity for the health of his soul, but though the Sermon on the Mount 'delighted [him] beyond measure,' he resisted the idea of Jesus as God's only begotten son and mankind's sole saviour. Yet it was in London that he 'crossed the Sahara of atheism,' to use his phrase in the autobiography.

For some time before his departure from India, he, Mehtab and some other lads had been attracted to a view that esteemed and equated dynamism, atheism, physical strength, meat-eating and freedom from superstition. In London he changed. Talking to him in 1907-8, Doke learned that Gandhi's London years 'helped . . . to sweep away the fragments of his boyish atheism' (40). We saw earlier that ahimsa did not feature in the values of London's Mohandas, but he found, or refound, a belief in God. And since his vegetarian friends were supportive of his vows, he may have felt an identity between his God and theirs.

He also knew, as he would openly say in a letter addressed to Indian students published in *The Vegetarian* in April 1894, that 'the English Vegetarians will more readily sympathise with the Indian aspirations,' adding, 'That is my personal experience.' He went on to state that 'the vegetarian movement will indirectly aid India politically also . . .' (*The Vegetarian*, 28.4.94; 1: 125ff.). These lines confirm the 'political' strand in London's Mohandas, and the proximity of that strand to his 'religious' position.

'While [an Indian student] is in England,' Mohandas would soon write, 'he is alone, no wife to tease and flatter him, no parents to indulge, no children to look after, no company to disturb. He is the master of his time . . . Moreover, the invigorating climate of England is by itself a stimulant to work . . . You cannot help working' (*Guide to London*; 1:71). Applying available time to 'constructive work' was a habit Gandhi acquired in London, and the Vegetarians supplied the channel.

But many Sundays were free nonetheless and held scope for more than 'constructive work.' An old lady noticing Mohandas struggling with a menu in French in a Brighton cafe had helped him to order a vegetarian meal, given him her London address, and invited Gandhi to dine with her every Sunday. The rest of the story is best given in Gandhi's own words:

She would . . . introduce me to young ladies and draw me into conversation with them. Particularly marked out for these conversations was a young lady who stayed with her, and often we would be left entirely alone together. I found all this very trying at first . . . But . . . in course of time [I] looked forward to every Sunday and came to like the conversations with the young friend.

The old lady went on spreading her net wider every day . . . Possibly she had her own plans about us. I was in a quandary. How I wished I had told the good lady that I was married! It is, however, never too late . . . I wrote a letter to her somewhat to this effect:

'Ever since we met at Brighton you have been kind to me . . . You also think that I should get married and with that view you have been introducing me to young ladies . . . I must confess to you that I have been unworthy of your affection. I should have told you when I began my visits to you that I was married . . . I was married while yet a boy, and am the father of a son. I am pained that I should have kept this knowledge from you so long . . . Will you forgive me?'

Almost by return post came her reply somewhat as follows: 'I have your frank letter. We were both very glad and had a hearty laugh over it . . . It is well that you have acquainted us with the real state of things . . . We shall certainly expect you next Sunday and look forward to hearing all about your child-marriage and laughing at your expense.'

We cannot be certain that the old lady harboured the designs that Mohandas suspected, and it is of interest that his acquaintance with her 'ripened into friendship and was kept up all through my stay in England and long after,' as he would say in the autobiography. Whether causing tears or laughter, Gandhi's confessions were something of a cement too.

❋

In the autobiography Gandhi has described the last leg of his 1891 journey and the news awaiting him:

The sea was rough . . . all the way from Aden. Almost every passenger was sick; I alone was in perfect form, staying on deck to see the stormy surge, and enjoying the splash of the waves. The outer storm was to me a symbol of the inner. But even as the former left me unperturbed, I think I can say the same thing about the latter. There was the trouble with the caste that was to confront me . . . [and] my [feeling of] helplessness in starting on my profession. And then, as I was a reformer, I was taxing myself as to how best to begin certain reforms. But there was even more in store for me than I knew . . .

I was pining to see my mother. I did not know that she was no more . . . The sad news was now given me . . . My brother had kept me ignorant of her death, which took place whilst I was still in England. The news was a severe shock to me. But I must not dwell upon it. My grief was even greater than over my father's death. Most of my cherished hopes were shattered. But I remember that I did not give myself up to any wild expression of grief. I could even check the tears . . .

He does not spell out the 'reforms' or 'hopes' but he is thinking of more than his career, though he is certainly thinking of that. He gives a fresh example of the ability to suppress pain and discloses both an anticipation of storms and a preparedness to face them, traits that suggest a leader in the making.

In later years, and right until the end, Gandhi made several references to his attitudes in boyhood and youth. For instance, in November 1947, when he heard painful accounts from Hindu and Sikh refugees and Muslims who felt threatened, he said: 'Right from childhood . . . I have made it a habit of hardening my heart instead of shedding tears. While hearing . . . angry or sorrowful tales . . . I steel my heart' (Prayer speech on 4.11.47; 89:471-2).

Two months earlier, discussing how individuals might be reformed, he had remembered, without naming him, Mehtab, whom in his boyhood he had tried to change — a bid from which he had drawn some lessons: 'It is not enough to be good. We must also be brave and at the same time have wisdom. Then from association with us even the bad people will become good . . . I have learnt this from my childhood' (19.9.47; 89:204).

He claimed, in October 1947, that he was 'a person who has been dreaming of freedom from his childhood days' (89:400); and in 1945 he said that he had kept 'an eye to truth' 'ever since I gave my word to my mother' (82:222). The vows of 1888 were thus seen as crucial even in the perspective of 1945. We can see this alongside a remark by Gandhi recorded by Pyarelal that whereas ahimsa and brahmacharya had required a 'struggle' from him, 'truth has always come natural to me.' 'It caused me a deep wrench every time I departed from it,' Gandhi added (*Early Phase* 1:213).

In a description of satyagraha that Gandhi composed in 1920, he claimed: 'For the past 30 years I have been preaching and practising satyagraha.'[5] This would place the start of satyagraha in 1890. We know, however, that the first of his satyagrahas was launched in the Transvaal in 1906. But in 1890 Gandhi had adhered, in the teeth of opposition, to his vows, and the 1920 remark may make sense if satyagraha is seen as a stand against harmful pressures, not just as a stand against a harmful law.

In old age Gandhi also recalled that the climate around him in his early years was sympathetic to Hindu-Muslim understanding. In October 1947 he said: 'Right from my childhood I have been taught that in Ramrajya or the Kingdom of God no person can be unworthy just because he follows a different religion' (89:300). And in January 1948 he once more remembered his boyhood hopes on the communal question as well as his unfamiliarity, until the London visit, with newspapers: 'When I was young I never even read the newspapers. I could read English with difficulty and my Gujarati was not satisfactory. I have had the dream ever since then [of] Hindus, Sikhs, Parsis, Christians and Muslims [living] in amity not only in Rajkot but in the whole of India' (on 14.1.48; 90:425).

A similar recall can be detected in a 1928 remark on the place of faith and prayer in his life. Defining prayer as 'a sacred alliance' against evil between man and God, he spoke of it as 'an experience extending over an unbroken period of nearly forty years' (on 20.12.28; 38:248). He is saying that the 'unbroken period' of faith began around 1889, which, as we have seen, is consistent with what we have found.

His recollections, in 1921 and later, of childhood objections to untouchability stand on their own. There is no reference to them in the London Diary or in the *Vegetarian* interviews. In the autobiography Gandhi describes the 1898 incident in Durban when he and Kasturba quarrelled over his stand against untouchability (and also, as he admitted, because of his attitude at the time that 'the wife was born to do her husband's behest'). Made in letters and at meetings at different times and in different places, Gandhi's references to his early unease about untouchability have the ring of truth. If the Diary and the *Vegetarian* pieces omit it, they also omit much else, restricted as they were to subjects such as the journey to England, or the foods and festivals of India. (However, there was, we saw, a reference to the scavenger.)

The older Gandhi also felt that he was predisposed early in life against violence and hate. In 1925 he said: 'My personal religion peremptorily forbids me to hate anybody. I learnt this simple yet grand doctrine when I was twelve years old through a school book, and the conviction has persisted up to now' (*Young India*, 6.8.25).

In 1946: 'Hatred can be overcome only by love. Counter-hatred only increases the surface as well as the depth of hatred. I am aware that I am repeating what I have many times stated before . . . Only I recited no copy-book maxim but definitely announced what I believed in every fibre of my being. *Sixty years* of practice in various walks of life have only enriched the belief . . .' (*Harijan*, 7.7.46).

'I have been a fighter for many years, *more than sixty years*. But I fight not with the sword but with the weapons of truth and nonviolence' (26.9.47; 89:247).

If the periods Gandhi mentions are to be taken literally, these quotes speak, respectively, of a Mohan who is twelve and seventeen years old. We know that nonviolence or ahimsa did not figure in Gandhi's remarks before or during his London spell, and in fact we noted his enthusiastic reference in London to 'the Indian shepherd' with his cudgel who was more than a match for a European with a sword. The quotes accord with the facts only if hate is delinked from violence, and nonviolence seen primarily in terms of courage. London's Mohandas may have been against hate, and we need not question Gandhi's memory of the impression made by the school book. We are aware that in London the Sermon on the Mount made a similar impact. But London's Mohandas was not against men bearing arms, and Gandhi stated in 1928 that it was reading Tolstoy's book *The Kingdom of God is Within You* in 1893-4 that brought home to him the futility of violence. 'I was at that time a believer in violence,' he added (37:261).

In *Hind Swaraj* (1909) he wrote that he himself, 'before now,' had used arguments in favour of using minimum force. In 1924 he said, 'As a coward, which I was for years, I harboured violence.'[6] Is he referring only to the meat-eating escapades with Mehtab and other friends and the bluster about driving out the British by force? Or to a belief that existed until he read Tolstoy's book? If the latter, then it means that a sequence of incidents, perhaps beginning with an encounter with Ollivant, the British Resident in Kathiawad, and continuing with the eventful journey between Durban and Pretoria, sparked violent thoughts in him that were calmed by Tolstoy's writing. Gandhi's picture, drawn in old age, of a commitment to non-violence that began in boyhood and continued unbroken and uncompromised throughout his life is not borne out by the record of his utterances or, as we saw in the opening chapter, by the positions he took in times of conflict. But he is not incorrect in claiming to 'have been a fighter' from early days. This he was from the start, a fighter who is always monitoring himself.

We saw that the young Gandhi had sensed or suspected a significant but difficult calling for himself. At times in later years he gave frank expression to this awareness. In January 1928, for instance, he wrote: 'My ambition is much higher than independence. Through the deliverance of India I seek to deliver the so-called weaker races of the earth ... *I can no longer hide the light under a bushel*. Mine is an ambition worth living for and worth dying for . . .' (*Young India*, 12.1.28).

In 1930 he said: 'I was born to destroy this evil government.'[7] Again in 1942 he said: 'How can I remain silent at this supreme hour and *hide my light under the bushel*?' (To AICC, Bombay, 8.8.42).

Eighteen years earlier, in 1924, he had said: 'As a rule, I do not read writings in the Indian Press about me whether they are laudatory or condemnatory. Praise I do not need as I am sufficiently proud of myself without outside help. Condemnation I refrain from reading lest the Hyde in me get the better of the Jekyll and do violence to my nonviolence' (*Young India*, 8.5.24). It is not the pride of face, skill or achievement to which he refers. He has in mind, I think, consciousness of a mission, and we are right to think that he felt it even in the late 1880s.

Facing, in 1920, the charge that he was more of a politician than a saint, he again recalled his boyhood: 'The critic regrets to see in me a politician, whereas he expected me to be a saint. Now I think that the word saint . . . is too sacred a word to be lightly applied to anybody, much less to one like myself . . . If I seem to take part in politics, it is only because politics encircles us today like the coil of a snake from which one cannot get out, no matter how much one tries. I wish therefore to wrestle with the snake, *as I have been doing, with more or less success, consciously since 1894, unconsciously, as I have now discovered, ever since reaching the years of discretion*' (*Young India*, 12.5.20).

The year 1894 is when he founded the Natal Indian Congress, but what is of greater interest is his 'discovery,' in 1920, that he had been wrestling with politics from his 'years of discretion.' Here he sees his meat-eating escapades as well as his London experience, including the keeping of the vows, as being at least in part 'political.' Not only does he concede the intertwining in his life of religion and politics, he sees the start of that intertwining in his boyhood. We have seen that there is a basis for such a perception.

Perhaps the strongest evidence of early signs of the future man lies in what Tryambakrai Mazumdar told Narhari Parikh in 1919. Parikh, an able young lawyer, had joined Gandhi's Ashram in 1917. He recorded Mazumdar's comment in a letter he wrote to Mahadev Desai, Gandhi's secretary from 1917. Mazumdar, we should remember, is the one who travelled with Gandhi to England in 1888 and awakened Gandhi in time in Portsmouth. This is what he said to Parikh after meeting Gandhi again in 1919:

Gandhi was obstinate since his childhood . . . He acted at once after thinking of something . . . Since his childhood that man has had divine strength . . . There is no one more truthful. But along with truth he has a lot of ego. Only what he says is the truth . . . I say it is like this, if you dislike it we go our different ways. But that is his beauty. He succeeds because of that. And his strength lies in the fact that he is a patron of the poor and the distressed. He is the one who goes to their huts and spreads compassion.

India is unhappy at present and so worships this saviour. Not only India, if he goes today to Egypt, people will shout 'Victory to Mahatma Gandhi.'. . . If anybody could comfort Germany and Russia, it is Gandhi. . .

We went to England together. He waited for me for some time. He went on rising and I just sat, doing nothing but eat . . . He is a real Mahatma. He told me now to serve . . . Oh, I forgot one thing. He said he was going to die of a blow by an Indian. [8]

Desai's comment is also of interest: 'Mazumdar's analysis is . . . very correct. The ego he is talking about is not the common ego but a subtle ego which is felt only when you search deeply and intensely . . . It may be that that ego is necessary for a spiritual life. I see that there is an evolution taking place in Bapu every minute.'[9]

'At the age of 20 or 21,' Gandhi said in 1947, 'it became my dream to attain . . . a state of mind [which] cannot be affected even in dire circumstanes or at the moment of death' (86:303). Also in 1947, he provided a glimpse of history which may be suggestive of the political thinking of Mohandas in his late teens or early twenties:

'The (1857) Sepoy War was quelled by means of superior force. Outwardly things quieted down but the hatred against an imposed rule went deep underground . . . The British established schools and law courts and Indians took to these with enthusiasm; they even cooperated in the diffusion of Western culture; but, in spite of this, they could never bear the insult or the degradation involved in political subjugation' (87:83).

＊

Let us return to 1891. Told of his mother's wish that he should placate chiefs of his caste who wanted him back in it, Mohandas took a 'purificatory' dip in the river at Nasik. This had the desired effect but, remembering Mohandas's cheeky words before the journey to London, leaders of one Modh Bania faction announced that the bar against him remained in force. His sister Raliat's husband (and therefore Raliat) and Kasturba's parents belonged to this subcaste. Though they were prepared 'secretly to evade the prohibition' and entertain the returning barrister, Mohandas would not 'as much as drink water' in their homes. Gandhi says that this 'scrupulous conduct' won him the goodwill of the subcaste even if not of the leaders, who continued to treat him as an outcaste. In his autobiography Gandhi writes that he did not 'feel even mental reservation' against these leaders, another instance of a capacity to bar an unworthy emotion.

However, young Gandhi departed from a principle he had 'scrupulously observed' during six luckless months in Bombay when he agreed, in Rajkot, to give a percentage of his fees as commission to a man who brought him legal work. This man was Mohandas's brother's partner, and the brother, Laxmidas, insisted on commission being paid. Gandhi wrote in the autobiography that he had 'deceived' himself and yielded.

He had failed as a trial lawyer in Bombay. Recalling a humbling courtroom experience, Gandhi wrote: 'I stood up, but my heart sank into my boots. My head was reeling and I felt the whole court was doing likewise.' He returned the fee his client had given him and withdrew. The Bombay venture was abandoned. In Rajkot he 'got along moderately well' by 'drafting applications and memorials' until the end of 1892, when he received what he calls 'the first shock of my life.' Charles Ollivant, the Raj's Political Agent in Kathiawad, had young Gandhi thrown out of his, Ollivant's, office.

Mohandas had known Ollivant in England, where the officer had seemed friendly enough. This fact excited Laxmidas, for Ollivant was examining an allegation that had blocked Laxmidas's advancement in Porbandar's princely court. Laxmidas pressed his brother to intervene with Ollivant. Declining at first, Mohandas advised his brother to 'submit a petition in the proper course.' It did not seem proper to him, Mohandas argued, to try to take advantage of an acquaintance in England. Laxmidas, who had helped finance Mohandas's training in England, answered:

> You do not know Kathiawad, and you have yet to know the world. Only influence counts here. It is not proper for you, a brother, to shirk your duty, when you can clearly put in a good word about me to an officer you know.

Giving in, Mohandas sought an appointment and got it. Gandhi has recorded what followed:

> I reminded him of the old acquaintance . . . . The Political Agent owned the acquaintance, but the reminder seemed to stiffen him. 'Surely you have not come here to abuse that acquaintance, have you?' appeared to be . . . written on his brow. Nevertheless I opened my case. The sahib was impatient. 'Your brother is an intriguer. I want to hear nothing more from you. I have no time. If your brother has anything to say, let him apply through the proper channel.'
>
> The answer was enough, was perhaps deserved. But selfishness is blind. I went on with my story. The sahib got up and said, 'You must go now.' 'But please hear me out,' said I. That made him more angry. He called his peon to show me the door. I was still hesitating when the peon came in, placed his hands on my shoulders and put me out of the room.
>
> The sahib went away as also the peon, and I departed, fretting and fuming. I at once wrote out and sent over a

note to this effect: 'You have insulted me. You have assaulted me through your peon. If you make no amends, I shall have to proceed against you.'

Quick came the answer through his sowar: 'You were rude to me. I asked you to go and you would not. I had no option but to order my peon to show you the door. Even after he had asked you to leave the office, you did not do so. He therefore had to use just enough force to send you out. You are at liberty to proceed as you wish.'

With this answer in my pocket, I came home crestfallen, and told my brother all that had happened. He was grieved but was at a loss as to how to console me. He spoke to his vakil friends, for I did not know how to proceed against the sahib. Sir Pherozeshah Mehta happened to be in Rajkot at this time, having come down from Bombay for some case. But how could a junior barrister like me dare to see him? So I sent him the papers of my case, through the vakil who had engaged him, and begged his advice. 'Tell Gandhi,' he said, 'such things are the common experience of many vakils and barristers. He is still fresh from England, and hot-blooded. He does not know British officers...Let him tear up the note and pocket the insult. He will gain nothing by proceeding against the sahib, and will very likely ruin himself.'

The advice was bitter as poison to me, but I had to swallow it. I pocketed the insult, but also profited from it . . . This shock changed the course of my life.

It is curious that so obviously significant an episode, the 'first shock' changing 'the course of his life,' to repeat his own phrases, has received relatively little attention. Erikson glides past it swiftly, and even Pyarelal seems to give it insufficient importance. We are struck, first of all, by the clarity with which Gandhi remembers the details of a thirty-three-year-old incident. Quoting Ollivant's answer sent through the sowar, Gandhi does not qualify it as being 'in effect' or 'more or less' what the Agent said. The suggestion is that the words reproduced were the words expressed. Gandhi had either preserved the note or memorized its contents.

We mark next that the episode comprises three blows to Gandhi's pride. Firstly, he falls from rectitude. He meets Ollivant for a wrong purpose. He knows it is wrong, is told it is wrong, but does not desist. He has fallen. Secondly, he is cast out. He, barrister and son to a Prime Minister, is ejected by 'a friend' of his British days. Thirdly, and this may have been the worst of the three humiliations, he is unable to carry out his threat. Ollivant challenges him to do so, but Gandhi feels he cannot. If in the future Gandhi tells the British that India is not their moral inferior and asks them to quit India even as Ollivant had asked Mohandas to quit his office, perhaps he is, among other things, responding to the trauma of 1892 and the guilt, rage and impotence into which it broke out. And perhaps that trauma should be seen against Mohandas's feelings of attachment about 'dear London' and 'its environments,' to which he had given expression only a few months earlier.

It is interesting to absorb the autobiography's narration of the episode. If Gandhi had done nothing else in his life but provide this honest and fair recollection of his humiliation, that would have sufficed to mark him out.

Any charm for Mohandas in the practice of law in Kathiawad was destroyed by the episode. Ollivant presided over the region's chief court, and Gandhi had no wish to salaam the sahib there. When, therefore, Abdulla & Co., a South Africa-based firm with Porbandar connections, wanted to know whether Gandhi would help with a case in South Africa, he at once offered to go. 'I wanted somehow to leave India,' he writes in the autobiography.

Ollivant had propelled him out of India into an unknown place and future; he had also fuelled Gandhi with powerful reflections and emotions. He had been 'at fault.' 'Never again!' he told himself. But Ollivant's 'impatience and anger were out of all proportion to my mistake [which] did not warrant expulsion.' But then, despite 'having . . . threatened to proceed against' Ollivant, Mohandas had been obliged 'to remain silent.' Mehta had said this was 'a common experience' for Indians. He, Gandhi, would dig out its cause and cure.

In 1924, Gandhi alluded to his youthful interest in writing and what overrode it: 'But at the earliest period of my life it became one of storm and stress. It commenced with a fight with the then political agent of Kathiawar. I had therefore not much time for literary pursuits' (*Young India*, 4.9.24). In 1915 he told Kalelkar: 'If I have given up anything for national service, it is my interest in English literature. Renouncing wealth and career was no sacrifice; I wasn't really interested in them. But I was completely fascinated by English literature.'[10] What fired him for 'national service,' or a fight for self-respect, was the Ollivant episode.

The Maritzburg incident took place within ten days of Gandhi's arrival in South Africa. Our look at the young man preceding it confirms Gandhi's 1939 assessment that, crucial as it was, Maritzburg was not the first of his 'creative experiences.'

Chapter 3

Violence

A FEW DAYS after partition and independence, a Black educator from the US, Stuart Nelson of Howard University, asked Gandhi about the communal violence of 1946 and 1947 that seemed to contradict the nonviolence of the Indian movement for freedom. Gandhi, who was in Calcutta at the time, replied that he now doubted the genuineness of that nonviolence. He felt Indians had 'harboured illwill and anger' against the British, while claiming to resist them nonviolently. Their resistance had been 'inspired by violence,' not by 'a respect for the better element in the English people which they were trying to awaken by self-suffering.'

Added Gandhi: 'The attitude of violence which we had secretly harboured, in spite of the restraint imposed by the Indian National Congress, now recoiled upon us and made us fly at each other's throat when the question of the distribution of power came up.' Implying that he had failed to see this 'secret violence,' Gandhi said that his 'vision had been clouded.'

These remarks were recorded by Nirmal Kumar Bose and published in his *My Days with Gandhi* (170-1). If something had clouded Gandhi's vision, what was it? Let us first note, however, that Gandhi's remarks are not quite fair to himself and the movement he led. There is no evidence that the same people took part in the nonviolent campaigns and the communal violence of 1946-7; and there is plenty of evidence that Gandhi was aware of Indian violence.

It is true, nonetheless, that the movement for freedom triggered a variety of power struggles of which the communal riots were a tragic and ugly manifestation. Aware of Indian divisions, Gandhi had waged a fight to unite Indians along with his bid to end British rule, but the goal of Indian unity eluded him. Tragically for everyone, communal suspicions and hates exploded in violence.

Gandhi knew well the face of Indian violence. In 1919, the year of Jallianwala, he had identified and attacked Indian violence along with the Raj's violence. During his 1921 noncooperation campaign, when Hindus and Muslims jointly attacked Parsis, Christians, Jews and Europeans in Bombay, Gandhi said: 'The swaraj that I have witnessed during the last two days has stunk in my nostrils' (*Young India*, 24.11.21). When Chauri Chaura occurred (1922), he suspended the campaign, admitted 'the brutal violence by the people,' and said: 'There is not as yet in India that truthful and nonviolent atmosphere which and which alone can justify mass disobedience' (*Young India*, 16.2.22).

Following his release in 1944 after a two-year imprisonment in Poona, he voiced disagreement with the violence that had marked the Quit India defiance that he had inaugurated. When Hindu and Muslim ratings in the Royal Indian Navy jointly mutinied in February 1946, Gandhi predicted that violence-inclined Hindus and Muslims would turn against one another. We have previously noted some of these reactions, as also Gandhi's awareness of violence against the 'untouchables.'

Thus Gandhi was not blind about Indian violence, but he tended to lose sight of it from time to time, or on occasion to disregard or risk it in his pursuit of national self-respect. The latter was his goal, not the eradication of Indian violence, no matter how much this violence pained or disgusted him. Certainly Gandhi's British antagonists never underestimated his passion for shaking off alien rule. Wavell, for instance, felt that Gandhi was far and away the 'most formidable' foe of the British Empire and that 'he certainly hastened the departure of the British, which was his life's aim.' The Viceroy also thought that a man like Lord Pethick-Lawrence, Secretary of State for India in 1946, was more of a pacifist than Gandhi

(*Journal*: 236,439 and 309). Penderel Moon spoke for many British when he wrote: 'The deliverance of India from British rule, which admittedly was Gandhi's chief political aim, would appear also to have been the dominant purpose of his life. He himself would have denied this.'[1]

'He himself would have denied this.' The sentence shows an awareness of, as well as a skepticism about, Gandhi's claim of a spiritual purpose. Wavell, Moon and others thinking like them felt the steel in Gandhi's nonviolent arm; they did not, or did not want to, feel the spiritual seeker. They seemed to think that anyone, Indian or British, who failed to locate his chief foe in Indian flaws, and an ally in the Raj trying to cope with the flaws, could not be a pursuer of 'truth.' To them Gandhi listened only to one inner voice, the political.

Many in the Raj were no doubt baffled by one who seemed resolved to wrest power from their hands but disdained to keep it in his. Numberless face-to-face encounters, analyses and intelligence reports had showed the Raj that Gandhi was not interested in money, office, pomp or power. He often laid down the law to his 'soldiers,' true, but this tendency to 'dominate' was not accompanied by any evident wish to grab or hold on to power, for Gandhi seemed to show no reluctance when, as he often did, he withdrew from 'generalship,' or resistance when, as also happened, Congress 're-tired' him from it. The Raj also possessed evidence that Gandhi spent much time and energy in talks or correspondence with individuals on their personal problems and in nursing the sick in his ashrams.

Those in the Raj who could not reject the evidence before them summed him up as 'strange,' but some denied it and called him a hypocrite. Wavell wrote that he felt 'malevolence' in Gandhi; he also thought that Gandhi's objective was 'the establishment of a Hindu Raj' (*Journal*: 439 & 314). Other Viceroys or Secretaries of State did not notice illwill, and there were several whites like Louis Fischer who said: 'He had no animus. He was incapable of hatred . . . He wanted to liberate India in order to liberate England from India.'[2]

I see him with his two inner voices, at times finding them in accord and at other times painfully torn between the two. He saw national self-respect as a spiritual or religious virtue, as 'truth'; sadly for him, he was also aware that national self-respect could cloak Indian cruelties. Hence the strain in his life. Again, in his capacity as the leader of a political movement he took some options that seemed irresistible or unavoidable but which troubled some of his closest friends; before long we shall look at some of these decisions.

Fear, hate and violence appear together, and in that order, in many of Gandhi's statements. In the autobiography, recalling the apprehensions of some of his European friends in South Africa over the nonviolent resistance he was planning, he writes: 'I found that the term "passive resistance" was too narrowly construed, that it was supposed to be a weapon of the *weak*, that it could be characterized by *hatred*, and that it could finally manifest itself as *violence*' (My italics). What he was planning, he says, was different: a battle by the strong, free of illwill and fully nonviolent. He coined a new name, satyagraha, for what he saw as a discovery.

Often his analysis of an incident of violence was in terms of preceding fear and hate. As he saw it, a cowardly person hated and was likely to turn violent, while a brave person was nonviolent. 'The bomb-thrower creates secret plots, is afraid to come out in the open,' he had said in Benares in 1916 (13:215); and we have previously seen the 1924 remark: 'As a coward, which I was for many years, I harboured violence.' He refers, I would guess, to the talk of driving out Englishmen at the boyhood meat-eating escapades, to his anger after the Ollivant episode, when he felt powerless to implement his threat, and to feelings in the wake of his early experiences in South Africa.

Yet the rooting of violence in fear cannot be a complete explanation. It cannot apply to those who may be tempted to violence for reasons other than cowardice. Anger induced by injuries to body or soul may turn to hate, vengeance and violence, without fear or cowardice entering the scene. This everyday route to violence Gandhi does not seem to focus on, though he cites several instances of anger and rage felt by him. How he conquered fear is a story he often tells: how he controlled anger has to be pieced together.

That India found freedom from fear through Gandhi is the verdict of many an Indian and non-Indian observer or contemporary; that India became hate-free or nonviolent because of him is no one's verdict. It may be true that the movement for independence led by him was largely and, in comparison with other liberation movements, remarkably peaceful; yet Gandhi's India did not shed violence. Reminding everyone of his early timidity and at times confessing even in later years to a lack of confidence in his fearlessness if attacked, Gandhi in fact faced threats, imprisonments, physical blows, mobs and opposition without flinching. He also inspired a great number of his compatriots to do likewise. His 1897 strides across the Durban mob that had threatened to lynch him (in the event he was kicked and beaten but saved by Mrs Alexander, wife of the police chief), and his 1939 walk through the ranks of sword-carrying foes in Rajkot in 1939 dramatized his personal bravery, as did other instances. His bare-chested, open-air, unprotected life amidst currents of hate also testified to it. His political forthrightness was likewise plain.

'Fearlessness — yes, I would say fearlessness was his greatest gift,' remarked Nehru in 1955. 'And the fact that the weak little bundle of bones was so fearless in every way, physically, mentally, it was a tremendous thing which went to the other people too, and made them less afraid.'[3] In 1928 Jawaharlal and Subhas Bose had personal experience of it — they were chastised for going back on their word; and Nehru and Azad felt it in 1942 when Gandhi asked them to leave their posts in Congress if they could not agree to Quit India.

Decades earlier, in 1897, F.A. Laughton, a white lawyer working for Dada Abdulla, Gandhi's first client in South Africa, had made this remark after watching Gandhi's attitude to the white crowd threatening to lynch him: 'Intimidation is out of the question because, if he knew the Town Hall were going to be thrown at him, I believe from what I saw that he would not quail.'[4]

India absorbed the courage Gandhi taught. She did not accept the futility of anger and hate that he also taught, and she did not understand how he himself coped with anger and hate. He seems to have done this in five ways. One, he strove to expel or suppress it. We marked an early ability to order his anger to silence and can look at new instances. In his first months in Pretoria (1893-4), a white barber refused to cut his hair and another white man, a police-man, 'pushed and kicked' Gandhi 'without the slightest warning.' The story is in the autobiography. 'I certainly felt hurt,' Gandhi said, referring to the barber's refusal, but he proceeded at once to buy 'a pair of clippers and cut my hair before the mirror.'

As for the incident with the policeman, a white friend of Gandhi, a man called Coates, had witnessed it. He offered to testify if Gandhi prosecuted the offender. 'I will not go to court for a personal griev-ance,' Gandhi said. At this Coates reprimanded the policeman who made an apology to Gandhi — 'for which,' Gandhi writes, 'there was no need. I had already forgiven him.' What he adds is also of interest: 'But I never again went through this street . . . Why should I unnecessarily court another kick? I therefore selected a different path.' In both cases he almost at once 'banishes' the hurt. A reflec-tion helped him: in India barbers did not serve the untouchables. 'I got the reward of this in South Africa, not once but many times, and the conviction that it was the punishment for our own sins saved me from becoming angry.'

The terse phrase 'not once but many times' alludes to the series of personal knocks that Gandhi received as an Indian in South Af-rica and as the leader of the Indian community there. He does not tell us of all of them, but we can see his years there as a continuous encounter with indignity.

We may note some additional claims he made about negating anger. In 1921: 'I have attained great capacity, I believe, for sup-pressing and curbing my senses' (*Young India*, 17.11.21). In 1927: 'Anger wells up in my breast when I see or hear about mis-deeds . . . All I can humbly claim is that I keep these passions and moods under fair subjection' (*Young India*, 14.7.27). In 1935: 'It is not that I do not get angry. I don't give vent to anger. I cultivate the quality of patience . . . and, generally speaking, I succeed' (*Harijan*,

11.5.35). In 1947: 'I am also a human being and feel enraged but I swallow my anger' (89:174). When G.D.Birla once asked him, 'Do you get angry?' Gandhi's reply was: 'Yes, I do. But I try to become a witness to my own anger.'[5] Anger had to be faced before it could be expelled.

Reflection was his second weapon against hate. But before we reflect more on his 'reflection,' let us note that in the incidents cited Gandhi not only lets go of his anger, he also lets go of the men who had caused it. They leave his life, never to return to it. A lack of illwill is part of his life, but reconciliation not necessarily. One reason why it is not is that Gandhi's world is, largely, that of the Indians of South Africa. He is glad to have European allies for the Indian cause and will work to enlist them, but his cause is Indian. In wanting to expel anger and in reflecting on the untouchables of India he is listening to Truth; in letting go of the two whites he is listening to India. Striving to reform everyone in South Africa may be a noble aim. It is not our Gandhi's dharma.

His reflection included a study of sacred writings of all backgrounds including his own, and under this head we may also include the role of the religiously-inclined friends he met or corresponded with. The year in Pretoria — immediately after Ollivant and Maritzburg — was perhaps crucial in this respect. He read scores of religious tracts and meditations, attended services, listened to devout Christians and had a significant correspondence with Rajchandra, the Bombay-based jeweller, poet and thinker to whom Pranjivan Mehta, his friend from London days, had introduced Gandhi in 1891, after their return from England. His religious thinking was clarified. Christianity was considered but not embraced. Loyalty to Hinduism was reaffirmed, as was his right to interpret it and to practise cooperation with persons of all faiths. Tolstoy's books were among those that 'made a deep impression.' 'I began to realize more and more the infinite possibilities of universal love.' In short, reflection confirmed the lesson in twelve-year-old Mohan's schoolbook that hate was forbidden and probably helped to melt it.

This melting, or dissolution, was his third counter against anger. He sought the dissolution through prayer and fasting. A role was also played by some European friends who not only stood by him in South Africa and India but also offered him prayerful love. Joseph Doke and his family, Henry and Millie Polak and Charles Andrews were among the whites who extended towards Gandhi a warmth that helped dissolve resentment towards a race that had hurt his country and himself personally. That evil and not evildoers had to be hated was a truth that his mind had accepted when he was young. People like the Dokes and Charlie Andrews took the truth to his injured heart. He would often recall, long after the experience, the calm that the singing of 'Lead Kindly Light' by the Doke family had brought to him in 1907 while he recuperated in the Doke home after an assault.

The nature of his reflection and praying and their results can be gathered from a selection of his remarks. In 1925: 'Mine is not an exclusive love. I cannot love Muslims or Hindus and hate Englishmen...By a long course of prayerful discipline, I have ceased for over forty years to hate anybody' (*Young India,* 6.8.25). Also in 1925: 'I feel like a caged lion . . . Things I omit to mention in the pages of *Young India* are buried deep down in my bosom and they are far weightier than those I advertise. But I do not fail to advertise them daily before the Unseen Power' (*Young India,* 12.11.25). In 1927: 'As I believe that silent prayer is often a mightier force than an overt act, in my helplessness I continuously pray . . .' (*Young India,* 22.9.27).

In 1928: 'I have learnt much from the West and I should not be surprised to find that I have learnt something about Ahimsa too from the West. I am not concerned what ideas of mine are the result of my foreign contacts' (*Young India,* 11.10.28). In 1934: 'East and West, South and North, are all one to me . . . The Harijan movement is really only the first step in my programme of breaking down all barriers whatever which divide man from man' (*Harijan,* 25.5.34).

No associate needing to meet him ever heard that Gandhi was unavailable because he was meditating; work was meditation to him. At times, however, he would escape from a discussion or a crowd for a few moments of solitary reflection and return with clarity and calm. The minutes in the bath and privy were treated as opportunities for reflection, as were any periods in the middle of the night when he could not sleep. His rosary was kept next to his pillow; on occasion he would sit up in the peace of the night and meditate or pray with the rosary's aid while his companions slept.[6]

Four, he deflected his and his people's anger. That emotion was to be directed at a system, at British rule, and sometimes at things such as foreign cloth, not at British men and women. Tagore, Andrews and others argued that this was not a safe response to anger, and we will look later at their debate with Gandhi. Here let us merely note that Gandhi presented deflection of hate as part of his strategy.

Finally, he sought to sublimate hate through satyagraha, which he said was a force of the spirit, of truth, of love. He and Indians agreeing with him would prefer dying to killing or injuring; if need be, they would die for their rights and also to save the lives of opponents.

'Fear not,' however, was simpler, more comprehensible and more attractive than 'hate not;' and though he succeeded a great deal, as far as he himself was concerned, in the suppression, dissolution, deflection and sublimation of anger, he was unable to coach India to do likewise. We can connect him, historically, to the conquest of fear, but not quite to the conquest of violence. A residue of undissolved resentment in his own life may have contributed to the failure.

Moreover, in certain forms at least, anger seemed to assist the struggle for national self-respect. As a leader of the masses, Gandhi had to remain 'in tune' with those he led, and we should not forget his remark to Nirmal Kumar Bose in August 1947 that his uniqueness if any was that he could 'almost instinctively feel what is stirring in the heart of the masses.'[7] And while a man of truth dissents from popular sentiment, a leader cannot cut himself off from it.

He did not deny an internal conflict. In 1921 he wrote: 'It is not possible for me, a weak, frail, miserable being to mend every wrong . . . The spirit in me pulls one way, the flesh in me pulls in the opposite direction' (*Young India*, 17.11.21). He is not referring here to fear, lust or greed. Those pulls he had tamed. He is too weak, he is saying, to take on everything. India and Indians must take precedence. In 1925 he again spoke of 'the eternal duel going on within me and which admits of no truce' (*Young India*, 18.6.25). In part, the duel was between pure truth and nationalism.

'My mission,' he says in 1940, 'is to convert every Indian, whether he is a Hindu, Muslim or any other, even Englishmen and finally the world to nonviolence for regulating mutual relations whether political, economic, social or religious' (*Harijan*, 13.1.40). The phrases 'even' and 'finally' reveal his priority, for which he claims religious sanction: 'I cannot find Him apart from the rest of humanity. My countrymen are my nearest neighbours' (*Harijan*, 29.3.36). He has to serve neighbours if he is to serve God; they happen to be Indians. 'For me,' he had written in 1924, 'the road to salvation lies through incessant toil in the service of my country and therethrough of humanity' (*Young India*, 3.4.24). India, he told himself and others, was his karmabhoomi.

He admitted the intensity of his nationalism. 'My nationalism, *fierce* though it is, is not exclusive, is not devised to harm any nation or individual,' he said in 1931 (*Young India*, 26.3.31, emphasis mine). A quarter century earlier, when Lord Curzon told Calcutta University that 'the highest ideal of truth is to a large extent a Western opinion,' Gandhi, thirty-five at the time and living in South Africa, reacted at once with a strong rejoinder in *Indian Opinion* and asked Curzon to apologize (*Indian Opinion*, 1.4.05). His comments on the Russo-Japanese war had been free of any racial tinge. In 1908, however, when he wanted to raise the pitch of satyagraha and enlist hardliners, he used racial language while invoking memories of that war. In the Gujarati *Indian Opinion* he wrote: 'When Japan's brave heroes forced the Russians to bite the dust of the battlefield, the sun rose in the east. And now it shines on all the nations of Asia. The people of the East will never, never again submit to insult from the insolent whites' (27.6.08; 8:324).

On the other hand, we should not forget the number of Indians who thanks to Gandhi abjured violent thoughts against Englishmen. Ghanshyam Das Birla, Vinoba Bhave and Kaka Kalelkar were three among them. All are on record about this; according to Vinoba, Gandhi quenched the volcano of his (Vinoba's) anger.[8]

Gandhi, the seeker after Truth and Love was also, and inseparably, an Indian seeker. Or an eastern seeker. At any rate a black or non-white seeker. His being non-white was integral to his identity, as integral as his Truth-search. He was not merely a man of truth and love striving to heal the world. He strove simultaneously — with satyagraha and as much freedom from illwill as possible — to right the wrongs done by the British to India. He was not blind to the wrongs that Indians did to Indians. The Truth he worshipped brought these wrongs before his eyes and against some of them he fought with passion; but he would not break himself loose from the fight for India's freedom, from what he himself called the 'coil' of politics.

Tolstoy, who shortly before his death in 1910 had called Gandhi's South African work 'most fundamental and important,' supplying 'most weighty practical proof' of the effectiveness of nonviolence, was uneasy about the nationalism he detected in Gandhi. He thought of it — too facilely, it must be said — as 'Hindu nationalism' and told friends in Russia that it 'spoiled everything.'[9] He and Gandhi agreed on nonviolence and bread labour but not on nationalism, which in Gandhi's case may also be seen as righteous indignation. Gandhi doggedly sought to make it as righteous as possible, to confine the indignation to 'the system,' and to treat Indian independence as only the stepping-stone to a new world. Yet a core of nationalism remained in him, rallying Indians, inspiring colonized people everywhere, hurting the British, disappointing men like Tolstoy, Tagore and Andrews — and veiling Indian ills, including violence, that preceded British rule and were to survive it.

It was this nationalist sediment that to some extent 'clouded his mind.' Though admitting its effect, he was not sorry. He told Nelson that but for the 'illusion' he had harboured, India would not have reached the point of independence (89: 62).

❋

With this proposition in mind, let us accompany Gandhi through some of the stages in his life, beginning with the Maritzburg episode. Gandhi's 1893 journey from Durban in Natal to Pretoria in the Transvaal, which is where his client Abdulla wanted him to be, was done in stages: by overnight train to Charleston, by coach to Standerton, by another coach the next morning to Johannesburg, and by train from Johannesburg to Pretoria. At Maritzburg (or Pietermaritzburg) station, en route to Charleston, he was ordered to leave the first-class compartment and go to the van. He refused, and was thrown out with his bags. He could still enter the van but did not. The train steamed away, leaving him with bitter thoughts on a cold night. Station officials had taken custody of his bags which contained his coat. He wanted his coat but, fearing another insult, did not ask for his bags.

He pondered returning to India but decided to battle it out. The first fight was for the right to travel first-class to Charleston the next day. He won it. At a stop in Pardekoph on the coach ride to Standerton, he was boxed in the ears and punched in the face by a white guard for refusing to sit on 'a dirty piece of sackcloth' on the footboard. The guard tried to push Gandhi out of the coach. Though 'he was strong and I was weak,' Gandhi had resolved to 'keep my hold even at the risk of breaking my wristbones.' Other passengers interceded and the guard relented with the warning 'to show you what I can do' at Standerton. Gandhi 'sat speechless and prayed to God to help me.' At Standerton Gandhi informed the coach company of his experience, demanded an assurance against its repetition on the leg to Johannesburg, and secured it.

After spending a night in Standerton with an Indian merchant, he took the coach to Johannesburg. On arrival in the big city he took a cab to the Grand National Hotel and asked for a room. 'The manager eyed me for a moment and politely saying, "I am very sorry, we are full up," bade me goodbye.' Gandhi went to an Indian shop where there was 'a hearty laugh over the story of my experience at the hotel.' Other Indians knew better than to ask for a room in a hotel. They told him that his intention to travel first-class to Pretoria was unrealistic.

They did not know our Gandhi. He first wrote a letter to the stationmaster in Johannesburg of his wish to travel first-class to Pretoria and then turned up in 'a frock-coat and necktie,' placed a sovereign on the counter and asked for a first-class ticket. The stationmaster was behind the counter. He issued the ticket on the condition, which was accepted, that Gandhi would not sue the railway company if anything happened en route.

The Johannesburg Indians were surprised at Gandhi's success but warned him of trouble on the leg to Pretoria. At Germiston a guard ordered him to move 'to the third class' but an Englishman, the only other passenger in the compartment, asked the guard not to 'trouble the gentleman.' 'If you want to travel with a coolie, what do I care,' said the guard to the Englishman, and walked away. At about eight in the evening Gandhi reached Pretoria, but it was a Sunday and the man alerted by Dada Abdul¹a did not find it convenient to meet the train. Not knowing where to go for the night, Gandhi tried to ask the man checking tickets at the exit when 'an American Negro standing nearby' broke into the conversation and offered to take Gandhi 'to a small hotel, of which the proprietor is an American.' 'I think he will accept you,' said the unknown, unnamed African-American.

Mr Johnston, the proprietor, agreed to have Gandhi provided he took his meals in his room, for if Gandhi ate with the others, 'my guests might be offended and even go away.' The condition was agreed to and Gandhi was in his room, expecting a tray, when Johnston entered and announced that the guests did not mind Gandhi joining them for dinner.

It was three nights and four days since he had left Durban. Getting to Pretoria was at least as testing an exercise as getting to London had been five years earlier; and his year in Pretoria was as important as his three years in London. His legal work taking only a part of his day, he read and reflected more in Pretoria in 1893-4 than at any other time in his life before or since, if we exclude the periods in jail. We have previously seen Gandhi's 1928 statement that studying Tolstoy in Pretoria cured him of thoughts of violence. Though he does not say so anywhere, it is a reasonable surmise that some of these thoughts were a fallout of the journey from Durban.

Gandhi also organized the Indians of Pretoria, asking them, in his first week in the city, to forget all distinctions of religion or language. For some months he regularly taught English to some of the Pretoria Indians, including a Hindu owning a small shop and a Muslim barber. In 1907-8 Doke would write, on the basis of what Gandhi told him: 'The twelve months spent in Pretoria were a distinct gain. He learned self-restraint . . . [and] to bear the insults which attached to his race and colour until . . . he almost gloried in them, and, gradually, pride of birth and education gave way before the humility of sacrifice' (45).

In Pretoria, for the first time in his life, Gandhi made a conscious attempt to understand Christianity and Islam, as well as an attempt to understand his own Hinduism intellectually. The exercise included a correspondence with Rajchandra Mehta in Bombay. Equally of interest is Gandhi's claim in the autobiography that 'there was now in Pretoria no Indian I did not know, or whose condition I was not acquainted with.' In Pretoria as elsewhere, in his mid-twenties as during other stages in his life, God and India were pulling him together.

According to Doke, Gandhi had 'admired the justice of British law' until his South African experiences. 'It is true that, now and then, some British official had shown himself brusque or overbearing, but nothing, so far, had happened to chill his loyalty' (44). (This no doubt was an allusion to Ollivant.) South Africa chilled that loyalty but did not kill it. To Gandhi an Indian was a white's equal in the Empire, and he demanded rights for Indians in South Africa in the name of the Empire.

Recalling the South African years, he would write in the autobiography: 'Hardly ever have I known anybody to cherish such loyalty as I did to the British constitution . . . ['God save the Queen'] used to be sung at every meeting that I attended in Natal . . . With a careful perseverance I learnt the tune . . . and joined in the singing . . . In those days I believed that British rule was on the whole beneficial to the ruled.' He thought the colour prejudice that he and the Indians encountered in South Africa was 'contrary to British traditions' and 'only temporary and local.' South Africa was unjust but the Empire was not, and London would correct South Africa. This was what he told himself and others each time Indians in South Africa were discriminated against or denied redress.

In a letter published in _The Englishman_ of Calcutta in 1902, he said: 'Imperialism is on the lips of everybody . . . How to weld the different parts of the British Dominions into one beautiful unbreakable whole is a problem which the greatest British politicians of the day are endeavouring to solve, and yet here is a colony (Natal) which is making invidious distinctions between one class of British subjects and another in a most aggravating manner' (3:251).

He also sought allies from among South Africa's whites but from a position of dignity. 'Every occasion when it was possible to cooperate with the Europeans on terms of equality and consistent with self-respect was heartily availed of,' he writes in _Satyagraha_.

Neither the satyagraha inaugurated in 1906 nor the imprisonments that followed in 1908 and 1909 altered Gandhi's view about the Empire. An article he wrote for the Gujarati _Indian Opinion_ on a 1906 voyage from South Africa to England describes the British character in glowing terms. Though not yet resorted to, satyagraha had been resolved upon by this time. Yet Gandhi wrote:

> The Englishman alone knows (_i.e., the Indian does not know_) to give orders and he knows how to take them. In his behaviour he is great with the great and small with the small. He knows how to earn money and he alone knows _(not the Indian)_ how to spend it . . . The Englishman in the war (_the Zulu war_) did all his work himself, trekked over long distances and felt happy with dry bread. Here on board the ship he does not do any work. He presses a button and an attendant stands before him. Why indeed should such a people not rule?
>
> The steamer is as big as a small town. There must be about a thousand persons on board, but there is no noise, no disorder. Everyone is absorbed in his or her work. Only the waves make music and remind us of their cease-

less action (*Indian Opinion* [Guj.], 17.11.06. Words in parentheses mine).

On this 1906 visit to England he had his first and last meeting, though by no means the last exchange, with Winston Churchill, then undersecretary for the colonies. In 1909 and 1931 Gandhi would again be in England. Whether he sought a meeting with Churchill in 1909 is not known. In 1931 Churchill refused to meet Gandhi. Published in 1908, Churchill's *My African Journey* touches on the Indians in South and East Africa. He notes that 'the native of British India will undoubtedly, wisely or unwisely, rightly or wrongly, be refused access in any large numbers to several South African colonies,' and wonders whether the Asiatics will or will not 'teach the African natives evil ways.'

Judging the interests of South Africa's whites and Indians to be 'irreconcilable,' Churchill refers to the 'appeals to force by mobs or empires to decide in a brutal fashion the brutal question' between the two races. It was Gandhi who in his talk with Churchill had 'appealed to the empire;' and Churchill, who covered the Boer War as a correspondent, had no doubt heard of the Durban mobs rallied against Gandhi in 1897.

Churchill also wrote in the book that 'the white artisan is invited to acquiesce in his own extinction...by a competitor (the Asian) whom, he believes, he could strike down with his hands.'[10] The words evoke the insecurity and hostility amidst which Gandhi was living. They also reveal the contrast between Churchill and Gandhi. Gandhi would not accept that Indian and white interests were irreconcilable. Equally importantly, he had evolved a non-brutal way of resolving the issue: disobey an unjust law, suffer the penalty, but refuse to 'strike down' your adversary.

We will return later to the Gandhi-Churchill relationship and mark meanwhile the toughness plus warmth that characterized the relationship between Gandhi and the South African leader Jan Smuts, who imprisoned and released Gandhi several times. A Pathan called Mir Alam and some other Indians dissatisfied with a settlement that Gandhi had made with Smuts in 1908 attacked him with a stick and an iron pipe, apart from kicking him. Gandhi would have been killed but for the fact that his companions, Thambi Naidoo and Essop Mia, shielded him and took some of the blows. The Doke family cared for the injured Gandhi in their home. Joseph Doke's daughter Olive recalled in 1946: 'Lights were turned low hoping the patient would rest but first there came a request from him that Mother and I would sing "Lead Kindly Light" for him. So outside his bedroom door we softly sang the beautiful hymn . . .'

Olive's brother C.M. Doke would remember what happened when, shortly afterwards, Gandhi was again arrested: 'Our friend trudg[ed] up the hill to the Fort (Johannesburg's gaol) beside a policeman. He was not handcuffed . . . My sister and I walked parallel to him on the other side of the road . . . We tried to attract his attention without letting his escort see us, but his face was straightforward. It was not until he reached the prison gate that he turned, saw us, and waved a hand, before the heavy doors closed on him . . .'[11]

Heavy doors between East and West rather than the wave of a hand seemed emphasized by the tract that Gandhi wrote after his next visit to England, which was in 1909, *Hind Swaraj*. We will look at *Hind Swaraj* in another chapter; here let us merely note that it was in part linked, as was the 1906 satyagraha decision, to a need Gandhi felt to outflank Indian groups thinking of taking to arms. In 1906 he had heard some Indians in South Africa speak of violence and of 'wreaking vengeance.' He had to choose, Gandhi later said, between 'allying himself to violence or finding some other method' of challenging legalized prejudice. And in 1906 as well as in 1909 he tried to reason in London with Indians advocating an armed route to independence.

Gandhi's 1909 visit yielded nothing, which is what he had expected, but a parallel visit that his friend Henry Polak made to India mobilized sympathy for the South African struggle. An incident that occurred on Polak's return to Durban reveals a less known facet of Gandhi's personality. Along with several co-workers, Gandhi was at the dock to welcome Polak back. As the ship closed in, Gandhi's nephew Chhaganlal greeted Polak, who was standing on the deck. A white dock employee asked Chhaganlal to move. Chhaganlal moved back some feet. 'Can't you hear?' the functionary shouted again, 'I said get out of here!' This was answered by a voice twice as thunderous that came from some yards away. '*He shan't move an inch!*' The voice was Gandhi's. The employee was escorted out by his colleagues.[12]

Gandhi had close and warm ties with his white associates in South Africa. Several of them lived, some with their families, on the two ashrams Gandhi had created, one near Durban, the Phoenix Settlement, and the other near Johannesburg, Tolstoy Farm. Many of the Europeans were given Indian names, with Bhai or Behn as a suffix; the multifaith and multiracial settlements had a definite Indian tenor. Gandhi's relationship with one of his European associates, Hermann Kallenbach, reveals the intimacy he was capable of. A gifted architect and a Jew, Kallenbach, who provided the land for Tolstoy Farm, felt that Gandhi had changed his life. Though the two met but rarely after Gandhi's return to India, Gandhi often wrote to Kallenbach, and some lines he sent at the end of 1917 give a flavour of the depth of this friendship: 'We may wither, but the eternal in us lives on . . . Thus musing . . . my thoughts went to you and I sighed, but I regained self-possession and said to myself, "I know my friend not for his form but for that which informs him." '[13]

The climax of Gandhi's time in South Africa was the 1913 satyagraha in which thousands of Indian men and women — the indentured, plantation workers, miners and others — took part, which was followed in 1914 by the Smuts-Gandhi agreement and the Indians' Relief Act, a compromise that brought some solid gains to the Indians. Leaving South Africa for the last time, after having given twenty years to it, Gandhi said in 1914 that the credit for the gains went to the humble Indian men and women who had died in the struggle, and added: 'I go away with no illwill against a single European.'[14]

❋

The Indian political figure Gandhi had been closest to, Gokhale, died within months of Gandhi's return to India. This was a blow comparable to the death of Mohandas's mother while he was a stu-

dent in London. Gokhale had befriended Gandhi on the latter's
visits to India in 1896 and 1901-2, spoken for the Indians of South
Africa, and spent some weeks in 1912 in their midst. In 1909, he
had evaluated Gandhi before a Congress session in Lahore in the
following remarkable terms:

> It is one of the privileges of my life that I know Mr Gandhi
> personally; and I can tell you that a purer, a nobler, a
> braver and a more exalted spirit has never moved on this
> earth ... [He is] a man among men, a hero among heroes,
> a patriot among patriots, and we may well say that in him
> Indian humanity at the present time has really reached its
> high watermark.[15]

This assessment was based on Gokhale's brief view of a twenty-
seven-year-old Gandhi visiting Pune in 1896, some weeks that the
two spent together in Calcutta in 1901-2, letters that Gandhi had
sent him since, and the description of Gandhi's personality and work
in South Africa provided by Henry Polak, who visited India in 1909.
It reveals the impact that Gandhi in his twenties and thirties made
on some close observers.

Heeding advice Gokhale had given, Gandhi spent the first year
after his return travelling, observing, listening. He had travelled
extensively even on the 1896 and 1901-2 visits to India, and his
intention to take part in the Indian national movement probably dates
back to 1894, when he successfully organized the Natal Indian Congress, if not earlier. From the start he looked upon South Africa as
a nursery and training ground for fighters for Indian independence.

He founded an ashram in Ahmedabad in 1915, gathered co-workers, took opportunities to apply satyagraha on local issues — the
hardships of peasants in North Bihar's indigo plantations, textile
workers in Ahmedabad, peasants in Gujarat's Kheda district, railway travellers — and won success and attention. Even those ridi-
culing him as a crank could not deny the newness he was bringing:
a willingness to say 'no' to the Raj's face. Until his emergence,
much of the defiance of the Raj was in secret, and those arrested

pleaded 'not guilty' to charges of breaking the law. As a result of what Gandhi did and advised, many Indians, including peasants, were saying they would defy an unjust law and take the punishment.

Another new element was the all-India outlook nurtured by Gandhi. His co-workers came from diverse parts; in each part visited by him, Gandhi strove to foster appreciation for other areas; in some ways he became an interpreter between India's various regions. In 1918, his initiatives for promoting Hindi or Hindustani as a link language included sending his eighteen-year-old son Devadas to Madras to teach the language to willing students in that city.

Simultaneously, Gandhi prepared the ground for tackling the Hindu-Muslim question and looked for potential Muslim allies. The Ali brothers, Shaukat and Muhammad, were in detention for alleged sympathy with Turkey, which was Germany's partner, and therefore the Empire's foe, in the World War being fought at the time. Gandhi opened correspondence with them. They had met him before their arrest and 'thought very highly' of him. Gandhi's remark to students in Calcutta, 'If I were for sedition I would speak out for sedition and take the consequences,' had 'impressed them very greatly.'[16]

Gandhi sought, at the same time, to befriend the Empire and its Viceroy, Lord Chelmsford, and, as we saw earlier, recruit soldiers for the Empire. Called by the Viceroy to a war conference in Delhi in April 1918, Gandhi asked Chelmsford to release the Ali brothers and instruct the Bombay government to concede the demands of the Kheda peasantry. On his part he would support recruitment at the conference. He did so by means of a single-sentence speech — uttered in Hindustani. It was probably the shortest speech the dignitaries had heard, and the first, at a state occasion, in an Indian language. Gandhi had converted his gesture towards the Empire into a stroke for Indian pride.

The labour to enlist recruits followed this conference, but to get a fuller idea of what was going on in Gandhi's mind we should look at what, in confidence, he had told Mahadev Desai (a prize recent recruit for his personal work) a month before the conference:

I have to cruelly suppress my urges. Ever since I read the history of the East India company, my mind refuses to be loyal to the British Empire and I have to make a strenuous effort to stem its tide of rebellion. The first thought that rises up in the mind is that the British should be driven out of India bag and baggage; but a feeling deep down in me persists that India's good lies in [the] British connection, and so I force myself to love them.

The same about Muslims. Though we do say that Hindus and Muslims are brothers, I cannot conceive of their being brothers right today. In this matter also, something within tells me that Hindus and Muslims are going to unite as brothers one day, that there is no other course open to them, and they have but to be brothers. If we go on remembering old scores, we would feel that unity is impossible, but at any cost we ought to forget the past.

History teaches us that these things have happened the world over . . . Not that all religious distinctions will be wiped out in future, but Hinduism will captivate Muslims by the power of its compassion, which is its very essence . . . We can win over the Muslims this very day if we are sufficiently imbued with the spirit of brotherly love. But it is difficult to predict just now the time when Hindus will rise to that height.[17]

A franker statement of emotion and objective cannot be had. The 'history of the East India Company' is no doubt a reference to the first volume of Romesh Dutt's *Economic History of India*, published in 1901. We may note that Gandhi speaks of his passion against the British presence in the present tense — his Pretoria reflections and all his subsequent efforts have neither eradicated the anger nor made him immune to fresh waves of it. He has to force himself to love them; the wonder is that he often succeeds. I do not think he lied when on leaving South Africa he denied any illwill against a single European, or was over-dramatic when speaking to Desai. His heart saw numerous comings and goings of anger, and clashes between anger and wisdom.

Though recruiting with ardour, he half sensed that he would soon have to rise against the Empire. At the end of June 1918 he told Desai: 'We stand on the threshold of a twilight — whether morning or evening we do not know. One is followed by the night, the other heralds the dawn.'[18]

As for the Hindu-Muslim question, let us also look at what Gandhi privately said to Desai four months later: 'It is the question of the Muslims that pricks me like a thorn. I wonder how I am going to be able to win them over to love and nonviolence! They are steeped in hatred.'[19] The Gandhi saying this is in the thick of his recruiting bid, and the hatred he has in mind here is more perhaps the anti-British emotion of Indian Muslims partial to Turkey (whose Sultan was then seen as the Khalifa, or chief, of all the Sunni Muslims of the world); but the Hindu-Muslim relationship is also, obviously, what he is thinking of.

What we get when the pieces are put together is the fairly staggering picture of a man intensely aware of great Hindu-Muslim, India-Empire and Muslim-British gulfs, and striving to bridge them all, the Indian-British one 'for India's good' and the Hindu-Muslim one 'because there is no other course open to them.'

To get an even fuller picture, let us look at what Gandhi had told Jamnadas Dwarkadas and Indulal Yagnik in Bombay in 1915. The two had invited Gandhi from Ahmedabad to give a talk on South Africa. Yagnik relates that the fact that Gandhi had walked from his Girgaum accommodation in Bombay to the Gaiety Theatre for the meeting had made him feel guilty. After Gandhi had spoken to a full hall, Yagnik got Dwarkadas to take Gandhi in a car to the station and accompanied them. During the ride Gandhi was asked if he expected a following for civil disobedience in India. Gandhi's answer was as follows:

> I am not very much worried about securing a large following. That will come in due course. But I do anticipate that a time may come when my large following may throw me overboard on account of my strict adhesion to my prin-

ciples — and it may be that I shall almost be turned out
on the streets and have to beg for a piece of bread from
door to door.[20]

Yagnik's is a critic's book; the quote is credible. It shows that Gandhi
was aware, within months of returning to India, that the palatable
and the unpalatable both would issue from his lips. By March 1919
Gandhi had indeed secured a huge, and nationwide, following. His
call for satyagraha against the Rowlatt Bills that sharply curtailed
freedom of speech had catapulted him to centre-stage; but after incidents in Ahmedabad in which an English sergeant was killed, he
suspended the fight, and on 14 April said to a meeting of two thousand near his Ashram: 'If a redress of grievances is possible only by
means of illwill for, and slaughter of, Englishmen, I for one would
do without swaraj and without redress.'[21]

The three years between February 1919, when Gandhi rocketed to
national leadership, and March 1922, when the Empire sentenced
him to six years in prison, saw resolves and acts that altered India.
Virtually every part of India and aspect of life was affected. The
ordinary Indian shed fear of the white ruler and became aware of
the famished or untouchable neighbour. The peasant came into focus. Women stepped out of their homes and stood on the battlelines.
Hindus and Muslims fraternized as never before. Together they
challenged the Empire.

Across the land, Indians draped themselves in khaddar or khadi,
handspun yarn woven on the hand loom, signifying new values. A
spinner of yarn added to his or her income, felt at one with toiling
Indians, learnt the dignity of labour. A khadi wearer enabled a poor
compatriot to earn bread with honour. Since the rough cloth was
conspicuous, it identified the wearer as a soldier in the battle being
waged; in Nehru's words, khadi became the livery of freedom. If
khadi knitted together the comfortable and the needy, Hindi or
Hindustani seemed to weave different parts of the land into one; and

liberty from liquor became a popular goal.

We know that the Hindu-Muslim partnership did not last. After independence khadi acquired other, less noble, connotations, whereas liquor acquired nobility. Hindi-Hindustani came to be looked upon with suspicion; and the rich-poor, caste Hindu-untouchable divides were to persist. But these erosions and distortions of later years do not negate what happened in India in 1919-22.

Gandhi's role was crucial to the period's resolves and acts. Thanks to a new constitution that the Amritsar session had authorized him to prepare, Congress became broader-based, more democratic and more efficient. He drew an array of talented individuals into national work, raised money from the poor and the rich, naming the donors and acknowledging receipt, and placed politics in a context of social and national regeneration. Thanks to the texture of the fight he led, Indians felt they were morally on the offensive, and the Empire on the defensive.

Integral to Gandhi's role was the man himself. Though he was frequently unwell during this period, his mental and physical energy was at its peak, as was his confidence. One of the numerous gifted individuals who joined him at this time, Pyarelal, saw in him 'a calm assurance of strength' and 'an access to some hidden reservoir of power which could find a way even through an impenetrable granite wall.' In 1948 Pyarelal recalled Gandhi's speech at the Amritsar Congress of December 1919, when Gandhi had asked for a condemnation of Indian violence.

Gandhi's voice, Pyarelal said, was 'full-chested and so distinct that it could be heard clearly to the farthest end of the vast gathering in that pre-mike era.' Added Pyarelal: 'Napoleonic in its brevity and force, every word of [the speech] is imprinted on my memory in letters of flame . . . "The Government went mad (Gandhi said) but our people also went mad. I say, do not return madness with madness but return madness with sanity, and the situation will be yours" '[22] Pyarelal was young, eager to believe and hungering for a purpose. Not everyone responded to Gandhi in 1919 and 1920 like him. But a remarkable number did.

At the Amritsar Congress, held within months of the Jallianwala massacre on a site adjacent to the blood-soaked ground, Gandhi's plea for cooperation with the Empire and the reforms it had proposed prevailed despite strong opposition. Jinnah, part of Congress until December 1920, had seconded Gandhi's resolution. Shortly after Amritsar, a senior official of the Raj in Gujarat, Frederick Pratt, who had dealt with Gandhi's 1918 satyagraha in Kheda, wrote as follows to Gandhi:

> A week or two ago when I read the account of your speech in the Amritsar Congress, in which you and Mr Jinnah were fighting the battle of trust and cooperation against suspicion and disappointment, I felt I would like to write...Our relations in the past have not been harmonious. Speaking for myself only, I feel sure there have been hard thoughts and hard words against you, which were not justified. But the future matters more than the past, and I wish to grasp the hand of fellowship and cooperation in the same spirit in which you extended it in your admirable speech.[23]

By now, however, Gandhi was moving towards rebellion, which began in May-June 1920. It was connected to London's response to the Punjab excesses and to the sentiment of India's Muslims about Turkey. In May 1920 the report of the Hunter Commission appointed to inquire into Jallianwala and related inhumanities was published. It confirmed all the sombre facts that Congress's inquiry, meticulously conducted by Gandhi, had revealed, yet drew tame conclusions. Moreover, though General Dyer, who had ordered the Amritsar shooting, was divested of his command, the House of Lords gave him a vote of approval and British admirers gave him a sword of honour and 20,000 pounds! All of Punjab and much of India was outraged.

The final terms for Turkey, defeated along with Germany, were also announced in May 1920. She was deprived of all her colonies and the Greek-majority areas it once controlled. Saudi Arabia, home to Mecca and Medina, was recognized as a free state under a pro-

British chieftain, Faisal. Palestine and Iraq, the former including Jerusalem and the latter Karbala, places almost as sacred to the Muslims as Mecca and Medina, were placed under British guardianship. The leaders of India's Muslims saw all this as an affront to Islam. In their view, suzerainty over Islam's sacred places belonged to the Sultan of Turkey, the Khalifa of the Muslim world; that Faisal was a Muslim was not good enough. Muslims in India took the line that unless they fought to restore the Khalifa's overlordship — his Khilafat — they would be party to the sacrilege that Britain had committed.

Later, this was shown to be a mistaken understanding of Islam. A British civil servant called J.W. Hore argued in a minute to the Secretary of State for India, Edwin Montagu, that 'there is no canon which lays down that the Sultan of Turkey is and always must remain the Khalifa.'[24] An old custom was not necessarily a canon. That Hore was right, and the leaders of India's Muslims wrong, was proved in March 1924 when Mustafa Kamal, who had seized power in Turkey, abolished the Khilafat and expelled the Sultan, and no Indian Muslim felt that Islam had been compromised.

This is the cool wisdom of hindsight. In 1920 India's Muslims were passionate about the sacrilege against the Khilafat. It was seen as betrayal too, for in the middle of the war the British Premier, Lloyd George, had promised that the Allies were not 'fighting to deprive Turkey of the rich and renowned lands of Asia Minor.' Relying on this assurance, a number of Indian Muslims had soldiered for the Empire against Turkey.

The Ali brothers were released towards the end of 1919. After attending the Amritsar Congress, Muhammad Ali went with a few other Muslims to London and pleaded for Khilafat. Lloyd George told them: 'Turkey slammed the gates in the face of an old ally . . . Germany has had justice, pretty terrible justice. Why should Turkey escape?'[25] India's Muslims saw this as a breach of promise.

We have seen that Gandhi had cultivated the Ali brothers from 1915 and spoken for them to the Viceroy. He sensed the strength of Muslim feeling on Khilafat earlier than most. The convergence of Khilafat and Punjab, triggering the simultaneous resentment against the Empire of Hindu, Muslim and Sikh India, seemed to him a divine design.

'This is an opportunity which is not going to recur for the next hundred years,' he said in Calicut in August 1920 (18:180). Amazingly, three profound aspirations of his now seemed realizable: Hindu-Muslim unity (if Hindus made common cause with Muslims); weaning Muslims from violence (if he obtained the concurrence of Muslim leaders to nonviolence); and the end of the British connection (if Hindus and Muslims jointly withheld their cooperation).

The last was his heart's desire but so far the head had overruled it. Now, in an India that felt rudely estranged by the Empire, he felt he had no choice. If he did not lead an all-Indian nonviolent fight, others would incite Muslims, Hindus and Sikhs to separate, violent risings. The chance of a lifetime seemed the only possible option; opportunity and compulsion spoke as one. The result was a Gandhi as certain as he was radiant.

Congress became his. His programme of noncooperation was adopted by Congress at a special session in Calcutta in September 1920 and at its annual session in Nagpur in December. At Nagpur Congress changed its goal from 'Swaraj within the Empire' to, simply, 'Swaraj.' Jinnah called this change unconstitutional and left Congress. In some though not all ways, he stuck to the Gandhi-Jinnah position of Amritsar. Annie Besant and Madan Mohan Malaviya joined Jinnah in dissent but every other Congress stalwart boarded the noncooperation train piloted by Gandhi. The tide of opinion was clear; even Tilak, jealous of the Hindu interest, had said at the end of May 1920 that 'Hindus would support' Muslim decisions on Khilafat.[26]

Congress now asked lawyers to withdraw from the Raj's courts, the aristocracy to give up their Raj-bestowed titles, politicians to boycott the Raj's councils, parents to remove their children from the Raj's schools, and everyone to wear khadi. The climax, said Gandhi, would be a refusal to pay taxes.

The hundreds of lawyers who gave up their practice included Motilal and Jawaharlal Nehru in Allahabad, Chitta Ranjan Das in Calcutta, Vallabhbhai Patel in Gujarat, Rajendra Prasad in Bihar and C. Rajagopalachari and T. Prakasam in Madras. Though not a lawyer, Khan Abdul Ghaffar Khan rose to fight the Raj in the North-west Frontier. In Calcutta Maulana Abul Kalam Azad, scholar and powerful Urdu writer, did the same. Those surrendering titles and medals included Hakim Ajmal Khan, one of Delhi's noted physicians, and Gandhi himself: he had received medals for raising ambulances for the Empire.

Thousands of bright youngsters walked out of the Raj's colleges. New national institutions absorbed many of them — the Kashi Vidyapith of Benares, Ahmedabad's Gujarat Vidyapith, the Jamia Millia of Aligarh, later moved to Delhi, Calcutta's Bengal National College (Subhas Bose, twenty-five at the time, left the Indian Civil Service to head it), the Patna National College, and the Swadhinata Vidyalaya of Madras.

Propaganda against liquor hurt the Raj's treasuries. In many Muslim homes Id was celebrated without beef. Orthodox Brahmins invited Muslims to meals in their homes. Muhammad Ali said: 'After the Prophet, on whom be peace, I consider it my duty to carry out the commands of Gandhiji.'[27] The Raj's surprise and concern were reflected in a remark that Lord Reading, successor to Chelmsford as Viceroy, made to his son about 'the bridge over the gulf between Hindu and Muslim' being created.[28]

❋

Some distinguished figures criticized noncooperation. Tagore found it 'negative.' He wanted a 'true meeting of the East and the West' and disapproved of 'the intense consciousness of the separateness of one's own people from others.' Gandhi replied that a negative was often necessary. Weeding was as important as sowing. The authors of the Upanishads described God in terms of 'neti' — 'not this.' 'The power of saying "no"' was important. Added Gandhi: 'Nor need the Poet fear that noncooperation is meant to erect a Chinese wall between India and the West. On the contrary, noncooperation is intended to pave the way to real, honourable and voluntary cooperation' (*Young India*, 1.6.21).

Tagore was not convinced. He did not like the students leaving colleges or the emphasis on spinning and khadi, and he recoiled from the burning of foreign cloth, an item added to the programme of noncooperation. In an article, 'The Call of Truth,' published in *Modern Review* in October 1921, Tagore said:

> Sparta tried to gain strength by narrowing herself down to a particular purpose, but she did not win. Athens sought to attain perfection by opening herself out in all her fulness — and she did win. Consider the burning of cloth, heaped before the very eyes of our motherland shivering and ashamed in her nakedness ... How can we expiate the sin of the forcible destruction of clothes which might have gone to women whose nakedness is actually keeping them prisoners, unable to stir out of the privacy of their homes?

Tagore said that in Gandhi 'divine providence has given us a burning thunderbolt of truth' and also that 'the Mahatma has won the heart of India with his love. Such a man should welcome the world and strive to unite it, not champion noncooperation or merely say "spin and weave, spin and weave".' The Poet spoke also of an impression of pressurization for noncooperation.

Gandhi answered with 'The Great Sentinel' in *Young India* (13.10.21). He welcomed the Poet's warning against bigotry and intolerance, asked non-believers to stay away from noncooperation and added:

> When there is war the poet lays down the lyre, the lawyer his law reports, the schoolboy his books.
>
> To a people famishing and idle, the only acceptable form in which God can dare appear is work and promise of food as wages. God created man to work for his food and said that those who ate without work were thieves. Eighty percent of India are compulsory thieves half the year. Is it any wonder if India has become one vast prison?
>
> Why should I who have no need to work for food spin?

Because I am eating what does not belong to me. I am living on . . . my countrymen. In burning my foreign clothes I burn my shame. I must refuse to insult the naked by giving them clothes they do not need instead of giving them work which they sorely need. I would give them neither crumbs nor cast-off clothing but work.

Our noncooperation is neither with the English nor with the West . . . We say to the English administrators: 'Come and cooperate with us on our terms.' A drowning man cannot save others . . .

True to his poetical instinct the Poet lives for the morrow and would have us do likewise. He presents to our admiring gaze the beautiful picture of the birds early in the morning singing hymns of praise as they soar into the sky. These birds had their day's food and soared with rested wings in whose veins new blood had flowed the previous night. But I have had the pain of watching birds who for want of strength could not be coaxed even into a flutter of their wings. The human being under the Indian sky gets up weaker than when he pretended to retire.

The hungry millions ask for one poem — invigorating food. They cannot be given it. They must earn it. And they can earn it only by the sweat of their brow. I do indeed ask the Poet to spin and weave.

The powerful sentences did not remove Tagore's skepticism. Charles Freer Andrews, close to both Tagore and Gandhi, also objected to the burning of cloth, which seemed to him 'a form of violence' and racial. Andrews said, too, that if Arabs, Armenians and others formerly ruled by Turkey wanted independence, that was no different from the Indian wish for freedom, which he supported.

The West supplanting Turkey's influence in former colonies was what he objected to, Gandhi replied. As for the burning of cloth, 'if the emphasis were on all foreign things, it would be racial, parochial and wicked.' But the emphasis was only on foreign cloth. Also: 'India is racial today. It is with the utmost effort that I find it possible to keep under check the evil passions of the people. The general body of the people are filled with illwill, because they are weak and hopelessly ignorant of the way to shed their weakness. I am transferring the illwill from men to things.'

Tagore and Andrews feared that Gandhi was abetting illwill. Gandhi claimed he was deflecting it. The Raj charged that the mob violence of 1919 had been sparked off by Gandhi's satyagraha. Gandhi said it occurred in areas where the Raj had not allowed him to go. When in the summer of 1921 the Moplahs of Malabar, Muslims tracing their ancestry to Arab immigrants, rose in revolt, first against the Government and then against their Hindu landlords, and killings and forced conversions took place, the Raj was quick to link the grisly episode to 'the incitements of Mohamed Ali, Shaukat Ali and those who think like them.' The Moplahs had never seen the Ali brothers, or Gandhi, and once more Gandhi said that he and those who thought like him would have pacified the Moplahs had they been allowed to go to them. In effect, Gandhi was claiming an authority to guide India in the Raj's place.

❋

The Raj, it looked, was shrinking. Indians seemed to give allegiance not to it but to Gandhi. Men like Muhammad Ali were often at his side, symbolizing the bridge seen by Reading. The Ali brothers had accepted nonviolence 'as a policy,' and this was enough for Gandhi, but some of their speeches were hot. The Viceroy complained to Gandhi, who said he would obtain regrets from the brothers or dissociate himself from the impugned remarks. Heeding Gandhi, the brothers publicly announced their regrets, but Montagu, the secretary of state, writing to the Viceroy, rightly surmised that the recantation at Gandhi's urging 'must have left very unpleasant thoughts in their mind.'[29]

Decline, meanwhile, was overtaking the Sultan of Turkey, the man India's Muslims were willing to die for. The Sultan was derided by Mustafa Kamal, Turkey's man of destiny, who had set up a government of his own. This brought a death sentence on Kamal's head from the Sultan's government. Gandhi and the Ali brothers sent messages to Turkey appealing for unity. When Kamal inflicted defeats on Greek foes, India's Khilafat committee praised him for his role in the preservation of the Islamic empire, not realizing Kamal's dislike for that empire. A Kamal-British clash seemed possible, and the Ali brothers declared in Karachi that serving or enlisting in the British army would violate Islam. They were arrested.

If the Ali brothers had 'uttered sedition,' said Gandhi, sedition was now 'the creed of the Congress.' He raised the tempo. Das, the Nehrus, Lajpat Rai, Rajagopalachari, Azad and numerous others broke laws and invited arrest. A boycott of an Indian tour by the Prince of Wales was declared. Also announced was a plan to withhold the land tax in Gujarat's Bardoli taluka. Bardoli had a large body of disciplined workers, including many trained in the South African satyagrahas. Moreover, it was part of the district of Surat. The first place in India to offer hospitality to the British, Surat, would now lead in farewelling them. In *Young India* Gandhi wrote of talukas 'throughout the length and breadth of India' seeking 'to plant the flag of swaraj' after it 'floats victoriously at Bardoli.'[30]

Yet 'violence in any part of the country' would jeopardize the movement, warned Gandhi. And he announced an indefinite postponement of the Bardoli defiance when violence occurred in Bombay during the visit of the Prince of Wales. Some Parsis, Anglo-Indians and Jews who had not joined the boycott were targeted by a mob of Muslims and Hindus. Saris were pulled and torn, caps were seized and burnt. In riots and police firing fifty-eight were killed, of whom fifty-three were Hindus or Muslims. Gandhi confronted the rioters in the streets, declared that the swaraj he saw 'stank in his nostrils' and that 'Hindu-Muslim unity had been a menace to the handful of Parsis, Christians and Jews,' and went on a fast. For the Muslims he had 'one special word': 'I have striven for Hindu-Muslim unity because India cannot live without it . . . The Muslims have to my knowledge played the leading part during the carnage. It has deeply hurt me' (*Young India*, 24.11.21). It was a remark he could not suppress and Muslims could not like.

Meeting in Ahmedabad at the end of 1921, its ranks greatly depleted by prison-courting, Congress resolved to launch the Bardoli defiance, and Gandhi reiterated the resolve in a letter to the Viceroy on 1 February. In Bardoli, in Gandhi's presence, 4000 men and women pledged themselves to stand firm 'unto death.' India was agog, but Gandhi called off the action when he heard of the Chauri Chaura episode of 5 February. A small police party had fired at a procession of noncooperators in Chauri Chaura in eastern U.P. Their ammunition exhausted, the policemen took refuge in their outpost. Violent men in the procession set fire to the outpost and hacked the fleeing constables to pieces. Twenty-two policemen were killed. Gandhi felt God had spoken through the incident. Another voice urged him to press on: " 'But what about your manifesto to the Viceroy . . . ?" spoke the voice of Satan. It was the bitterest cup of humiliation . . . "Surely it is cowardly to withdraw the next day after pompous threats to the Government and promises to the people of Bardoli." '

This voice was rejected, and to the shock of his allies, lieutenants and followers, 30,000 of whom were behind thick walls for implementing Gandhi's campaign, that campaign was halted.

Demoralization followed shock, and the Raj did what so far, for fear of uncontrollable unrest, it had refrained from doing. It arrested Gandhi. He bared his heart in impromptu remarks he made at his trial before reading a prepared statement. Accepting responsibility for 'the Bombay and Chauri Chaura occurrences,' he added:

> I knew that I was playing with fire. I ran the risk and, if I was set free, I would still do the same...I wanted to avoid violence. Nonviolence is the first article of my faith. It is also the last article of my creed. But I had to make my choice. I had either to submit to a system which I considered had done irreparable harm to my country, or incur the risk of the mad fury of my people bursting forth when they understood the truth from my lips (*Young India*, 23.3.22).

The heart he bares is in conflict. It makes a choice and takes a risk.

Then, after Chauri Chaura, it makes another choice and takes another risk, this time of demoralization. Gandhi's heart paid the price of having more than one goal.

Turkey under Mustafa Kamal abolished the Khilafat and expelled the Sultan. With no Khilafat to fight for, India's Muslims no longer needed Hindu backing. Hindus continued to need Muslim support for Swaraj, but Khilafat's demise made Muslims less enthusiastic and more suspicious. Now they saw Hindus as rivals rather than partners, and recalled earlier fears that Swaraj might mean Hindu rule. The bridge that had made the Raj anxious began to crack.

Muhammad Ali's biographer Afzal Iqbal writes: 'Thus the movement ended in apparent failure. But things were never the same again. These events formed a psychological watershed in the development of modern India.'[31]

Talking to a British journalist in November 1923, Lord Lloyd, Governor of Bombay when Bardoli was called off, gave this assessment: '[Gandhi] gave us a scare. His programme filled our gaols. You can't go on arresting people for ever, you know, not when there are 320 million of them, and if they had taken the next step and refused to pay our taxes, God knows where we should have been. Gandhi's was the most colossal experiment in the world's history, and it came within an inch of succeeding. But he couldn't control men's passions. They became violent, and he called off his programme.'[32]

Against these assessments must be set the many-sided criticism of Gandhi's role over Khilafat. From the Muslim side it was charged that Gandhi had incited the Muslims to fight the British and then dropped them. Hindu critics accused Gandhi of appeasing Muslim extremism. Secular criticism focussed on the use of a religious issue for a political aim. British critics, as also Tagore and some Indian moderates, underlined the violence that Gandhi could not prevent.

The critics set down what they saw from their different standpoints. They could not stand where Gandhi stood, or see what he saw. He stood on what he believed was the rock of India; and he saw as an Indian, not as a Hindu or a Muslim. With heat, hammer and chisel — through self-denials, fasts, suppressions and sublimations

— he had moulded himself to be loyal to every Indian but not confined to any section of India, to any single caste, community or region.

He thought that the fates had brought Indian liberty and Hindu-Muslim unity within reach; all that was needed was the application of Indian will. But Turkey let him down, as did Indian demonstrators, the former by rejecting Khilafat and the latter by rejecting nonviolence. He did not read Turkey right and was over-optimistic about popular discipline. Passion about India, the nationalism that Tagore had spotted and warned against, had blinkered him, but his hand was also forced by the sentiment of the Indian people. Neither anti-Muslim nor anti-Hindu, he was passionately and impatiently pro-independence.

So was much of India. The striking thing, nonetheless, is Gandhi's solitariness on the Indian rock. Some criticized him from a Hindu peak, and others from a Muslim tower, but no one proposed an Indian alternative, or another strategy for Indian independence. Some Britons said that there was no such thing as an India on which anyone could stand — that Gandhi stood on a fancy. Openly or secretly, many Hindus and Muslims subscribed to this view, but Gandhi believed he belonged to an India richer than a Hindu or a Muslim India.

The argument of Tagore was that Gandhi should have stood on the rock of humanity, calling out simultaneously to Indians and the British, Turks, Greeks and Armenians, and everyone else. Then there would have been no disillusionment from Turkey or from Indian demonstrators. But then there would not have been an Indian freedom movement either.

※

We need not go into the Salt March of 1930 and what it triggered across India, the biggest defiance after the noncooperation of 1920-22, except to note its remarkably nonviolent character and to recall Churchill's resentment at the talks Gandhi had with Irwin, the Viceroy, in the wake of the revolt. Churchill found it 'nauseating' and 'alarming' to think of the 'half-naked' Gandhi 'striding up the steps of the viceregal palace to parley on equal terms with the representative of the King-Emperor.' When Gandhi and Irwin reached a settlement, and Gandhi agreed to attend a Round Table Conference in London on India's future, Churchill lamented that 'the lawless act' had 'now been made lawful' and appeasement extended to those who had 'inflicted such humiliation and defiance as has not been known since the British first trod the soil of India.'[33]

A vignette from a Delhi press conference where Indian, British and American journalists talked with Gandhi reveals his manner and mind in March 1931. Q: 'Will you press for Purna Swaraj (complete independence) at the Round Table Conference?' Gandhi: 'We will deny our existence if we do not press for it.' Q: 'What was that which turned the tide in the negotiations?' G (*smiling*): 'Goodness on the part of Lord Irwin and perhaps (*a bigger smile on his face*) equal goodness on my part as well.' Q: 'Do you expect to achieve Purna Swaraj in your lifetime?' G: 'I do look for it most decidedly. I still consider myself a young man of 62.'

Q: 'Do you prefer the English people as a governing race to other races?' G: 'I have no choice to make. I do not wish to be governed but by myself.' Q: 'Would you agree to become the Prime Minister of the future Government?' G: 'No. It will be reserved for younger minds and stouter hands.'[34]

❋

We will look at some aspects of the London visit, including the meeting with the King-Emperor himself, but there may be value, before that, in a glance at an attempt at the end of 1928 to rebuild the Hindu-Muslim bridge. From Congress had emerged the Nehru Report, named after the chairman of the committee that prepared it, Motilal Nehru. This was a response to the Raj's claim that India's different groups and communities did not agree on a future constitution.

In the Report, Muslims were offered three new Muslim-majority provinces — Sind, by being detached from Bombay, of which it was then a part, and the N.W.F.P. and Baluchistan, by the conferment of local powers denied to them in the Raj's scheme. Also offered was the removal of 'weightage' for non-Muslim minorities in the Punjab and Bengal. (By a 1916 agreement between Congress and the Muslim League, which the Raj had implemented and which accepted communal electorates, minorities enjoyed 'weightage' — a proportion higher than their numbers warranted — in provincial councils. Among other things, this resulted in an equality between Muslims and non-Muslims in the council of Muslim-majority Punjab, and something like a minority for Muslims in the council of Muslim-majority Bengal.) Finally, the Nehru Report offered Muslims a twenty-five per cent quota in a central assembly, which accorded with the national Muslim percentage. As a quid pro quo, Muslims were expected to forgo communal electorates and weightage for Muslims in Hindu-majority states.

While a few Muslim leaders accepted the Nehru Report, more rejected it. A group led by Jinnah and Muhammad Ali offered to endorse it, inclusive of joint electorates, if a few improvements were made: an increase to thirty-three per cent of Muslim seats in the central assembly, continuance of weightage for Muslims in Hindu-majority provinces, and in the Punjab and Bengal not only the removal of weightage for Hindus and Sikhs but a guarantee by statute of Muslim majorities. Behind the last demand lay a fear that poverty and lack of education would restrict Muslim voting in the two provinces.

At a crucial discussion in Calcutta at the end of 1928, these demands were rejected. Motilal Nehru, however, said that Muslims could have twenty-seven instead of twenty-five percent in the central assembly. Jinnah and Muhammad Ali regarded the Calcutta response as 'a parting of the ways.' Their demands were turned down because of a lack of assurance that Muslims as a whole would be content with the Jinnah-Ali demands.

Left to himself, claimed Jinnah, he would accept the Nehru Report, dropping his demands. He said in Calcutta: 'Would you be content if I were to say, I am with you?'[35] Left to himself, Gandhi would have accepted the Jinnah-Ali demands. He said so to Jinnah in Calcutta, but added that the Sikhs had made it clear to Congress that they would back out if concessions to Muslims in the Punjab went beyond the Nehru proposals.[36] Leaders alone could not rebuild the bridge.

Muslim attitudes hardened after the Calcutta failure. This was reflected in low levels of Muslim participation in the 1930 defiance — except in the N.W.F.P. where, under the leadership of Khan Abdul Ghaffar Khan, nonviolent Pathans 'took over' the town of Peshawar for five days in April.

✳

It was the opportunity to affect popular opinion in Britain rather than any faith in the Round Table Conference (RTC) that took Gandhi to London in 1931. In India, Irwin had been replaced as Viceroy by Willingdon, a hardliner, and the RTC was packed with Indian delegates opposed to Gandhi. With their aid London 'proved' that significant sections in India disagreed with Gandhi and preferred the Raj.

But Gandhi had his own strategy. He stayed among London's poor in Bow in the East End of London, went to Lancashire to meet textile workers hurt by India's boycott of foreign cloth, spent time among teachers and students in Oxford, Cambridge, the London School of Economics, and Eton, and gave interviews to the press. Newspapers found his clothes (the short dhoti and, if the weather required it, a sheet or shawl to cover his chest) and need for goat's milk irresistible. Inevitably, their stories extended to the man and the Indian struggle. What he said through the press or face to face helped undermine belief in the nobility of Britain's involvement with India. Thus he told a group in Oxford: 'The long and short of it is that you will not trust us. Well, give us the liberty to make mistakes . . . I do not want you to determine the pace (of Indian self-government). Consciously or unconsciously, you adopt the role of divinity. I ask you for a moment to come down from that pedestal' (45:227).

'How far would you cut India off from the Empire?' he was asked in Oxford. 'From the Empire entirely, from the British nation not at all,' was the answer. India would be a partner, but 'on equal terms' (45:229). To the students of Eton, he said; 'It can be no pride to you that your nation is ruling over ours. No one chained a slave without chaining himself' (45:222).

Living in Kingsley Hall, Muriel Lester's settlement in Bow in East London, Gandhi and his party — Mahadev Desai, Mira Behn, Pyarelal and Gandhi's son Devadas — walked morning and evening, prayed morning and evening, received callers, and went out calling. Now sixty-two, Gandhi kept late hours and slept little. His aim was to reach as many Britons as possible.

Residents of Bow crowded their windows and balconies to look at the strange figure walking along their streets. Gandhi visited a woman in a hospital and a sick man in his home in Bow when he heard that the patients wanted to see him. Children pestered parents until they were permitted to join Gandhi on his early morning walk. Gandhi 'was delighted and took his walk with them, their rosy faces like apples, and big red scarves round their necks.' The children called him 'Uncle Gandhi' and 'were sad to see he had no socks on and used to try to make him wear warmer clothes!'[37]

Behind Gandhi walked Sergeants Evans and Rogers, assigned by Scotland Yard to 'protect' the guest. Albert Docker, a Bow resident, would recall: 'They (the sergeants) used to come back wiping their brows with sweat, trying to keep up with Mr Gandhi. It was a marvellous way, the way he did step out and make them actually run.' Evans and Rogers went wherever Gandhi went and kept the hours he did. Their charge stretched and won them.

At a 'joy night' in Kingsley Hall, a woman called Martha Rollason patted Gandhi 'on the shoulder' and said: 'Come on, Mr Gandhi, let's have a dance.' Muriel Lester noticed that Gandhi 'looked awfully pleased to be asked.' He turned to Lester and said, 'You'll have to teach me to dance.' Gandhi also said, according to Pyarelal, 'Yes, I shall certainly dance,' and then, pointing to a stick in his hand, added, 'This shall be my partner.' He remembered the dancing lessons he had taken in London in 1889, and was greeted by a man who had taken the lessons with him, Mr Charles, now the maitre at the Dorchester Hotel.

It was Andrews's idea that Gandhi should meet with the Manchester workers hurt by the Indian boycott. He told them that the boycott was linked to khadi and meant to assist poor Indians and was not anti-Manchester. He was heard with sympathy and some even cheered him.

Bernard Shaw and Charlie Chaplin came to meet him; Jan Smuts was in London and tried to be of help; and there were talks with British politicians. Gandhi attempted to meet Churchill but the Englishman was not willing. When a relative of Churchill's, Clare Sheridan, came to do a painting of Gandhi, the latter told her: 'You are a cousin, then, of that man who doesn't wish to know me, Winston Churchill. He refused to meet me. You must tell him . . . that now you've met me I am not as bad as reputed. And will you tell him that I'm sorry I can't talk with him, but I have very kindly feelings towards him.'[38]

Unless he intended to infuriate Churchill, Gandhi would have done better to stop after 'as reputed.' Only a saint could have 'very kindly feelings' towards a reviler, which is what Churchill had recently been towards Gandhi; and there was no evidence that Churchill wanted to acknowledge Gandhi as a saint. If he received the full message, Churchill would have ascribed mischief and insincerity to the sender.

With politicians of another type, Gandhi was more successful. A Labour MP, J.F. Horrabin, noticed Gandhi's 'twinkling smile' on several occasions — Gandhi 'twinkled,' Horrabin wrote, at the cartoonist David Low, whom Horrabin had taken to meet Gandhi, at a Tory MP 'with a highly aggressive manner,' and at others. Later, 'Mr Gandhi twinkled for a couple of hours,' Horrabin adds, 'when, in my Gower Street flat, he sat surrounded by a small crowd of journalists.'[39]

Gandhi's easternness, and his unique definition of it, emerged when at a meeting with Quakers he was asked if he ever found the spirit he was seeking in any western books. He replied at once: 'Yes. For instance, when my friend Henry Polak gave me Thomas a Kempis's *Imitation of Christ*, I read it through at a sitting and I thought I was reading an eastern book.' Q: 'You mean a universal book?' Gandhi: 'Well, when I use the term eastern, I mean universal' (1.12.31; 48:370).

King George V was reluctant to welcome Gandhi at Buckingham Palace, to which all RTC delegates were invited for an afternoon reception. 'What!' he had exclaimed to Samuel Hoare, Secretary of State for India, 'Have this rebel Fakir in the Palace after he has been behind all these attacks on my loyal officers!' Courtesy prevailed and Gandhi was invited to the Palace; and courtesy also prevailed when, despite reluctance, Gandhi went to it. He went in what he always wore. Asked later whether he felt comfortable about his dress, Gandhi replied: 'The King had enough on for both of us.'

Hoare introduced Gandhi to George V. After speaking some innocuous sentences, the King asked, 'Why did you boycott my son?' 'Not your son, Your Majesty,' said Gandhi, 'but the official representative of the British crown.' Then the King, who, according to Hoare, 'evidently thought it was his duty to caution Gandhi on the consequences of rebellion,' uttered 'a grave warning': 'Mr Gandhi, I won't have any attacks on my Empire!' Hoare says he held his breath but 'Gandhi's savoir-faire saved the situation.' He said to the King: 'I must not be drawn into a political argument in Your Majesty's Palace after receiving Your Majesty's hospitality.'[40]

'With an eye and mind as pointed as a needle he penetrated in a moment any sham.'[41] This was Hoare's description of Gandhi's performance in political conversations, but there was no chance of the RTC succeeding. Gandhi said in London that he expected another round of struggle and a fresh spell in jail. But in his final speech to the RTC he said that he was glad he came, for he had felt 'human affection' in England. He added:

My thanks to all, from Their Majesties down to the poorest men in the East End where I have taken up my habitation. I am carrying with me thousands upon thousands of English friendships. I do not know them, but I read that affection in their eyes as early in the morning I walk through your streets. All this hospitality, all this kindness, will never be effaced from my memory no matter what befalls my unhappy land (1.12.31; 48:367).

The children of Kingsley Hall had given Gandhi some little toys on his birthday, 'a woolly lamb, a little doll's cradle, and some other things.' Muriel Lester saw that as Gandhi left England, 'these toys, with his delicate hands, he carried in his own fingers all the time, and gently always put them on the window-sills of every carriage that we changed into, and then on the Channel steamer crossing.' Evans and Rogers also he could not forget. At Gandhi's urging, HMG arranged a Roman holiday for them while Gandhi was in the Italian capital on his way back. After his return to India, Gandhi, expecting to be arrested any moment, sent them, in remembrance of their relationship, English watches located and bought in Bombay.

Chapter 4

East vs. West

FROM THE END of 1939, three struggles simultaneously stirred the subcontinent, featuring the Allies against the Axis, Congress against the Raj, and the Muslim League against a united India. Three passions stirred Gandhi's heart, one for nonviolence, another for freedom, and a third for a united India. As far as nonviolence was concerned, three questions stirred Gandhi's mind: a peaceful end of the world war, India's participation in that war, and securing Indian independence through nonviolence.

Gandhi knew that these three questions were not going to be resolved to his satisfaction. Though he addressed occasional messages to the Czechs, the Jews, the British, the Americans, the Japanese and even Hitler, there is no evidence of any serious bid on his part to bring the war to a halt. If India vindicated nonviolence on her soil, she would speak to the world, not otherwise. Such was his stand. Having claimed universal relevance for nonviolence, he had to make appeals to the warring sides. He did not expect them to be heeded, but they strengthened his hands for a nonviolent fight for Indian freedom.

Nor did Gandhi make a serious attempt to block Congress's efforts to cooperate with the Raj in the world war. Though distancing himself from Congress's resolutions in 1940 and 1941-2 that offered cooperation in the war in exchange for the substance of independence, he did not stand in the way. When the offers were turned down, Congress returned to Gandhi.

For a year from the end of 1940, he was able to organize a notable campaign that united nonviolence and freedom. In this programme of Individual Civil Disobedience (ICD), carefully selected individuals invited arrest by reciting the unlawful sentence, 'It is wrong to help the British war effort with men or money.' Vinoba Bhave, who had joined Gandhi in 1916 and was soon thereafter hailed by the latter as one giving to Gandhi's Ashram more than he received in it, was, by Gandhi's choice, the first to offer arrest, and Jawaharlal the second. About 15,000 courted arrest under ICD, a campaign personally directed by Gandhi. It saw no violence and made Congress's point without impeding the war against Germany. At its conclusion, however, Britain was not better disposed towards Indian independence, and India not less anti-British. The end of ICD coincided with Japan's attack on Pearl Harbor and the start of its sweep across the Pacific.

The possibility of Westminster Abbey and the Houses of Parliament being bombed had moved Gandhi. He told Viceroy Linlithgow that personally he was for nonviolent support to Britain. He was also 'disconsolate' that 'God should allow' the war and that his nonviolence seemed 'almost impotent.' But he added that 'at the end of [his] daily quarrel with God' the answer comes that impotence 'is in men,' not in God or nonviolence (Press statement of 5.9.39, 70:162).

Gandhi's concern for England was not typical. Expending emotion and lives for the Union Jack or the Empire was not the desire of Indians, and lack of enthusiasm turned to dislike when Britain's intention to control rather than trust India became apparent. Sweeping constitutional changes at the height of war were acceptable in Europe. A union with England could be offered to France to wean her away from the pull and menace of Germany. In India, however, the policy of His Majesty's Government was to control the territory and manage the war.

The Congress Working Committee rejected Gandhi's line and demanded to know Britain's stand on Indian independence before spelling out its stand on the war. In 1950 Patel told his friend and biographer Narhari Parikh that this was a mistake that opened the door for an understanding between the Raj and the Muslim League, but in October 1939 Patel was one with Nehru, everyone else in the Working Committee and the national mood in turning down Gandhi's proposal.[1]

The Raj turned towards Congress's foes. The pique of some in the Raj at Congress's denunciations over the years, a section's antipathy to the very idea of Indian independence, in some a belief that Congress would be unfair towards minorities, and dislike of the notion of 'a bargain' in a time of war combined to produce this outcome.

Linlithgow was frank with his King: 'As soon as I realized that I was to be subjected to heavy and sustained pressure designed to force from us major political concessions as the price of Congress's cooperation in the war effort, I summoned representatives of all the more important interests and communities in India, including the Chancellor of the Chamber of Princes and Mr Jinnah . . . and interviewed them one by one . . . a heavy and trying task, but well worth the trouble.'[2]

Jinnah's words provide corroboration. He said in March 1940: 'Up to the time of the declaration of war, the Viceroy never thought of an important party . . . The Viceroy never thought of me.'[3]

Linlithgow's recourse to Divide and Rule is also confirmed by what he wrote to Zetland, Secretary of State for India. 'I had one or two rather anxious moments,' he said, 'when Jinnah, Jawaharlal and Gandhi were discussing the situation together.'[4] Fortunately for Linlithgow, Jinnah was not attracted to an alliance with Congress. He indicated to the Raj that the Muslim League would back the war effort provided the Raj made no independent deal with Congress; and also that the League would wait for Indian independence. He could take this attitude because, influenced by the League's campaign, many of India's Muslims looked upon the Hindu rather than the Briton as the foe.

The hero of the Muslims in 1920 and 1921, Gandhi was seen as their enemy twenty years later. In March 1940 Pakistan was formally demanded, and in August 1940 Linlithgow was authorized by HMG to state that Britain would 'not contemplate transfer of their present responsibilities to any system of government whose authority is directly denied by large and powerful sections in India's national life.' That this meant the grant by HMG of a veto to Jinnah was confirmed by Leopold Amery, Zetland's successor as secretary of state, who told Parliament that 'the foremost among these elements stands the great Muslim community of ninety million, constituting a majority both in Northwestern and Northeastern India.'

No settlement with the Raj now seemed possible without a settlement with Jinnah; and no settlement with Jinnah seemed possible without a compromise over the Pakistan demand. Congress leaders eager for power or for a chance to join the Allies in defence of China and Russia tried to ignore or wish away this truth, but it stared Gandhi in the face. He saw Jinnah, veto in hand, blocking his path to India's Muslims, and he saw Churchill and Linlithgow, pencils in hand, ready to divide India. He also saw the Indian militant, bomb or dagger in hand, ready to strike at Englishmen.

The Cripps Mission of 1942, undertaken when Japan, having captured Singapore and Rangoon, stood at India's gate, confirmed Gandhi's fears. Churchill had sent to India his cabinet colleague Stafford Cripps, a Labour leader friendly to Nehru, not to respond to Indian demands but to demonstrate his 'flexibility' over India to Roosevelt, the American President who seemed to believe in the right of nations to be free. Churchill was confident that Congress and the League would not agree; by way of abundant caution, he had also privately instructed Linlithgow and Wavell, the Commander-in-Chief in India, not to agree to any Cripps-Congress deal without Churchill's cabled consent.

Attractive on the surface, Cripps's proposals were in fact perturbing. He offered full Dominion status after the war and, right away, a national government of the leading political parties. His plan also laid down that after the war every Indian province would have the right to secede; and envisaged a post-war constituent assembly comprising elected members as well as nominees of India's princes. Gandhi took one look at the proposals and left Delhi for his Ashram at Sevagram, but the Working Committee sought an agreement. The talks collapsed when Cripps was unable to confirm that the Viceroy would only be a constitutional head in the proposed national government, or that an Indian Minister of Defence would have more than nominal powers. The fact that Congress leaders had not made an issue of the secession clause was not lost on Gandhi.

✳

Thus far Gandhi had refrained from embarrassing Britain in the middle of the war. He had also feared the degeneration of a disobedience campaign into communal clashes. Now he felt he had no choice. All he had hoped and worked for seemed in danger. Defiance now would perhaps lead to some violence; he would enjoin nonviolence and hope that departures from it would be few; but he could suppress himself no longer. Britain and Japan were speaking with guns, warships and bombs. He too would speak, on India's behalf, and two words would be enough: 'Quit India.' If he did not speak, galloping events would crush his vision.

He said the idea came to him on his day of silence and implied that the inner voice had spoken. But Quit India's meaning is not hidden. It was a strike for national self-respect, India's oneness and the Gandhian vision. At the end of May 1942 he said to about a hundred students who had offered him their services: 'If I continue to wait, I might have to wait until doomsday . . . In the meantime I may be enveloped and overwhelmed by the flames of violence spreading all around' (on 28.5.42, 76:155-61).

By 'the flames of violence' he meant the world war and, even more, the images, destructive of his vision, that appalled him. Unimpressed by the fine print of Cripps's proposals, Gandhi interpreted Britain's intentions from day-to-day happenings in India and from Churchill's utterances. Trusting its Indian officials less and less, the Raj was importing experts when knowledgeable Indians were available. And though Churchill's plain words, 'I have not become the King's First Minister in order to preside over the liquidation of the British empire,' were not uttered until November 1942, he had declared in September 1941 that the Atlantic Charter would not apply to India. Gandhi told G.D. Birla during Cripps's visit of his assessment that Churchill had resolved not to '"abandon [India] voluntarily".[5]

In the fortnight preceding his 9 August arrest, Gandhi tried to address several audiences. In a firmly-worded letter 'To Every Japanese' (*Harijan*, July 26), which, interestingly enough, was published in the Japanese press, he spoke of Japan's 'merciless devastation' of China, said that free India would 'let the Allies retain their troops in India,' and added that if Japanese troops entered India 'we will not fail in resisting you with all the might that our country can muster' (76:309-12). The statement about Allied troops remaining in India had been demanded by Nehru for the sake of China and Russia, and of Congress's image in the world, and Gandhi had agreed to it.

'To American Friends,' Gandhi wrote that Quit India was not anti-Allies. 'After having imbibed and assimilated' the messages of Thoreau, Tolstoy and Ruskin, declared Gandhi, he could not possibly be 'guilty of approving Fascism or Nazism, whose cult is suppression of the individual and his liberty' (*Harijan*, 9.8.42; 76:357-9). Gandhi's British friends had told him that Quit India was being seen in Britain 'as a most cruel stab in the back.' His reply was that he had 'passed many sleepless nights' and his heart was 'agonized' but 'some form of conflict was inevitable.' Even so he was acting 'in the spirit of pure friendship.'[6]

He told Muslim friends that Congress would be content with a transfer of power to a Muslim League government if the League backed Quit India (Letter of 8.8.42; 76:382).

The AICC had been summoned on 7 and 8 August in Bombay to decide on Quit India. On 6 August Gandhi told the Press that he 'definitely contemplated an interval between the passing of the (Quit India) resolution and the starting of the struggle' (76:375). As in previous satyagrahas, he would inform the Viceroy of Congress's demand, seek a meeting and then decide the next move. His personal relationship with Linlithgow entitled him to hope that the pattern might be repeated, and he would stress the relationship in his AICC speech.

Now, however, and for the first time, it was an Empire at war that he was challenging. To Vinoba, Mashruwala and a few other close colleagues, Gandhi said on 26 July: 'This time we have to finish the entire work in three or four days' (76:334). And on 3 August, in a note for his English friend Horace Alexander, Gandhi wrote: 'British authority would deal summarily with the movement' (76:362). Yet Gandhi kept insisting until his arrest that Linlithgow would give him time.

Demanding nonviolence from Quit India supporters, he nonetheless indicated that incidents of violence would not halt his campaign this time. He told Vinoba and the others: 'Supposing a nonviolent struggle has been started at my behest and later on there is an outbreak of violence, I will put up with that' (76:334). This message was duly conveyed to the Viceroy. Gandhi's emissary, Mira Behn, plainly told Laithwaite, the Viceroy's secretary: 'On this occasion (Gandhi) would do his very utmost to ensure nonviolence, but he would not feel justified in calling off the movement because cases of violence occurred' (76:322).

On 7 August Gandhi spoke to the All India Congress Committee: 'I stick to the principle of nonviolence as I did before. If you are tired of it, you need not come with me . . . If there is the slightest communal taint in your minds, keep off the struggle . . . We must remove any hatred for the British from our hearts. At least in my heart there is no such hatred . . . At a time when I am about to launch the biggest fight in my life, there can be no hatred for the British in my heart . . . You should not resort to violence and put nonviolence to shame . . . If you don't understand this it will be better if you reject this resolution.'

Criticizing those 'who do not mind the advent of the Japanese,' Gandhi said: 'The coming of Japan will mean the end of China and perhaps of Russia too . . . If that happens I would hate myself.' Then he referred to the French and Russian revolutions and suggested that India's would be different: 'Though theirs was a fight for the people, it was not a fight for real democracy . . . My democracy means every man is his own master. I have read sufficient history and I did not see such an experiment on so large a scale for the establishment of democracy by nonviolence' (76:377-81).

After the resolution was passed on 8 August, Gandhi delivered perhaps the most stirring speech of his life. Speaking first in Hindi and then in English, he praised the courage of those who had voted against the resolution, recalled his 'lifelong aspiration' for Hindu-Muslim unity, said that Congress wanted independence not for itself or the Hindus alone but 'for all the forty crores of the Indian people,' and poured out his passion:

> I want freedom immediately, this very night, before dawn, if it can be had . . . Fraud and untruth today are stalking the world. I cannot be a helpless witness to such a situation. I have travelled all over India as perhaps nobody in the present age has. The voiceless millions in the land saw in me their friend and representative, and I identified myself with them to the extent that it was possible for a human being. I saw trust in their eyes which I now want to turn to good account in fighting this Empire based on untruth and violence.
>
> How can I remain silent at this supreme hour and hide my light under the bushel? Shall I ask the Japanese to tarry a while? If today I sit quiet and inactive, God will take me to task for not using up the treasure He had given me, in the midst of the conflagration that is enveloping the world.
>
> Everyone of you should, from this moment onwards, consider yourself a free man or woman, and act as if you are free. Here is a mantra, a short one, that I give you. You may imprint it on your hearts and let every breath of yours give expression to it. The mantra is: 'Do or Die.' We shall either free India or die in the attempt.
>
> I will now write to the Viceroy . . .

In his English speech Gandhi recalled his friendship with Lord Linlithgow:

> It is a friendship which has outgrown official relationship . . . There has sprung up a personal bond between him and myself. He once introduced me to his daughter. His

son-in-law was drawn towards me . . . And yet let me
declare here that no personal bond will ever interfere with
the stubborn struggle which, if it falls to my lot, I may
have to launch against Lord Linlithgow.

Then there is the sacred memory of Charlie Andrews
which wells up within me at this moment. The spirit of
Andrews hovers about me . . . I enjoyed his confidence.
There were no secrets between us. We exchanged our
hearts every day . . . He is unfortunately gone. He was a
fine Englishman. I know that the spirit of Andrews is
listening to me.

I want Englishmen, Europeans and all the United Nations to examine in their heart of hearts what crime India
has committed in demanding independence today. I ask:
is it right for you to distrust us? Even if the whole of the
world forsakes me, I will say, 'India will wrench with
nonviolence her liberty from unwilling hands.'

Conceding 'a fundamental difference between Fascism and even this
imperialism which I am fighting,' Gandhi said, 'Do the British get
from India all they want? What they get today is from the India
which they hold in bondage. Think what a difference it would make
if India was to participate as a free ally . . .'

Britain was fighting for herself, not for India. Two months earlier, Gandhi had written: 'India is not the home of the British people.
If they are overwhelmed they will return from India every man,
woman and child, if they have facilities enough to carry them, even
as they returned from Singapore, Malaya and Rangoon' (*Harijan*,
7.6.42; 76:166).

'Where shall I go, and where shall I take the forty crores of India? How is this vast mass of humanity to be aflame in the cause of
world-deliverance unless and until it has touched and felt freedom?
I have therefore pledged Congress and the Congress has pledged
herself that she will do or die.'

❋

He wanted freedom before dawn; he was arrested before dawn. Mahadev Desai and his host G.D. Birla had predicted the event but Gandhi thought that the reference to Linlithgow in his speech would delay it. Before he was driven away in the police car, Gandhi asked Pyarelal to convey his 'parting message to the country': 'Let every nonviolent soldier of freedom write out the slogan "do or die" on a piece of paper or cloth and stick it on his clothes, so that in case he died in the course of offering satyagraha, he might be distinguished by that sign from other elements who do not subscribe to nonviolence' (76:403).

All the leaders were put away. In a few days the whole of India seemed to erupt. Almost every town and every village found its men and women of the hour. Widespread, powerful and in places violent, Quit India was described by Linlithgow to Churchill as 'by far the most serious rebellion since that of 1857.'[7] The Empire suppressed the rising, but Indian independence was now not in any doubt, and Congress was positioned, irremovably, to take the succession from the Raj.

The warmth in the Gandhi-Linlithgow relationship had been genuine and two-sided. Writing to Amery in February 1943, Linlithgow referred to Gandhi's 'very many likeable qualities' and said, 'My personal relations with him have always been very good' (8.2.43; TOP 3:639). Shortly before the war, Linlithgow had been helpful over a dispute of Gandhi's with the Rajkot durbar; and he had shown interest in Gandhi's rural schemes. Yet Linlithgow was as loyal to the Empire and to Churchill as Gandhi was to Indian honour and to Congress.

Five days after his arrest, Gandhi wrote to Linlithgow charging him with 'precipitating the crisis' (14.8.42; TOP 2:702-5). Added Gandhi: 'However much I dislike your action, I remain the same friend you have known . . . [and] a sincere friend of the British people . . . Congress seeks to kill imperialism as much for the sake of the British people and humanity as for India.'

Some weeks later, learning that a son of Irwin had been killed in the war, Gandhi wrote to Linlithgow of the 'sad but heroic death of the Hon. Peter Wood in action,' and asked the Viceroy to convey 'congratulations as well as condolences on the sad bereavement to the father' (5.11.42; TOP 3:209). As Linlithgow well understood, this was how Gandhi was taking the deaths in the Quit India battle. His faithful ally and secretary, fifty-year-old Mahadev Desai, had died in his lap, and word of killings elsewhere in the country was reaching him.

At the end of 1942, giving the date as 'New Year's Eve' and his place as 'Detention Camp,' Gandhi wrote to the Viceroy: 'Contrary to the Biblical injunction, I have allowed many suns to set on a quarrel I have harboured against you, but I could not allow the old year to expire without disburdening myself of what is rankling in my breast against you. I had thought we were friends and should still love to think so. However, what has happened since the 9th of August last makes me wonder' (TOP 3:439-40).

This intriguing opening, suggestive of an appeal from one heart to another, was followed by the declaration that he would fast for twenty-one days unless Linlithgow convinced Gandhi of his error. Gandhi knew, of course, as did Linlithgow, that a fast of this length by the seventy-four-year-old prisoner would attract the attention of the whole of India, and that India would be convulsed if he were to die. After consulting advisers, Governors and the India Office in London, Linlithgow replied that in fact it was Gandhi who had let the other man down, and cited the killings and destruction in Quit India's name. Gandhi rejoined: ' You throw in my face the murders . . . I see the fact of murders as clearly I hope as you do . . . The Government goaded the people to the point of madness. They started leonine violence in the shape of the arrests' (29.1.43).

Linlithgow's counter, again prepared after careful consultation, was quite strong. He charged Gandhi: 'There is evidence that you and your friends expected this policy to lead to violence; and that you were prepared to condone it; and that the violence that ensued formed part of a concerted plan, conceived long before the arrest of Congress leaders.' Linlithgow went on to describe the threatened fast as 'political blackmail,' adding, within brackets, 'Himsa,' using the Hindi word (5.2.43; TOP 3:588).

The fast was 'an appeal to the Highest Tribunal for justice,'

Gandhi replied. As for the charge of expecting, condoning and planning violence, Gandhi said: 'I have seen no evidence in support of such a serious charge' (7.2.43; TOP 3:615-6). Undertaken in February and March 1943, the fast had the effect that Gandhi and Linlithgow had anticipated. Three of Linlithgow's Executive Council resigned and the Viceroy had to work hard to prevent other defections. From behind barbed wires, the Empire's prisoner had once more managed to set off a tremor.

In September it was announced that Linlithgow was leaving and that Wavell would succeed him. Gandhi wrote (27.9.43; TOP 4:324):

> Dear Lord Linlithgow: Of all the high functionaries I have had the honour of knowing, none has been the cause of such deep sorrow to me as you have been. It has cut me to the quick to have to think of you as having countenanced untruth and that regarding one whom, at one time, you considered as your friend. I hope and pray that God will some day put it into your heart to realise that you, a representative of a great nation, have been led into a grievous error. With good wishes, I still remain, Your friend, M.K. Gandhi.

The insinuation of plotting violence was an untruth. Rumours deliberately circulated in America and Britain that Gandhi had pro-German or pro-Japanese leanings were lies too. The Viceroy must have known the allegations to be false, for despite strenuous efforts, the Raj had been unable to come up with any evidence linking a violent incident of 1942 to any senior Congress leader, let alone to Gandhi. No pro-Axis leanings could be shown either. We have seen, however, that Gandhi had expected some violence; and he had privately said that cases of violence would not halt his struggle.

What cut Gandhi to the quick was a mix of the Raj's distortions and his own unease. And the latter was an inevitable result of the old conflict between pure truth and nationalistic truth. Friends in England such as Horace Alexander and Agatha Harrison had been saddened by Quit India, he knew; and he must have heard that Henry

Polak had turned critical. 'Walking alone' in alienation from cherished friends was not an agreeable exercise. For India's identity and Congress's survival he had to launch Quit India; but there was no way in which Quit India could remain wholly nonviolent.

Understanding this, Linlithgow threw the ball back into Gandhi's court (7.10.43; TOP 4:381):

> Dear Mr Gandhi: I am indeed sorry that your feelings about any deeds and words of mine should be as you describe. But I must be allowed, as gently as I may, to make plain to you that I am quite unable to accept your interpretation of the events in question. As for the corrective virtues of time and reflection, evidently these are ubiquitous in their operation, and wisely to be rejected by no man. Yours sincerely, Linlithgow.

To complete the picture of Gandhi's attitude to the British during the war, we may note that during Cripps's 1942 visit, when Gandhi was moving from discontent to rebellion, he spoke to Birla of a lingering warmth towards the Empire, which he said he wanted 'to mend, not end.'[8] Also relevant are Gandhi's 1940 remarks in the wake of the death of Charlie Andrews:

> When we met in South Africa we simply met as brothers and remained as such to the end. It was not a friendship between an Englishman and an Indian. It was an unbreakable bond between two seekers and servants . . . At the present moment I do not wish to think of English misdeeds. They will be forgotten, but not one of the heroic deeds of Andrews will be forgotten so long as England and India live. If we really love Andrews's memory, we may not have hate in us for Englishmen . . . (*Harijan*, 13.4.40).

Shortly after his release in the summer of 1944, Gandhi wrote a letter to an English friend, the Quaker Carl Heath, that revealed both an inner turmoil and a turning to God: 'Though in the midst of a raging storm, I often hum to myself, "Rock of Ages, cleft for me, let me hide myself in Thee" ' (78:290, 13.11.44).

❀

There was pride and sorrow in Churchill's and Linlithgow's war, the Second World War. Evil regimes were confronted and defeated, and nations in chains freed, but not without sadness in families across the world. Quit India, Gandhi's last war, also offered pride and sorrow. It saved India's self-respect and made freedom inevitable but a price was paid in blood and tears. Mahadev Desai, Kasturba, who died in detention in 1944, and Maulana Azad's wife Zuleikha, who died in Calcutta while her husband was a prisoner at Ahmednagar Fort, were contributions to a large sacrifice.

Meeting Churchill in England in 1935, Ghanshyam Das Birla had found that the British leader was uneasy about his refusal to meet Gandhi in 1931. 'It was then rather awkward,' Churchill said, adding, 'Mr Gandhi has gone very high in my esteem since he stood up for the untouchables.' Receiving Birla's report, Gandhi authorized Birla to write to Churchill that he retained 'a good recollection of Mr Churchill when he was in the Colonial Office.' This was a reference to their 1906 meeting in London. In 1937 Birla again met Churchill in London and was asked to 'give your leader my greetings.'[9] But if there was any chance of a Gandhi-Churchill understanding, it was torpedoed by Hitler's war.

Smuts of South Africa was dining with Churchill on 7 August 1942, when the AICC began its Quit India deliberations in Bombay. Lord Moran, Churchill's physician, entered the conversation into his diary:

> Smuts spoke of Gandhi: 'He is a man of God. You and I are mundane people. Gandhi has appealed to religious motives. You never have. That is where you have failed.'
> PM (with a great grin): 'I have made more bishops than

anyone since St. Augustine.' But Smuts did not smile. His face was very grave.[10]

When Gandhi was arrested, Winston Churchill 'pouted' to Moran: 'We have clapped Gandhi into gaol.' Gandhi's release in May 1944 followed consultations between New Delhi and London. He had been seriously ill with malaria and dysentery, and the Raj did not want to take chances. Eight weeks after the release, Churchill, according to the Viceroy's diary, sent Wavell 'a peevish telegram to ask why Gandhi hadn't died yet' (*Journal*: 78).

In the spring of 1945, Churchill spoke to Wavell of dividing India into 'Pakistan, Hindustan and Princestan.' That summer British voters sent Churchill into opposition. When he called again on Churchill, Wavell was exhorted to 'keep a bit of India' even if independence was unavoidable (*Journal*: 120 and 168). Jinnah established a line to Churchill, who exerted his influence in Partition's favour. Two weeks after independence and Partition, Churchill's son Randolph met Gandhi in Calcutta and asked about his ideas on a reunion of Pakistan and India. Gandhi's answer was that while he continued to consider Partition a sin, reunion was a question not for him but for 'the people of both states.' If they 'voluntarily wished to be one, there would indeed be nothing like it' (89:268).

But in August and September 1947 the people of the two states witnessed killings that prompted some formidable words from Randolph's father:

> The fearful massacres which are occurring in India are no surprise to me. We are, of course, only at the beginning of these horrors and butcheries, perpetrated upon one another with the ferocity of cannibals, by the races gifted with the capacities for the highest culture and who had for generations dwelt side by side in general peace under the broad, tolerant and impartial rule of the British Crown and Parliament. I cannot but doubt that the future will witness a vast abridgement of the population throughout what has for 60 or 70 years been the most peaceful part of the world, and that at the same time will come a retrogres-

sion of civilisation throughout these enormous regions, constituting one of the most melancholy tragedies which Asia has ever known (89:253).

At his prayer meeting on 28 September, Gandhi summarized Churchill's speech and commented on Churchill's standing and role: 'Mr Churchill is a great man. He belongs to the blue blood of England. The Marlborough family is very famous in British history. He took the helm when Great Britain was in great danger after the Second World War started. No doubt he saved the British Empire from a great danger at the time.'

Then he took Churchill to task: 'If he knew that India would be reduced to such a state after freeing itself from the rule of the British Empire, did he for a moment take the trouble of thinking that the entire responsibility for it lies with the British Empire? . . . Mr Churchill has been too hasty in his sweeping generalisation. India's population is several millions. Of these a few lakhs have taken to the path of barbarism.'

Sweeping as Churchill had undoubtedly been, Gandhi knew that he himself was neither fair nor impartial in laying 'the entire responsibility' for India's killings on the Raj. Addressing his people, Gandhi added:

Many of you have given ground to Mr Churchill for making such remarks. You still have sufficient time to reform your ways and prove Mr Churchill's prediction wrong...
Had the people continued to listen to me as they did before the negotiations for freedom started, there never would have been that show of barbarism which Mr Churchill has described with such relish and gross exaggeration (89:253-5).

A week later Churchill repeated his remarks. Gandhi said Churchill was playing domestic politics and trying to discredit the Labour government which had conceded Indian independence. Gandhi went on:

Supposing Mr Churchill comes back to power, would he give us an ultimatum that he is going to enslave us again, and attack us? Let us see how he does it . . . The British are not going to return. They cannot come back. But if other powers under the U.N.O. come here for investigation, we will not be able to stop them. If then we continue to be mad and lose our heads, we will lose our freedom to them (On 5.10.47; 89: 289-90).

In November Churchill announced that the Tories would oppose the Burma Independence Bill. Violence in India, he said, would be repeated in Burma. Gandhi advised a group of Burmese callers 'to profit' from Churchill's remarks and 'without being angry to so conduct their affairs as to falsify Mr Churchill's forebodings' (On 8.11.47; 89:501). The Gandhi-Churchill exchange ends with this remark.

The lights were on Asia. What would it say to the West? To Asian leaders meeting in New Delhi at Nehru's invitation, Gandhi revealed himself, four months before independence, as a distinctive defier and peculiar would-be conqueror of the West. He told them that India's wisdom could be found in an untouchable's 'humble cottage in a humble village,' not in 'Delhi, Bombay, Madras, Calcutta, Lahore.' Killings in the Punjab and Bihar were in the news. 'The carnage that is going on before our very eyes is a shameful thing,' Gandhi admitted. But he recalled that men from the East had taken wisdom to the West:

The first of these wise men was Zoroaster. He belonged to the East. He was followed by the Buddha who belonged to the East — India. Who followed the Buddha? Jesus, who came from the East. Before Jesus was Moses who belonged to Palestine though he was born in Egypt.

After Jesus came Mohammed . . . I do not know of a single person in the world to match these men of Asia.

If you want to give a message to the West, it must be the message of love and the message of truth. I want you to go away with the thought that Asia has to conquer the West through love and truth . . .

In this age of democracy, in this age of awakening of the poorest of the poor . . . you will complete the conquest of the West not through vengeance because you have been exploited, but with real understanding (87:190-3).

Elizabeth, daughter of the English monarch and granddaughter of George V, whom Gandhi had met in 1931, was married three months after Indian independence to Philip, nephew of Mountbatten. At the request of India's leaders, Mountbatten had stayed on as Governor General. Francis Watson of the BBC has recalled an incident in connection with England's royal wedding: 'When his own country stood poised between consummation and chaos . . . the old man with nothing he called his own but his stick and his spinning-wheel, his faithful watch and a few other carefully guarded trifles, went to Lord Mountbatten and asked what he could send as a wedding gift to Princess Elizabeth and Prince Philip.'[11]

In consultation with the Mountbattens, Gandhi decided he would send a small table-cloth woven from yarn his hands had drawn on a charkha. He requested Mountbatten to carry the present (9.11.47; 89:507):

Dear Lord Mountbatten: This little thing is made out of doubled yarn of my own spinning. The knitting was done by a Punjabi girl who was trained by Abha's husband, my grandson. Lady Mountbatten knows Abha. Please give the bride and the bridegroom this with my blessings, with the wish that they would have a long and happy life of service to men. Yours sincerely, M.K. Gandhi.

In prayer, Gandhi used to say, his mind was not proof against distraction, but it was when he spun. What Elizabeth and Philip received from him was the creation of his purest toil. Also, he shared with them what bound him to India's hungry and ill-clad, the thread made by hand. He shared it at a time when the cold the refugees were facing was daily on his mind; and if the Punjabi girl who knitted 'this thing' was, as is probable, a refugee, then the gift also involved the subcontinent's displaced. Pain was woven into that piece of lace. And love too.

Yet national self-respect was never dethroned. Any suggestion that things were better before freedom riled him. When a Delhi Maulana said to him on 11 January 1948 that he wanted a passage to England, the remark helped spark Gandhi's last fast. He would only break it, Gandhi said, when Muslims in Delhi felt secure; when that happened, he added, Hindus and Sikhs in Pakistan would also experience relief. The Maulana who had made the wounding remark called on the fasting Gandhi and heard strong words: 'I had no answer to give you then. Now I can face you ... I shall say to the Government: "Here are the unfaithful Muslims who want to desert India. Give them the facility they want." ' The Maulana said he was sorry if his words had hurt Gandhi. Retorted Gandhi: 'That would be like the Englishman who kicks you and at the same time goes on saying, "I beg your pardon." Do you not feel ashamed of asking to be sent to England? And then you said that slavery under the British rule was better than independence under the Union of India. How dare you, who claim to be patriots and nationalists, utter such words?'

Begun on the morning of 13 January, the fast ended on the evening of the eighteenth. At 5.45 a.m. on the eighteenth, well before the decision to break the fast, Gandhi wrote on a consequence of the Indo-British encounter, the use of English in India. Asked why *Harijan*, published in English, was continuing, Gandhi replied in his journal:

> I cannot discontinue the English *Harijan* ... My contact
> with the West is also widening. I was never opposed to
> the British or to any Westerner nor am I today ... So

> English will never be excluded from my small store of knowledge. I do not want to forget that language nor give it up. [However], it cannot become our national language or the medium of instruction . . . The rule of the English will go because it was corrupt, but the prevalence of English will never go (*Harijan Sevak*, 25.1.48; 90:441-3).

A group of men came to his prayer meeting two days later to kill him. The plan miscarried but one of them threw a bomb and damaged a wall near where Gandhi was seated. He was apprehended. The next day Gandhi spoke about him, and also about the violence that had accompanied Quit India in 1942:

> You should not have any kind of hate against the person who was responsible for this (the blast). He had taken it for granted that I am an enemy of Hinduism . . .
>
> A correspondent writes that when I was in jail in 1942 people had indulged in acts which were sometimes violent . . . It is true that there was violence in the country following my imprisonment . . . Had the country then remained wholly nonviolent, we would not have been in the plight we are in today (21.1.48; 90:472-4).

But we have found that a purely nonviolent Quit India movement was an improbability, and that Gandhi knew it. Nine days after the incident of the bomb Gandhi was killed. God was on his lips when he collapsed. Since he was striding towards the little spot where he had prayed every evening for about five months, we may assume that God was in his heart as well. Knowing him, we can assume also that close to God in that citadel resided Indian self-respect, freed as far as possible of all anger and hate.

Chapter 5

'Hind Swaraj'

HIND SWARAJ IS a text for its times, not a text for all time. I for one am unable to accept the sweeping statement: 'The tendency of the Indian civilization is to elevate the moral being, that of the Western civilization is to propagate immorality. The latter is godless, the former is based on a belief in God' (Ch.13). The torch held by *Hind Swaraj*'s author does not throw an even light on the terrain under examination. Some portions remain in darkness while the shape of others is distorted or exaggerated. Yet no study of the historic encounter between the Indian and Western civilizations can ignore *Hind Swaraj*; neither can any study of the working of Gandhi's mind.

This is a mind that among other things anticipates the future, including his own role, with uncanny accuracy. In *Hind Swaraj* Gandhi writes in 1909 that Bengal, partitioned in 1905, 'will be reunited,' and that the split in the Indian National Congress that had occurred amidst much bitterness in 1907 'will not last long.' He expects (Ch.1) that people of his views will in due course be 'using that body' (the Congress), and adds: 'I do not expect my views to be accepted all of a sudden. My duty is to place them before readers . . . Time can be trusted to do the rest.'

He describes the kind of Indians who can speak the plain truth to the British. They should have 'real love' and no fear, believe that Indian civilization is 'the best' and the European variety 'a nine days' wonder,' be intensely dissatisfied with India's 'present pitiable condition,' and, 'having experienced the force of the soul within themselves,' neither 'cower before brute force' nor 'on any account desire to use brute force.'

Having spelt out the requirements, he says: 'If there be only one such Indian . . . the English will have to listen to him.' The last sentence of the book reads as follows: 'I have endeavoured to explain [swaraj] as I understand it, and my conscience testifies that my life henceforth is dedicated to its attainment.' The author of *Hind Swaraj* has no doubt about satyagraha's triumph, his personal commitment and his future role.

Gandhi was keenly aware, if not prescient, on another score. Summarizing for his friend Polak's benefit the idea that he was about to present in *Hind Swaraj* — ideas that he said had 'taken a violent possession of me' — Gandhi touched on the tension between England and Germany. He said that the relationship between England and an industrialized and militarized India would be no more than 'an armed truce' — 'even as it is between, say, Germany and England, both living in the Hall of Death in order to avoid being devoured, the one by the other' (Letter to Polak, 14.10.09; 9:479). This was five years before the Great War.

The West confronted Gandhi politically through the Empire and culturally through its civilization. His break with the latter came in 1909, eleven years before his break with the Empire. As Gandhi said to Polak in the 1909 letter referred to, his objections to modern civilization were 'not new.' In a piece in the *Natal Mercury* published at the end of 1894, a twenty-five-year-old Gandhi had written pejoratively of 'the dazzling and bright surface of modern civilization' (3.12.94; 1:139-40). The following year, the *Natal Advertiser* published (1.2.95) a letter in which Gandhi spoke of 'the utter inadequacy of materialism [and of] . . . a civilization [whose] greatest achievements are the invention of the most terrible weapons of destruction.'

When an accident occurred in 1903 in the Paris Metro, Gandhi again wrote in *Indian Opinion* of 'the tinsel splendour of modern civilization' (20.8.03; 3:414-5). In 1904, after reading on a train Ruskin's *Unto This Last* lent to him by Polak, Gandhi established his Phoenix settlement outside Durban, and moved *Indian Opinion* from Johannesburg to Phoenix, revealing a distaste for city life. In 1905 he wrote about Tolstoy and his beliefs in *Indian Opinion*, quoting with approval the Russian's views against accumulating wealth, returning evil for evil, wielding a gun or political power, and setting up large cities (2.9.05). So *Hind Swaraj* was not sudden, even if it was sharp.

Yet we should note three sets of influences that, in the end, drew *Hind Swaraj* out of Gandhi. The first was disillusionment with the politics and society of South Africa and England. Protection of white power was the bottomline for South Africa's politicians. As for white citizens, the ones in Johannesburg had no time, Gandhi wrote, 'to look at anyone else.' Greed for gold could be heard in the roar of the Johannesburg batteries, which, as Doke wrote in his biography of Gandhi, 'are never still. Night and day, and every night and every day, without rest, the crushing of the great machinery goes on' (6). Devanesen dramatizes but is not wholly wrong when he writes, 'The gold mines on the Rand were largely responsible for the Mahatma's firm conviction that Western civilization is essentially selfish and materialistic,' and adds:

> In Johannesburg where the pursuit of wealth was almost a religious passion, Gandhi chose a life of poverty. In streets where there was fear in men's eyes, he learned to look death in the face. In a place where the mining compounds were oppressive reminders of the power of Johannesburg to tear men from their homes and render them outcasts, Gandhi broke up his own family only to recreate it in a wider way in the Phoenix Settlement. In a city that denied the brotherhood of man, he learned how to affirm that all men are brothers.[1]

Gandhi's disillusionment with the great and powerful of Britain was crystallized during four months he spent in London in 1909. The South African colonies were about to join in a Union of South Africa, a combined Dominion less likely than the Transvaal or Natal to heed any advice that London might give in favour of the Empire's

Indian subjects living in South Africa. Gandhi and Hajie Habib, a Johannesburg merchant, took leave from an incomplete satyagraha in South Africa, where some of their colleagues were in prison, to plead in London with the Empire's custodians, but the latter were distracted by the pull of summer holidaying and a budget crisis. Smuts and Botha were in London to finalize the Union and the Dominion, but Morley, the Secretary of State for India, was not even aware of their presence until Gandhi urged him to intercede with them.[2]

Other aspects of life in England also seemed to jar. In a letter to *Indian Opinion*'s readers, Gandhi wrote: 'The more experience I have of meeting so-called big people or even men who are really great the more disgusted I feel . . . Everyone appears preoccupied with his own affairs' (*Indian Opinion*, 21.8.09). Invited to a banquet for Turkish parliamentarians visiting London, attended by about 300, Gandhi disliked the smoke and alcohol in the air and wrote to Polak of the occasion's 'refined savegery' (9:308). The news of a flight over the English Channel by the French aviator Louis Bleriot did not impress Gandhi; and he drew the attention of his readers to the chemical adulteration of jellies and processed foods coming to light in England (*Indian Opinion*, 8.1.10).

Though Gandhi managed to secure for his cause the active (but private and unpublicized) intervention of a former Governor and Viceroy in India, Lord Ampthill, and through Ampthill the goodwill of a more famous ex-Viceroy, Lord Curzon, the British government took care not to trouble Smuts and Botha with the question of South Africa's Indians.

Before leaving South Africa, Gandhi had advised 'everyone not to expect anything from the deputation,' and to pin their hope on satyagraha alone. Though not unexpected, the reaction hurt Gandhi. The effect on him can be seen in the difference between a picture postcard that he sent to his third son Ramdas from the *Kenilworth Castle* en route to London — 'I am on this steamer,' Gandhi wrote on the card — and the letter written to Ramdas from the *Kildonan Castle*, which brought him back to South Africa: 'Do not be annoyed with your father because he is not bringing anything for you. I did not like anything. What could I do if I did not like any European article? I like everything Indian.'[3]

Writing from London to his cousin Khushalchand in India, Gandhi favourably contrasted jail-going in South Africa with negotiating in Britain, and spoke of 'how strong the passions of attachment and enmity in one's mind are' (7.9.09; 9:391-2). Though he does not specify, the enmity seems to refer to Britain. Gandhi appears to have solved his personal problem, purging himself of guilt, by deflecting his negative thoughts to Britain's civilization. In *Hind Swaraj* he prescribes this course to militants eager 'to expel the English force by arms': 'Your hatred against them ought to be transferred to their civilization' (Ch.14).

The four 1909 months spent in London also saw Gandhi confirmed in his faith in satyagraha and the simple life. He wrote from London that the only thing that interested the people he was meeting was the news of jail-going by Indian satyagrahis in South Africa. At public gatherings at the Emerson Club and in Hampstead, his speeches evoked a warm response from non-establishment Britons. At the Emerson Club he said that South Africa's 'grim prisons' were the gateways to the 'garden of God' where the 'flowers of self-restraint and gentleness' sprang 'beneath the feet of those who accept but refuse to impose suffering.' At Hampstead he said it was 'utterly impossible' for him to accept that East and West would never meet; but a fruitful meeting would only follow a rejection of modern civilization. To Polak he wrote that the occasion was 'a splendid success' (9:477-82).

Britain's women suffragists were active in picketing during Gandhi's visit. He saw their revolt as evidence of modern civilization's failure. He built links with several of their leaders and admiringly described their struggles in *Indian Opinion* but added that the suffragist cause suffered when members resorted to violence.

The Rangoon-based Dr Pranjivan Mehta, Gandhi's friend from the late 1880s when both were students in England, joined Gandhi during his 1909 visit. The two saw a lot of each other, staying in the same hotel in London and travelling together to Louth, where Mehta's son was put in school, and to Whiteway, a Tolstoyan settlement in the Cotswolds. Gandhi wrote to Polak: 'I think [Mehta] is convinced now that ours is the right plan' (26.8.09; 9:368). Gandhi's faith seemed bolstered by Mehta's conversion to his views. Later he would say that *Hind Swaraj* was largely a reproduction of conversations between him and Mehta.[4]

A book Gandhi read in England would be recommended at the end of *Hind Swaraj*. On 8 September he wrote to Polak: 'I was reading last night a very illuminating book by Edward Carpenter — *Civilization, its Cause and Cure* . . . Now you know in what direction my thoughts are drawing me.' But the most satisfying confirmation was the one Gandhi received from Leo Tolstoy. Mehta had shown Gandhi a copy of what seemed to be a writing by Tolstoy. Entitled *Letter to a Hindoo*, it was addressed to Taraknath Das, then editing in Vancouver, Canada, a magazine advocating violence called *Free Hindustan*.

In reply to a request from Das for an article, Tolstoy had written this 513-page epistle, which argued that Indians should resist England nonviolently and reject her civilization instead of accepting it. Because, perhaps, of its length or opinions, the letter was not published by Das. Gandhi sent the copy that had reached him to Tolstoy, sought confirmation that it had been authored by him, and asked for permission to publish it. Tolstoy's reply was immediate: Gandhi could publish it. Mehta making the money available, Gandhi had 20,000 copies printed in England. On his voyage back to South Africa, Gandhi would translate Tolstoy's letter into Gujarati and also write *Hind Swaraj*. In his preface to Tolstoy's Letter, he described the Russian as 'one of the clearest thinkers in the western world, one of the greatest writers, one who, as a soldier, has known what violence is and can do,' and quoted Tolstoy:

> A commercial company enslaved a nation comprising 200 million people! . . . What does it mean that 30,000 people, not athletes but rather weak and ill-looking, have enslaved 200 millions of vigorous, clever, strong, freedom-loving

people? Do not the figures make it clear that not the English but the Indians have enslaved themselves?

The truth of these words, Gandhi said, was unquestionable. Added Gandhi: 'India . . . will cease to be nationalist India . . . when it goes through the process of civilization in the shape of reproduction on that sacred soil of gun factories and hateful industrialism' (10:4-5). In April of the following year Gandhi sent his *Hind Swaraj* to Tolstoy. The ailing Russian seemed thrilled by it and by accounts sent by Gandhi of the South African satyagraha. Writing back to Gandhi, Tolstoy referred to the Transvaal satyagraha as 'most fundamental and important,' supplying 'most weighty practical proof' of what the two believed. In November 1910 Tolstoy died. According to Martin Green, the communication to Gandhi was 'Tolstoy's last long letter' (199).

More surprising was the confirmation Gandhi found in G.K. Chesterton. Gandhi reproduced in *Indian Opinion* an article by Chesterton published in the *Illustrated London News* in September 1909. In it Chesterton said:

> When I see . . . the views of Indian nationalists, I get bored and feel dubious about them. What they want is not very Indian and not very national . . . There is a great difference between a people asking for its own ancient life and a people asking for things that have been wholly invented by somebody else . . . Suppose an Indian said: 'I wish India had always been free from white men and all their works. Everything has its own faults and we prefer our own. Had we our own institutions, there would have been dynastic wars; but I prefer dying in battle to dying in hospital . . . If you (the British) do not like our way of living, we never asked you to do. Go, and leave us with it.
> Supposing an Indian said that, I should call him an Indian nationalist. He would be an authentic Indian . . .

But the Indian nationalists whose works I have read go on saying: 'Give me a ballot box. Give me the judge's wig. I have a natural right to be Prime Minister. My soul is starved if I am excluded from the editorship of the *Daily Mail*.' Now this is not so difficult to answer . . . Even the most sympathetic person may say in reply: 'What you say is very fine, my good Indian, but it is we who invented all these things' (*Indian Opinion*, 8.1.10; 9:425-7).

Chesterton went on to speak of 'a conflict between two complete civilizations' and said: 'The right of a people to express itself, to be itself in action, is a genuine right. Indians have a right to be and to live as Indians. But Herbert Spencer is not Indian; his philosophy is not Indian philosophy.'

Spencer was cited on the mastheads of *Free Hindustan* and the *Indian Sociologist*, the organ of London-based Indian militants whom we will discuss shortly. Here we need only note that Gandhi found Chesterton's reflection of some of his views congenial. Observing the 'conflict between two complete civilizations,' Gandhi too felt that India had 'to be itself in action.' *Hind Swaraj* was the result.

Anxiety had contributed to it too, anxiety about the route of assassination to Indian independence. On 2 July 1909, eight days before Gandhi's arrival in London, Sir Curzon Wyllie, ADC to Morley, the Secretary of State for India, was shot dead at a London reception hosted by the National Indian Association in a South Kensington hall. Wyllie, who had served in India, had arrived as a guest. The assassin was an Indian student, Madanlal Dhingra. A Parsi doctor, Cowasji Lalkaka, who tried to interpose himself between Wyllie and Dhingra, was also killed.

Men linked to India House, a centre started by Shyamji Krishnavarma, an ex-divan of Udaipur and founder-editor of the *Indian Sociologist*, had influenced Dhingra. One of them was Vinayak Damodar Savarkar, who authored the text of the deed's defence found on Dhingra's person. A cook at India House and eyewitnesses gave evidence that led to Dhingra's hanging on 17 August. The *Indian Sociologist* wrote that patriotic homicide was not murder, but Krishnavarma, the editor, had slipped away to France. In his absence the printer of the journal, an Englishman, was given a prison term. Appalled by the killing and its justification, Gandhi wrote a note for *Indian Opinion*:

> It is being said in defence of Sir Curzon Wyllie's assassination that it is the British who are responsible for India's ruin, and that, just as the British would kill every German if Germany invaded Britain, so too it is the right of any Indian to kill any Englishman . . . The analogy of Germans and Englishmen is fallacious. If the Germans were to invade Britain, the British would kill only the invaders. They would not kill every German whom they met. Moreover, they would not kill an unsuspecting German, or Germans who are guests (*Indian Opinion*, 14.8.09; 9:302).

In Gandhi's view, those who incited him were guiltier than Dhingra, who committed his deed 'in a state of intoxication.' He may have been courageous, he knew he was inviting death, but the courage too was the 'result of intoxication.' Added Gandhi:

> Even should the British leave in consequence of such murderous acts, who will rule in their place? Is the Englishman bad because he is an Englishman? Is it that everyone with an Indian skin is good? If that is so, there should be [no] angry protest against oppression by Indian princes. India can gain nothing from the rule of murderers — no matter whether they are black or white. Under such a rule, India will be utterly ruined and laid waste. *This train of thought leads to a host of reflections* (*Indian Opinion*, 14.8.09; emphasis mine).

Gandhi had talked at length with Krishnavarma and his associates during his 1906 visit to England, when he spent two nights at India House. In 1909 some of the London-based Indian militants contacted him, which aroused suspicion about Gandhi in British minds. Gandhi hoped to win the militants to his way; Ampthill, who told Gandhi of the suspicion, could understand this. At least two of the militants were converted, T.S.S. Rajan and V.V.S. Aiyar, though Aiyar's change only occurred in 1915, after both he and Gandhi had returned to India. Padmanabhan's biography of Aiyar (NBT, New Delhi) quotes him: 'When I met [Gandhi] in London [in 1909], I only thought of him as addicted to Truth and as one with *tejas* (radiance). That was a time when I had faith in the sword. At that time Gandhiji urged that there was something more potent than violence, namely spiritual strength. He also asked us to think about his new method of passive resistance, satyagraha. It took a good number of years for us to gain faith in that.'

On 24 October, Vijayadashami day, Gandhi spoke as the chief guest at a subscription dinner arranged by the militants. The request to speak was 'accepted unhesitatingly,' as Gandhi put it in a letter to Polak [9:504]. He would 'talk on the uselessness of violence.' Rajan, a medical student, met Gandhi for the first time on the day of this dinner. As Rajan recalled in 1946:

> I had a great veneration for those young men who talked loudly of revolution leading to freedom for India. A handful as we were, we became a dreaded lot in the Indian world that lived and moved about in London. Vinayak Damodar Savarkar was our chief, and the late V.V.S. Aiyar his lieutenant.
>
> We decided [on] bringing together all Indian students scattered about Great Britain just to remind ourselves of our national solidarity in an alien land. Over one hundred and twentyfive students agreed to partake in the subscription dinner . . . A part of us volunteered to do the cooking, and we entered on our duties in the underground cellar and kitchen, . . . early in the day.
>
> At about 2 p.m. a small, thin, wiry man with a pleasant face joined us in work and was making himself very useful. He volunteered to do the washing of plates and clean-

ing of vegetables with such gusto that we were only too willing to give him the joy of his performance. Hours rolled on, and there was no abatement in the work turned out by this man. Later, when Mr Aiyar turned up in the kitchen, we [came] to know that our announced worker was Mr Gandhi, the great man of Indian South Africa, the president of our evening function. It took my breath away . . . He continued his work well on into the evening when he helped us to lay the tables and the plates and serve the dinner we had prepared. At long last . . . did he consent to sit at the head of the table and preside over the function . . . I found greatness in the Mahatma of the future . . . long before the world knew him.[5]

Gandhi had imposed two conditions before agreeing to preside: the dinner would be vegetarian, and there would be no controversial politics. Gandhi, Hajie Habib, Virendranath Chattopadhyaya and Savarkar spoke. On Vijayadashami the Ramayana was the obvious theme. Gandhi and Savarkar emphasized different aspects of the story.

Two other accounts of this dinner are available, one a later recollection by Asaf Ali, a student at the time, and the other a report, obviously written by Gandhi, in the *Indian Opinion* of 27 November 1909. According to Ali, the gathering was more interested in Savarkar than in Gandhi. The former was 'by far the most arresting personality' in the Indian student community, and 'a flaming ring of violent revolutionarism' had been built around him.[6] Ali recalled that Gandhi's words on the occasion were 'calm, unemotional, and devoid of rhetoric.' Gandhi's interest in the young men comes across from the *Indian Opinion* report:

The dinner was cooked by volunteers from among Indian students of medicine and law. One of them was a very active fellow. He has struggled against odds in order to become a barrister. The same volunteers waited at the table. Mr Hajie Habib proposed a toast to India, and was

supported by Mr Chattopadhyaya. Mr Savarkar delivered a spirited speech on the great excellence of the
Ramayana (*Indian Opinion,* 27.11.09; 9:498-9).

In a letter to Ampthill, Gandhi referred to the militants' views: 'I
have endeavoured specially to come into contact with the so-called
extremists who may be better described as the party of violence.
This I have done in order if possible to convince them of the error of
their ways . . . One of them came to me with a view to convince me
that I was wrong in my methods and that nothing but the use of
violence, covert or open or both, was likely to bring about
redress . . . Everywhere I have noticed impatience of British rule. I
have practically met no one who believes that India can ever become free without resort to violence . . . The information I have
given Your Lordship is quite confidential and not to be made use of
prejudically to my countrymen' (30.10.09; 9:508-10).

A letter that Gandhi wrote to Gokhale also conveyed his concern
that most Indians he had met in London looked to violence (11.11.09;
9:531-2). 'I came in contact with every known Indian anarchist in
London,' Gandhi would later say, adding that *Hind Swaraj* was
'written in answer to the Indian school of violence and its prototype
in South Africa.'[7] In 1938 Gandhi said that *Hind Swaraj* was 'a
faithful record of conversations I had with workers, one of whom
was an avowed anarchist.' Two years later Gandhi revealed that
'the anarchist' was his 'dear friend Dr Pranjivan Mehta': 'All the
argument in the book is reproduced almost as it took place with
him. I stayed with Dr Mehta for a month. Although he loved me, he
thought I was foolish and sentimental. But I did place my point of
view before him. It appealed to his heart. His attitude changed. So
I said let me write down the argument.'[8]

'In the summer of 1909, Gandhi knew more about the realities of
armed conflicts than any of the passionate revolutionaries who talked
to him so earnestly.'[9] This verdict by Devanesen seems valid. The
Gandhi of 1909 had seen the Boer and Zulu wars from close quarters; he had made a careful study, as Devanesen points out, of the
volumes by Kaye and Malleson on the 1857 rising; some of his

fellow-satyagrahis in South Africa had given their lives; and there had been at least three violent attacks on his person in South Africa, by whites in Durban, by Indians in Johannesburg and by an African cell-mate in a Transvaal prison. (The last incident, described in the *Rand Daily Mail* of 5.10.09, can be seen in 9:565.) Thus the Gandhi of 1909 was 'no weakling whose stomach was likely to turn at the thought of blood,' to quote Devanesen again (367). Much experience and reflection lay behind Gandhi's remark at the Emerson Club that war 'demoralizes those who are trained for it. It brutalizes men of naturally gentle character. It outrages every beautiful canon of morality. Its path of glory is foul with the passions of lust, and red with the blood of murder. This is not the pathway to our goal' (On 8.10.09. *Indian Opinion*, 12.2.10).

Gandhi's disquiet about violence also came across in his comment on the September 1909 killing by a Korean of Prince Hirobumi Ito, a former Japanese Premier involved in the occupation of Korea:

> The Japanese hold power in Korea as the British do in Egypt and India . . . Of course, Japan is not in Korea to oblige her . . . [Japan] grabbed it. The Korean people were in no way pleased with this. They have always regarded Japan with hatred . . . But Japan, having once tasted Russian blood, was certainly not likely to pull out of Korea so easily. Such is always the intoxication of power. Those who wield the sword generally perish by the sword . . . Some of our young men believe that the British can be driven out of India by killing [some of them]. Even if this is possible, it is not worth doing. Some things in Japan are commendable, but her imitation of Western ways does not deserve to be admired.
>
> In subjugating Korea, Ito used his courage to a wrong end. But those who fall under the spell of the Western civilization cannot help doing so. If Japan is to rule, defend and expand herself through force, she has no option but to conquer neighbouring lands. The conclusion to be drawn from this is that those who have the welfare of the

people at heart must lead them only along the path of satyagraha (9:424-5).

This is the thesis of *Hind Swaraj*. Violence and Western civilization go together, as do satyagraha and Indian civilization. Violence is evil. It expands and multiplies, and is inseparable from the greed of Western civilization. Self-sacrifice in place of violence, and the pitting of soul force against brute force, is the right way; it is also the Indian way. If the 1906 Zulu war had given birth to satyagraha, the *Hind Swaraj* thesis was sparked by Gandhi's disillusionment and anxiety of 1909 coinciding with Tolstoy's espousal of nonviolence, Carpenter's depiction of civilization as a disease, and Chesterton's desire for a native nationalism from India. The conversion of Mehta and the interest of militants like Rajan indicated to Gandhi that a doctrine that combined satyagraha with the simple life would appeal to elements in India. Tolstoy had linked violence with Western civilization; Gandhi would ask India, in the name of her own soul and her own past, to reject the imported mix.

The Gandhi of 1909 was quite well known. Doke's biography was published that year. Other accounts were soon to follow. Visiting India while Gandhi was in England, Henry Polak had added to the awareness of Gandhi and the South African struggle. Asked to send a message for the end-1909 session of the Indian National Congress, Gandhi presented his latest conclusions:

> For the many ills we suffer from in India, passive resistance is an infallible panacea . . . It is the only weapon that is suited to the genius of our people and our land, which is the nursery of the most ancient religions and has very little to learn from modern civilization — a civilization based on violence of the blackest type, largely a negation of the Divine in man, and which is rushing headlong to its own ruin *(Indian Opinion*, 27.11.09; 9:508).

As he neared the end of his visit to England, Gandhi became surer of his findings and aired them freely. He wrote to Ampthill that

India would have to reject modern civilization, and a large group of eminent Britons and Indians who assembled at the Westminster Palace Hotel to bid him farewell were told that it would be 'utterly impossible' for him to give his allegiance to 'an Empire in which he was not to be trusted . . . as an equal to any other member of the Empire.' He sought British goodwill but added that his true reliance was in satyagraha. He tended to treat satyagraha and the simple life as synonyms, and violence and modern civilization likewise. Not everyone accepted the linkages as inherent. Ampthill for one wrote to him: 'I confess that I do not fully understand your arguments' (1.11.09; 9:508-10).

Half the affected population in the Transvaal had taken part in the satyagraha — women, youngsters, including the poor and the illiterate; they were fighting for the principle of equality and not for any benefit for themselves; they were taking suffering but had resolved not to inflict it; it was, Gandhi said in a letter to Tolstoy and in his speech at the Westminster Palace Hotel, 'one of the greatest struggles of modern times.' If it succeeded, Gandhi wrote to Tolstoy three days before his departure from England, it might 'serve as an example to the millions in India and to people in other parts of the world who may be downtrodden, and will certainly go a great way towards breaking up the party of violence, at least in India' (10.11.09, 9:528-9).

Here Gandhi claims global rather than merely national relevance for his doctrine, but we can see that violence in India was much on his mind. In a letter he sent to Gokhale the following day, inviting the leader from Poona to assist the satyagraha struggle in South Africa by joining it, Gandhi said: 'An early success will break up the violence movement in India' (11.11.09, 9:531-2).

On the voyage from England to South Africa in the *Kildonan Castle*, Gandhi wrote *Hind Swaraj*, in Gujarati, and also translated Tolstoy's *Letter to a Hindoo* into Gujarati. The 30,000-word *Hind Swaraj* was written in one ten-day stretch on the 'good, strong, stamped stationery of the ship.'[10] Some of the manuscript is in Gandhi's left hand, used when the right was tired. In the preface, also written on the ship, Gandhi said: 'I have written because I could not restrain myself. I have read much, pondered much during the stay of four months in London . . . These views are mine and yet not mine. They are mine because I hope to act according to them. They are almost a part of my being. But they are not mine, because . . . they have been formed after reading certain books. That which I dimly felt received support from these books. The views I venture to place before the reader are . . . held by many Indians not touched by what is known as civilization, but . . . they are also held by thousands of Europeans.'

The way in which the text flowed onto the ship's notepaper and the confidence it exudes suggest that *Hind Swaraj* was felt by Gandhi to be something in the nature of a discovery, fusing insights that had seemed unconnected until then. The clear-cut formulation that only nonviolence suited the genius of India whereas violence was insepa-rable from western civilization held considerable promise. It would strengthen Gandhi in any confrontation with the Empire and in his clash with the Indian school of violence, a realization that may have accelerated the script's flow. The 'host of reflections' he had spoken of in August no doubt included some with a bearing on strategy.

Indian Opinion published the Gujarati *Hind Swaraj* in two long instalments in December. In January 1910 it appeared in book form. The Raj in India banned its distribution. Gandhi responded by pub-lishing an English edition at the end of March 1910.

This look at *Hind Swaraj*'s origins perhaps makes its wholesale attack on modern civilization and blanket defence of the Indian more understandable, even if the attack and the defence remain unaccept-able in their extreme form. Before discussing *Hind Swaraj*'s ex-tremism, let us note some of its insights obscured by our awareness of the extremism.

We can start with Gandhi's comment on history. He says that history is commonly taken to mean 'the doings of kings and emper-ors' or 'a record of the wars of the world.' It ignores what the citizen does and skips periods of peace. 'Hundreds of nations live in peace. History does not and cannot take note of this fact. His-tory is really a record of every interruption of the even working of the force of love or of the soul . . . Soul force, being natural, is not noted in history.' Yet it is real and active, and but for it the wars of the world would have finished the world.

Then there is Gandhi's view of the Indian nation. *Hind Swaraj*'s 'Reader,' representing Gandhi's militant critic, asks: 'You have said that passive resistance is a speciality of India. Have cannons never been used in India?' Replying as 'Editor,' Gandhi says: 'Evidently in your opinion India means its few princes. To me it means its teeming millions on whom depends the existence of its princes and our own.'

Hind Swaraj's rebuke and challenge to 'lawyers,' 'doctors,' and 'the wealthy' is, as Anthony Parel points out, a reminder to the elite of their duties and privileged status. The reminder remains valid across the decades, and the politicians, intellectuals and activists of our time may do worse than to soak themselves in fifteen words, each of a single syllable, from *Hind Swaraj*: 'Those in whose name we speak we do not know, nor do they know us' (Ch. 13).

Of similar aptness is Gandhi's remark to the 'freedom-loving' Reader: 'I believe that you want the millions of India to be happy, not that you want the reins of government in your hands' (Ch. 15).

Hind Swaraj's nation is not the state. Its author accords a smaller role in the rise of a nation to the guns and swords of rulers than to the compassion described in Tulsidas's verse, and to fearless peasants and citizens. 'That nation is great which rests its head upon death as a pillow' (Ch. 17).

Also, Gandhi's nation includes all the races and faiths found in India. He admits conflicts among them but stresses India's capacity to accommodate a variety of newcomers and viewpoints. 'In reality,' says Gandhi, 'there are as many religions as there are individuals; but those who are conscious of the spirit of nationality do not interfere with one another's religion . . . In no part of the world are one nationality and one religion synonymous terms; nor has it ever been so in India.'

Gandhi sees religion as an Indian's private affair but he also sees India as a deeply religious land as well as a multi-religious one. While underlining pluralism and tolerance, *Hind Swaraj* does not ignore the role of religion in India. Again, the swaraj of *Hind Swaraj* is both a personal and a national matter. An individual's swaraj, a citizen's self-rule over himself or herself, and India's swaraj go together.

'At the time of the writing of *Hind Swaraj*,' says Parel, 'Gandhi was painfully aware that those who cared for the nation, such as the apostles of violence, did not care for the soul; and that those who cared for the soul, did not care for the nation. Gandhi sought to purge modern Indian nationalism of its reliance on brute force, and to instill in the minds of those who cared for the soul the need to become civic minded as well.'[11]

We can note, too, the frankness of *Hind Swaraj*'s answer to the question, 'Why was India lost?': 'The English have not taken India; we have given it to them. Recall the Company Bahadur. Who made it Bahadur? Who assisted the Company's officers? Who was tempted at the sight of their silver? Who bought their goods? History testifies that we did all this.'

As for *Hind Swaraj*'s stand on 'progress,' some sentences make sense eighty-five years after they were written:

As men progress, they shall be able to travel in airships and reach any part of the world in a few hours. Men will not need the use of their hands and feet. They will press a button, and they will have their clothing by their side. Another button, and they will have their newspaper. A third, and a motor car will be waiting for them. They will have a variety of delicately dished up food. . . Formerly, when people wanted to fight one another, they measured between them their bodily strength; now it is possible to take away thousands of lives by one man working behind a gun from a hill. This is civilization.

Formerly, men worked in the open air . . . Now they are obliged to work, at the risk of their lives, at most dangerous occupations . . . There are now diseases of which people never dreamt before, and an army of doctors is engaged in finding out their cures . . . Formerly, people had two or three meals consisting of home-made breads and vegetables . . .

Hind Swaraj's case on means and ends and against violence is compelling.

> If I want to cross the ocean, I can do so only by means of a vessel; if I were to use a cart for the purpose, both the cart and I would find the bottom . . . The means may be likened to a seed, the end to a tree; and there is the same inviolable connection between the means and the end as there is between the seed and the tree . . .
>
> To use brute force, to use gunpowder . . . means that we want to force our opponent to do that which we desire but he does not. And if such a use of force is justifiable, surely he is entitled to do likewise by us . . .
>
> Do you not tremble to think of freeing India by assassination? . . . Whom do you suppose to free by assassination? The millions of India do not desire it . . . Those who will rise to power by murder will certainly not make the nation happy. . .

Though adjudging Indian civilization superior to the white man's, *Hind Swaraj* opposes racial hate. It cites Britons such as Hume and Wedderburn who 'lashed us into action' for Indian swaraj, or gave 'body, mind and money to the same cause.' Like service, tyranny too has no colour. 'You will admit,' Gandhi tells the Reader, 'that the people under several Indian princes are being ground down. The latter mercilessly crush them. Their tyranny is greater than that of the English.'

Frankness of this kind coupled with Gandhi's free acknowledgment of his debt to men like Tolstoy gives *Hind Swaraj* a human and universal flavour that transcends its extremism. This flavour is also seen in the comment on majorities and minorities. 'Many examples can be given in which acts of majorities [were] found to have been wrong and those of minorities to have been right. All reforms owe their origin to the initiative of minorities in opposition to majorities' (Ch. 17).

Hind Swaraj's proud and staunch nationalist is plainly also a citizen and lover of a wider world, and I cannot resist reproducing the line from Walt Whitman that Devanesen quotes in his discussion of *Hind Swaraj,* a line which, as Devanesen rightly says, 'could have come from Gandhi': *'I have look'd for equals and lovers, and found them ready for me in all lands; I think some divine rapport has equalized me with them.'*

To examine whether *Hind Swaraj* is reasonable and holds the scales even, a lengthy quotation is called for. It is taken from Chapter 13, 'What is True Civilization?':

> I believe that the civilization that India has evolved is not to be beaten in this world. Nothing can equal the seeds sown by our ancestors. Rome went, Greece shared the same fate; the might of the Pharaohs was broken; Japan has become westernized; of China nothing can be said; but India is still, somehow or other, sound at its foundation . . .
>
> Civilization is that mode of conduct which points out to man the path of duty. Performance of duty and observance of morality are convertible terms. To observe morality is to attain mastery over our mind and our passions . . . If this definition is correct, then India, as so many writers have shown, has nothing to learn from anybody else . . .
>
> We notice that the mind is a restless bird; the more it gets, the more it wants; and still remains unsatisfied . . . Our ancestors saw that happiness was largely a mental condition . . . The rich are often seen to be unhappy, the poor to be happy . . . Observing all this, our ancestors dissuaded us from luxuries and pleasures. We have managed with the same kind of plough as existed thousands of years ago . . .
>
> We have had no system of life-corroding competition . . . It was not that we did not know how to invent machinery, but our forefathers knew that if we set our hearts after such things, we would become slaves and lose our moral fibre. They therefore after due deliberation

decided that we should only do what we could with our hands and feet . . . They further reasoned that large cities were a snare . . . and that people would not be happy in them, that there would be gangs of thieves and robbers, prostitution and vice flourishing in them and that poor men would be robbed by rich men. They were therefore satisfied with small villages.

They saw that kings and their swords were inferior to the sword of ethics, and they therefore held the sovereigns of the earth to be inferior to the rishis and the fakirs . . . This nation had courts, lawyers and doctors, but they were all within bounds. Everybody knew that these professions were not particularly superior; moreover these vakils and vaids did not rob people; they were considered people's dependants, not their masters. Justice was tolerably fair. The ordinary rule was to avoid courts . . .

Reader: It would be all right if India were exactly as you have described it, but it is also India where there are hundreds of child widows, where two-year-old babies are married, where twelve-year-old girls are mothers and housewives, where women practise polyandry, where the practice of Niyoga obtains, where, in the name of religion, girls dedicate themselves to prostitution, and in the name of religion sheep and goats are killed. Do you consider these also symbols of the civilization that you have described?

Editor: You make a mistake. The defects that you have shown are defects. Nobody mistakes them for ancient civilization. They remain in spite of it . . . We may utilize the new spirit that is born in us for purging ourselves of these evils. But what I have described to you as emblems of modern civilization are accepted as such by its votaries . . .

In no part of the world, and under no civilization, have men attained perfection. The tendency of the Indian civilization is to elevate the moral being, that of the Western civilization is to propagate immorality. The latter is god-less, the former is based on a belief in God. So under-standing and so believing, it behoves every lover of India to cling to the old Indian civilization even as a child clings to the mother's breast.

There is no doubt that civilization means restraint, and that harm has been caused by cities, competition and litigation. Others may hold that competition invigorates, courts settle disputes and cities enrich the mind, and that civilization lies in the enjoyment in mod-eration of life's good things. Nonetheless, *Hind Swaraj*'s perspec-tive on these subjects remains useful. It is harder to accept that the plough's sameness over the ages proves the wisdom of Indian soci-ety, or that innovations that assist the body must hinder the soul.

Does the evil of materialism reside in matter, and machinery, or in the human heart, in the attitude of that heart to other human be-ings, and in the human mind, whose inventions may heal or destroy? Once or twice Gandhi admits the blessings of progress. In his cri-tique of civilization (Ch. 6), he says: 'Formerly, special messengers were required and much expense was incurred in order to send let-ters; today, anyone can abuse his fellow by means of a letter for a penny. True, at the same cost, one can send one's thanks also.' However, *Hind Swaraj*'s tendency is to ignore the benefits that change can confer, and to confuse the spirit of materialism with science or technology.

Gandhi treats Indian defects as deviations or aberrations from a sound mainstream, and sees poison at the core of western civiliza-tion, surely a slanted view. It goes against what he had written in *Indian Opinion* in 1906: 'Is it not a fact that between Mahomedan and Hindu there is a great need for toleration? Sometimes one is inclined to think it is even greater than between East and West. Let not strife and tumult destroy the harmony between Indians them-selves' (*Indian Opinion*, 8.9.06; 5:414).

Here he admits a bigger gap within India than between East and West, and he was capable throughout his life of attacking Indian evils in strong language. We will see something of that when, later in this work, we examine his views on caste. But in *Hind Swaraj* he seems driven by a need to separate East from West and to prove the former's superiority.

Caste is not mentioned in *Hind Swaraj*. Oppressive princes and selfish elites are referred to; the weak citizen appears to be the object of Gandhi's concern; the sufferings of women are separately seen, and in the discussion on satyagraha Gandhi points out that both men and women can offer it (Ch. 17). But the untouchables are not mentioned. Nor is caste.

It was an issue of which Gandhi was deeply aware. His well known tussle with Kasturba in 1898, when he asked her to leave their house before she shamed him back to his senses, had been connected with untouchability and caste. In 1905 he wrote in *Indian Opinion* that in his eyes there was no distinction between Brahmins and untouchables (*Indian Opinion*, 20.5.05; 4:430), and there had been other expressions by him on the question. The fact that *Hind Swaraj* was a record of his talks with Pranjivan Mehta may have had something to do with the absence — the question may not have featured in the talks. (This may be the reason for other omissions such as the racial prejudice of white South Africa.)

Two other explanations are possible. Gandhi may have felt in 1909 that the subject was sensitive and called for silence. Did he perhaps also feel that admission of untouchability practised over the centuries would hurt his picture of Indian civilization?

Gandhi's attitude to *Hind Swaraj* in later years is of interest. His answer to queries was that he stood by it. He might change the language here and there, he would say, but it contained his beliefs. Yet at the height of his noncooperation campaign in 1921 he took care to state that the swaraj of *Hind Swaraj* was not what 'I am today aiming at.' He was not, he said, launching a campaign against railways and hospitals. His goal was 'parliamentary swaraj in accordance with the wishes of the people of India.'[12]

At the end of 1938, when a new edition of *Hind Swaraj* was published, the text was preceded by an introduction by Gandhi's secretary and close colleague, Mahadev Desai, who clarified that Gandhi was opposed not to machines as such but to their enslaving man. In his preface to a 1938 edition Gandhi wrote that *Hind Swaraj*'s publication in 1909 had 'stopped the rot that was about to set in among some Indians in South Africa.' That is, it prevented a slide to violence. Gandhi intriguingly added: 'The reader may balance against this the opinion of a dear friend, who alas is no more, that it was the production of a fool.'

The remark is intriguing not because Gandhi hides the name of 'the dear friend.' Mahadev Desai has informed us that it was Gokhale, who read *Hind Swaraj* when he visited South Africa in 1912. What is curious is Gandhi's keenness to pass on Gokhale's verdict to the reader, a keenness that may suggest an unease in Gandhi's own mind about the book's extremism.

'My life is my message.' So said Gandhi in 1945 when a Black journalist from U.S.A. asked him for a message. If we go by what Gandhi did and how he lived, then it is obvious that his aim was to modify modern civilization, not to uproot it. In *Hind Swaraj* he attacks railways, law courts and hospitals, yet he did not hesitate to use the railways to spread his anti-Raj views, a British-run hospital to have his appendix removed (in 1924) and his legal skill to safeguard Indian interests in negotiations with the Raj. Of course, he walked whenever he could; more than most, he practised naturecure and used mudpacks on himself and other willing patients; as a lawyer in South Africa he produced a series of out-of-court settlements. He believed in the open air and the good earth and in turning enemies into friends; but he was not hostile to the nineteenth and twentieth centuries.

In June 1920 he translated for *Navajivan*, his Gujarati journal, an item in the *Bombay Chronicle* claiming that 'the Hindus invented the decimal system, Geometry and Algebra were first developed in India, and so too Trigonometry,' that 'the first five hospitals to be built were in India,' that 'the physicians of ancient Europe used Indian drugs,' that 'the Ramayana and the Mahabharata still remain unrivalled,' and so forth, and added his comment:

> I do not know how far these statements are true but this I know, that if the late Justice Ranade were alive today and

heard such talk of India's past glory, he would certainly
have asked, 'So what?' . . . Where is the man who can
write the Ramayana today? . . . Where is the ability of
those days? . . . We have added nothing to the drugs discovered thousands of years ago, nor do we even have ad-
equate knowledge about those mentioned in the ancient
books (20.6.20).

But perhaps it is beside the point to ask whether *Hind Swaraj* holds
the scales balanced. We know that it was not prompted by a study
of civilizations. It erupted from their clash, and cannot be understood apart from it. While advancing some stimulating reasons for
his thrusts against railways, law courts and hospitals, Gandhi shows
most passion when he argues that the three utilities helped Britain to
entrench its rule over India. 'But for the railways, the English could
not have such a hold on India' (Ch. 9). 'The greatest injury they
(the lawyers) have done to the country is that they have tightened
the English grip' (Ch. 11). 'The English have most certainly used
the medical profession for holding us' (Ch. 12).

We should note the striking similarities between *Hind Swaraj*
and Gandhi's Quit India pronouncements thirty-three years later.
Rejection was the note on both occasions, of the West in 1909, of
the Raj in 1942. In 1942 he asked Britain to go, leaving India to
chaos or God. His language was similar to what he had quoted
from Chesterton in 1909, while his *Hind Swaraj* thoughts were crys-
tallizing. As we have already seen, Chesterton had said that to him
an Indian nationalist was one who would speak as follows to the
British: 'Everything has its own faults and we prefer our own . . . If
you do not like our way of living, we never asked you to. Go, and
leave us with it' (9:427). That last sentence was Gandhi's 1942
call.

Asked by 'Reader' about 'the condition of our country,' 'Editor,'
the Gandhi of 1909, replies: 'It is a sad condition. In thinking of it
my eyes water and my throat gets parched.' When 'Reader' refers
to 'the Pax Britannica,' 'Editor' replies: 'You may see peace if you
like; I see none . . . The present peace is only nominal, for by it we

have become emasculated and cowardly . . . It is better to suffer the Pindari peril than that someone should protect us . . . I should prefer to be killed by the arrow of a Bhil than to seek unmanly protection' (Ch. 8). This is very much the language of Quit India. In *Hind Swaraj*'s final chapter, Gandhi adds: 'If the English vacated India bag and baggage, it must not be supposed that [India] would be widowed . . . If we must fight amongst ourselves, it is better that we do so. There is no occasion for a third party to protect the weak . . . You (the British) may fear Russia; we do not. When she comes we shall look after her. If you are with us, we may then receive her jointly' (Ch. 20). In 1942 he said identical things, substituting Japan for Russia.

Hind Swaraj was a warrior's manifesto, not a scholar's survey. It was the East's assertion of identity in a world and an age dominated by the West, and Gandhi's assertion of himself before an India undecided between petitioning and bomb-throwing. Helping India to stand upright, let go of the bomb and look the West in the eye, *Hind Swaraj* also triggered a worldwide celebration of indigenous cultures.

The perspective outlined nine decades ago by *Hind Swaraj* is now widely held. Thus an American student of nature and cultures writes of 'the despair of the [American] Indian as all that was beautiful in his past was pulled down and hidden by the curtain of white civilization,' and adds: 'This civilization has put the whole earth in terrible danger by its over-exploitation of living things, by its burning of fuels that pollute the air, by its poisoning of the waters, its creation of erosion and deserts, by its corruption of governments and men. Are automobiles, airplanes, superhighways and all the other fancy gadgets that have seemed so important to us, really worth more . . . than a livable, beautiful earth?'[13]

As we have seen, this was very much the language of *Hind Swaraj*. Though opposed to Western civilization, and in spite of its extremism, *Hind Swaraj* finds an echo in many minds including in the West, because of its defence of nature and native civilizations, and its sympathy for the underdog everywhere.

'Those from the West should not consciously or unconsciously lay violent hands upon the manners, customs and habits' of the East, or 'tear the lives of the people of the East by its roots,' Gandhi said in 1927 in Sri Lanka; but he added that Eastern 'manners, customs and habits' could be questioned if they were 'repugnant to fundamental ethics' (*Young India*, 8.12.27).

If slights to the East got under his skin, so did the darts of Truth. Always. Therefore, while fervent, insightful and in some ways prescient, *Hind Swaraj*, a child more of national self-respect than of Gandhi's other passion, Truth, cannot be taken as his last word. It has to be corrected by his appraisals elsewhere of traditional India's weaknesses and the modern West's strengths.

Chapter 6

Gandhi and his God

IN *HIND SWARAJ* Gandhi cites the Gujarati proverb that translates into 'As is the God, so is the votary.' If the proverb contains truth, an examination of his God may tell us something about Gandhi. We will attempt it in this chapter. In the process we will look also at Gandhi's hardness and tenderness, his relationships with Kasturba and their sons and with women, and his preoccupation and experimentation with chastity.

For a start, Gandhi's God is good. In *Hind Swaraj* and throughout his life Gandhi deduced God's goodness from the world's survival: 'In spite of the wars of the world, it still lives on' (Ch. 17). 'In the midst of death, life persists; in the midst of untruth, truth persists; in the midst of darkness, light persists. Hence I gather that God is Life, Truth, Light. He is Love. He is the Supreme Good' (*Young India*, 11.10.28).

On numerous occasions in his life Gandhi paused to note God's kindness to him. He was led to a brothel in Rajkot and another in Zanzibar but God saved him, he said. In between these two incidents, Gandhi felt God saved him when he was on the verge of crossing the limit in Portsmouth, during his time as a student in England. His friend Tryambakrai Mazumdar warned Gandhi on the threshold of wrong and Gandhi desisted. Through Mazumdar God had saved him, Gandhi thought.

If Gandhi's God saved, He also provided. When in 1915 Gandhi's first Indian ashram in Kochrab in Ahmedabad seemed on its last legs, with members and supporters opposed to Gandhi's decision to admit a family of 'untouchables', and funds fully exhausted, a young industrialist called Ambalal Sarabhai drove up, handed Rs 13,000 to Gandhi, and left as silently as he had arrived. To Gandhi this was God the Good acting through Sarabhai.

Two years earlier, in South Africa, an army of volunteers much larger than Gandhi had expected assembled for his satyagraha march. They had to be fed and lodged but 'there was not a copper in my pocket,' Gandhi would later recall. 'No fear, said I, if God wills it, He will carry it forward. Then money began to rain from India.'[1]

Gandhi's sense of the goodness of God survived the killings and the partition that accompanied freedom. He lost his will to live on but not his belief in God's goodness and wisdom. In October 1947 he wrote:

> If I had the impertinence openly to declare my wish to live 125 years, I must have the humility, under changed circumstances, openly to shed that wish. And I have done no more, no less. This has not been done in a spirit of depression. The more apt term perhaps is helplessness. In that state I invoke the aid of the All-Embracing Power to take me away from this 'vale of tears' rather than make me a helpless witness of the butchery of man become savage, whether he dares to call himself a Muslim or Hindu . . . Yet I cry, 'Not my will but Thine alone shall prevail.' If He wants me, He will keep me here on this earth yet awhile (*Harijan,* 12.10.47).

In January 1948, he said: 'I am in God's hands. If He wants me to live, I will not die. I do not want my faith in God to weaken' (*Harijan,* 18.1.48). In 1936 he had written that he did not fret over his inability to explain 'why, if God is a God of mercy and justice, He allows all the miseries and sorrows we see around us,' adding, 'If we could solve all the mysteries of the universe, we would be co-equals with God' (*Harijan,* 13.6.36). In 1934 he had said that God was 'proving for me His greatness and goodness every day . . . I can't even count the blessings; they are so many. For even the so-called sorrows and pains He sends descend like blessings.'[2]

Walking through ravaged Noakhali in the winter of 1946-7, Gandhi continued to note God's blessings. To his grandniece Manu, who joined him in Noakhali on 19 December and assisted him until his death, he said on 10 January 1947: 'Just observe how God sustains me. Though I sleep at 10 or 11 p.m., rise at 2 or 2.30 a.m., do my work at high pressure and get no rest at all, I carry on somehow! That itself is a wonder' (*Ekla Chalo Re* [*ECR*], Manu Gandhi's diary, pp.89-90).

Reaching the minds and hearts of Noakhali's Muslims was his goal. Only they could restore the confidence of the victimized Hindu minority. Thanks to steady propaganda, some Muslims saw him as an enemy and refused to return his salutations as he walked past them. Others, however, were touched, and some confessed crimes against Hindus.

'The Rama whom I adore is God Himself,' different from any historical Rama, Gandhi said in Noakhali. 'He always was, is now and will be for ever.' Verses in Rama's praise were part of his public prayers. In the village of Paniala, Manu inserted the line 'Ishwar Allah Tere Naam' ('Ishwar and Allah are Your names') in the salutation to Rama. When Gandhi observed that Paniala's Muslims had responded positively to the insertion, Manu explained that she had borrowed the line from a recitation by a Brahmin in Porbandar's Sudama temple. Asking Manu to sing the line 'daily from now on,' Gandhi said: 'God Himself breathed it into your mind. How wonderful are His ways! My faith in His divine powers grows from strength to strength' (*ECR*:91-2). Thus Gandhi's God was not only good; He was actively good, inspiring the faithful.

Sending his co-workers to different villages in Noakhali, Gandhi kept only two or three with him. With them he walked from village to village, singing Tagore's song 'Walk Alone' and covering 116 miles in seven weeks. On 20 December he said to Manu: 'Let us do everything entrusting it to God . . . Have the fullest faith in Rama and hand over this mission to Him' (*ECR*:12-3).

'The Infallible Caretaker' and 'the Never-failing Watchman' were other descriptions of God the good by Gandhi. 'God is with us and looks after us as if He had no other care besides,' he wrote. 'How this happens I do not know. That it does happen, I do know.'[3]

❋

He invoked many a witness to prove God's love, among them Tulsi, Nanak, Kabir, Chaitanya, Narsinh Mehta, Ramdas, Tukaram and Mira (through their songs), and also Paul of Tarsus. On the Hindu New Year's day in 1917, falling on 15 November, he wrote to his nephew Maganlal from Motihari in Bihar, where he was assisting exploited peasants: 'What shall I send you for a gift on this bright and happy day? I would like to give you what is wanting in you, in me, in many others.' What was wanting was love or charity. Gandhi quoted from Paul's First Letter to the Corinthians, closing with 'And now abideth faith, hope, charity; but the greatest of these is charity.' Then he said:

> Read this, chew the end, digest it. Read the original in English; translate it into Hindi. Do all you can, strain your neck and eye, but get a glimpse of this love or charity. Mira was stabbed with the dagger of love and she really felt the wound. If we too can get at this dagger . . . we can shake the world to its foundations. Though I feel I have something of that love, I am painfully conscious every moment how very shallow it still is. I weigh and find myself very much wanting . . . Only yesterday I saw I had no room in my heart for those who would not let me have my way.[4]

Love moves him. Gandhi realizes his need for it and wants it, yet we should note too the link he makes between love and power. 'If we can get at this dagger, we will shake the world.' God the good is also, and quite importantly, the God of power. And though stirred by love, Gandhi spoke more often of ahimsa or nonviolence. In 1936 he told a group of Black visitors from the U.S.A. why:

> In spite of the negative particle 'non', [nonviolence] is no
> negative power. Superficially we are surrounded in life
> by strife and bloodshed, life living upon life. But . . . it is
> not through strife and violence but through nonviolence
> that man can fulfil his destiny . . . Ahimsa means love in
> the Pauline sense, and yet something more, although I know
> Paul's beautiful definition is good enough for all practical
> purposes . . . Love in the English language has other con-
> notations too, and so I was compelled to use the negative
> word. But it does not express a negative force (62:198-
> 202).

Apart from its sensual meanings handicapping 'love,' the word was
inadequate for Gandhi in situations of conflict, or when, as he put it,
'life lived upon life.' Nonviolence or ahimsa was love plus struggle,
whereas by itself love might suggest an absence of struggle. Denying that nonviolence was a negative force, Gandhi separated it from
hate; but he would never divorce it from struggle.

Gandhi's was a movement of power against an empire of power,
and against which the Muslim League had pitted its own power. In
his confrontations Gandhi sought to tap people's power and also
some of what he believed to be God's power. Hindu tradition was
rich with accounts of power won by renunciation. Prahlad, for instance, had by his application earned from Indra the sovereignty of
the three worlds. Gandhi did not desire sovereignty but, wanting to
eject Britain's sovereignty over India and prevent Jinnah's sway
over India's Muslims, he resorted to renunciation. His striving for
perfect chastity or brahmacharya was at least partly linked to the
power it was believed to bestow, and Nirmal Kumar Bose, the professor of anthropology who accompanied him on the Noakhali trek,
seems to have heard Gandhi saying, 'If I can master [brahmacharya],
I can still beat Jinnah' (Quoted in Erikson: 401).

His renunciation was aimed at 'capturing' Noakhali's Muslims
and Hindus 'with love,' Gandhi told Manu (11.2.47; *ECR*:143-4).
If he captured Noakhali's Muslims, the drive for Pakistan would
lose strength. There would be a 'complete disappearance of antipa-

thy between Hindus and Muslims,' he said, 'when my heart grows into a full-blown flower of perfection' (ECR: 67-8).

Perfection and power seemed interchangeable terms to him. They were Godlike attributes. 'She feared no man, because she feared God only,' Gandhi wrote in 1926 about Emily Hobhouse (*Young India*, 15.7.26). Here implying that love of God removed fear of man, elsewhere Gandhi seemed to suggest that the opposite sequence was also true if not truer, that only the removal of fear made love possible. 'Love is the epitome of strength,' he wrote in 1918 to a Danish friend, Esther Faering, adding: 'Love flows the freest when there is entire absence of fear.'[5] On such occasions Gandhi worshipped the God of courage or strength and found love, rather than the other way round.

No matter how hard to reach, perfection had to be sought and was the source of irresistible power. 'Life for me would lose all interest if I felt I could not attain perfect love on earth,' he had said to Faering in 1917.[6] In 1921 he wrote: 'As a perfect man I should take note of [the miseries of neighbours], prescribe a remedy, and compel adoption by the force of unchallengeable truth in me. But as yet I see through a glass darkly ...' (*Young India*, 17.11.21). He repeated the thought four years later: 'When I am a perfect being, I have to simply say the word and the nation will listen. I want to attain that perfection by service' (*Young India*, 13.8.25). Fifteen years thereafter he held the same view. With 'perfect brahmacharya,' he wrote, 'I should have but to think of a thing and it would happen' (*Harijan*, 20.1.40).

Though willing to speak soberly of 'perfection,' of his wish to attain it and of the perfect man's potency, Gandhi was not deluded into thinking that he had come within touching distance of it. To the end of his days he continued to hold that he was but an ordinary and weak human being. His eyes seemed steady whether facing the perfect man of his imagination or his own imperfect self.

God was 'a Living Power that is changeless, that holds all together, that creates, dissolves and recreates' (*Young India*, 11.10.26). He was All-Powerful yet patient. 'Perfection is the attribute of the Almighty, and yet what a great democrat He is! What an amount of wrong and humbug He suffers on our part!' (*Harijan*, 14.11.36). An interpretation of Jesus given by Gandhi in 1918 in a letter to Sushil Kumar Rudra, a Christian, shows the importance Gandhi gave to power: 'Jesus had the power to consume his enemies to ashes but he refrained and permitted himself to be killed, for he so loved, etc . . . ' Where others saw Christ's love, Gandhi focussed also on his strength (28.7.18).

Gandhi's interest in power, in the men of power and in the Power over power emerges from what he wrote on the twentieth day of a twenty-one-day fast for Hindu-Muslim unity he undertook in 1924: 'Man is nothing. Napoleon planned much and found himself a prisoner in St. Helena. The mighty Kaiser aimed at the crown of Europe and is reduced to the status of a private gentleman. God had so willed it. Let us contemplate such examples and be humble . . .' (25:222-3).

Until earlier in the year Gandhi had been in prison; two years earlier he was judged close to a position to topple the Raj. Like the Kaiser he had aimed at the crown, if only to remove it. After the lines quoted Gandhi added that the words of a song that he and his colleagues had been singing during the fast 'better express my state than anything else I can write.' It was one of Tulsidas's songs, an appeal from 'a sinner of old' to One who 'protects the weak' and can 'remove the sin and misery of mankind.'

Thus Gandhi also worshipped the God of humility, and that is how he addresses God in a prayer he once wrote for a Briton living in India. In the autobiography and in numerous utterances during his life Gandhi speaks of wanting to humble himself. Man should be 'less than dust' and 'become a cipher' if he would see God (*Young India*, 25.6.25). Yet anything divided by a zero is infinity. Gandhi grasped the power of humility. In practical terms he saw that the Indian people would empower one who humbled himself. A renouncer would obtain both spiritual and political power.

In Noakhali he renounced most of his companions, sending them away to strife-torn villages. He renounced a base, staying with whoever offered a roof. Among his hosts in forty-seven Noakhali villages were washermen, fishermen, cobblers and weavers. He renounced the mobile hut that his friend Satis Das Gupta had brought for him, a contraption simple to take apart, carry and put together. Das Gupta's gesture touched Gandhi but he would not use the 'palace.' He renounced security. 'There is the One . . . above all of us who will look after me, and He is able enough,' Gandhi wrote in a letter to Vallabhbhai Patel (*ECR*:55).

He renounced his chappals and walked barefoot. When Manu saw the inevitable cuts and protested, Gandhi replied: 'We don't go to our temples, mosques or churches with shoes on . . . We tread on that holy ground where people have lost their loved ones . . . How can I wear chappals there?' (*ECR*: 54). He took assistance from Manu, Nirmal Kumar Bose and one or two others, but performed many chores himself, including darning a shawl and a handkerchief late in the night.

Conscious of the cold, Manu one evening heated the water for Gandhi to wash his hands and face with before retiring. Noticing its temperature, Gandhi said: 'Where people don't have twigs for baking their rotis, you want me to wash my face with warm water? I can understand heating water for bathing, but not for this' (*ECR*:111-2). And when Jawaharlal Nehru came to Noakhali for a couple of nights at the end of December, Gandhi had his commode moved to the hut that Nehru was using. Jawaharlal sent it back.

Compassion, considerateness and an understanding of how Noakhali's people could be won motivated these acts of renunciation; and we should remember that Narsinh Mehta's *Vaishnava Janato*, with its theme of understanding another's pain, topped the list of Gandhi's favourite prayer songs. Yet Gandhi also sought to plug himself into the power of God. One of his American friends, the author and evangelist E. Stanley Jones, noted that a set of opposing qualities met in Gandhi. He was of East and West, the city and the village, a Hindu influenced by Christianity, simple and shrewd, candid and courteous, serious and playful, humble and self-assertive. According to Jones, the blend gave 'a sweet savour.' 'But,' Jones added, 'while the savour is sweet, the preponderating impression he leaves is not sweetness, but strength.'[7]

❋

If Gandhi's God was one of love, perfection and power, He also at times seemed a remote God. No doubt Gandhi often spoke of the closeness of God to man, 'closer than nails are to fingers,' and of his certainty about God. 'I am surer of His existence than of the fact that you and I are sitting in this room,' he said (*Harijan*, 14.5.38). Yet he also perceived a vast abyss between imperfect man and perfect God: 'Since He is knowable, we search. It may take a billion years before we find Him. What does it matter?'[8] Seeing God or coming 'face to face with God' was an 'endless process,' requiring 'birth after birth,' he said in 1939. He quoted Sankaracharya who, Gandhi wrote, 'likened the process to the attempt to empty the sea by means of a drainer small as the point of a blade of grass' (*Harijan*, 7.10.39).

He told Manu in February 1947 that perfect purity might take 'years or even ages' but it had to be worked for until one's last breath (*ECR*: 128). Believing in God, heeding the truth in one's heart, renouncing for God and for effectiveness, all this was possible for humans and necessary; but seeing God or attaining perfection was a different matter. In 1921 he described the acute tension in him between the hunger for perfection and the awareness of his imperfections:

> My soul refuses to be satisfied so long as it is a helpless witness of a single wrong or a single misery. But it is not possible for me, a weak, frail, miserable being, to mend every wrong or to hold myself free of blame for all the wrong I see . . . This struggle resolves itself into an incessant crucifixion of the flesh (*Young India*, 17.11.21).

The lines show Gandhi's aspiration, sense of responsibility, and pain, all of a high degree. He sought perfection to heal his world, and was miserable at his failure. His God is almighty and compassionate but has left it to humans to remedy the world. God saves the faithful in spite of their errors and provides for them, but reforming nations is the task of men and women. God is far and unlikely to intervene. This last sentence is not Gandhi's but seems to follow from some of the things he said.

But perhaps it is useful to stress that Gandhi's God is remote only when perfection is sought, when the seeker wishes to mould the world to his desire. Where the seeker is reconciled to his frailty, Gandhi's God is near and helpful. Gandhi has left many passages like the following:

> God has always come to my rescue . . . My courage was put to the severest test on 13th January 1897 when . . . I went ashore and faced the howling crowd determined on lynching me. I was surrounded by thousands of them. I was pelted with stones and kicked, but my courage did not fail me. I really cannot say how the courage came to me. But it did. God is great (*Harijan, 1.9.40*).

In his life there were other occasions for courage. In 1939 in the princely state of Rajkot — Mohan's Rajkot, where Karamchand had been the dewan — a 600-strong mob armed with sticks and swords attacked a prayer-meeting he was holding, broke up the congregation as well as the cordon of unarmed volunteers trying to defend Gandhi, and surrounded him from all sides. Gandhi had blessed a movement for reforms in the Rajkot regime; the attackers were the regime's supporters. Bal Kalelkar, the twenty-six-year-old son of D.B.('Kaka') Kalelkar, Gandhi's associate from 1915, was with Gandhi in Rajkot. He recollected the incident seven years later:

> I suddenly noticed that Bapuji's whole body began to shake violently. It was not out of fear; his face could tell how free from fear he was; the physical reaction was his revolt against the disgusting atmosphere of violence. Suddenly he closed his eyes and started praying: I could hear him saying Ramnam with an intensity of devotion that could never be surpassed. I joined him in his prayer and to keep time to our chanting of God's name I started patting my hand on his back . . .

> The prayer worked. When Bapuji reopened his eyes there was a new strength that had appeared then like magic. In a firm tone he asked all the volunteers to quit the place at once and leave him absolutely alone at the mercy of the hired goondas ... Then he called the leader of the gang who was busy breaking up the congregation and told him that he was absolutely at his disposal if he cared to argue out his point; if not, would he tell what he proposed to do next? To everyone's amazement the thugs' violence melted like ice ... The leader of the gang stood before Bapuji with folded hands ... That evening Bapuji walked all the way home with one hand on the shoulder of the leader of the gang.[9]

Mahadev Desai's account of Gandhi's initial reaction in this incident refers to a 'sudden' attack of 'indescribable pain' near the waist, 'an old symptom that seizes him whenever he receives an acute mental shock.'[10] As Devanesen points out (314), the violence on Gandhi over the years had affected his system; yet restored by will and prayer he could walk unarmed and unprotected through armed and hostile lines. In 1947 Gandhi recalled the role of fear in his early life and connected courage with God:

> I was cowardly by nature. I was frightened to sleep in the dark. To sleep alone in a room was an act of bravery for me. I hope I have lost that cowardliness. Yet I do not know what would be my state if I lost my way and had to wander alone in a thick forest on a dark night and if I were to forget that God was ever with me (*Harijan*, 15.6.47; 88:101).

❄

'Who knows in how many places I must be guilty of hardness of heart?' Gandhi wrote to Romain Rolland in 1928 (14.2.28). Those close to him felt this hardness; also, he spoke of God as 'the hardest taskmaster I have known on this earth.'[11] Gandhi's strictness was love's bitter medicine, or the hardness of an Ashram rule, or his norm for a public worker. At other times, however, it was a loss, under pressure, of temper or patience.

In January 1947, during the Noakhali trek, he once asked Manu to walk back alone a couple of miles or so to retrieve a pumice stone left behind by her after she had scrubbed his feet with it. The stone had been given by Mira Behn and used by him for over twenty years. It was Manu's responsibility, Gandhi said, to find it, and doing it by herself would test her courage.

Manu has described the incident in her diary. She walked back from the village of Narayanpur to look for the missing object. Though an old woman had thrown the stone away, Manu found it and hurried back to Gandhi. Saying, 'Take your stone!' she threw the thing before Gandhi, who laughed. In her diary, Manu wrote: 'I was knocked out and he laughed!' Gandhi told her she had passed a test. Later in the day Gandhi said to her:

> If scoundrels had seized and killed you I would have danced with joy, but I would not have liked it a bit if you had run back out of fear . . . You could not have realized the risk I took in sending you. I said to myself, 'This girl sings "Walk Alone" with enthusiasm but has she digested the song?' . . . You can see how hard I can be from today's incident. I also realized it (*ECR: 75-7*).

No doubt Manu was tested but it was an upset mind, not a cool one, that had ordered her to take the test. The last two sentences indicate a measure of contrition, which is also suggested by Gandhi's concern, recorded by Manu, about her rest and nourishment during the hours after she returned with the stone. But he does not admit the ill temper that triggered the episode. 'My nature dislikes any change in my routine,' he said to Manu the following day while discussing something else, but the admission may explain the ill temper.

'I have been sticking on to [this] shaving tackle given me by a loving sister,' Gandhi had said in 1936 to a group of teachers who called on him while he shaved in Sevagram. He would not be shaved by the local barber, Gandhi explained, because the barber refused to serve the untouchables of the village; and he did not procure an Indian razor because he did not wish to hurt the sister's feelings. 'But there it is, the compromise is there,' said Gandhi (*Harijan*, 5.9.36).

Kalelkar relates how in 1915 in Bombay he found Gandhi searching anxiously for a pencil. Kalelkar's offer of a pencil he was carrying was declined, Gandhi explaining that the missing pencil had been presented to him by 'Natesan's young boy in Madras.' When a joint search by Gandhi and Kalelkar finally produced the pencil, Kalelkar saw that 'it was less than two inches long.'[12] Gandhi's 1947 attachment to the stone too was surely linked to the person who gave it, as well as to long usage.

The language about dancing with joy over another's courageous death was one he often used, especially when the alternative was surrender to evil. Since he used it in respect of those close to him, it often revealed, paradoxically enough, his attachment. What he means in the present case, I think, is that he wanted Manu to prefer death to surrender but longed for her safety; that he could not bear the idea of anything happening to her but had decided to accept the worst. He was too proud, however, to admit his error in forcing the errand on Manu.

Summoning equanimity and faith, he would repulse his attachments, angers and anxieties. He was a firm foe of such feelings and willed himself to conquer them. On a handful of occasions he applied the drastic remedy of hitting himself — e.g. on a night journey by train between Gorakhpur and Kashi in 1921, when crowds demanding his darshan had made sleep impossible for him and, what to him was worse, for Kasturba and Mahadev. After his pleadings and shouts failed to pacify the darshan-seekers, he hit himself thrice. After the second stroke, a companion asked him: 'What will be our plight if you yield to anger?'

It is from Gandhi's own account that we know of the incident. In the account he does not appear to regret the self-blows. In fact, after saying that it is a man's duty every time to control his anger, he adds: 'When, however, a person simply cannot control his anger, the best way to work it off is to strike oneself.' And he recalls a previous incident: 'On one occasion I atoned for my own lapse. I had committed such a sin that I felt suddenly shocked at it and was aflame with anger with myself. I rose and struck myself hard blows and only then did I have peace' (*Navajivan*, 20.2.21; 19:374). He does not say what the sin was.

The reference to the companion's remark indicates an unease in Gandhi about the remedy of hitting oneself, and we should mark his advice to Madalasa Agrawal in 1946: 'Do not lose your temper with anybody, not even with yourself' (24.8.46; 85:200).

❋

We have seen that Gandhi sought to suppress his angers chiefly by acts of will and in his own strength. Though, as he said, he daily 'advertised' before God his need for aid, and, as we have found, often spoke to others of his angers, self-reliance was the dominant note. Greatly developed as this was in his case, it could not wholly or instantly dissolve his angers.

At times, therefore, those near him were hurt. Until she fully understood him, Kasturba sometimes spoke, as Gandhi recalled, of 'a poison' in Gandhi's heart (53:117). This was her reaction to the uneliminated angers in Gandhi, sparked when he did not get his way with her or with others. In 1914 Gandhi said in a letter: 'Even Gokhale used to tell me that I was so harsh people were terrified of me.'[13] Gokhale probably said this in 1912, when he spent several weeks with Gandhi in South Africa.

We know that Gandhi's renunciation of wealth and comfort and the changes in his lifestyle did not please Kasturba. His fasts and imprisonments made her insecure. His refusal to give his children the Western education he had himself received pained her. When, in 1920, khadi became his passion, Kasturba said, 'First he coaxed me to wear socks and boots (in 1896, when he took her to South Africa). Then he coaxed me to discard them (before their return to India). Now he wants me to wear several yards of this thick heavy stuff!' (Light khadi came much later.)[14]

'Well, how do you like the spiced vegetables?' Gandhi once asked, addressing some women from his Ashram who after experimenting with wholly unspiced pumpkins had started spicing them again. Kasturba butted in: 'You had better keep quiet on the subject. Remember when every Sunday you would ask me to prepare some delicacies for you and you would gulp them down lustily?'[15] Perhaps she was referring to Bombay 1891-2 or Durban 1897-8.

It took effort on her part to accept her husband's position on untouchability but harder for her was the presence of women near Gandhi. Many of them were educated and capable of sharing areas of his life that she could not enter, for she had from the start resisted his attempts to educate her. The camaraderie, warmth and laughter between Gandhi and his women co-workers flowed inevitably from his nature and from his resolve to live for and with a 'family' much larger than the joint families that Kasturba was familiar with. Just as inevitably, Kasturba was hurt. But over time she seems to have conquered her feelings until she became a fellow-worker and fellow-fighter with him, going to prison in support of his campaigns. Her courage made up for her lack of schooling.

In early 1920, Gandhi, who had turned fifty the previous October, felt strongly drawn towards a gifted woman three years younger than him who wrote, spoke and sang compellingly. Related to Tagore, Sarladevi was the wife of Ram Bhuj Dutt Chaudhri, a man of standing in Lahore. Catapulted in 1919 to national leadership and investigating the Punjab atrocities in 1920, Gandhi found and enjoyed Sarladevi's company, and was attracted by her personality and promise. For a while thinking that they were meant for each other and meant together to shape India to a new design, Gandhi wondered about a 'spiritual marriage,' without being clear about its meaning.

In June 1920 he forsook the idea. Later he said that the thought of Kasturba had saved him, and also that the love of younger ones like his son Devadas, secretary Mahadev Desai and nephew Mathuradas Tricumji had prevented him from 'rushing into hellfire.'[16] Rajagopalachari too seems to have discussed the question with Gandhi, and a letter he wrote to Gandhi on 12 June, 1920, appears to be a response to a telegram from Gandhi signifying a change in his relationship with Sarladevi. 'My dearest Master,' Rajagopalachari said, 'Had your telegram. Words fail me altogether. I hope you have pardoned me' (*Rajaji* 1:85). The text of Gandhi's telegram is not available.

The change was shattering for Sarladevi, who said that she had 'put in one pan all the joys and pleasures of the world, and in the other Bapu and his laws, and committed the folly of choosing the latter.'[17] A letter he sent her in December contained these lines: 'Have we that exquisite purity, that perfect coincidence, that perfect merging, that identity of ideals, the self-forgetfulness, that fixity of purpose, that trustfulness? For me I can answer plainly that it is only an aspiration. I am unworthy to have that companionship with you. I require in me an infinitely higher purity than I possess . . . This is the big letter I promised. With dearest love I still subscribe myself, Your L.G.' (19:107). The initials stood for Law Giver, the title with which she had rebuked him.

Fifteen years later he said to Margaret Sanger that he had 'nearly slipped' after meeting 'a woman with a broad, cultural education' but had fortunately been freed from a 'trance'.[18] The reference was undoubtedly to the 1920 relationship with Sarladevi.[19] In March 1947 Gandhi recalled an episode that perhaps involved Sarladevi, who was not named. To Amrit Kaur he wrote:

> With one solitary exception I have never looked upon a woman with a lustful eye. I have touched perhaps thousands upon thousands. But my touch has never carried the meaning of lustfulness . . . I would like those who have felt otherwise, if there are any, truly to testify against me. Even the one solitary instance referred to by me was never with the intention of despoiling her. Nevertheless my confession stands that in that case my touch had lustfulness about it. I was carried away in spite of myself and but for God's intervention I might have become a wreck (87:108).

The love between Gandhi and Kasturba seemed to deepen over the years. Sometimes it showed in little gestures. Gandhi might pat Kasturba's cheek when the moment of separation arrived, which, thanks to his treks and prisongoing, was often. Or, in her illness, he would caress her head or be found 'running his fingers through her hair.' [20] Or, and this was very seldom, he would recall how during their marriage ceremony, when each was thirteen, they had held each other's hands 'lovingly and for long.'[21] Or, and this happened very often, when Kasturba tenderly served him a meal, or nursed and massaged him.

The climax of their partnership was the eighteen months they spent together as the Empire's prisoners in the Aga Khan's mansion in Pune. Kasturba was unwell and certain that she would not see the outside world again. Once when a fellow-detainee, Dr Gilder, was allowed to receive some mangoes for his wedding anniversary, Kasturba asked Gandhi, 'How many years have we been married?' 'Why,' Gandhi replied, 'do you also want to celebrate your anniversary?'[22] Kasturba laughed along with the others, but all the rich sadness of a life squeezed into a mission was summed up in the question and the laughter.

Kasturba died in Gandhi's arms in prison, another sign to him of God's goodness. Missing her more than he had thought, Gandhi appropriated the little stool on which Kasturba used to rest her head as, sitting up, she coughed in her bed. It became his dining table for the rest of the detention. 'If I had to choose a companion for myself life after life,' Gandhi said, 'I would choose only Ba.'[23] Despite the shocks and hardness she had to endure and her transformation from Kastur to Ba (Mother), Kasturba would probably have spoken similarly, and meant it.

We will look later, in the discussion on Gandhi and caste, at an 1898 incident involving Kasturba, untouchability and Gandhi that he never ceased to regret. According to Narayan Desai, son of Mahadev, Gandhi 'used to relate this incident with tears in his eyes.'[24] Narayan Desai has described another incident involving Gandhi, Kasturba and their eldest son Harilal, who nursed deep grievances against his father, rebelled, and saddened both his parents by his rootless life and problems with liquor. On one of their journeys, Gandhi, Kasturba and their party heard a cry at a railway station, 'Mata Kasturba ki jai!' — 'Victory to Mother Kasturba!' This was not a cry normally heard; the man raising it was Harilal.

'He was emaciated,' Desai reports. 'His front teeth were gone. His hair had turned grey. From a pocket of his ragged clothes, he took out an orange and said, "Ba, I have brought it for you." Breaking in, Bapu said, "Didn't you bring anything for me?" "No, nothing for you. I only want to tell you that all the greatness you have achieved is because of Ba. Don't forget that!"

'Ba . . . promised to eat the orange. Then she . . . pleaded with Harilalkaka to come with us. Harilalkaka's eyes were full of tears. "Leave off such talk, Ba. There's no way out of this for me." As the train pulled away, Kasturba remembered that neither she nor anyone else had offered Harilal anything. He "must be dying of hunger," Kasturba said. From outside the compartment amidst the cries of "Gandhiji-ki-jai," another faint cry could also be heard, "Mata Kasturba ki jai."[25]

In 1947, three years after Kasturba's death, Gandhi used the words his son had used while speaking to a visitor from South Africa: 'It is because of her (Kasturba) that I am today what I am,' he said. Added Gandhi:

> It was that illiterate woman who helped me to observe all my vows with utmost strictness and kept me ever vigilant. Similarly in politics also she displayed great courage . . . She was a devout Vaishnavi [who] regularly observed sacred days . . . but she loved the Harijan girl (in the Ashram) as much as she loved Manu or Devadas's Tara . . . In the fast of 1943 . . . I was nearly at death's door, but she never cried or lost courage, but kept up other people's courage and prayed to God. I can see her face vividly even today.[26]

In another incident, when asked by Gandhi why she was late for an Ashram task, Kasturba had replied that she was readying a meal for a journey that their third son Ramdas was making. Admitting on further questioning that she might not have delayed herself for the sake of other Ashramites, she added: 'But truth to tell, they are not to me like Ramdas . . . You are indeed very hard on me.' Gandhi replied that there was nothing wrong in her loving Ramdas but the Ashram was not their family home. Its rules applied to all; their children could not expect special treatment. 'Remember, the whole world is watching and expecting great things from us.'[27] They had to be, and seem, fair and just.

The incident helps us to see Gandhi's 'reasonable' hardness even if Kasturba did not wholly accept the reasoning. He had to show onlookers and those whose hopes had been aroused that his Ashram did not practise double standards. That meant a withholding of favours for Kasturba's sons. Throughout a general on war duty, Gandhi had to be hard to remain credible with his troops and their sympathizers.

Less defensible was the sort of hardness that made him say to Kasturba on one occasion in South Africa that the illness from which she was suffering was 'largely due' to her dislikes and suspicions.[28] A remark by Kasturba had nettled him into making the statement, but it was the type of statement he sometimes also made to Harilal, who responded by becoming more rebellious.

A turning point in Harilal's life was Gandhi's decision to make over a scholarship for studies in London given by his friend Pranjivan Mehta 'for the education of one of your sons' first to a Parsi youth called Sorab Adajania and next to Harilal's cousin Chhaganlal. Gandhi had obtained Mehta's permission for this allocation but Harilal accused his father of seeking a reputation for saintliness at his sons' expense.

Gandhi knew that his sons were bitter. To his second son Manilal he wrote in 1918: 'Just as I became myself the victim of my spiritual experiments, so did Ba and you, the sons. But Ba has seen the wisdom of my experiments . . .'[29] Harilal retained his resentment but with time the others overcame it, recognizing what the father had tried to do for them, and for others, even though regret at not receiving formal schooling remained.

Their mother's complaint when they were young was that Gandhi was trying to make them saints before they could become men. Yet Gandhi could not have sent his boys to western-style schools while attacking western civilization, or while recommending bread-labour, settlement-life and an alternative to what to him was a materialistic system of education. He believed in what he had found in Ruskin and Tolstoy and felt that the Phoenix Settlement and the Tolstoy Farm possessed the ambience his sons and other youngsters needed. The schooling he and his associates arranged for the youngsters could have been better organized; the frequent prison-going of the 'teachers' affected it; but it was not, judging by the results, a disaster.

For some time Harilal was Gandhi's hope. Bright, outgoing and handsome, he joined some of his father's South African satyagrahas, spending two six-month terms in prison. These were rough spells and may have played a role in his largely sad future. The Gandhi-Harilal relationship is a subject in itself and not one that I will attempt to examine in any detail. No doubt the father was hard, unfeeling and moralistic at times, yet his sustained attempt to regain his son should also be recognized. He wrote to his son as painstakingly and as often as he could, a letter a day in some phases, and enlisted friends and relatives towards his son's restoration. On occasion he wrote breezily, as in February 1919, when he was recuperating from a troubling illness. Addressing the letter 'To the Satyagrahis' Firm,' the description that Harilal and his prison-going companions had acquired in South Africa, Gandhi said:

> Just as I was beginning this letter, I had to make my room a court of justice. The accused was Rasik, the complainant an innocent dog. Through its howls it had loudly complained that somebody had thrashed it. My inquiry revealed that Rasik seemed to be the culprit. The accused confessed his crime and, on further questioning, his previous offences. The judge (myself) pardoned all his crimes, but he was warned . . .
>
> As I am writing this, Kantilal is holding the inkpot. He and Ramiben are reading the letter as it is being written

and trying to improve upon it. The accused also is crouching behind one of the legs of the four-poster. Little Manu was giving out her shrieks of laughter at regular intervals, but now she is crying to be lifted on to my bed.[30]

Kanti, Rami, Rasik and Manu were all Harilal's children, staying at the time with Gandhi and Kasturba in the Ashram in Ahmedabad. Three months earlier Gandhi had written to Harilal, 'I am often ashamed of the meanness of my mind,' and offered to give his son 'the fullest benefit of my experiences' if he joined the father.[31] But there were also letters that exhorted, or expressed pain or disappointment. The relationship was never restored.

In 1924, a reference by Gandhi to his 'own dearest relatives' was immediately followed by this remark: 'Sometimes love's anguish left deep scars on the loved ones, but it left much deeper ones on the lover's bosom' (Young India, 4.9.24). He hurt dear ones from a sense of duty, and not always from love, but because of the latter he saw the hurt and agonized over it.

Harilal had turned up from nowhere to see his mother when she lay dying in the Pune detention camp. After his father's death he appeared just as suddenly in the home in New Delhi of his youngest brother, Devadas. Harilal would not admit it, but Devadas concluded from the timing of his visit and from what he did not say that he came 'to share our sorrows.'[32]

Manilal, who died in 1956, played a valuable role in South Africa with Indian Opinion and in the nonviolent struggle for racial justice. Visiting India in the winter of 1945-6, he could not help reminding his father of his failure 'to take care of his real family.' After listening, near Gauhati, to his son, Gandhi said to one of his young helpers, Sudhir Ghosh: 'Why don't you take Manilal to Shillong tomorrow for a trip? It is a pretty place. Do go to Shillong for the day and take Manilal with you and enjoy yourselves. It must be boring for you to spend all your time with an old man.'

Ghosh and Manilal went up to the beautiful hill town where the Indian manager of a hotel told them that only Britons could be served. Manilal commented to his father that South Africa was more enlightened than Shillong. Ghosh writes: 'Gandhiji looked sad but there was no trace of resentment in him. He was only unhappy because our fun was spoilt by some hotel manager.'[33]

Ramdas, the third son, was married in the Sabarmati Ashram in 1928. Gandhi addressed his son, the bride and the Ashramites. He 'was nearly moved to tears' when he referred to his sons. Ramdas was advised to be the bride's 'true friend' and 'not her master.' Added Gandhi: 'We are pledged to poverty. You will both earn your bread in the sweat of your brow as poor people do. I have given you no gifts except a pair of *taklis* (spindles), and a copy of my dearly beloved Gita and *Bhajanavali* . . . Let the Gita be to you a mine of diamonds.'[34]

It was not comfortable being Gandhi's son. At the height of the end-1921 riots in Bombay, Gandhi announced that he had called back Devadas from Gujarat 'to be sent out as a "sacrifice" for slaughter by the rioters, should a fresh outbreak occur.'[35] However, Devadas has written of the other side. He was around twenty and leaving for a course in Benares when Gandhi 'suddenly stepped forward and with great love kissed me on the forehead.' 'God alone is the witness of the deep love between father and son,' Devadas added.[36]

In the last week of his life Gandhi said to his son, who had informed him that he was taking Pyarelal home to dinner, 'But do you ever think of inviting me?' He said this 'with great laughter'; but the exchange can perhaps be bracketed with Kasturba's query in respect of wedding anniversaries.[37] Before going to sleep on the last night of his life, Gandhi encouraged Devadas, who usually turned up for some minutes at his father's bedtime, to linger.

❋

Gandhi is revealed, too, in his relationship with the industrialist, Ghanshyam Das Birla, who was twenty-one when he first met Gandhi in Calcutta in 1915. Unharnessing the horses in Gandhi's carriage, Birla and some others had pulled the carriage to the residence of Gandhi's host. Birla has recalled:

I informed him that I would . . . send him a monthly dona-
tion . . . 'Fine,' he replied. Look what I did — it was very
silly of me! I said, 'Very good, then, I'll expect a monthly
letter from you.' He retorted saying, 'Does that mean I
have to come to you with a begging bowl every month?' I
felt so ashamed.

I asked Gandhiji, 'If I write to you, will you reply?'
'Of course,' he said. Just to test him, I wrote him a letter
four or five days after he'd left. He replied — on a postcard.

Birla has also related a conversation at four in the morning 'in the
bitter winter of 1926' at a railway station in Delhi, where Birla,
whose wife Mahadevi was very ill, had gone to see Gandhi, who
was arriving on his way from the Punjab to Ahmedabad. Birla ('in
a warm, easy way'): 'Will you be stopping over?' Gandhi: 'No, I
have to be on my way.' Silence from Birla. G: 'Why did you ask?'
B: 'Oh, nothing.' G: 'No, you had a reason.' B: 'I mean, there's a
lady, she's on her deathbed. She desires your darshan, but you're
not stopping over, so how can I ask you to come.' G: 'I won't stop
over but I'll come with you.' B: 'It's bitterly cold, and the place is
nearly twelve miles from here.' G: 'Nothing to worry about. I'll
come and catch my train at the next station.' Arguments from Birla.
G: 'Not one word more. Get inside the car.'

Birla's recollection continues: 'In those days we didn't have the
closed cars we do now. It was really wintry, and imagine the icy
wind along with it [for] ten miles through the jungle. Arriving, he
asked the ailing lady, "How are you?" Her eyes opened in surprise . . . She said, "You are here, I am so happy. I know my death
is near. It was my great desire to have your darshan. That wish is
now fulfilled, I can die in peace." He replied, "Take God's name
and be at peace." He stayed there ten minutes and boarded his train
at the next station . . . Such was the man who captivated me.'[38]

A letter he received from Lajpat Rai in August 1927 was cited by
Birla. It said: 'The best man to learn manners from is Mahatma

Gandhi. His manners come very near perfection, though there is nothing perfect in this world. Great as he is, the greatest of us all, he is very particular in his behaviour towards his friends and coworkers.'[39]

❈

In Noakhali, Nirmal Kumar Bose had noted what he described as Gandhi's 'daily ministrations on behalf of love' and 'the extreme tenderness with which he regarded each individual' relating woes to him.[40] Hindu women who had lost their husbands and homes, the sick child of a Muslim villager, a rheumatic adult, and a young man unable to choose between a girl he loved from another caste and his conservative father — these were the kind of people on whom he spent himself. He strove to heal the sick and wipe the women's tears but said that courage rather than consolation was what he wished to offer. Bose saw that while meeting one group of bereaved women, 'Gandhiji's face hardened, and he said that they must recover their courage.'[41]

Wanting to move beyond solace to a restoration of relations, he asked Muslims to welcome the Hindus back and the Hindus to return to their homes. But he admitted another reason for steeling himself to accounts of barbarities: 'I say I cannot bear it' (On 19.9.47 in Delhi; 89:204). Some weeks later he spoke of 'the countless [refugee] women at Kurukshetra . . . still wearing the clothes [in] which they had arrived' from Pakistan, and added: 'I cannot even bear to hear about these things — who knows what will happen if I have to see these things?' (89:456, 1.11.47).

'Tears won't bring back the dead,' he firmly told bereaved Hindu women in the village of Jagatpur in Noakhali who had wept before him. After they left he said to Manu that the picture of the women would stay before his eyes; that evening, records Manu, he refused to eat anything other than a lump of jaggery (ECR: 69).

His softer side was also revealed in his reactions in Delhi to the rain and to winter's approach, and in the zeal with which he collected blankets for the refugees. There were occasions when he broke down, as in Bihar, when he saw pieces of human flesh sticking on walls.[42] To be of use, however, he had to toughen his heart, and he asked the victims to toughen their hearts for the sake of their families and themselves.

Warmth was not a new trait. It was in a prison in Pune in 1932 that he heard that Pranjivan Mehta — his friend from London days, the unnamed 'Reader' with whom Gandhi debates in *Hind Swaraj*, and the donor of the scholarship that Harilal did not get — had died in Rangoon. In a wire to Mehta's son, Gandhi referred to the doctor's 'commercial integrity, lavish hospitality and great generosity,' and added: 'I feel forlorn without lifelong faithful friend.' To Mehta's nephew he wrote: 'A beautiful nest is in danger . . . I had no greater friend than Doctor in this whole world. But I am unable to do anything from here (Pune's Yeravda jail) to keep his nest whole, and that makes me unhappy' (50:327-9).

Warders and prison officials received friendship and, at times, treatment at his hands. Kalelkar, a fellow-prisoner, relates that Dattoba, a cook in Yeravda, overcame a limp in 1930 thanks to Gandhi's care and prescriptions, and that Major Quinn, an Irish jail chief to whom Gandhi gave Gujarati lessons, carried in his shirt pocket a piece of paper on which Gandhi had written: 'Be kind to prisoners. If provoked, swallow your anger.'[43] The day after Quinn had failed to appear for a Gujarati class, Kalelkar, who had discovered the reason, conveyed it to Gandhi: 'He had to supervise a hanging.' Gandhi, who knew that the noose was close by, turned pale and sick.[44]

Translating, for Mira, the Ashram book of bhajans into English, obtaining, on a train journey, a tray of tea for Mahadev while the exhausted secretary slept, sending flowers round to Kalelkar, securing yoghurt for Kripalani, picking, from a gift of chikoos, the plumpest two for Mahadev — it was in acts of service that Gandhi's love found expression.[45]

✳

Hardness is conveyed by some of Gandhi's remarks to Hindus and

Sikhs who had left Pakistan for India, including some who had been his friends or associates in West Punjab, Sind and the Frontier. Gandhi seems to rebuke them for having escaped instead of fighting, and for leaving behind poorer and weaker Hindus who had no means of escape. Where they might have expected a welcome, the escapees seemed to receive an admonition.

'The leaders were able to come easily with their families,' he told Lalji Mehrotra, who had left Karachi, 'but the poor helpless villagers are in a sad plight . . . If even one of them (the leaders) had died there, I would have danced for joy . . . In all that I tell you, I attach no blame to you' (89:378-9, 21.10.47).

Yet Gandhi's recorded words misrepresent his true emotion. His eyes conveyed to the escapees his understanding as well as his gladness at their passage from danger. The words uttered reflected his sadness at the destruction of his vision of Hindu-Muslim co-existence as well as his concern for the ones continuing in insecurity.

'If many had fled, leaving neighbours to their own fate,' he said in Noakhali in the 1946-7 winter, referring to prominent Hindus who had moved to Calcutta, 'they did not deserve to be called leaders. The seats (on peace committees) would have to be occupied by barbers, washermen and the like, who were as much interested in the preservation of their life and property as the rich.'[46]

Forty years earlier, Millie Polak, the wife of Henry Polak, had noticed that Gandhi's views did not drain his warmth. Shortly after discussions on sex-abstinence that she had had with Gandhi, during which she had disagreed sharply with him, 'one of the members of the little settlement at Phoenix,' Polak would recall, 'gave birth to a child.' She added:

> I purposely refrained from speaking of the matter when I visited Phoenix two or three days later . . . After a short while, and having talked of other things, [Gandhi] said in a surprised voice, 'You have not asked about the mother and the babe. Don't you want to see them?' He then came with me to see the baby and talked in a quiet, joyous way to the mother; and I realized in a flash that, even as a

woman does, he differentiated betwen abstract principles and human needs and affections.[47]

Among those who met Gandhi during the final weeks of his life was G.D. Khosla, a judge who wanted advice in respect of evacuee property for which he had been made responsible. Khosla, who was meeting Gandhi for the first time, has left an account:

> I began to tell him of my assignment, and the difficulties I had encountered. It was a long story and Gandhiji listened patiently without interrupting me . . . There was no mysterious or hypnotic force to which I was being subjected . . . Gandhiji was listening to me just as any other man might . . . He spoke in a calm, matter of fact way. What I heard was not a command but a simple statement of truth . . . He did not seem to be making a final pronouncement . . . He did not digress into a high-falutin' moral discourse but kept to the practical problem I had put before him.
>
> Realization came to me that this man had only one sentiment in his heart and that was the sentiment of love . . . When he looked at me, I noticed a softness in his eyes and I felt ashamed.[48]

Dilip Kumar Roy, the poet, also saw Gandhi in this last phase and for a few evenings sang at Gandhi's prayer meetings. He recorded: 'After the meeting I made my last obeisance on the lawn. He looked at me tenderly with his gentle sad eyes and said: "It was good, that song." "I know you had a special liking for that song." He sighed. "When do I hear you next? Tomorrow?" "I must fly tomorrow for Calcutta."

'He smiled. "Well, well! If you must, you must, and there's an end of it. But I will miss you tomorrow . . ."' Roy, something of a critic and one of those who regretted Gandhi's unwillingness to withdraw into a world of meditation, adds: 'When I left him, my eyes were moist with tears. I was moved by him as never before.'[49]

The American writer, Vincent Sheean, also commented on Gandhi's tenderness in January 1948. After a talk with Gandhi, Sheean sought another interview. Sheean records that Gandhi, who agreed to slot it, 'added very gently, in a voice that would have melted the heart of an enemy (and I was no enemy), "If there is no time, you will understand." ' A sense that Gandhi 'understood' and 'wanted to help me' touched Sheean.

Gandhi spoke to Sheean of what the Gita and the Sermon on the Mount meant to him, and explained the Ishopanishad verse that was part of his daily prayer: 'Renounce the world and receive it back again as the gift of God. And then covet not.' Gandhi told Sheean that the seemingly superfluous last bit was full of meaning, for a renouncer can be tempted, after surrender and acceptance, to covet again. Sheean thought that Gandhi's words reached out 'from the depths to the depths.'[50] Their tone had been wrung from experience. We have seen that Gandhi knew the meaning of coveting after renunciation.

❋

'They usurp the function of the Godhead and indulge in novel experiments. They write about their own researches in most laudatory terms and hypnotize us into believing them.' This is Gandhi writing in *Hind Swaraj* (Ch. 10) of the British attitude towards India and in particular of the historical analysis that claimed to prove the impossibility of Hindu-Muslim friendship. Yet perhaps no British experiment was as novel or daring as the one through which Gandhi sought to test his brahmacharya or purity.

Purity was a corollary of Gandhi's belief that 'you cannot possibly divide your love for Truth and God with anything else' (*Young India*, 31.12.31). One not wholly free from lust or attachment could not serve God or humans, and freedom from lust meant control over thoughts as well.

In 1945 and in the last year of his life he tested his purity by asking some married or unmarried ashram women to lie down beside him at night. If he or his partner in the experiment felt tempted, then his brahmacharya was flawed. There was no seclusion. Other associates slept near and around him, and any doors were always open. (Sometimes he slept in a verandah with no walls.)

The experiment was known to many and Gandhi showed no reluctance to discuss it orally or in correspondence. In Noakhali he referred to it in at least one of his prayer talks. But his associates kept the experiment out of *Harijan*, and in Noakhali Nirmal Kumar Bose, who used to translate Gandhi's talks into Bengali, chose not to translate the reference to the experiment. Some associates disapproved of it, others were baffled, and most wanted to avoid a public debate.

Plainly, the experiment was dangerous for the personalities and reputations of its participants. The women involved saw him as a Mahatma or a saint and could not be said to have participated after mature or independent thought. Some husbands were not fully consulted in advance and one of the participants, his unmarried grandniece Manu, was only seventeen in Noakhali. Also, the experiment contained the possibility of hazardous or mischievous emulation.

Though, following objections and discussions, Gandhi discontinued the experiment in 1945, he did not accept that he had been wrong; and he resumed it in 1947, this time chiefly with Manu. India's 1946-7 killings and the looming partition caused Gandhi to look within himself for a weakness to explain the misfortunes around him; and he also seems to have thought that perfecting his brahmacharya, including by testing himself, would enhance his power over events.

He told Manu that the life of one who kept his body as 'a holy temple for God' would speak as 'a poem of exquisite spiritual beauty,' and also that 'a full-blown flower of perfection' would banish communal hate.[51] As we saw, Bose appears to have heard Gandhi saying, 'If I can master this, I can still beat Jinnah.'

He entertained discussion and at times sought views on the experiment but reserved the right to follow his convictions. Pained by the experiment and unable to approve of it, some of his closest associates, including Kishorelal Mashruwala, Narhari Parikh and Swami Anand, parted company with Gandhi; Mashruwala relinquished his charge of the *Harijan* weeklies. In a letter to Vinoba Bhave, Gandhi referred to his 'co-workers' pain' but added that his own mind was 'becoming firmer than ever.' 'Please let me have your view,' he said to Vinoba (86:453). But there was no indication that he would heed Vinoba's or anyone else's opinion. Vinoba replied that while he could not quite agree with Gandhi, he had no wish to argue.

The experiment was a factor in the departure from Noakhali of Parasuram, who had been assisting Gandhi as a stenographer. To Parasuram, who had evidently written that he could not continue his association unless Gandhi renounced the experiment, Gandhi said: 'I cannot concede your demands . . . I like your frankness and boldness. My regard for your ability as a typist and shorthand writer remains undiminished . . . I shall always be interested in your future and shall be glad to hear from you when you feel like writing to me . . . You are at liberty to publish whatever wrong you have noticed in me and my surroundings' (86:300).

Accompanied by Kedar Nath, who had a following as a spiritual teacher, Swami Anand went to Bihar in March 1947 to discuss the question with Gandhi, who while discontinuing the experiment had retained the right to resume it. The talks produced no change in opinion. 'I am not so lost as you seem to think,' Gandhi told Anand and Nath. 'You do not seem to regard a lapse in respect of truth, nonviolence, nonstealing etc. to be so serious a matter. But a fancied breach in respect of brahmacharya . . . upsets you completely.' He added that apart from one instance, which he did not describe but was perhaps related to Sarladevi, he had 'never sought the company of a woman with a view to satisfying my passions' (87:99).

He sought God's or Godlike power but with the awareness that God was watching him. In 1938 he wrote: 'There is not a moment when I do not feel the presence of a Witness whose eye misses nothing and with whom I strive to keep in tune' (*Harijan*, 24.12.38). In February 1947 he said to Manu in Noakhali: 'Here I want to be tested to the fullest extent possible. If I fail the examination it will be under God. I want no testimony apart from God's. If there is any deceit, even if hidden from us, the world will come to know of it' (*ECR*:143-4). In his search for power from the God of power,

Gandhi played with fire, but he did not play God.

We can side with a Gandhi not impressed with those who were upset by 'a fancied breach' of chastity but untroubled by hates and frauds, yet over the decades no one had been keener than him in projecting chastity as a norm, and in any case the experiment was supposed to be for tapping chastity's power. In some ways the testing recalled the boy Mohan's meat-eating in Rajkot in Sheikh Mehtab's company, which too was linked to a search for power for driving out the British.

But the practice also seemed connected to attacks of shivering that Gandhi experienced in his seventies. Gandhi referred to the shivering, as did Manu and some other participants. Erikson found, or remembered, a similar episode in an earlier era. It related to a king 'old and stricken in years' who was unable to feel any warmth though covered at night with many clothes, whereupon a young woman called Abishag, a Shunammite, 'was brought to the king.' She 'cherished the king, and ministered to him, but the king knew her not' (Kings I:3,4). We do not know whether Gandhi was aware of the precedent involving David.

We may note, too, that several women felt a 'woman' or 'mother' in Gandhi. We have seen Millie Polak's remark about Gandhi's womanlike reactions. Manu wrote a book called *Bapu My Mother*. Mira Behn and Premabehn Kantak made similar references. On his part Gandhi was keen to have a woman's heart and felt he had acquired it. 'I know you have not missed the woman in me,' he wrote to Sarojini Naidu in 1932 (51: 17.9.32). In 1936 he wrote to Pyarelal about the latter's sister Sushila: 'As in the case of others, in Sushila's case also my attempt has been to be a mother and a father.'[52]

Over his life he mothered a large number, including many women. It seems legitimate to link this, as Nirmal Kumar Bose, among others, has done, with Gandhi's relationship with his mother. He had said to Mahadev Desai in 1918 that he would not easily believe that anyone had 'tasted the joys of parental love as much as I' or 'loved his father or mother more than I.' 'My claim in this matter is very high,' he added.[53]

A depth of feeling is suggested by his autobiography's lines about his mother's death: 'I was pining to see my mother . . . The news was a severe shock to me. My grief was even greater than over my father's death. Most of my cherished hopes were shattered.' Though he could not have realized the connection himself, what his mother had poured into Mohan came out as Gandhi's nonviolence and in his personal warmth.

Gandhi hoped, so Bose surmises, that the women nestling against him would feel their mother. Yet, just as with Putlibai the boy Mohan gave love apart from receiving it, Gandhi in old age, father of his nation, seems to have required warmth as much as he offered it. Dilip Kumar Roy noticed Gandhi's 'inner isolation' and 'laughter fraught with pain,'[54] and Bose wrote of Gandhi's 'daily need of a contact with the earth of humanity,'[55] but it is Erikson who most clearly speaks of Gandhi's need for 'maternal solace' — 'a need to be held and reassured, especially at the time of his finite loneliness' — while also recognizing Gandhi's 'need to be a perfect and pure mother' (404-6).

An entry in Manu Gandhi's Noakhali diary accords with Erikson's insight. A 'very old man, not a leader or a prominent person but an ordinary man' was desperately eager for Gandhi's darshan but unable to cross the river to the village Aloonia, where Gandhi was camping. Requested to go to the old man, Gandhi agreed. Manu writes: 'After the evening prayer we crossed the Dakaria river . . . The beautiful river flowed amid lush greenery. The sky was clear, it wasn't too cold, and the sun wasn't too strong. It was a journey of five to seven minutes. During those minutes Bapuji placed his head in my lap, closed his eyes and took a nap . . . Both banks were lined with human throngs and dense trees . . . Right in the middle, the world's great figure lay asleep in my lap, while the boatman rowed his boat. My hand was on Bapuji's forehead' (*ECR*: 160). Manu adds, 'Those moments of my life became blessed.' Yet she was giving as much as she was receiving.

If these explanations sound reasonable, we should still remember Gandhi's 1947 remark, 'God alone knew men's hearts,'[56] and also what he had said in 1932 to Andrews: 'After all, the intention behind an act is the final criterion, and that God alone can know, not even the author of the intention.'[57]

❋

Gandhi worshipped truth as well, invoking that norm oftener than any other, with ahimsa in second place. His preference from the late twenties for 'Truth is God' over 'God is Truth' is well known, but his truth had at least four meanings: truth as the universe's Reality (the *sat* or satya of Hindu thought), truth about facts, truth to a vow or resolve, and the truth of the voice within. Gandhi saw *sat* as all-powerful and benevolent. In the end the world's Reality favoured peace and harmony even if realpolitik seemed to foster strife in the short run: 'The world rests upon the bedrock of Satya or Truth. Asatya meaning Untruth also means 'non-existent'; and Satya or Truth means 'that which is.' If untruth does not so much as exist, its victory is out of the question. And Truth being "that which is" can never be destroyed.'[58]

Discourses on *sat* were not rare in India but Gandhi was uncommon in his insistence on factual truth. In South Africa he took 'steps . . . to save the (Indian) community from the habit of exaggeration' and any 'force in the arguments of the Europeans was duly acknowledged' from his side (*Satyagraha*: 48). He was strict over facts in 1919 when Jallianwala occurred and in 1946 and 1947, when sufferers bombarded him with accounts of atrocities by 'them.' Bose noticed his passion for the precise truth in Noakhali. It is evident also in his remarks in Calcutta and Delhi in 1947-8. This was more than a fad for accuracy. He felt he had to respond to events and so needed to know just what the events were. Also, India had to be protected from the fires that exaggeration could invite. Accuracy, on the other hand, 'brings home the guilt to the accused' (*Young India*, 23.2.22).

A journalist's duty was spelt out in 1925: 'I may not write in anger or malice. I may not write idly. I may not write merely to excite passion . . . Often my vanity dictates a smart expression or my anger a harsh adjective. It is . . . a fine exercise to remove these weeds. The reader sees the pages of *Young India* fairly well dressed-up and is inclined to say, "What a fine old man this must be!" Well, let the world understand that the fineness is carefully and prayerfully cultivated' (*Young India*, 2.7.25).

Vows were crucial to him, beginning with the solemn word about meat, wine and women that Mohan gave to his mother before leaving for London. Josiah Oldfield's reaction was that here was an Indian willing to put truth before his life. Later came the vows of poverty and brahmacharya taken in the Zulu country, the vows of silent periods, the vow against milk which, to his lasting guilt, he broke by taking goat's milk, the vow about khadi, and the 1930 vow not to return to his Sabarmati ashram until swaraj was won, among others. His fasts were vows, too, of course.

Here too we can connect him to his mother, an oft-fasting and vow-taking woman. In this case Gandhi was aware of the connection: 'Fast[ing] is in my blood and my bones. I imbibed it with my mother's milk. My mother fasted if someone was ill in the family, she fasted if she was in pain, she fasted in season and out of season. How can I, her son, do otherwise?' (*Harijan*, 8.4.39).

But he justified vows on general grounds: 'A life without vows is like a ship without anchor, or like an edifice that is built on slipsand instead of solid rock. A vow imparts stability, ballast and firmness to one's character' (*Young India*, 22.8.29). He warned, of course, that vows should be taken not 'in a fit of passion' — in indignation or wrath — but calmly and 'with God as witness' (*Young India*, 21.1.19).

In the play that moved him as a boy, Harishchandra prefers death for himself and his loved ones over departure from his vow of truth. He became Gandhi's model. When his second son Manilal, then ten, lay seriously ill with typhoid and pneumonia in Bombay — this was in 1901, before Gandhi was summoned back to South Africa — a Parsi doctor prescribed chicken broth, which Gandhi's vow precluded.

Wondering whether parents had the right 'to inflict their fads on their children,' Gandhi 'softened' or 'weakened,' he tells us in the autobiography, to the extent of asking the boy for his opinion. Manilal said he would leave it to Father. Deciding to keep to his vow, Gandhi resorted to hydropathy, wrapping the boy in a steaming sheet and covering him with two blankets. The boy's temperature was 104 degrees, and his dry body burned 'like hot iron.' Kasturba was present but there is no record of what she said. Leaving the boy in her charge, Gandhi went out for some minutes to walk in Chowpatty and pray. Returning with 'my heart beating within my breast,' Gandhi heard his boy speak.

'You have returned, Bapu?' 'Yes, darling.' 'Do please pull me out. I am burning.'

'Are you perspiring, my boy?'

'I am simply soaked. Do please take me out.' Gandhi felt the forehead and found it covered with sweat. The temperature was coming down. He 'thanked God.' Engaging the boy in conversation, Gandhi kept him wrapped for some more minutes and then 'undid the pack and dried his body.' Then 'father and son fell asleep in the same bed, and each slept like a log.' Whether the boy's recovery was due to 'God's grace, or to hydropathy, or to careful diet and nursing' was, in Gandhi's view, God's secret, but he had kept his vow.

Some of his friends were troubled by the vows. When in 1924 he announced that he would fast for twenty-one days, Muhammad Ali, then his close associate, said that God would not mind the withdrawal of an oath taken in haste. Andrews thought that a vow could cramp a soul in its stride towards 'something new and unexpected and original,' and J.C. Kumarappa felt that 'the vow-maker is on a moral plane, not on the spiritual.'[59] Gandhi commented that Andrews felt free to do the will of God as he perceived it to be from moment to moment. Such an attitude might suit Andrews, but 'I should be undone.'[60]

His vows helped Gandhi to regulate and chart his life. To an extent they made it secure. He was always quoting Newman's 'One step enough for me' and 'I do not ask to see the distant scene,' but a vow or a fast seemed to offer him firm ground for the next step. 'I know the path,' he said in 1926. 'It is straight and narrow. It is like the edge of a sword. I rejoice to walk on it. I weep when I slip' (*Young India*, 17.6.26). He is committed — and secure. He 'knows the path.' God or his conscience might have dictated the path. Thereafter the burden is his.

One can, to simplify, say that Gandhi tended to trust himself, his will and his vows, for the immediate future, and God for the longer term. When, in 1936, John Mott asked him, 'What affords you the greatest hope and satisfaction?' Gandhi gave a reply that may have surprised the missionary: 'Faith in myself born of faith in God ' (*Harijan*, 26.12.36). Gandhi did not spare himself in his division of labour with God. He had to do his best and his utmost, if necessary fast or throw himself into danger, before leaving everything in God's hands. And his praying seemed to relate more to what he should do than to what God should.

As for the fasts, George Woodcock summarises the view of many in saying that they 'put in question the very possibility of succeeding in nonviolent action without some kind of coercion. They succeeded against Indians not from the power of truth but because they could not bear the guilt of causing his death.'[61] Gandhi admitted the coercion but likened it to the 'coercion' that Christ exercised from the Cross. There was nothing wrong, he said in 1933, if people did 'the right thing under the pressure of love' and even if they did not enjoy doing it. They would see its soundness later (To Father W. Lash on 5.2.33; 53:228-9).

His parents' love had restrained him, he said, when he was a boy, and the loving pressure of younger ones had saved him from error when he was fifty. So he would not protest if love for him caused caste Hindus to alter their attitudes to the untouchables. Yet he only rarely supported fasts by others, unless they were short ones for health or expiation. He said in 1939: 'The weapon of fasting can easily savour of violence unless it is used by one skilled in the art. I claim to be such an artist in this subject' (*Harijan*, 11.3.39).

His own fasts were either for self-purification or for a wider purpose (against violence or untouchability or the Raj's one-sided propaganda), but the denial also seemed to renew him. His 1918 fast in defence of Ahmedabad's textile workers gave him, he said at the time, 'days of peace, blessing and spiritual uplifting.'[62] He would say identical things about all his fasts. On the twentieth day of his twenty-one-day fast in 1924 he said, 'Presently from the world of peace I shall enter the world of strife' (*Young India*, 9.10.24). When his last fast ended in January 1948, he said, 'From calm I have entered storm' (90:468).

Gandhi the karmayogi, in Andrews's words (written to Tagore) 'a saint of action rather than of contemplation,' striving for a 'love which works,'[63] an activist labouring to lighten the burden of the oppressed who said he carried a cave inside him and so did not need to retire to one in order to reflect, this Gandhi always found peace, sometimes much-needed peace, when he fasted. At such times he found more time for that interior cave, others were less inclined to pull him out of it, and having made his decision he could, while fasting, throw all his burdens onto God's shoulders.

Physically he often found his fasts hard to bear. 'I have dreaded fasts,' he said in 1939 (*Harijan*, 18.3.39). 'Let no one imagine,' he remarked earlier, 'that I do not suffer. These fasts are bearable only because they are imposed upon me by a Higher Power, and the capacity to bear the pain also comes from that Power' (*Harijan*, 24.8.34).

The last sentence brings us to Gandhi's truth as the voice within. Asked in Lausanne in December 1931, 'What is truth?' Gandhi answered: 'A difficult question, but I have solved it for myself by saying that it is what the voice within tells me' (48:405).

In 1933 he remarked that to him 'the voice of God, of conscience, of truth, or the inner voice or the still small voice mean one and the same thing' (*Harijan*, 8.7.33). Whatever or Whoseever this voice was, 'I have been a willing slave to this most exacting Master for more than half a century,' he said (*Harijan*, 6.5.33). Eleven years earlier he had declared that 'the only tyrant I accept in this world is the still small voice within' (*Young India*, 2.3.22).

In his last speech in South Africa, after referring to sufferings that Indian satyagrahis had undergone in South African prisons, he spelt out what the prayer of his Johannesburg friends, of whom he spoke with great feeling, should be: that 'the approbation of their own conscience' would remain for Gandhi and Kasturba their 'first, second and last' concern.[64] He struck the same note in August 1942, when at his urging Congress resolved for Quit India:

> There is something within me impelling me to cry out my
> agony. I have known exactly what it is. That something
> in me which never deceives me tells me now: 'You have to
> stand against the whole world, although you may have to
> stand alone . . . Do not fear. Trust that little thing in you
> which resides in the heart and says: Forsake friends, wife,
> all, but testify to that which you have lived for and for
> which you have to die' (*Bombay Chronicle*, 9.8.42).

'That little thing' could propel Quit India, and also an ordinary
apology. Manu Gandhi records an apology he made to her in the
pre-dawn hours of 10 January 1947. Evidently Gandhi had accused Manu of something. What it was is not mentioned. But this
is what he said on 10 January: 'I tell you I was absolutely wrong in
accusing you. I am so much older than you. I am your grandfather.
What pardon can I seek from you? Still there is nothing wrong in
my asking for it.' He added that while it was a wonder that God had
kept him going thus far, his end could come any moment. He wanted
to make his confession before it came (*ECR*: 65).

Truth as loyalty and as the peremptory voice within had come
together thirty-nine years earlier when Gandhi was in a Johannesburg
prison. He and the other satyagrahis were packed tight (150 in a
dorm meant for 51), forced to dig up unyielding ground in fierce
heat, and underfed. For a spell Gandhi was thrown into a cell with
'wild, murderous-looking, vicious' criminals who tried to frighten
him with obscene gestures. Dwelling on lines from the Gita helped
Gandhi to accept 'the sufferings that may befall me.'

When an Indian fellow-prisoner fainted from exhaustion, and
Gandhi poured water on his face to revive him, he remembered that
it was his call that had led to the ordeals of the satyagrahis. A voice
within assured him, Gandhi later recalled, that he had not been mistaken in issuing that call or in enjoining loyalty to their vow. Torture, fainting and death were not proof of error.[65]

In the South African prisons Gandhi's heart or lips cried out to

God for strength to face his torments. These prayers were answered. 'I have found Him nearest at hand,' Gandhi would later say, 'when the horizon seemed darkest — in my ordeals in jails when it was not all smooth sailing for me.'[66]

Gandhi's passion against forced conversions was a corollary of the value he placed on the right even of the weakest to his or her beliefs. In Noakhali, Bose noticed Gandhi's indignation at a Maulvi whose reaction to an incident where some Hindus had converted to Islam to save their lives was to point out that they were alive. Gandhi told the Maulvi to his face that he was amazed that God allowed someone with his views to become a scholar of Islam.[67] The Maulvi's apathy at the coercion against Hindus angered Gandhi, yet he knew that not many were likely, if it came to the test, to prefer death to disloyalty or deception.

In the Noakhali village of Fatehpur, Gandhi told the Muslims that it was 'child's play' to 'harass the Hindus here, as you Muslims are in the majority,' but was it 'just and honourable?' (86:328). To Manu he said that she should have the courage to speak the truth clearly. 'Whether the truth hurts or pleases another cannot be our anxiety,' and 'if ever we find anyone slandering us, we should dance with joy.' We should speak to others as our conscience directs, of course observing 'rules of decorum and language' (ECR:79). Truth was indeed Gandhi's God.

Two weeks before his death he again explained his preference for 'Truth is God': 'In the name of God we have indulged in lies, and in massacres of people, without caring whether they were innocent or guilty, men or women, children or infants . . . I am not aware that anybody has done these things in the name of Truth' (On 18.1.48. 90:452).

*

The God of or in the poor, Daridranarayan, God the cleaner and God the servant, these too Gandhi worshipped, and if we are struck with the variety of his God, we should remember also his curiosity about Him. This erupted early and no doubt before 1893 when from South Africa he sent a letter to his friend Rajchandra Mehta, the jeweller and poet whose self-mastery Gandhi admired. Gandhi, twenty-four, asked:

> What is God? Is He the creator of the universe? What is moksha (deliverance)? Who is the author of the Gita? Is God the author? . . . Does any merit accrue from the sacrifice of animals? What do you think of Christianity? The Christians hold that the Bible is divinely inspired and that Christ was an incarnation of God, being His son. Was He? Were Rama and Krishna God Himself or only a part of Him? Who were Brahma, Vishnu and Shiva? (1:90-91).

His friend sent some answers to Gandhi but he had to tap life for more, and we have taken a glimpse of what he found. Instead of looking for the older Gandhi's literal answers to the questions in the 1893 letter — questions sparked by his encounters with Christian missionaries — we have tried to understand the God that Gandhi turned to and spoke of as he faced himself and his world.

Three additional points may be touched upon. Firstly, Gandhi's God was very much the creator of the universe. Ever since a friend in South Africa, Herbert Kitchin, took him to an observatory, Gandhi was interested in the stars. They were 'a stepstone to the knowledge of God,' he said in prison in 1932.[68] A few days later he said: 'When we look at the sky we have a conception of infinity, cleanliness, orderliness and grandeur which is purifying for us. Man may land on planets and stars and find that life there is much the same as on earth.'[69]

In 1924 he had said that he saw 'Him and His mercies' in creation. 'When I admire the wonder of a sunset or the beauty of the moon, my soul expands in worship of the Creator' (*Young India*, 13.11.24). Elsewhere he remarked that 'the star-studded sky . . . has bewitched me, mystified me and sent me into the most wonderful ecstatic thrills imaginable.'[70]

Secondly, Gandhi's God was of and for all. In 1909 he asked

rhetorically in *Hind Swaraj*: 'Is the God of the Muslim different from the God of the Hindu? . . . Wherein is the cause for quarrelling?' (Ch.10). Almost forty years later he said in Noakhali: 'God is One, though called by different names . . . The God of the Muslims is the same as the God of the Hindus.' And also, as we have already seen: 'The Rama whom I adore is God Himself.'[71]

Finally, Gandhi the man of will loth to burden God was in the end resigned to His Will. He had deep longings for himself and his people, and powerful desires assailed him from time to time, to live, to die, to achieve political or national goals. 'Yet I cry, "Not my will but Thine alone shall prevail" ' (*Harijan*, 12.10.47).

That was said in October 1947. Three months later Gandhi died while walking to his prayers. His hands came together in salutation to those in front of him, including the man who fired three bullets into his chest, and his lips parted to utter the name of God: 'Rama!' We may say, then, that while dying Gandhi worshipped the God of forgiveness, the God of all and also God the bountiful, who answered Gandhi's longing to die remembering Him. The designer of such a death was God the Dramatic Artist.

Chapter 7

The Colour Line

'DID THE SOUTH African Negroes take part in your movement?'

The question was put to Gandhi in February 1936 by Howard Thurman, then dean of Rankin Chapel in Howard University. With his wife Sue Bailey Thurman, who was a historian and a singer, and another Black couple from the U.S.A., Edward and Phenola Carroll, Thurman had been invited by Gandhi to Bardoli, where the meeting took place. Gandhi's reply was as follows: 'No, I purposely did not invite them. It would have endangered their cause. They could not have understood the technique of our struggle nor could they have seen the purpose or utility of nonviolence' (62:199).

Thurman's question has since been asked by several others. It is natural, in the 1990s, to wonder why Indians and Africans did not combine or coordinate their struggles against white supremacy during Gandhi's time in South Africa, which commenced over a century ago. However, the question thrown at him during that time was of an opposite kind: Was he not giving ideas to the Africans? We have seen that in 1907 Winston Churchill had cited white fears of Africans learning 'evil ways' from the Indians (*African Journey*: 37). A year later Jan Smuts warned his constituents in the Transvaal that Indian defiance could one day lead to 'Kaffir' or African defiance.[1]

Published in 1909, Doke's book says that Gandhi's resistance 'has been bitterly attacked by many politicians, chiefly because they imagine that it places a new weapon in the hands of the natives'

(102). Adding that 'Mr Gandhi has frequently replied to this,' Doke summarizes Gandhi's arguments. We can see the prophetic character of Gandhi's thought:

> If the natives in any crisis adopt this method of meeting what they believe to be injustice, rather than resort to force, we ought to be devoutly thankful. It would mean that the gun and the assegai would give place to peaceful tactics. Men who see far believe that the problems which are connected with the natives will be the problems of the future and that, doubtless, the white man will have a stern struggle to maintain his ascendancy in South Africa. When the moment of collision comes, if, instead of the old ways of massacre, assegai and fire, the natives adopt a policy of passive resistance, it will be a grand change for the colony.
>
> The right to vote in political affairs . . . will be the great solution of questions connected with passive resistance. The one triumphant way . . . is to deal justly with the natives, and to give them, directly or indirectly, a voice in the settlement of those questions which concern their welfare . . . If the natives accept the doctrines which are now so prevalent amongst the Indian community, South Africa need not fear the horrors of a racial uprising. It need not look forward to the necessity of maintaining an army to keep the natives in awe.

'Passive resistance,' Gandhi added, 'has come to stay. Well, thank God for that — it is the herald of peace' (Doke: 102-3).

Yet Thurman's question remains, and Gandhi's 1936 answer calls for analysis. He seems to suggest that the Africans would have invited repression, or more of it, by joining hands with the Indians. This makes sense, of course, and it is also true, though Gandhi does not say so in his reply to Thurman, that an alliance would have hurt the Indian cause too. The Indians' white allies (in the media, church and the professions) would have been alienated, and the authorities would have hit the Indians harder.

The reply also suggests that the Africans would have had diffi-

culty in understanding or accepting nonviolence. The bloody nineteenth century clashes in South Africa may have influenced such a
view — after a succession of battles, Zululand was annexed only in
1897, after Gandhi's arrival. But that view has to be set against
Gandhi's claims about the universality of nonviolence as well as his
statement to the Thurmans and the Carrolls at the end of their 1936
meeting: 'Well, if it comes true it may be through the Negroes that
the unadulterated message of nonviolence will be delivered to the
world' (62:202). In 1936 he expressed a belief in the Negroes'
capacity for nonviolence that he seemed to lack while in South Africa, his views cited by Doke notwithstanding. In his concluding
remark in 1936, he spoke of 'the Negroes' and not only of American
Negroes.

Discussing South Africa with the Thurmans and the Carrolls,
Gandhi probably recalled the unnamed stranger, an American Black,
who had noticed his difficulty at Pretoria station in 1893 and found
a lodging for him. It was an intercession that Gandhi never forgot.
He put it in his autobiography, though it is unfortunate that Gandhi
failed to give posterity the name of his benefactor.

The belief that Africans would not take easily to nonviolence
was not confined, in Gandhi's South African period, to him. The
American-educated Zulu leader John L. Dube, who helped found
the African National Congress and started a settlement in Phoenix
before Gandhi set up his Ashram there, seemed to share the perception. We gain this information indirectly, from a report of a 1914
conversation between Dube and W.W. Pearson, who had gone to
South Africa, along with C.F. Andrews, to assist Gandhi. Where
Pearson's account was first published is not known; but Ravjibhai
Patel, a Gandhi associate in South Africa, reproduced it in his *The
Making of the Mahatma*.

Calling on Dube, Pearson evidently asked him why the Africans
had not emulated Gandhi's satyagraha. In reply Dube recalled a
scene he had witnessed of a group of poor Indians near Durban
facing police brutalities with a forbearance and nonviolence that
had 'amazed' Dube. (This would have been in 1913, the year when
the Indians' satyagraha reached its climax.) Dube told Pearson that

Gandhi had been able to tap a vein in the Indian character that he was not sure existed in the Africans.[2]

Interviewed in 1976, Selby Msimang, an ANC founder member, thought that the African leadership of Gandhi's time 'would, in any case, have found Indian politics too radical to countenance an alliance.'[3] But an alliance was also excluded by Gandhi's aim while in South Africa, which was Indian equality with the whites under the British crown rather than an end to British or white rule. No African or Indian articulated the latter goal during his South African time. As for his goal, alliance with Black South Africans would only have damaged it.

Since being pushed below the white man's status and being pushed closer to the African's meant the same thing, Indians objected to being clubbed with the Africans. 'We are classed with the natives of South Africa,' Gandhi protested in 1896 (2.8). Sympathetic whites also complained that Indians were 'despised as coolies and treated as Kaffirs' (*Cape Times*, 13.4.1889; 2:49).

Though there was no partnership and little dialogue, many Africans offered a silent applause and a silent blessing to the Indian satyagrahis. Aware that Gandhi had stood up to the conquerors of Black South Africa, men like John Dube expressed their admiration at the time, and other Black leaders in later decades.

We can look at Nelson Mandela's 1995 comment: 'Gandhi had been initially shocked that Indians were classified with Natives in prison . . . All in all, Gandhi must be forgiven these prejudices and judged in the context of the time and the circumstances.'[4]

We must, however, recognize that Gandhi, who could see himself as an 'interpreter' between the Indians and the whites (*Natal Advertiser*, 14.1.1897; 2:163), did not attempt to play that role between the Indians and the Africans. His associates were Indian, white (including Jewish) and at times Chinese but never African. Nonetheless his times with the Africans during the Zulu 'rebellion' had meant much to him, and he could not forget that his brahmacharya vow, which to him was also a vow to live for others rather than for himself or his family, was made while he was carrying and tending wounded Africans.

There is every evidence that he warmed to the Africans. In the opening pages of *Satyagraha*, written in an Indian prison in 1922, he writes with feeling of their huts, food, clothes and languages, and admiringly of their height, broad chests, 'round and bright eyes' and 'muscular calves,' adding: 'The Creator did not spare himself in fashioning the Zulus to perfection . . . If we ask a Zulu to which of the various races inhabiting South Africa he will award the palm for beauty, he will unhesitatingly decide in favour of his own people, and in this I would not see any want of judgment on his part. The physique of the Zulu is powerfully built and finely shaped . . .' (*Satyagraha*: 19).

Gandhi wrote, too, that the Africans 'have a perfect grasp of the distinction between truth and falsehood.' He conceded that the Indian trader, while more courteous than his white counterpart, 'might not miss the opportunity, if it offered, of cheating his Negro customer;' but if detected, added Gandhi, the trader could be roughly handled by the Negroes. In Gandhi's assessment, while the big-framed African feared even a white child because of the white man's bullet, Indians were afraid of the Africans. Prabhudas Gandhi remembers anxious conversations in Phoenix between his father Chhaganlal and Kasturba about reports of Zulus marching towards the Ashram, which stood in the heart of the Zulu country, in the wake of the Zulu 'rebellion' (1906); but he also claims that Gandhi was seen as a friend and servant of the Zulus despite his role on the British side in the revolt.[5]

Gandhi's empathy for the Africans is apparent in a letter he sent to *The Times of Natal* in October 1894, a response to what he obviously saw as an attempt to run down Indians in African eyes: 'The Indians do not regret that capable Natives can exercise the franchise. They would regret it if it were otherwise. They however assert that they too, if capable, should have the right. You, in your wisdom, would not allow the Indian or the Native the precious privilege under any circumstances, because they have a dark skin' (*Times of Natal*, 26.10.1894; 1:136).

Two years later he said that Indian traders had found a 'valuable customer in the native of South Africa' (2:95), and wrote to the

Times of India of 'a picnic party of European children [who] used Indian and Kaffir boys as targets and shot bullets into their faces, hurting several inoffensive children' (*Times of India*, 20.10.1896; 2:87). *Hind Swaraj* (1909) refers to 'the extinction of the Negroes of Australia' and warns that country's whites that those who take to the sword could perish by it (Ch. 17). In *Satyagraha* he praises the white South African writer, Olive Schreiner, because 'she knew no difference between her Negro servant and herself,' and adds that 'whenever the rights of the Negroes were in danger,' the Schreiners and some others he names, all belonging to the Cape, 'stoutly stood up in their defence.'

In 1911 he wrote to Maganlal about the Africans with whom he was digging the ground at Tolstoy Farm: 'I for one am a farmer and wish you to become farmers . . . I prefer this work . . . I regard the Kaffirs, with whom I constantly work these days, as superior to us. What they do in their ignorance we have to do knowingly. In outward appearance we should look just like the Kaffirs' (August 1911; 10:308). (This may have been the last time that he used the expression 'Kaffir.') The allegation of ignorance reveals a limitation in Gandhi. However, Gandhi's appraisal of the Africans as 'superior to us' is also of some interest. We can look, too, at a Phoenix scene recorded by Andrews:

> He (Gandhi) was there with the little children around him . . . Mrs Gandhi and her sons had not been released from prison and so he was there alone. One baby girl, belonging to an 'untouchable' family in India, nestled in his arms, sharing her place there with a weak little invalid Muslim boy who sought eagerly to gain his special notice. A Zulu Christian woman had stayed for a while to take food with us on her way to the Zulu mission on the hill . . . [6]

Such scenes with Africans in them are rare in accounts of Gandhi's South African years. We have mentioned the political reasons but socially, too, there was no African-Indian interaction; an African woman dining with Indians was an unusual event. (When I visited

South Africa in 1993, exactly a century after Gandhi's arrival there, the picture did not seem vastly altered.)

An important role was probably played by Gandhi's character trait of restricting himself to 'his' field or waters. His swadharma, the duty enjoined on him, was towards the Indians. He was aware of a larger humanity but would serve it indirectly. One's swadharma was not dictated by birth. If it was, everybody would be forever rooted to his or her home, village and country. Gandhi did not argue with non-Indians like Henry Polak, Hermann Kallenbach, Sonja Schlesin, Albert West and Joseph Doke who claimed a swadharma of assisting the Indian cause and paid a price. Doke's son, Clement Doke, recalled that neighbours 'cut us completely for so breaking caste as to entertain a black man'[7] — when they sheltered Gandhi after he was assaulted by Mir Alam. Well aware of such consequences, Gandhi took and in some cases sought non-Indian help. Yet he saw his own calling as being first to India and Indians, and thence to others.

Apparently there were occasions when Gandhi discussed politics with African leaders. After returning to India he recalled some of these meetings but they are not mentioned in *Indian Opinion* or in Gandhi's South African letters, which suggests that political conversations with Africans fell outside his main agenda. In 1929 'a highly educated African from South Africa' mentioned to Gandhi the 'apathy of educated Africans towards their race' and said: 'We are crushed, trampled upon and oppressed. We do not know which way to turn.'

According to Pyarelal, who reported the interview in *Young India* without naming the South African, a 'deeply touched' Gandhi replied: 'I had occasion to discuss this subject with the Natives while I was in South Africa. I told them that they had got to help themselves and always to work in the hope that help would come to them from somewhere when the hour for it arrived.' Saying to his visitor that public workers had to 'turn the searchlight inward' and reform themselves first, Gandhi offered 'to take six young men here free of charge and give them a full course of training here' (*Young*

India, 28.3.29; 40:61-4). The idea does not seem to have material-ized.

Ten years later Gandhi again recalled his talks with Africans in South Africa. This was when Rammanohar Lohia proposed that an AICC resolution on the Indian struggle in South Africa should in-clude a call for a joint non-white front. Responded Gandhi: 'I yield to no one in my regard for the Zulus, the Bantus and the other races of South Africa. I used to enjoy intimate relations with many of them. I had the privilege of often advising them . . . But it was not possible to amalgamate the two causes' (Bombay, 26.6.39; 69:376-9). Not yet, that is. The hour for it would arrive before long.

Meanwhile we should note that Gandhi was ahead of his time in speaking of himself and other Indians as 'kala' or 'kalo' ('black'). We have previously seen that he did this over the 1906 Zulu rebel-lion, and it would help our study of Gandhi and the Blacks if we looked again at his comments on the events that triggered the rebel-lion.

> Important events, the effects of which will not be forgot-ten for many years, took place in Natal last week . . . The Kaffirs in Natal rose against the poll-tax. Sergeants Hunt and Armstrong were killed in the revolt. Martial law has been declared in Natal . . . Some Kaffirs were prosecuted under the martial law and 12 of them were condemned to death . . . The Kaffirs from neighbouring areas and their chiefs were invited to witness the execution, which was to take place on March 29.
>
> Twelve lives have been taken for two. The 12 Kaffirs were blown to death at the mouth of a cannon on Monday . . . It is only the Blacks who stand to lose by this. They have no vote. Where they have it they cannot use it effectively, so that the colonial authority will place greater restrictions on them, and they alone will get jus-tice who ingratiate themselves with it.
>
> Great changes are likely to take place in South Africa during the coming years. The Indians and other Blacks

have much to ponder and they must act with circumspection' (*Indian Opinion* [Guj.], 7.4.06; 5;266-7).

Though 12 Kaffirs were put to death, the rebellion, instead of being quelled, has gathered strength . . . The dead
(in the clash with Bambata, the deposed chief) included
those who had shot the 12 Kaffirs. Such is the law of
God . . . Bambata is still at large. There is no knowing
how all this will end.
    What is our duty during these calamitous times in the
colony? It is not for us to say whether the revolt of the
Kaffirs is justified or not. We are in Natal by virtue of the
British power. Our very existence depends upon it. It is
therefore our duty to render whatever help we can (*Indian
Opinion* [Guj.], 14.4.06; 5:281-2)

Once more we see him anticipating the future with clarity. He may
not have mixed much socially with the Africans, but he is clear
about their supreme political relevance. A key sentence, the clue to
his strategy, is the one about 'Indians and other Blacks' having 'much
to ponder' and needing to 'act with circumspection.' He controls
but does not conceal his fury at white overkill or his sympathy with
the Blacks. He does not veil a warning to white power. As for the
Indians, their response should be governed by the question of 'our
very existence.' If they are not to commit suicide, Indians should
swallow the bitter pill and help the British power against the rebels.
The Zulus too, belonging to 'the other Blacks,' should think of 'the
great changes' hidden in the future, and act wisely rather than im-
pulsively. The advice is of a boatman who knows the waters and is
concerned about the passengers. Most of all, perhaps, he is concerned about the Indians among them, but the Blacks and the whites
are not forgotten.
    Shyamji Krishnavarma's *Indian Sociologist*, voicing militant
Indian opinion from London, attacked Gandhi's role over the rebellion as 'disgusting' (Green: 160), but Gandhi never admitted it as
an error. 'My heart was with the Zulus,' he wrote in his autobiography, and he recalled an uneasy conscience, but he felt the deci-

sion he made was inescapable. If they had withheld support to the government, the Indians would have put at risk all their meagre rights, including the right to live in South Africa.

Three weeks before the Zulu episode, Gandhi had spelt out his line that each aggrieved race in South Africa had to fight on its own. The issue that invited his comment was a petition on behalf of the Coloured, the mixed-race community conspicuous in the Cape Colony but present in most parts of South Africa; but the comment had, and was clearly intended to have, a wider bearing. In the English *Indian Opinion* Gandhi said:

> It is true that British Indians and other coloured people have much in common regarding their grievances, but they have little in common regarding the points of view from which each section can urge its claims . . . Whilst, therefore, the Indian and non-Indian sections of the coloured communities should, and do, remain apart, and have their separate organisations, there is no doubt that each can give strength to the other in urging their common rights (24.3.06; 5:242-3).

In the journal's Gujarati section Gandhi wrote: 'The two should fight out their cases, each in their own appropriate way. We can cite the Proclamation of 1858 in our favour, which the coloured people cannot. They can use the powerful argument that they are the children of the soil . . . We can petition the Secretary of State for India, whereas they cannot . . .' (24.3.06; 5:243).

That 'the powerful argument that they are the children of the soil' would one day be resolutely advanced by the largest component of the coloured races, the African, was implicit in Gandhi's statement. As he saw it, Africans, Indians and the Coloured had common grievances and rights, but they would hurt rather than help one another by joining hands before the time was ripe.

Occasionally, however, he came out with the sort of comment that would be common fifty or sixty years after his departure from South Africa. When a white group demanded that Natives should be barred from travelling upper class in the railways, Gandhi wrote: 'If separate carriages are to be provided for different races, logically there should be compartments for Natives, Chinese, British Indians, Cape Coloured, Boers, English, Germans and so on' (*Indian Opinion*, 5.11.04; 4:292-3).

Gandhi's encounters with African warders and fellow-prisoners are part of the story. He met friendly faces but also, as we have seen earlier, a few murderous and fearsome ones. On one occasion he was grabbed, lifted and tossed but 'fortunately,' as Gandhi would recall later, 'I was able to catch hold of one of the doors and saved myself from a nasty fall.'[8]

Fourteen years after this incident, Gandhi befriended an African in Yeravda Jail in Pune, a Somali called Adan who had been made a warder. Indulal Yagnik, a fellow-prisoner with Gandhi, recorded an incident involving Adan:

> One evening our Negro warder from Somaliland was bitten by a scorpion on his hand. He gave a shout. Mr Gandhi was quickly on the spot . . . He first asked for a knife to cut the wound and to let out the poison. But he found the knife dirty. So missing no moment he quickly washed the area round the wound and applying his lips to the wound began to suck out the poison. He went on spitting after sucking and eventually stopped when Adan felt relief.[9]

His strategy was gradually, almost imperceptibly, changing. In 1926 he declared in *Young India* that he could not think of 'justice being done to Indians, if none is rendered to the natives of the soil' (22.7.26; 31:181-2). When, in 1928, a few Indians in South Africa objected to a plan to send Indian students to Fort Hare College, established for Africans, as 'humiliating and a degradation,' Gandhi, writing in *Young India*, likened the sentiment to what 'is expressed by the South African whites in respect of ourselves,' and said: 'Indians have too much in common with the Africans to think of isolating themselves from them. They cannot exist in South Africa for any length of time without the active sympathy and friendship of the Africans' (*Young India*, 5.4.28; 36:190).

Meeting Gandhi in January 1939, the Rev. S.S. Tema, a Black Minister of the Dutch Reformed Mission and a member of the African National Congress, sought his views on the African struggle in South Africa and on an African-Indian alliance. Gandhi said the need was for an African leadership that was selfless, content to live in poverty, and willing to give up 'European dress and manners.' 'You must become Africans once more,' Gandhi added.

He was equating European culture with selfishness, and the non-European, African in this case, with its opposite, as he had done in *Hind Swaraj*. It was not a line that appealed to educated Africans, who wanted to embrace many of the ideas and styles brought by the West while resenting white supremacy.

As for a united non-white front, Gandhi said to Tema:

> It will be a mistake. You will be pooling together not your strength but weakness. You will best help one another by each standing on its own legs. The two cases are different. The Indians are a microscopic minority. They can never be a menace to the white population. You, on the other hand, are the sons of the soil who are being robbed of your inheritance . . . Yours is a far bigger issue. It ought not to be mixed up with that of the Indian.
>
> This does not preclude the establishment of the friendliest relations between the two races. The Indians can help you by always acting on the square with you. They may not put themselves in opposition to your legitimate aspirations, or run you down as 'savages' while exalting themselves as cultured people to secure concessions . . . at your expense.

When Tema asked whether the Africans should adopt violence or nonviolence, Gandhi advised 'nonviolence of the brave, not of the coward.' (Narrating to Louis Fischer in 1946 the story of a Negro clergyman with 'a Herculean frame' who when insulted by a white man said, 'Pardon me, brother,' and sneaked into a compartment for Blacks, Gandhi said, 'This is not nonviolence. It is a travesty of Jesus's teaching. It would have been more manly to retaliate' [*Harijan*, 4.8.46; 85:10-11].)

Tema raised the possibility of 'one or two of our young men, who we are hoping will become leaders, to come to you for training.' 'It is quite a good and sound idea,' replied Gandhi. But there is no record of any ANC member joining Gandhi's Ashram (*Harijan*, 18.2.39; 68:272-4).

At an AICC meeting in Bombay in June 1939, Gandhi said that if the rights of Indians in South Africa 'conflicted with their (the Africans') vital interests,' he would advise 'the forgoing of those rights' (26.6.39; 69:376-9).

The forties saw a more perceptible change in his line. In June 1946 he wrote in *Harijan*: 'It is time white men learnt to treat every human being as their equal . . . It has been repeatedly proved that given equal opportunity a man, be he of any colour or country, is fully equal to any other' (*Harijan*, 30.6.46; 84: 371-3). This was different from his 1911 reference to the superiority of African 'ignorance.' However, he took care to point out that 'the whites of South Africa too are our brethren, being children of the same God' (In Delhi, on 21.6.46; 84:355-6).

He told a delegation of South African Indians in 1946 that a common front with the Africans should not be ruled out, and the following year he sent a message to South Africa via Dr Y.M. Dadoo and Dr G.M. Naicker, leaders of the Indian community, supporting 'political cooperation among all the exploited races in South Africa . . . if it is wisely directed and based on truth and nonviolence' (*Harijan*, 25.5.47; 87:492). Circumspect as ever, and mindful of South Africa's complexity, Gandhi was also aware that yesterday's inexpediency can become tomorrow's necessity.

❋

Gandhi's *Satyagraha in South Africa*, dictated to Yagnik in Yeravda, says of African-Americans: 'The Negroes of the United States have accepted western civilization. They have embraced Christianity. But the black pigment of their skin constitutes their crime, and if in the Northern States they are socially despised, they are lynched in the Southern States on the slightest suspicion of wrongdoing' (146).

Gandhi wrote a detailed sketch of Booker T. Washington for one of the first issues of *Indian Opinion*. In this 1903 article, Gandhi traced Washington's hardships, faith, perseverance and contribution, and said that his was an example 'worthy to be followed' by 'all of us who care to study his life.' Added Gandhi: 'The life of our hero would perhaps rank higher than that of any British Indian, for the simple reason that we have a very great past and an ancient civilization' (10.9.03; 3:437-40). The rich tribute, which is doubtless how Gandhi saw it, was vitiated by the implied comment on African civilization, about which Gandhi seemed to know very little.

The first public reference by an American Black to Gandhi was probably made in 1917 when Hubert H. Harrison, an intellectual 'who taught on the streets and in the lecture halls of Harlem,' wrote an essay touching on Gandhi's call for Indian self-reliance. This is the finding of Sudarshan Kapur in his valuable study, *The African-American Encounter with Gandhi* (Kapur:13). Direct contact between Indian nationalists and American Blacks was established by Lajpat Rai, who visited the United States for three weeks in 1905 and lived there as an exile between 1915 and 1920. Noting a common sentiment for racial equality in British-ruled Indians and America's Blacks, as well as 'some analogy' between 'the Negro problem in the U.S.A. and the problem of the depressed classes in India,' Lajpat Rai met some of Black America's most distinguished leaders including Booker T. Washington, W.E.B. Du Bois, George Washington Carver and John Hope.

From 1920, Haridas Mazumdar spoke about Gandhian nonviolence from several American platforms, including some provided by Marcus Garvey, who sought to unite the world's Negroes. A Jamaican who had moved to U.S.A. in 1916, Garvey sent a cable to Gandhi supporting the latter's 1921 campaign. To a cheering rally of American Blacks in August that year, Garvey said: 'If it is possible for Hindus and Mohammedans to come together in

India, it is possible for Negroes to come together everywhere' (Kapur:19).

Du Bois had concluded by 1903 that 'the problem of the twentieth century is the problem of the color-line — the relation of the darker to the lighter races of men in Asia and Africa, in America and the islands of the sea' (Kapur: 10). In August 1921, Du Bois's journal, *The Crisis*, published the entire text of Gandhi's 'Open Letter to Every Briton in India.' After Gandhi's arrest and trial the following year, *The Crisis* wrote: 'White Christianity stood before Gandhi the other day and, let us all confess, cut a sorry figure' (Kapur:40). Throughout the twenties the African-American discourse featured Gandhi and his programme of nonviolent noncooperation. Events such as the success of the Bardoli satyagraha led by Vallabhbhai Patel and the death of Lajpat Rai, both occurring in 1928, were marked by the Black Press.

In July 1929 *The Crisis* published on its front page a signed message from Gandhi, possibly the first he addressed directly to American Blacks. He may have been encouraged to send it following a report from C.F. Andrews, who had visited America earlier that year, mentioning an 'indescribably real and deep' sympathy for him among Black Americans (Kapur:75). Said Gandhi:

> Let not the 12 million Negroes be ashamed of the fact that they are the grandchildren of slaves. There is no dishonour in being slaves. There is dishonour in being slaveowners ... Let us realize that the future is with those who would be truthful, pure and loving (Kapur:39).

Kapur points out that 'Watch the Indian People' and 'We need a Gandhi' were some of the thoughts articulated among American Blacks in the twenties and the thirties. Thus the *Chicago Defender* said in an editorial in 1932: 'What we need in America is a Gandhi who will fight the cause of the oppressed. One who like Gandhi can divorce himself from the greed for gold, one who can appreciate the misery of the oppressed' (5.11.32; Kapur:66). As the comment indicates, the perception of Gandhi as a self-denying fighter had entered the African-American psyche. In 1931, Gandhi's visit in a peasant's dhoti to the King in England drew from the *Pittsburgh Courier* the comment that Gandhi was 'an unusually brilliant man' because he would not 'bow to the conventions of European civilization' (Kapur:53).

Gandhi was brought closer to Black Americans in 1934 when two of his English followers, Madeleine Slade (Mira Behn) and Muriel Lester, visited America. Accounts of Black America's interest in him provided by Slade and Lester may have played a part in the keenness with which Gandhi received the Thurmans and the Carrolls in 1936. He wrote inviting them to meet him in Bardoli and came out of his hut to welcome them when they arrived. Mahadev Desai told Thurman that he had never seen Gandhi 'greet a visitor so warmly' in all his years with the Mahatma (Kapur:88).

Thurman later recalled that Gandhi asked 'persistent, pragmatic questions about American Negroes, about the course of slavery, and how we had survived it ' (Kapur: 88). Gandhi also wanted to know whether the prejudice against colour was growing or dying out, and whether American law recognized marriages between Blacks and whites (62:198-202). The discussion turned to the possibility of one or a few overcoming brutality with nonviolence, and the relationship between love and nonviolence, with Gandhi explaining (as we saw in a previous chapter) that nonviolence was love in the Pauline sense plus a fearless struggle against wrong.

When Sue Bailey Thurman asked how she should act if her brother was lynched before her very eyes, Gandhi suggested noncooperation with the lynching community unto self-immolation, with 'faith remaining undimmed while life ebbs out, minute by minute.' He added: 'My answer may not convince you, but I am striving very hard . . . and my faith will not diminish.' At the end of the meeting Gandhi asked for a Negro spiritual. The visitors sang two while Gandhi and his associates 'bowed their heads in prayer.'

He was invited to America — 'for Negroes . . . We need you badly.' Gandhi replied that he had to 'make good' his message in India first, adding that he would go 'the moment I feel the call within me.' It was when Thurman referred to the similarity between what

Gandhi had spoken to them and the message of the Negro spirituals that Gandhi said that possibly the Negroes would deliver nonviolence to the world (Kapur:87-91; also 62:198-202).

A year later, two leaders of Black opinion, Benjamin E. Mays and Channing H. Tobias, called on Gandhi in Wardha. Tobias asked: 'What word shall I give to my Negro brethren as to the outlook for the future?' Replied Gandhi: 'With right, which is on their side, and the choice of nonviolence as their only weapon, if they will make it such, a bright future is assured' (64:229-30; Kapur:100).

In a letter he addressed to President Roosevelt in July 1942, explaining Quit India, Gandhi said that the Allied declaration of 'fighting to make the world safe for freedom of the individual and for democracy sounds hollow so long as India, and for that matter Africa, are exploited by Great Britain and America, and America has the Negro problem in her own home' (1.7.42; 76:264-5). A few days earlier, *Harijan* had published Gandhi's remark to the American journalist, Preston Grover: 'You have yet to abolish slavery ... Yes, your racial discrimination, your lynch law and so on. But you don't want me to remind you of these things' (21.6.42; 76:212).

Representatives of Britain in America met with some success in 1942 when they tried to portray Quit India as a bid to sabotage the war against Japan, but Black America drew inspiration from India's 1942 movement. Writing in a leading Black newspaper, the *New York Amsterdam News*, Rebecca West said, 'England has at last got its lesson from India. "Independence or nothing," says Mahatma Ghandi.' West urged 'colored leaders in this country' to tell America that 'it cannot win' without equality to the Negroes (Kapur:105-6).

It was an African-American journalist, Deton Brooks Jr., of the *Chicago Defender*, who, in the summer of 1945, elicited one of Gandhi's famous remarks by asking for a message for Americans. 'My life is its own message,' Gandhi replied, adding, 'If it is not, then nothing I can now write will fulfil the purpose' (Kapur:125; and 80:209).

Also meeting Gandhi in the summer of 1945, Frank Bolden of the National Negro Press Association found himself answering Gandhi's questions about the condition of Negroes in America. 'All during our discourse,' Bolden wrote, 'I noticed the great Mahatma's face registering first sorrow, then disgust, then agreement, followed by humour, and ending with pleasure' (Kapur:126-7).

When, that same year, the United Nations met in San Francisco for its charter conference, Gandhi spoke from India of 'the terrible deceptions and fraud' of war and added that there could be no peace for the world without 'universal freedom and equality of coloured races and nations' (Kapur: 127).

Perhaps the last African-American to meet Gandhi was William Stuart Nelson, Dean and Vice President of Howard University, who spent some time with Gandhi in Noakhali in January 1947 and again in Calcutta in August of that year, just a few days after Indian independence. It was to Nelson that Gandhi made the significant remark quoted earlier in this work about the hate that had infiltrated the freedom movement and spilled over in communal rioting.

After Nelson sang 'O God Our Help in Ages Past' at Gandhi's evening prayer in a Noakhali village, Gandhi explained the hymn's meaning to the people present. Stirred by the occasion and by his conversation with Gandhi, Nelson wrote in March 1947 of Gandhi's 'extraordinary spiritual and intellectual qualities' and 'complete mastery over the material demands upon his life,' adding that 'his mind met our problems most directly and constructively' (Kapur:135).

If Thurman in 1936, Brooks in 1945 and Nelson in 1947 evoked Gandhi's inmost thoughts, they should be seen in a long line of Gandhi's African-American interlocutors, beginning with the unnamed Black American at Pretoria station and extending to Mordecai Johnson, who visited India after Gandhi's death and in 1950 gave a speech on him in Philadelphia that, in the phrase of Martin Luther King Jr., 'electrified' King (Kapur:147).

Bayard Rustin has recorded, referring to a November 1957 conference for civil rights when King and fifty-nine other Black leaders of the South accepted the motto, 'Not one hair of one head of one white person shall be harmed,' that 'as King and I left [the conference], we discussed a prophetic statement made by Gandhi.'[10] This, as Rustin tells us, was the remark made to Thurman in 1936.

Chapter 8

Castes and Outcastes

THE PITCH TO which Gandhi's passion for independence from Britain rose in his 1920-2 campaign was equalled only once thereafter, in 1942. At the peak of that first struggle, of which Jallianwala was an important trigger, Gandhi said:

> What crimes for which we condemn the government as Satanic have not we been guilty of towards our untouchable brethren? . . . We make them crawl on their bellies; we have made them rub their noses on the ground; with eyes red with rage, we push them out of railway compartments — what more than this has British rule done? What charge that we bring against Dyer and O'Dwyer may not others, and even our own people, lay at our door? (On 13.4.21; 19:572).

This was spoken at a Suppressed Classes Conference in Ahmedabad. In an article in *Navajivan*, his Gujarati journal, Gandhi used stronger words. Cruelties to the untouchables did not merely equal the Punjab atrocities; they constituted 'an outrage grosser than that in the Punjab against which we have been protesting.' 'We . . . segregate them . . . drive them to live on the outskirts of the village, [are] not concerned whether they live or die . . . give them food left over by others.' It was nothing but 'Dyerism' to think that 'an untouchable cannot live in our neighbourhood and cannot own land

[and] . . . must, on seeing us, shout, "Please keep at a distance, do not touch me" ' (19:331).

In a *Young India* article in November 1920 he likened the untouchables to slaves and those practising untouchability to slaveowners: 'We have become "pariahs of the Empire" because we have created "pariahs" in our midst. The slaveowner is always more hurt than the slaves. We shall be unfit to gain swaraj so long as we keep in bondage a fifth of the population' (19:20). The suggestion that Indians in South Africa were paying for Indian untouchability was repeated by him throughout his life: 'Has not a just Nemesis overtaken us for the crime of untouchability? Have we not reaped as we have sown?' (*Young India*, 19.1.21). 'We who are responsible for Indian untouchability are ourselves victims of it in South Africa. It is a case over again of "the biter bitten" ' (*Young India*, 30.12.26). 'Our sins have a strange way of coming home to roost. We turned a portion of ourselves into pariahs and today the whites of South Africa are doing the same to our compatriots there' (Speech to AICC, Bombay, 7.7.46; 84:422-3).

At times he spoke of wider consequences: 'See what we have done, are still doing, to the suppressed classes! If "Kaffir" is a term of opprobrium, how much more so is "Chandal!" In the history of the world religions, there is perhaps nothing like our treatment of the suppressed classes . . . God does not punish directly. His ways are inscrutable. Who knows that all our woes are not due to that one black sin?'

In 1920 Gandhi recalled that when, on a visit to India from South Africa (this would be in 1896 or 1901), he recounted to Gokhale the plight of Indians in South Africa, Gokhale had called it 'the fruit' of the untouchability in Hindu society. Gandhi had 'immediately agreed' (Speech by Gandhi in Nagpur, 25.12.20; 19:149). In fact the thought had occurred to him earlier. In 1894, when a Pretoria barber refused to cut his hair, Gandhi quenched his resentment by remembering that 'we do not allow our barbers to serve our untouchable brethren.' He was 'rewarded' in South Africa, he writes in the autobiography, 'not once but many times, and the conviction that it was the punishment for our own sins saved me from becoming angry.'

A fierce attack by orthodoxy on a decision in October 1920 by the Gandhi-inspired university, Gujarat Vidyapith, not to recognize schools that excluded 'untouchables' uncovered the origin of Gandhi's stand against untouchability. Using the press, the post and whispering campaigns, the critics alleged that Gandhi had imposed the decision under the influence of Christians like C.F. Andrews, and declared that they would oppose his movement against the Raj if the decision was not annulled.

Gandhi was inundated with letters. In December 1920 he answered them in *Navajivan*: 'The advice I receive from one and all is that if I do not exclude Antyajas (the untouchables) from the national schools, the movement for swaraj will end in smoke. If I have even a little of the true Vaishnava in me, God will also vouchsafe me the strength to reject the swaraj which may be won by abandoning the Antyajas. The resolution (against excluding Antyajas) . . . is not mine but that of the senate (of the Vidyapith) as a whole. I welcome the resolution. Had the senate not passed it, it would have been guilty of adharma' (5.12.20; 19:73).

In November he wrote in *Young India* that the senate had 'counted the cost when it refused to bend before the storm,' and added: 'We may not cling to putrid customs and claim the pure boon of swaraj' (*Young India*, 24.11.20; 19:20). For a while he ignored the charge of acting under Andrews's influence; as he saw it, the issue was the Vidyapith's decision and its merits, not its origin. At the end of January, however, he wrote to Andrews on the subject, and in April he spoke publicly about it.

To Andrews he said:

My dearest Charlie . . . I must not keep one thing from you. The *Gujarati* is endeavouring to weaken my position on the question by saying that I have been influenced by you in this matter, meaning thereby that I am not speaking as a Hindu but as one having been spoiled by being under your Christian influence. This is all rotten I know.

I began this work in S.A. — before I ever heard of you and I was conscious of the sin of untouchability before I came under other Christian influences in S.A. The truth came to me when I was yet a child. I used to laugh at my dear mother for making us bathe if we brothers touched any pariah. It was in 1897 that I was prepared in Durban to turn Mrs Gandhi away from the house because she would not treat on a footing of equality Lawrence who she knew belonged to the pariah class and whom I had invited to stay with me . . . With deep love, Mohan (From Calcutta, 29.1.21; 19:288-90).

The public reference to his early days came in his talk to the Suppressed Classes Conference:

I regard untouchability as the greatest blot on Hinduism. This idea was not brought home to me by my bitter experiences during the South African struggle. It is not due to the fact that I was once an agnostic. It is equally wrong to think — as some people do — that I have taken my views from my study of Christian literature. These views date as far back as the time when I was neither enamoured of, nor was acquainted with, the Bible or the followers of the Bible.

I was hardly yet twelve when this idea had dawned on me. A scavenger named Uka, an untouchable, used to attend our house for cleaning latrines. Often I would ask my mother . . . why I was forbidden to touch him. If I accidentally touched Uka, I was asked to perform the ablutions, and though I naturally obeyed, it was not without smilingly protesting.

I was a very dutiful and obedient child and so far as it was consistent with respect for parents, I often had tussles with them on this matter. I told my mother that she was entirely wrong in considering physical contact with Uka as sinful.

While at school I would often happen to touch the 'untouchables', and as I never would conceal the fact from my parents, my mother would tell me that the shortest cut to purification after the unholy touch was to cancel the touch by touching any Mussalman passing by. And simply out of reverence and regard for my mother I often did so, but never did so believing it to be a religious obligation . . .

The Ramayana used to be regularly read in our family. A Brahmin called Ladha Maharaj used to read it. He was stricken with leprosy, and he was confident that a regular reading of the Ramayana would cure him, and indeed he was cured. 'How can the Ramayana,' I thought to myself, 'in which . . . an "untouchable" took Rama across the Ganga in his boat, countenance the idea of any human beings being untouchables?'

The story of Uka explains Gandhi's lifelong tendency to focus more on scavengers than on other, and larger, untouchable groups. We will soon look at Gandhi's reaction to untouchability in South Africa, but it may be useful to see more of the Ahmedabad speech, which contains several ingredients of his position. The lines quoted at the start of this chapter were part of it, as are the following:

[It] does not mean that I expect you to cease to have misgivings about the Hindus. How can they deserve to be not mistrusted having wronged you so much? . . .

I met the untouchables (in Nellore) and I prayed that day as I have done today . . . If I have to be reborn, I should be born an untouchable, so that I may share their sorrows, sufferings, and the affronts levelled at them, in order that I may endeavour to free myself and them from that miserable condition.

You must not ask the Hindus to emancipate you as a matter of favour. Hindus must do so, if they want, in their own interests. You should make them feel ashamed by your own purity and cleanliness . . . I have come in contact with the untouchables all over the country; and I have observed that immense possibilities lie latent in them of which neither they nor the rest of the Hindus seem to be aware. Their intellect is of virginal purity.

You should now cease to accept leavings from plates, however clean they may be represented to be. Receive grain only — good, sound grain, not rotten grain — and that too only if it is courteously offered . . . The Hindus are not sinful by nature — they are sunk in ignorance . . . May God give you strength to work out your salvation (13.4.21; 19:569-75).

The emotion in the 'I should be born an untouchable' statement should not blind us to its realism. Gandhi knew that his not being born an untouchable was a liability, for it was hard for untouchables to trust an outsider. Already some of them had attacked him. He had touched on the criticism in his talk. ('I was told in Bombay that some of you are opposed to noncooperation and believe that salvation is only possible through the British Government.') To be assailed only from one side was seldom Gandhi's fate.

After three years in South Africa, Gandhi, twenty-six at the time, came to India in 1896 to collect his family from Rajkot and to inform Indians of the difficulties of their compatriots in South Africa. Plague had broken out in Bombay and there was fear that Rajkot would catch it. Gandhi's services were accepted by the princely state and he was taken on the sanitation committee. 'The committee,' Gandhi writes in the autobiography, 'had to inspect the untouchables' quarters also.' But only one member was willing to accompany Gandhi to the untouchables' homes. 'To the rest it was something preposterous to visit those quarters.' Gandhi found that the little homes of the untouchables were well-swept and tidy, 'the few pots and pans clean and shining.' There was more filth in 'the upper class quarters.'

The story of the Gandhi-Kasturba quarrel over cleaning the chamber pot used by Gandhi's office assistant staying in their Durban home, 'a Christian born of untouchable parents,' need not be given here in any detail. It is contained in the autobiography, where Gandhi recalls 'her chiding me, her eyes red with anger, and pearl drops streaming down her cheeks, as she descended the ladder, pot in hand.' Gandhi shouted against her anger, she shouted back, and Gandhi dragged Kasturba to the gate 'with the intention of pushing her out,' when Kasturba uttered some hometruths and a 'really ashamed' Gandhi shut the gate. This incident, which took place in 1898, if we go by the autobiography, or in 1897, if we go by Gandhi's letter to Andrews quoted above, is proof above all of Gandhi's temper and coerciveness on the occasion, though we should remember what can be easily overlooked, that we owe our knowledge of the incident entirely to Gandhi's confession. Gandhi's opposition to untouchability is also suggested by the episode.

It took Kasturba time and effort to accept her husband's stand on the subject. Others close to Gandhi were also unwilling or critical, one of them being Laxmidas, Gandhi's brother. In a letter he wrote to Srinivasa Sastri in 1932, Gandhi recalled his dispute with Laxmidas, who died in 1914:

> I remained in banishment from my eldest brother for, I think, fourteen years. Year after year he sent me curses by registered post. I rejoiced in his curses . . . Six months before his death he saw that I was in the right. One of the reasons for his wrath was this very question of untouchability (20.9.32; 51:101-2).

Not much of the Laxmidas-Mohandas correspondence seems to have survived. However, Laxmidas would have known of his brother's 1896 visit to Rajkot's untouchables. Perhaps, too, Kasturba supplied an account of the Durban episode to members of the joint family when she and her husband were in Rajkot in 1901, but we cannot be sure.

At the Calcutta Congress of 1901, where he spoke on South Africa, Gandhi was 'face to face with untouchability.' To some delegates 'even the sight of others, whilst they were dining, meant pollution.' Gandhi tried personally to cope with the appalling insanitation at the Congress but 'found no one to share the honour with me' (*Experiments*). Back in South Africa, he wrote in *Indian Opinion* in 1905 that in his eyes there was no distinction between Brahmins and untouchables (4:430). Two years later he referred, in a letter, to 'the wicked superstitions about untouchability' (6:435). When satyagraha sent many Indians to prison, he rebuked as cowards those prisoners who refused to eat food touched by untouchables or to sleep near them (9:181). And he warned a Tamil meeting against reproducing in South Africa the strong caste divisions of their Madras province (12:495). Work among South Africa's indentured or ex-indentured Indians, often of low or 'untouchable' caste, also revealed, and shaped, his outlook on caste and untouchability.

✳

But it was John Ruskin's *Unto This Last* that firmly converted Gandhi to social equality. Henry Polak, who had sought out Gandhi because of the latter's work against the plague in Johannesburg, lent a copy of the book to Gandhi while seeing him off on a train from Johannesburg to Durban in 1904. 'The book was impossible to lay aside,' Gandhi would recall. 'It gripped me . . . I could not get any sleep that night.'

From the book Gandhi drew three conclusions: the individual's good is contained in the good of all; a lawyer's work is no more valuable than a barber's; a life of labour is the life worth living. According to Gandhi, the first he already knew, the second he had dimly realized but the third had never occurred to him. 'I arose with the dawn, ready to reduce these principles into practice' (*Experiments*).

The Phoenix Ashram was an immediate outcome but we should not underestimate the book's impact on Gandhi's mind, which henceforth would refuse any admission to ideas of high and low, or superiority and inferiority. In 1908 he translated *Unto This Last* into Gujarati under the title *Sarvodaya*, or the good of all. More has been heard of the ethical norms that Gandhi tried to foster in his ashrams than of the social equality and bread labour on which he insisted. These were part of the code for the Phoenix settlement, which was near Durban; for the Tolstoy Farm that Gandhi later established outside Johannesburg on land provided by Kallenbach; and for the satyagrahis of South Africa when they marched, camped or were imprisoned together.

We get a flavour of Phoenix from the account of his first day there by Ravjibhai Patel, who had joined the Ashram in 1912 at the age of twenty-four: 'The breakfast consisted of (home-baked) bread . . . jelly of orange peels, and wheat porridge. At 7 a.m. (after breakfast) farming commenced. Gandhiji called for two hoes. He took one and gave me the other. I was holding a hoe for the first time in my life. We began preparing plant beds for fruit trees.'[1]

The Satyagraha Ashram that Gandhi established in Ahmedabad in 1915, within months of his return from South Africa, had the abolition of untouchability as one of its aims. Ashramites were required to take a vow against it. But untouchability was not Gandhi's only foe. Alien rule was another, as was Hindu-Muslim discord.

Part of Gandhi's genius lay in his clear and early grasp of the interconnection of the three enemies. Instinctively if indistinctly he had shown this understanding in his first meeting in Pretoria in 1893 and even in some of his expressions as a student in London. The interconnection was both practical and moral. Hindus did not deserve freedom from alien rule if they treated a portion among them as untouchables, and caste Hindus were unlikely to get it if opposed by the untouchables. If they fought each other, Hindus and Muslims would, likewise, neither merit nor attain independence from Britain.

There was another angle to the interconnection. Even if they wanted to, India's British rulers were not really in a position to protect the untouchables from the caste Hindus, or Hindus and Muslims from one another: in any sustained test, neighbours were going to be more relevant than the fragile network of the Raj's authority. And if not justice but extension of its rule was Britain's aim, it would favour or drop a community (Muslims, caste Hindus or untouchables), according to political need. In these tricky waters, any boatman rowing towards Indian political independence, or the removal of high and low, or Hindu-Muslim unity, required great wisdom. A boatman wanting to reach all three ports needed infinite wisdom.

Elsewhere we quote the view of Britons like Wavell and Penderel Moon that Gandhi's dominant aim was Indian independence, or, as Wavell would at times allege, Congress or caste Hindu supremacy in independence's name. At times Ambedkar spoke similarly. My finding is different. I see Gandhi struggling to reach all three goals, and to ensure that independence came to India as a whole, not to caste Hindus or Congress.

Gandhi referred to the interconnection in a letter to Srinivasa Sastri in September 1915, after a storm had broken over Gandhi's decision to admit an untouchable family to his Ashram:

> When I took in Naiker, Mrs Gandhi did not 'kick'. (This appears to be a reference to accepting a lowborn youth who may possibly have come in the party from South Africa.) Now I had to decide whether I was to take in a grown-up Dhed with his wife (Dheds were 'untouchables.'). I decided to take him and she rebelled against it and so did another lady in the Ashram. There was quite a flutter in the Ashram. There is a flutter even in Ahmedabad.
>
> I have told Mrs Gandhi she could leave me and we should part good friends . . . I might have at no distant time to carry out the idea of shifting to some Dhed quarter and sharing their life with the Dheds . . . [The incident] is of importance to me because it enables me to demonstrate the efficiency of passive resistance in social questions, and when I take the final step, it will embrace swaraj, etc (23.9.15; 13:127-8).

We will not here ask whether Gandhi wants to embrace social questions because of swaraj, or swaraj because of social questions, or both because of something else, but merely note that he wishes to embrace the two together. Not only Kasturba but Gandhi's chief hope and a key associate from South African days, Maganlal Gandhi, opposed the admission of Dudabhai, the untouchable in question. A terse entry in Gandhi's diary for 11.9.21 states: 'Santok refused to eat. I too, therefore' (13:179). Santok was Maganlal's wife. She reacted to Gandhi's decision, he to her attitude.

Kasturba yielded and stayed but Maganlal and Santok packed their bags, said goodbye and left the Ashram, only to return later having 'washed their hearts clean of untouchability,' as Gandhi would recall afterwards (50:222). Dudabhai and other Ashramites were roundly abused when they tried to take water from a neighbourhood well. Money ceased to come to the Ashram. To associates who had remained in Phoenix, Gandhi wrote: 'At first we thought the entire Ashram would be outcast and that may yet happen.' But the tide turned. Ambalal Sarabhai appeared quietly and gave Rs 13,000, and Dudabhai and his wife, showing considerable patience and forbearance, found growing acceptance from inmates and visitors.

Five months later, Gandhi made one of his strongest statements. He was addressing the YMCA in Madras on his Ashram's vows. When he came to the one against untouchability, he said: 'Every affliction that we labour under in this sacred land is a fit and proper punishment for this great and indelible crime that we are committing' (16.2.16; 13:232-3).

The following year he presided over the Gujarat Political Conference and a parallel Social Conference, where at Gandhi's suggestion, a number of the untouchables had gathered along with caste Hindus. Abbas Tyabji, Vithalbhai Patel and others were seated near him. An agent of the Raj's police took notes. According to the agent, Gandhi said:

> Beside me there are lawyers and doctors, I believe, and other gentlemen; we have today joined hands with the so-called backward classes; now we are sure to get swaraj. (Hear, hear.) We, Hindus and Muhammadans, have become one; here we are in association with this Dhed community. Do not suppose that that community belongs to a lower status; let the fusion take place between you and

that community, and then you will be fit for swaraj . . .

Where is the difference between us and this community? There is the same heart, the same nose, the same
tongue, the same feeling, everything the same. (Cheers.)
Where there is a divided heart, there Ramachandra cannot be. There is no Imam. (Laughter.) But I am sure He
is here. (Hear, hear.) . . . I now call upon the Hon'ble Mr
Patel to speak (5.11.17; 14:71-2).

The moral and political linkages are spelt out in plain language.
The political message was captured by the police agent but missed
by the journal *Gujarati*, which however quoted Gandhi as saying:
'Where there are hypocrisy, falsehood, inequality and the notion
that certain persons may not be touched, Vishnu, Khuda or Rasool
cannot be present' (11.11.17; 14:73).

Apart from spelling out the interconnection, Gandhi speaks here
as a caste Hindu and to caste Hindus, though fully aware of the
untouchables present, and asks the caste Hindus to initiate the fusion. There was an immediate reaction in *Gujarati* and elsewhere.
Gandhi was accused of defying Hindu scripture; and it was claimed
that the orthodox position related to dirt, not to people.

In a response that set a pattern he would follow, Gandhi reiterated his stand, refuted his critics' reasoning, questioned the view
that every ancient verse was infallible, and sought to reassure caste
Hindus that he was their friend though obliged to adminster bitter
medicine:

Ravana was a rakshasa but this rakshasi of untouchability is even more terrible than Ravana . . . Even the slavery
of the Negroes is not worse than this. This religion, if it
can be called such, stinks in my nostrils. This certainly
cannot be the Hindu religion.

I shall put up a lone fight, if need be, against this hypocrisy. Alone I shall undergo penance and die with His
name on my lips . . . [If ever I] say that I was mistaken . . .
in calling untouchability a sin of Hinduism, you should

take it that I am frightened, that I cannot face the challenge . . . You should take it, in that event, that I am in delirium.

The dirt that soils the scavenger is physical and can be easily removed. But there are those who have become soiled with untruth and hypocrisy, and this dirt is so subtle that it is very difficult to remove it . . .

I shall continue to be my own guru. The path is arduous, certainly, but in this sinful age it seems to [be] the right one . . . I appeal to you to share in the sacred work that was taken up at Godhra . . . so that sixty million people may not break away from us in despair.

It is no good quoting verses from Manusmriti and other scriptures in defence of this orthodoxy. A number of verses in these scriptures are apocryphal, a number of them are quite meaningless . . . This movement will not cause the system of Varnashrama (caste-and-stage-in-life) to disappear. It aims at saving it by doing away with its excesses (14:73-7).

❈

What then was Gandhi's aim? To save the Hindu caste system? To preserve Hindu numbers? To win the untouchables over to his side against the British? Or was he bidding, as Gandhi claimed, to remove 'a stain on India's forehead,' even perhaps to wipe bitter tears away? I see the Varnashrama remark as sugarcoating for his pill for caste Hindus. He wants them to swallow his reforms. And perhaps the most important thought in the passages quoted is the one about the duty to weigh ancient verses. Repeating it soon afterwards, Gandhi wrote that verses from scripture 'cannot be above reason and morality' (14:345).

When a Christian missionary asked him whether it was 'love of the cause or the love of the people' that moved him, Gandhi replied that love of people brought the question of untouchability into his life: 'My mother said, "You must not touch this boy, he is an untouchable." "Why not?" I questioned back, and from that day my revolt began' (69:201). But if we see Gandhi as a humanitarian, as a man of compassion, we cannot see him solely as such. Mopping up the bitter tears of India's untouchables was not the only goal of his life. He wanted India free; he also wanted Hindu-Muslim friendship.

We sense in Gandhi a resolve to refute the notion that nationhood was a gift the British were giving to India. John Strachey had given expression to it in 1888: 'This is the first and most essential thing to learn about India — that there is not, and never was an Indian, or even any country of India, possessing according to European ideas, any sort of unity, physical, political, social or religious.'[2]

Gandhi had decided that he would be the Indian, and demonstrate the India that men like Strachey denied. He would bring all Indians together, Hindus and Muslims, caste Hindus and untouchables. Again and again he returned to the linkage. Whether India was 'fit for Swaraj' depended on the removal of untouchability. 'If slaveowners can be said to be fit, he said in 1918, 'then perhaps we are' (14:345). In a preface to a collection of Gujarati poems about the treatment of untouchables he wrote: 'Shri Padhiar has given a heart-rending picture which cannot but fill the reader with horror to the very roots of his being.' Significantly, he wanted the text 'read out to men and women in their millions, in the same way that works like the Bhagavat are read out to them in every square' (14:344-5).

His attitude was also revealed in Bijapur in 1918 where, at what was supposedly an untouchables' conference, he was asked at midnight to move a resolution asking Britain to accept the Congress-League political demands. Twice Gandhi asked if any untouchables were present. Finding there were none, he refused to move the resolution. Caste Hindu wellwishers of untouchables had no right to speak for them. 'He who demands swaraj must give swaraj to others,' he said, adding: 'I would ask you to give up all this play-acting and . . . offer prayers at this midnight hour so that our sinfulness, our hardness of heart, may disappear' (14:386-7).

At the end of 1920, at his instance, Congress made the removal of untouchability an integral part of its political programme. But in the 1920-2 campaign, noncooperation with the Raj and the Hindu-Muslim question acquired greater salience. Men like Andrews were troubled. Gandhi's reply to him shows the dilemma of one with more than a single goal and also, once more, his prescience:

> You are doing an injustice to me in even allowing yourself to think that for a single moment I may be subordinating the question [of untouchability] to any others . . . It is a bigger problem than that of gaining Indian independence but I can tackle it better if I gain the latter on the way. It is not impossible that India may free herself from English domination before India has become free of the curse of untouchability . . . Do you know that today [the orthodox] who are opposing me in Gujarat are actually supporting the Government and the latter are playing them against me? (29.1.21; 19:288-90).

After saying in 1917 that 'the caste system is a hindrance' (14:17), Gandhi seemed, until the mid-thirties, to defend caste in the form of the Varnashrama system while attacking untouchability. He suggested that the concept of the four ashramas or stages in life, of the brahmachari or student, the grihastha or householder, the vanaprastha or member of a community wider than one's family, and sanyasi or renouncer, was useful and 'capable of worldwide application.' He claimed value, likewise, in the notion of the four varnas or castes of, respectively, the Brahmin (teacher), Kshatriya (protector), Vaisya (merchant) and Sudra (worker).

As Gandhi saw it, the varnas were set by birth though changeable 'by a person choosing another profession.' However, if sons remained in the father's profession, there would be less competition and strife in the world — provided everyone took 'only a living wage and no more.' He thus makes a statement about the varnas being set by birth, qualifies it, adds a rider to the qualification, and finally attaches a proviso to the rider! Subjected to heavy and successive correction, his statement surely loses force — at his own hands.

Two other points he made seemed to rule out the practical relevance of his defence of varnas or castes. He said that while at first there were four varnas, the number of castes and subcastes now was legion. As if to underline this confession that his defence of caste was only theoretical, he made a second point. Restoring the pure varna system was like 'an ant trying to lift a bag of sugar' or 'like Dame Parkington with her mop, trying to push back the Atlantic Ocean.' It was a way of saying that his pure varna system was an impossible dream.

The idea of sons following their caste or hereditary occupation was deservedly attacked, and Gandhi was reminded that neither he nor his sons had lived by it. This was a charge that he could not refute and did not wish to. The 'caste system' he was 'defending' was nonexistent. Attacks on his 'defence' by foes of the caste system only assured caste Hindus that Gandhi was not their enemy, which he was not.

Whether Gandhi saw all this is not easy to say. His astuteness was always underestimated. What is certain is that his instinct guided him to press for one reform at a time but as a protector of Hindu society. In the early twenties he said that his attack on untouchability did not mean that he was pushing for interdining or intermarriage between castes. By 1932 he said that intermarriage was 'not a sin.' In 1935 he directly criticized the caste system and said, 'The sooner public opinion abolishes it, the better' (16.11.35; 62: 121). Towards the end of his life he said that 'a marriage could be celebrated in his presence only if one of the parties was a Harijan and the other a caste Hindu' (See 50:213fn.).

Thus his demands on Hindu society escalated gradually, but his insistence on equality was of early origin, never underplayed and independent of any theory of caste or varna. In 1932 he wrote:

> My impression is that there was no idea of high and low when the varna system was discovered. No one is high and no one is low in this world . . . No matter what was the position in ancient time, nowadays . . . society will not willingly admit any such claim to superiority [except]

under duress. The world is now wide awake.

All have not equal talents, equal property or equal opportunity. Still all are equal . . . The varna system implies
the obliteration of all distinctions of high and low.

The equality on which he never yielded was that of each person's
worth as a person, the equality of the humanness of every man,
woman and child, the equality of every soul the Creator made. This
equality society and the polity had to recognize.

Light was thrown on Gandhi's thinking on caste and untouchability by Nehru. He told Tibor Mende in January 1956:

I spoke to Gandhi repeatedly: why don't you hit out at the
caste system directly? He said that he did not believe in
the caste system except in some idealized form of occupations and all that; but that the present system was thoroughly bad and must go. I am undermining it completely,
he said, by my tackling untouchability . . . If untouchability goes, he said, the caste system goes. So I am concen-
trating on that . . .

All the old reformers . . . just functioned in the air while
this man powerfully moved the masses and created huge
social changes. So he made untouchability the one thing
on which he concentrated, which affected ultimately the
whole caste system.

Mende asked if Gandhi could be called 'a genius in finding the common denominator.' 'There was more than that,' replied Nehru. 'The
genius [lay] in finding . . . the weakest point of the enemy, the breaking of his front.'[3] Thus Gandhi is candid, in the remarks quoted by
Nehru, about his dislike of the caste system and strategy for finish-
ing it. He would have united pro-orthodox ranks if he had commenced with an attack on caste. He chose to zero in on an evil none
could defend.

❈

There are some similarities in Gandhi's approach to untouchability and caste, and Lincoln's to slavery and race. Both spoke of punishments earned for iniquity, by India for untouchability and the United States for slavery. However, the removal of his nation's iniquity was the sole aim of neither. Lincoln said that his 'paramount object' was 'to save the Union,' not the destruction of slavery. We have seen that Gandhi refused to concede that independence was more important to him than the removal of untouchability; but we know of phases in the freedom movement when untouchability went to the back burner.

Neither Lincoln nor Gandhi moved as fast for reform as abolitionists desired, choosing imperfect positions because the available alternatives seemed worse. Each wanted to carry out reform, not merely pronounce it, and needed, therefore, to carry along a minimum of whites in one case, and caste Hindus in the other. Each described his people's iniquity in words of fire and shame; but each was a responsible statesman in addition to possessing a prophet-like tongue, and had to choose among the possibles.

While justice was a passion with both, neither could ignore the claim of order. Abolition of slavery would have been a gesture in the wilderness if the Union or the nation of the United States had not been preserved; abolition of untouchability could have destroyed the untouchables if everything about every caste Hindu had been assailed, and all caste Hindus provoked and polarized. Both Gandhi and Lincoln insisted that reform would benefit all parties. 'In giving freedom to the slave, we assure freedom to the free — honourable alike in what we give and what we preserve,' said Lincoln. Gandhi similarly assured caste Hindus that they and Hindu society would emerge stronger after doing justice to the untouchables.

Both were accused of promoting intermarriage. 'I protest, now and forever,' said Lincoln, 'against that counterfeit logic which presumes that because I do not want a Negro woman for a slave, I do, necessarily, want her for a wife.' Gandhi's response was first a denial and then, in his final years, an acceptance of the charge. Both, finally, rejected malice. Lincoln's rejection is contained in a celebrated sentence, Gandhi's in his courtesy towards those who cursed him for going too fast or attacked him for not going far enough.

Also of interest are the similarities between the cases of India's untouchables and South Africa's Indians, apart from the moral connection drawn by Gandhi of one injustice inviting another. If Gandhi demanded that the Empire protect Indian equality, Ambedkar, the 'untouchable' who became Gandhi's great adversary, demanded the Empire's protection for the rights of untouchables in India.

When, as he sometimes did, Gandhi asked the untouchables to win over their caste Hindu neighbours, did he remember Chamberlain's 1902 statement that since London had little control over the governments in South Africa, Indians there should placate the Europeans if they wished to live in their midst? The satyagrahas that Gandhi led in South Africa were later matched by satyagrahas by Indian untouchables against caste Hindus, which were capable of undermining India's defiance of the Raj. He had to ensure that the two struggles helped each other when they could just as easily neutralize each other.

Gandhi's description of an encounter with an untouchable in Orissa in 1927 enables us to focus more on his approach:

> It was at Bolgarh, 31 miles from the nearest railway station, that, whilst I was sitting and talking with Dinabandhu Andrews, a pariah with a half-bent back, wearing only a dirty loincloth, came crouching in front of us. He picked up a straw and put it in his mouth, and then lay flat on his face with arms outstretched. He then raised himself, folded his hands, bowed, took out the straw, arranged it in his hair, and was about to leave.
>
> I was writhing in agony whilst I witnessed the scene. Immediately the performance was finished, . . . I began to talk to him. He was an 'untouchable' living in a village six miles away, and being in Bolgarh for the sale of his load of faggots and having heard of me, he had come to

see me. Asked why he had taken the straw in his mouth, he said that this was to honour me. I hung my head in shame.

Gandhi, who had ascertained that the man drank liquor and ate carrion 'because it was the custom,' proceeds with his account: 'I asked him for a gift. He searched for a copper about his waist. "I do not want your copper," I said to him in my misery. "I want you to give me something better." "I will give it," he replied. "The gift I want you to give me is a promise never again to take that straw in your mouth for any person on earth; it reduces a man's dignity to do so; never again to drink, because it reduces man to the condition of a beast; never again to eat carrion, for it is against Hinduism, and no civilized person would ever eat carrion."

'"But my people will excommunicate me if I do not eat carrion and drink," the poor man said. "Then suffer the excommunication and if need be leave the village." The downtrodden, humble man made the promise. If he keeps it, his gift [would be] more precious than all the rupees that generous countrymen entrust to my care' (*Young India*, Dec. 1927).

The man's abasement wounds Gandhi's sense of human dignity, his Hinduness and his Indianness. He wants the untouchable to stand erect before men, liquor and carrion. But he also puts in a word for Hinduism — and informs *Young India's* readers, who are mostly caste Hindus, that he has done so.

Gandhi tried to reason with orthodoxy. He held long talks with high priests in different parts of the country. His argument was that custom was not religion but the interlocutors did not budge. Only after his 1932 fast did a shift of some sort occur; but we should take a brief look at the Vykom (or Vaikkam) satyagraha of 1924-5. This focussed on a longstanding denial to untouchables of the use of public roads adjacent to a temple and Brahmin residences in the town of Vykom in the princely state of Travancore.

'Muslims might use the roads, Christians, even dogs — but not untouchables.'[4] The denial had withstood sustained local protests. In 1924 a satyagraha commenced, first taking the form of entering the forbidden streets and then of peaceful picketing of barriers erected by the state government to enforce the denial 'legitimized' by custom. When rains flooded the area, the state's police were provided with boats to enable them to implement the bar; the satyagrahis stood in waist-deep water to continue their protest.

Gandhi backed the satyagraha, went to Vykom, talked unsuccessfully with the leaders of orthodox opinion, and negotiated with Travancore's ruling circles. He also met Sri Narayana Guru, the religious leader of the Ezhavas, large in number but suppressed in the Malayalam country. An active part was played in the satyagraha by E.V. Ramaswami Naicker, who spoke of the removal of untouchability as 'the cornerstone of our Mahatma's programme.'[5] Confident of support outside orthodox ranks, Gandhi suggested a referendum of caste Hindus in the area. The proposal was rejected.

The satyagraha was kept up. Violence was kept out. After months of endurance, the government of Travancore threw open prohibited roads on three sides of the temple, keeping the street on the eastern side closed to outcastes and non-Hindus. The victory was partial. But Indians across the land had followed the satyagraha, and orthodoxy was effectively discredited by its resistance to a demand for bare humanity.

Another milepost in the untouchable movement was the 1927 Mahad satyagraha. On 20 March, Dalits gathered in Mahad for a Kolaba Zilha Bahishkrut Parishad (the Kolaba district conference of the boycotted), surged forward and drank from the Chawdar tank, from which untouchables were barred despite a resolution of the Mahad municipality for its opening to all. According to Gail Omvedt, scholar of the Dalit movement, Ambedkar, who had conceived the gathering, had 'direct action in his mind from the beginning' but this was not revealed to many and the action had the element of surprise. The drinking of the tank water, a riot that followed, and the subsequent 'cleansing' of the tank by horrified Brahmins made news throughout Maharashtra.

Later in the year, between 10,000 and 15,000 Dalits gathered again in Mahad. A copy of the Manusmriti was burned on this occasion. Ambedkar, says Omvedt, 'had a soft spot' for Gandhi at this juncture, though he was disappointed that Gandhi was 'not giving as much weight to untouchability removal as to Hindu-Muslim unity.' The tent for the December rally 'featured Gandhi's photo.' Two years earlier Ambedkar had said at a Bahishkrut Parishad in Belgaum: 'Where no one else comes close, the sympathy shown by Mahatma Gandhi is by no means a small thing.'[6]

✳

One way to thwart Gandhi's bid for independence was to bring together India's Muslims, princes and untouchables, three groups uncomfortable in different ways and degrees about Congress inheriting the Raj. Added to other sections opposed to Congress, such an alliance would spell a majority. To retain or obtain support from the three groups thus became Gandhi's need. Broadly speaking, he succeeded with the untouchables and the princes but failed with the Muslims. This is the context for the Gandhi-Ambedkar debate.

A conference in London in 1931 revealed their clash. HMG had invited representatives of a number of Indian interests to confer with one another and their British rulers. An exhibition in London of Indian rivalries was not likely to advance the cause of independence, but after much hesitation Gandhi took part, mainly in the hope of influencing popular opinion in Britain. He did not expect the conference to endorse Congress's demand for independence.

In London Ambedkar asked for, and Gandhi opposed, a separate electorate and reserved seats for the untouchables in any new constitution for India. Separate electorates for Muslims and Sikhs were included in the 1916 Lucknow Pact between Congress and the Muslim League which Tilak and Jinnah had helped forge and Gandhi had backed. But Gandhi refused to accept a division of the Hindu electorate. It would destroy the slender bridge he had helped construct between caste Hindus and untouchables, impede the reform that had commenced amongst caste Hindus, and expose untouchables to heightened hostility. At the conference he said:

It (the separate electorate for scheduled castes) means the

perpetual bar sinister. I would not sell the vital interests
of the untouchables even for the sake of winning the freedom of India. I claim myself in my own person to represent the vast mass of the untouchables . . . I claim that I
would get, if there was a referendum of the untouchables,
their vote, and that I would top the poll. And I would
work from one end of India to the other to tell the untouchables that separate electorates and separate reservation is not the way to remove this bar sinister, which is the
shame, not of them, but of orthodox Hinduism.

Let this committee and let the whole world know that
today there is a body of Hindu reformers who are pledged
to remove the blot of untouchability. Sikhs may remain
as such in perpetuity, so may Mohammedans, so may
Europeans. Will untouchables remain untouchables in
perpetuity? I would far rather that Hinduism died than
that untouchability lived.

Therefore, with all my regard for Dr Ambedkar, and
for his desire to see the untouchables uplifted, with all my
regard for his ability, I must say in all humility that the
great wrong under which he has laboured and the bitter
experiences that he has undergone have for the moment
warped his judgment. It is not a proper claim which is
registered by Dr Ambedkar when he seeks to speak for
the whole of the untouchables of India.

Referring to 'the two divisions' in every village that separate electorates would entrench, Gandhi suggested that those demanding a
separate electorate 'do not know their India, do not know how Indian society is today constructed.' He ended with a declaration: 'I
want to say with all the emphasis that I can command that if I was
the only person to resist this thing, I would resist it with my life'
(48:297-8).

During a discussion at Friends House, the Quaker centre, he was
more candid: 'The untouchables are in the hands of superior classes.
They can suppress them completely and wreak vengeance upon the

untouchables who are at their mercy. I may be opening out my shame to you. But . . . how can I invite utter destruction for them? I would not be guilty of that crime' (48:258).

It was a scenario that had a counterpart in U.S.A. As Bayard Rustin put it in 1971, 'recent American history' has 'time and again' proved 'with brutal clarity' that 'if Negroes engage in violence as a tactic, they will be met with repression, that if they follow a strategy of racial separation they will be isolated.'[7] Though he never proposed violence, Ambedkar was advocating separation.

There were additional reasons for Gandhi's stand. He did not want Congress weakened against the Raj. A separate untouchable electorate would help divide-and-rule elements in the Raj. Gandhi's nationalist pride was also involved. The untouchables turning to the British to secure their position in India hurt that pride. His political goal and nationalist pride fused with his concern for the untouchables to produce the impassioned reaction.

Interviewed by the BBC in 1955, Ambedkar said that Gandhi's true motive was political: 'All this talk about untouchability was just for the purpose of making the untouchables drawn into Congress . . . Secondly, you see, he wanted that the untouchables should not oppose his movement. I don't think beyond that he had any real motive of uplift.'[8]

The records do not substantiate this assessment and Ambedkar himself seems to have spoken in a different vein at other times. Keer writes in his biography of Ambedkar, for instance, that Ambedkar 'acknowledged' Gandhi's 'humanitarian service to the untouchables' (182). In any case, all the evidence suggests that in South Africa and India, Gandhi opposed the notions of untouchability and high-and-low with a directness and conviction not perhaps equalled by any caste Hindu or many untouchables of his time. The claim of opposition to untouchability as a boy is Gandhi's own but it was often made and has the ring of truth. Even if it is disregarded, the rest of the evidence is conclusive.

Yet, as we have seen, Indian unity and Indian self-respect too were powerful considerations with him. The man behind the London declaration is not merely a servant of the untouchables. He is not just the chief of Congress. He is not only the leader of the independence movement. He is, or wants to be, India's boatman.

Ambedkar's sense of self-respect equalled Gandhi's. He welcomed caste Hindu intervention in untouchable affairs about as much as Gandhi welcomed British intervention in Indian affairs. In London he was forty to Gandhi's sixty-two years. Though Gandhi had known of him for some time, he first met Ambedkar only some weeks before the London conference. Until then he had thought that Ambedkar was a Brahmin reformer enraged at the treatment of untouchables.[9]

In London Gandhi tried to win Ambedkar, and sent Devadas to him to arrange a meeting. A message he addressed to Sir Mirza Ismail, also a participant in the conference, shows Gandhi's anxiety: 'It will be a great triumph of yours if you can convert Dr A. Having suffered like him in S.A., Dr A. always commands my sympathy in all he says. He needs the gentlest treatment' (22.10.31; 48:208).

In a speech to the Indian Majlis, Gandhi spelt out his sympathy: 'I have the highest regard for Dr Ambedkar. He has every right to be bitter. That he does not break our heads is an act of self-restraint on his part . . . The same thing happened to me in my early days in South Africa where I was hounded out by the Europeans wherever I went. It is quite natural for him to vent his wrath' (48:224). Did Gandhi see that it was also natural for Ambedkar to seek British support, even as Gandhi had sought it for Indians in South Africa?

At another London occasion Gandhi said that Ambedkar 'has a right even to spit upon me, as every untouchable has, and I would keep on smiling if they did so.' But Congress, he claimed, had wider support among the untouchables than Ambedkar. This was because they 'know the work that the Congress is doing for them and they know that, if they cannot succeed in making their voice felt, I would be prepared to lead a campaign of civil resistance on their behalf and paralyse the Hindu orthodox opposition . . . On the other hand, if they were to be given separate electorates . . . it would divide the Hindu community into armed camps and provoke needless opposition' (48:161).

Gandhi was aware of his handicap. As a questioner told him in London, 'The great stubborn fact against you is that you are not an untouchable.' 'I know it very well,' Gandhi replied, adding that though he claimed to represent untouchables at the London conference, in the legislatures they should have 'their own representatives drawn from their own class' (48:161).

This was a hint that he might agree to reserved seats. But a separate electorate he would oppose. 'Look at the history of Europe. Have you got separate electorates for the working classes or women? With adult franchise, you give the untouchables complete security. Even the orthodox Hindus would have to approach them for votes' (48:224).

Passion, confidence and irreverence marked Ambedkar's performance in London. He rejected Gandhi's right in respect of the untouchables. Other delegates said that Gandhi could not speak for Muslims, Christians, Anglo-Indians and India-based Europeans. Though he was committed to smiling when attacked, the volley of suspicions directed at him hurt Gandhi. On 8 October, after heated exchanges in the conference's Minorities Committee, Gandhi told William Shirer, the American journalist: 'This has been the most humiliating day of my life.'[10]

On 13 November 1931, the Minorities Pact was announced. Signed, among others, by Ambedkar and the Aga Khan, the Pact demanded separate electorates for Muslims, untouchables, Christians, Anglo-Indians and Europeans. Within hours Gandhi made the declaration, quoted earlier, that he would 'resist' a separate electorate for the untouchables 'with my life.' HMG reserved judgment on this but made it clear that Gandhi's demand for independence would not be conceded.

❋

Within a week of returning to India, Gandhi was imprisoned. He had announced the resumption of disobedience. Tens of thousands followed him to jail or received blows from the Raj's police. Following his truth, Ambedkar continued to press for a separate electorate. Six months after the London conference, he was in that metropolis again, urging HMG not to yield to Gandhi.

Writing from prison in March 1932, Gandhi had reminded the British Premier, Ramsay MacDonald, of his oath. In August HMG announced that the untouchables would have a separate electorate. In September Gandhi said, from prison, that he would fast unto death.

HMG made it plain that it would revise its award only if caste Hindus and the untouchable leadership agreed on an alternative. He wanted, Gandhi said in explanation of his fast, to 'sting the Hindu conscience.' If the Hindu mass mind was not prepared to banish untouchability, it should sacrifice him 'without the slightest hesitation.' Added Gandhi, 'My life I count of no consequence. One hundred lives . . . would, in my opinion, be poor penance done by Hindus for the atrocious wrongs they have heaped upon helpless men and women of their own faith.'

Many sent telegrams pleading with Gandhi not to fast. Replying to C. Rajagopalachari, Gandhi said: 'I expect you to rejoice that a comrade has a God-given opportunity for a final act of satyagraha in the cause of the downtrodden.'

He warned caste Hindus that this was but the beginning. Henceforth 'an increasing army of reformers' would resist 'social, civic or political persecution of the Depressed classes.' The issue was of 'transcendental value, far surpassing Swaraj.' His son Devadas was advised to say that 'as his father's son' he would rather 'forfeit his father's life' than see the suppressed classes injured. Devadas spoke as urged.

To the scheduled castes, Gandhi clarified that he would accept reserved seats, though he doubted their usefulness. He hoped they would forgo the separate electorate.

The fast began inside the prison on 20 September. The first response came from a conference of caste Hindu leaders in Bombay which resolved that 'one of the earliest Acts of the Swaraj Parliament' would be to guarantee to untouchables equal access to 'public wells, public schools, public roads and all other public institutions' (53:130). To save Gandhi's life one caste Hindu leader after another asked for a change in customs. Across India temples were opened overnight to untouchables. Brahmins and untouchables dined together. Padmaja Naidu wrote of 'a catharsis' cleansing Hinduism of 'the accumulated corruption' of centuries, and Tagore spoke of a 'wonder' happening 'before our very eyes.' The assessments were exaggerated but the changes were dramatic enough.

The Raj permitted negotiations around Gandhi's bed under a mango tree in the jail compound. Allowed to join her fasting husband, Kasturba said to him: 'Again the same old story!'

Ambedkar came. His first words were, 'Mahatmaji, you have been very unfair to us.' 'It is always my lot to appear to be unfair,' replied Gandhi. Pyarelal, who saw the proceedings, writes in *The Epic Fast* that 'the redoubtable Doctor, strongly supported by his colleagues, fought every inch of the ground.' Ambedkar said afterwards that he was called upon 'to save the greatest man in India' and also to 'safeguard the interests' of the untouchables.

Gandhi's acceptance of reserved seats had given the negotiations a good start. If this had been announced in London, Ambedkar claimed, agreement would have been reached there, but we cannot be sure. 'If you devote yourself entirely to the welfare of the Depressed Classes, you would become our hero,' said Ambedkar to Gandhi. And he confessed that he was 'surprised, immensely surprised' that there was 'so much in common' between Gandhi and him.

'My cry will rise to the throne of the Almighty God,' Gandhi had said before starting his ordeal. Arriving at Yeravda, Tagore 'approached Gandhiji's prostrate form and burying his face in the clothes on Gandhiji's breast, remained in that position for several minutes, overcome with emotion.'

Agreement was reached on the seventh day. Untouchable leaders and caste Hindu leaders signed an accord to which Gandhi had agreed; HMG sent word that it would be honoured; and Gandhi broke his fast, sipping orange juice handed to him by Kasturba.

From behind bars a prisoner had jolted a nation's customs and imposed his will on an empire. The Yeravda or Poona Pact, as it came to be known, gave the scheduled castes double the seats that

HMG had offered and merged caste Hindus and untouchables in a single stream. The world seemed to marvel, and a writer in the *Boston Globe* said that 'the debt he (Gandhi) undertakes to settle is the debt of the human conscience to other human consciences.'

After the fast was broken, Gandhi suggested that 'a meeting of hearts' had taken place, conveyed his 'Hindu gratitude' to Dr Ambedkar, Rao Bahadur Srinivasan and Rao Bahadur M.C.Rajah, the untouchable leaders, and said, referring to them: 'They could have taken up an uncompromising and defiant attitude by way of punishment to the so-called caste Hindus . . . If they had done so I at least could not have resented their attitude and my death would have been but a trifling price exacted for the tortures that the outcasts of Hinduism have been going through for unknown generations. But they have chosen a nobler path and . . . have followed the precept of forgiveness' (All quotes from Pyarelal's *Epic Fast*). Ambedkar gave 'a large part of the credit . . . to Mahatma Gandhi himself,' but the Yeravda spirit was not destined to last.

Despite Ambedkar's exhortation, Gandhi could not devote himself 'entirely' to the cause of the untouchables. Andrews, who wrote in October 1932 that love for the untouchables 'may be said to be the deepest thing in all his (Gandhi's) life,' invited Gandhi, in 1933, to do just what Ambedkar had asked. Suggesting that Gandhi had 'been trying to serve two masters,' Andrews urged him to concentrate on untouchability removal 'for the whole remainder of your life, without turning to the right or to the left.' He conceded that an alien government might try to hinder such an enterprise by Gandhi but reminded Gandhi that he had said 'again and again' that with untouchability Indians 'are not fit to attain Purna Swaraj.'[11]

In August 1931 Gandhi had in fact made a disturbing forecast of life after swaraj: 'If we came into power with the stain of untouchability unaffected, I am positive that the "untouchables" would be far worse under that "Swaraj" than they are now, for the simple reason that our weaknesses and our failings would then be buttressed by the accession of power' (2.8.31, in Ahmedabad; *Epic Fast*: 303).

However, Gandhi did not heed the advice of Andrews. For all his feelings for the untouchables, he could not jettison the rest. Nor could he drop his passions for freedom and Hindu-Muslim unity. Ambedkar, on the other hand, was clear that 'social democracy was more vital than independence from foreign rule.'[12]

There was a difference also in the path to social democracy. To say that Ambedkar favoured caste confrontation while Gandhi did not would be simplistic and unfair to both. Gandhi did not rule out satyagrahas against the upper castes and supported some; on his part Ambedkar strove for caste Hindu support. However, Gandhi laid greater stress than Ambedkar did on the risks of confrontation; and he did not give a positive value to hatred that Ambedkar at times ascribed to that emotion.

In the preface to his *Ranade, Gandhi and Jinnah* (1943), Ambedkar said: 'I hate injustice, tyranny, pompousness and humbug, and my hate embraces all those who are guilty of them. I want to tell my critics that I regard my feelings of hatred as a real force. They are only the reflex of the love I bear for the causes which I believe in.' In this statement Ambedkar admits and explains his emotion of hate and calls it 'a real force' without directly extolling it. Gandhi too admitted his angers, and we know that angers can turn to hates. But Gandhi disliked his anger, whether directed at compatriots or Englishmen, and sought to banish, sublimate or deflect it. Gandhi would have conceded that Ambedkar had greater grounds for anger but he would not have endorsed anger.

Both Gandhi and Ambedkar prescribed self-respect to the untouchables. Gandhi asked them to spin and earn. Ambedkar stressed political self-reliance. Gandhi placed the onus of reform on the caste Hindu conscience, Ambedkar on untouchable striving. Finally, while Gandhi hoped to draw the untouchables towards Congress and the freedom movement, Ambedkar wanted them mobilized by and for themselves alone. Their clash was unavoidable, even though a longer view may see them as allies in social change.

❋

Damaging orthodoxy, the fast and the Pact also restored the morale of the freedom fighters languishing in British jails. Jawaharlal Nehru and others who had been sceptical about the fast acknowledged Gandhi's feat but continued to question the 'diversion' from the goal of independence. Their advice to Gandhi was the opposite of Ambedkar's and Andrews's. Gandhi's response was a journal called *Harijan*. (*Young India* had folded in 1932, a victim of the Raj's repression.) Partly relieved by the 'diversion' but not quite believing it, the Raj allowed Gandhi to edit the journal from prison. He said it would eschew politics as long as he was a prisoner. When the sentence ended, he felt free to use it for all his goals.

From 1931, 'Harijan' had been Gandhi's term for 'untouchable' in *Navajivan*, his Gujarati journal, which also perished in 1932. Under 'Why "Harijan",' the opening issue of the journal, which was soon followed by the Hindi *Harijan Sevak* and the Gujarati *Harijanbandhu*, Gandhi explained:

> It is not a name of my coining. Some years ago, several 'untouchable' correspondents complained that I used the word 'asprishya' in the pages of *Navajivan*. 'Asprishya' means literally untouchable. I then invited them to suggest a better name and one of the 'untouchable' correspondents suggested the adoption of the name 'Harijan,' on the strength of its having been used by the first-known poet-saint of Gujarat (Narsinh Mehta) . . . I thought it was a good word.
>
> 'Harijan' means 'a man of God.' All the religions of the world described God preeminently as the Friend of the friendless, the Help of the helpless and the Protector of the weak . . . In India who can be more friendless, helpless or weaker than [those] classified as untouchables? If, therefore, any body of people can be fitly described as men of God, they are surely these helpless, friendless and despised people.
>
> Not that the change of name brings about any change of status, but one may at least be spared the use of a term which is itself one of reproach. When caste Hindus have of their own inner conviction . . . got rid of the present-

> day untouchability, we shall all be called Harijans, for
> caste Hindus then will have found favour with God
> (11.2.33; 53:266-7).

Asked by Gandhi to send a message for *Harijan's* opening number,
Ambedkar replied that he did not think that Hindus would 'treat any
message from me with respect.' But he sent a 'statement.'
Ambedkar's letter and statement were published, along with a comment by Gandhi.

In his statement Ambedkar said: 'The outcaste is a by-product
of the caste system. There will be outcastes as long as there are
castes. Nothing can emancipate the outcaste except the destruction
of the caste system.'

Gandhi commented:

> Dr Ambedkar is bitter. He has every reason ... Outside
> India he is received with honour and affection but in In-
> dia, among Hindus, at every step he is reminded that he is
> one of the outcastes of Hindu society ... [Yet] there are
> today thousands of caste Hindus who would listen to his
> message with ... respect and consideration ...
>
> As to the burden of his message ... untouchability is
> the product, not of the caste system, but of the distinction
> of high and low ... The attack on untouchability is thus
> an attack on this 'high-and-low'ness. The moment un-
> touchability goes, the caste system itself will be
> purified ... ' (*Harijan*, 11.2.33; 53:259-61).

Orthodox opposition was fiercer and at times physical. When, after
his release, Gandhi campaigned across India against untouchability, sanatanists waved black flags and shouted slogans against him.
In Pune, a car thought to be carrying him was bombed; Gandhi was
not in it but seven others were injured. His meetings were broken
up. His character was reviled in pamphlets. In Benares his portrait
was burnt. In Karachi a man with an axe was apprehended before
he could use it against Gandhi.

Those with close ties to him took offence. His sister Raliat voiced displeasure. An old family friend, Ranchhoddas Patwari, whose loan had helped with Gandhi's voyage to London in 1888, sought precise replies to eighty-eight questions, predicted that Gandhi's stand against untouchability would destroy his position in the country and wreck Congress, suggested that Gandhi had 'completely forsaken dharma,' and finally spoke of a break between them.

Answering every question and argument, Gandhi said that Patwari would revise his views one day. Alluding to a trait that Patwari would have remembered from the 1880s, Gandhi added: 'I hope you don't doubt my intention or ability to adhere to a decision firmly made.' He also said: 'It was my elders who joined themselves in a mutual bond with the Patwari family . . . for half a century and I, for my part, will not break it' (53:13-24 and 304).

This mix of courtesy and firmness characterized his replies to the sanatanists. When one styled as a Vedanta scholar said that 'sanatanists do not hate untouchables but hate their customs and daily actions,' Gandhi answered in *Harijan*: ' "Hate" is perhaps the wrong word. I should use the word "despise." If to relegate a body of people to distant locations, to regard their touch, approach or sight as pollution, to throw at them the leavings of one's food, to deny to them the use of public roads and institutions, even the use of public temples, is not to despise them, I do not know what the word "despise" means' (25.2.33; 53:405).

Yet an uncanny sense told him that the sanatanists were isolating themselves, and that the bulk of the Hindu community would follow him. To Jawaharlal he wrote: 'The fight against sanatanists is becoming more and more interesting if also increasingly difficult... The abuses they are hurling at me are wonderfully refreshing. I am all that is bad and corrupt on earth. But the storm will subside. For I apply the sovereign remedy of ahimsa — non-retaliation. The more I ignore the abuses, the fiercer they are becoming. But it is the death dance of the moth round a lamp' (15.2.33; 53:309-10).

His nine-month 1933-4 Harijan tour, ending in Kashi, covered 12,504 miles and took him to Maharashtra, the present Madhya Pradesh, South India, Bihar, Assam, Orissa and Uttar Pradesh. Huge

258 THE GOOD BOATMAN

crowds of caste Hindus and untouchables heard him. On this trail he did not target the Raj but it was understood by all, caste Hindus, untouchables, the Raj and Gandhi himself, that he symbolized swaraj. Rallying round him for the Harijan cause also meant a chance to declare for swaraj, which was important when many Congress bodies were still banned.

The calamitous earthquake of January 1934 hit Bihar during the campaign. A storm was raised when Gandhi suggested that the disaster, which reduced towns to ruins, tore Bihar's earth and set off floods, was Providence's punishment for untouchability. Tagore accused Gandhi of encouraging irrationality but Gandhi did not correct himself. Assisting the quake's victims involved him fully; but he was not going to drop the focus on untouchability.

❊

The Harijan movement faciiitated the switch in Congress's strategy from defiance of the Raj to measured cooperation with it. Congress took part in the 1937 elections to provincial assemblies. No party could equal Congress's performance in the seats reserved under the Poona Pact for the untouchables. Ambedkar's followers won 11 out of 15 seats in Bombay but Congress was comfortably ahead everywhere else. Of the 20 reserved seats in the U.P., Congress won 16. In Bihar it got 11 out of 15, and in Madras 26 out of 30.

Ambedkar ascribed Congress's success to the caste Hindu vote but the truth was that Gandhi and the freedom movement had found a response among the scheduled castes. This became even more obvious nine years later, when Congress swept the Scheduled Caste seats in the 1945-6 polls. By this time Quit India had taken place, and Ambedkar's image had been damaged by his being a Member of the Executive Council that sought to suppress Quit India.

From time to time, and with increasing directness, Ambedkar threatened that he and his followers would exchange the Hindu faith for another. His words activated many a missionary, Christian, Muslim, Sikh and Buddhist. Gandhi seemed opposed to any change of faith by anyone. He said all religions contained common truth and, conveyed as they were by humans to other humans, some imperfections. Unable to see the point in a change of religion, he also feared strife from competition among religions for numbers. 'This proselytization will mean no peace in the world,' he said to Andrews in 1936.[13]

His unambiguous advice to Christian missionaries was to live their faith — to serve and identify with the people they went to — but not convert or even want to convert. When, in 1933, Ambedkar publicly declared that his thoughts seemed to be leading him away from the Hindu fold, Gandhi said:

> If this doctrine of utmost superiority and utmost inferiority, descending from father to son for eternity, is an integral part of Hinduism . . . then I no more want to belong to it than does Dr Ambedkar. But . . . there is no superiority or inferiority in the Hinduism of my conception (on 14.2.33; 53:306).

On another occasion Gandhi said that religion was 'not like a house or a cloak, which can be changed at will.' It was 'a more integral part of one's self than one's body.' As for conversions, Gandhi urged Ambedkar to consider the reaction of caste Hindus, amidst whom, 'for good or ill,' the untouchables found themselves.[14]

Gandhi's ultimate appeal was not to the principle of loyalty but to the mind and the soul: 'I invite Dr Ambedkar to shed his bitterness and anger and try to learn the beauties of the faith of his forefathers. Let him not curse Hinduism without making an unbiased study of it, and if it fails to sustain him in the hour of need, by all means let him forsake it' (14.2.33; 53:307).

Ambedkar's reply was that the Hinduism which the Dalits found around them was alienating. He had hoped, he said, that Gandhi would 'attain dictatorship in social affairs,' but Gandhi had refused to strive for it. 'India wants,' added Ambedkar, 'a dictator like Kemal Pasha or Mussolini in social and religious matters.'[15] When, eight years after Gandhi's death, Ambedkar took hundreds of thousands of his people from Hinduism to Buddhism, he spoke of a word he had evidently given to Gandhi. This was that when the time came, he would 'choose only the least harmful way for the country.' By adopting Buddhism he had ensured, Ambedkar said, that the conversion would not dislocate India.[16]

❋

Between 1937 and 1946 Gandhi was at the receiving end of unrestrained attacks from Ambedkar. Gandhi and the Congress were deceiving and suppressing the untouchables; Gandhi was not frontal and thoroughgoing enough in his criticisms of caste; and so on. 'Caste Has to Go' was Gandhi's title to an article he wrote in *Harijan* in November 1935. The article discussed the best way 'to destroy caste' and stated: 'The sooner the better' (*Harijan*, 16.11.35; 62:121-2). But Ambedkar was not satisfied.

Electoral disappointments and vilification for joining the Raj's governing council in 1942 sharpened his assaults. Gandhi answered some of the criticism and encouraged Rajagopalachari and K. Santhanam to deal with the rest. He was acknowledging the significance in Ambedkar's critique, and he continued to acknowledge the oppression that influenced the language of persons like Ambedkar.

On independence Gandhi advised Nehru and Patel to include Ambedkar in the new nation's first cabinet. When there were objections, Gandhi reminded Jawaharlal that power was coming 'to India, not to Congress.'[17] According to G. Ramachandran, 'both Nehru and the Sardar were not in favour, saying that this man had been attacking and maligning the Congress.' In Ramachandran's view, Gandhi saw Ambedkar's inclusion as an 'atonement' that India had to make to her untouchables.[18]

Ambedkar's skills had also influenced Gandhi. On 26 July, when talent was being mobilized for the first government, Gandhi said: 'We should utilize the services of everyone. After all they are our countrymen, aren't they? They have not become our enemies because they served the British Government. How a person like Girijashankar Bajpai abused me in 1942! . . . Should we spurn him if he wants to help us now? The loss shall be ours . . . If we seek the advice of such . . . persons, they will show their genius.'[19] Gandhi would have used identical language in support of Ambedkar's inclusion. Jagjivan Ram, a Congress member of the interim government, continued in the new cabinet, which thus had two Scheduled Caste (SC) leaders in it. In deference to Gandhi's wishes, Congress governments from 1937 onwards had included SC members.

One of Ambedkar's biographers, C.B. Khairmode, has referred to a conversation in Bombay in December 1946 between Ambedkar and Muriel Lester, one of Gandhi's English friends. Lester had been present at a Gandhi-Ambedkar meeting in London in 1931. She evidently informed Ambedkar that 'Gandhi was keen that the Congress should include Ambedkar in the Central cabinet and use his learning and leadership . . .' According to Khairmode, after Lester had given Gandhi an account of her talk with Ambedkar, Gandhi asked Patel and Nehru to invite Ambedkar into the cabinet.[20]

Gandhi's wooing of Ambedkar at this stage is confirmed by a statement he made in east Bengal in February 1947. Regretting the Muslim League's boycott of the Constituent Assembly, Gandhi added: 'Dr Ambedkar was good enough to attend the Assembly' (3.2.47; 86:426).

None had a greater role than Ambedkar in the construction of the Indian Constitution, but it is legitimate to see the rights it guarantees to the weak and the underprivileged as proof of Gandhi's commitment to them. He had pledged these rights in London in 1931, at the Karachi Congress earlier that year, and on numerous other occasions. Led by his colleagues and followers, the Constituent Assembly enshrined the rights at the heart of the Constitution. If we regard what the Assembly resolved to do as an index of what the people desired, and consider that caste Hindus were a large and influential component of India's people, this meant caste Hindu acceptance of untouchable rights. Our survey shows that a vital part was played in this acceptance by Gandhi's sustained battle.

❋

In the last two years of his life, Gandhi lived as much as he could in untouchable settlements: in New Delhi amidst sweepers in the Balmiki colony, in Noakhali in the homes of weavers, cobblers and fisherfolk. 'They bathe us with love,' Manu wrote in her Noakhali diary (*ECR*: 108). But Gandhi never lost sight of the reality in grassroots India. We have previously seen the letter he wrote in August 1946 to Vallabhbhai Patel:

> Who are the people who beat up Harijans, murder them, prevent them from using wells, drive them out of schools and refuse them entry into their homes? They are Congressmen. Aren't they? It is very necessary to have a clear picture of this   (1.8.46; 85:102).

Underscoring his acceptance of intermarriage, he said in Patna in April 1947 that he had 'long ago made it a rule not to be present at or give his blessings for any wedding unless one of the parties was a Harijan' (24.4.47; 87:350). When, two months after Gandhi's death, Ambedkar married a Brahmin doctor, Patel wrote to him: 'I am sure if Bapu were alive he would have given you his blessings.' Replied Ambedkar: 'I agree that Bapu, if he had been alive, would have blessed it.'[21]

In October 1947, after independence, Gandhi still felt, as he had done half a century earlier, that 'what we are suffering . . . is the consequence of the evil of untouchability' (26.10.47; 89:416). It was in South Africa that his inner voice had first suggested this connection to Gandhi. There he had been told by a friend — 'his mother was a Frenchwoman and his father an Englishman,' Gandhi recalled — a story that Gandhi relayed to leaders from Asia gathered in New Delhi in April 1947:

> There were three scientists who went out from France in search of truth . . . One of them found his way to India. He began to search. He went to the so-called cities of those times. He saw the so-called high-caste people, men and women, and he felt at a loss. Finally he went to a

humble cottage in a humble village. That was the cottage of a Bhangi (cleaner), and there he found the truth he was in search of (2.4.47; 87:191-2).

Less than three months later Gandhi dealt with a question put to him: 'Who will be the President of the Indian Republic? Should we not have Jawaharlal Nehru?' Said Gandhi:

If I have my way, the first President of the Indian Republic will be a chaste and brave Bhangi girl. If an English girl of 17 could become the British Queen and later even Empress of India, there is no reason why a Bhangi girl of robust love of her people and unimpeachable integrity of character should not become the first President . . .

She should be chaste as Sita and her eyes should rad-iate light. Sita had such radiance that Ravana could not touch her . . . If such a girl of my dreams becomes President, I shall be her servant . . . I shall make Jawaharlal, Sardar Patel and Rajen Babu her Ministers and therefore her servants (27.6.47; 89:223-5).

Though referring to Sita and Victoria, Gandhi may also have had Joan of Arc, young, unlettered and radiant, in mind. We have been that France and the wise Bhangi were together in his thoughts.

In September 1947 Gandhi returned to Delhi from Calcutta, where a fast by him had saved lives and restored some trust. Refugees from Pakistan were occupying the Balmiki colony space that he had become use to. Patel and others decided that he would have to live at Birla House. Gandhi thanked the Birlas, admitted that they had met his expenses at the Balmiki colony, but added that he was 'greatly pained' at the change of lodging (10.9.47; 89:167).

In December 1947 he spoke of the Harijans in Sind: 'If only Harijans were left behind in Sind and caste Hindus went away . . . the only condition for life then would be complete slavery and ultimate acceptance of Islam . . . [My correspondent] says if they (the Harijans) want to stay together at one place, they are not left in peace. Forced labour is extracted from them. They are told to clean lavatories, do the sweeping and so on.' Added Gandhi:

> A Bhangi should not be forced to clean lavatories today. If he can become a barrister, why should he be stopped? They must be free to act according to their inclination . . . [The Harijans in Sind] must be allowed to go about their business unhampered, otherwise they should be allowed to leave . . . If they say they have embraced Islam it is not to be accepted. It is only fear that makes them say so. All such conversions should be considered null and void (3.12.47; 90:167-9).

In December 1947 he backed a fast by Sane Guruji that enabled Harijans to enter Maharashtra's famed Pandharpur temple. When some priests started a counter-fast to revive the bar, Gandhi criticized them and expressed his view that 'as long as the Harijans were barred from the temple, it had not been really consecrated' (30.12.47; 90:327). Three days before his death he wrote an article for *Harijanbandhu* deploring the bar against Harijans in some Jain and Swaminarayan temples in Gujarat.

His last utterance in relation to the untouchables was about a Harijan basti in Ajmer. Rajkumari Amrit Kaur, the Health Minister, had seen it and described its pitiable condition to him. Gandhi referred to it in his post-prayer speech on 27 January:

> We have secured our independence but it is of no value if we cannot stop such a thing. And it can be done in a day. Can we not provide a piece of dry land for the Harijans? If they must remove garbage, . . . must they be also made to live in it? . . . We have become heartless (27.1.48; 90:508).

Right till the end, then, Gandhi was conscious of the difference between swaraj and humanity.

Chapter 9

Partition

IN THIS CHAPTER we will accompany Gandhi as India journeyed towards Independence and arrived also at Partition. We will look at his strategies and tactics to free India in unity, his mood, striving and discourse as Partition first loomed on the horizon and then seemed unavoidable, and the reasons for his failure to prevent it.

Gandhi's bid should be seen against the India he inherited. In his novel *Anandmath*, published when Gandhi was thirteen, Bankim Chandra Chatterjee had suggested that British rule was providential in design and destined to protect Hindus from Muslims. Similarly, Sayyid Ahmad Khan, who judged in 1857 that 'British sovereignty cannot be eliminated from India,' said at the time of the founding of the Indian National Congress: 'Now suppose that all the English were to leave India. Then who would be the rulers of India? Is it possible that two qaums — the Muslim and the Hindu — could sit on the same throne? Most certainly no . . . One of them will conquer the other . . .'[1]

Bankim did not speak for all Hindus, and on the Muslim side Badruddin Tyabji, for one, dissented from Sayyid Ahmad, but the notion of only two parties in conflict, one British and the other Indian, did not reflect Indian reality. John Strachey's poser about the India and the Indian comparable to European counterparts was easy to resent but hard to dispose of. The dispute over partitioning Bengal, occasioning the most fervent anti-Raj protests between the 1857 Rising and the emergence of Gandhi, found Hindus and Muslims ranged against one another. Hindus hated the 1905 partition, Muslims its 1911 annulment. Muhammad Ali said in 1911 that he was afraid of the 'Hindu symbolism and battlecries' in the Swadeshi campaign of the opponents of Bengal's partition.[2]

Other divides were almost as sharp. The outcastes were nervous about power moving from British to caste Hindu hands. In the South and in Maharashtra, lower castes were joining hands against Brahmins. Ruling more than 500 states, India's princes seemed suspicious of their subjects and of Congress's intentions. Owners of agricultural land were suspicious, if absentee lords, of tillers, and fearful, if small cultivators, of losing their holdings to town-based creditors. Communities coveting army or police jobs felt threatened by one another. For protection against rivals or adversaries, each Indian group, communal, caste or class, was inclined to turn to the Raj, thereby strengthening its hegemony, even while disliking its alienness and burden. Uniting Indians for dislodging it was a large and difficult project.

History offers both harmony and disharmony in Hindu-Muslim relations. In 1888, Lord Dufferin, the Viceroy, thought that India's 'most patent characteristic' was 'its division into two mighty political communities as distant from each other as the poles asunder.' Twelve years later, however, the Deputy Commissioner of the district of Rohtak in the Punjab noted that 'the Hindu and Mohammedan Jats and Hindu Goojars and Mohammedan Goojars think more of the common ancestors from whom they have descended than the fact that he is a Hindu or the other is a Mohammedan, and live in the same village with as much peace and good feeling towards one another as if they were members of the same race and religion.' Nine years later the *Economist* of London recorded the relevant truth that 'the political atom in India is not the individual but the community.'[3]

Evidence that Britain was glad of Indian divisions and used them is conclusive. A few quotes will suffice here. We can start with the well known entry in the diary of Lady Minto, the Viceroy's wife, that separate Muslim electorates (introduced in 1909) would mean the 'pulling back of 62 million people (the Muslim population at the time) from joining the ranks of the seditious opposition.' In 1925, Birkenhead, the Secretary of State, wrote to the Viceroy: 'I have placed my highest and most permanent hopes in the eternity of the communal situation.'

Churchill sent a message in 1937 to Linlithgow, the Viceroy, that he hoped that Muslims would be 'a counter-check' on Congress and that 'the Princes' India will preserve a separate entity.' He wanted, Churchill added, to 'preserve the British Empire for a few more generations in all its strength and splendour.' Any effort to 'unite' India was to Churchill 'distressing and repugnant in the last degree.'[4] Two years later, Linlithgow frankly told Zetland, the Secretary of State, that he was anxious to 'shepherd all the Muslims into the same fold,' that is, out of the Gandhi-led movement.[5]

A segment of Hindu opinion believed strongly in Hindu-Muslim incompatibility. Presiding at the 1937 session of the Hindu Mahasabha, Savarkar spoke of 'centuries of cultural, religious and national antagonism between the Hindus and the Muslims' and added: 'India cannot be assumed today to be a . . . homogeneous nation, but on the contrary there are two nations . . . the Hindus and the Muslims.'[6] In 1939, the chief of the Rashtriya Swayamsevak Sangh, Golwalkar, said that 'the real danger' was that Hindus had allowed themselves 'to be duped into believing . . . our old and bitter enemies (Muslims) to be our friends.' In his view, Muslims had 'either to merge themselves in the national race . . . or to live at the sweet will of the national race.' In the 1910s, 1920s and 1930s, men like Golwalkar and Savarkar warned Hindus that they were 'a dying race.'[7]

As for princely India, a leading ruler, the Jamsaheb of Nawanagar, said in 1946: 'Why should I not support the [Muslim] League? Mr Jinnah is willing to tolerate our existence, but Mr Nehru wants the extinction of the Princes.'[8]

Every critical phase of the freedom effort showed the trickiness of the exercise. We can look, for example, at Gandhi's response to the outbreak of the Second World War. In September 1939, Congress was in control in most Indian provinces, following elections held in early 1937, with British Governors possessing contingency powers. The centre was entirely British-run but the logic of power-sharing in the provinces pointed to a similar future arrangement in New Delhi. A delicate Congress-Raj compact overseen by Gandhi seemed capable of achieving a smooth if gradual transfer of power from British to Indian hands, though the Muslim League, after performing poorly in the 1937 elections, had succeeded in persuading many Muslims that Congress Raj was Hindu Raj. By stepping into Poland and inviting war, Adolf Hitler destroyed the carefully-nurtured Congress-Raj relationship.

The war was now the Raj's first priority but it ranked lower than independence in Indian hearts. Hitler might be more evil than the British but they, not he, ruled over India. Loss of office if Congress did not cooperate in the Raj's war, or loss of its standing among the Indian people if it did — this seemed the choice before Congress.

'I have never felt the weight of responsibility as heavily as I do today,' Gandhi said in *Harijan* (4.11.39; 70:315). Journeying from Wardha to Simla, he told Linlithgow, the Viceroy, that though he could not speak for Congress, his 'own sympathies were with England and France.' Referring to the meeting in a press statement on 5 September, Gandhi added:

> I told him that I could not contemplate without being stirred to the very depth the destruction of London . . . And as I was picturing before him the Houses of Parliament and the Westminster Abbey and their possible destruction, I broke down . . . It almost seems as if Herr Hitler knows no God but brute force and . . . will listen to nothing else. It is in the midst of this catastrophe without parallel that Congressmen and all other responsible Indians individually and collectively have to decide what part India is to play in this terrible drama (70:162).

Wanting, accordingly, to forge an Indian rather than a Congress response, Gandhi invited Jinnah, president of the Muslim League and a harsh critic of Congress, and Subhas Bose, who following a sharp dispute with Gandhi had resigned his Congress presidency and left Congress, to join in discussions. Jinnah did not come and Subhas, who did, proposed noncooperation with the war, but before continuing with the story let us note that on his way to Simla Gandhi was told by a big crowd at Delhi's railway station, 'We do not want any understanding' (70:161), and was attacked for his press statement. He was shedding 'no tears for the possible destruction of the monuments of Germany,' sympathizing 'with England and France and not with Germany' and doing 'an injustice to Hitler.' Gandhi replied that 'Herr Hitler is responsible for the war' and that his 'sympathy for England and France' was 'reasoned.' However, he clarified that his sympathy had 'no concrete value.' It was for the Working Committee to decide Congress's policy. The exchange evokes India's conflicts and dilemmas in 1939, and some of the shoals on her voyage to independence.

Jawaharlal was clear that Congress should break with the Raj unless independence was assured to India. Gandhi's suggestion that Congress should offer unconditional nonviolent support to Britain was shot down by the Working Committee. Patel and everybody else opposed it.

Gandhi wooed Jinnah. In a *Harijan* article published in early October, he recalled how Jinnah had once been 'the rising hope of the Congress,' and said that his role could 'not be forgotten.' The Muslim League was 'a great organization.' In New Delhi there were meetings involving Gandhi, Jinnah, Nehru, who was named chairman of a Congress committee (consisting of Patel, Azad and himself) formed to respond to the Raj's war policies, and Prasad, who had taken over as Congress president from Subhas. For a moment it seemed that Congress and the League might speak with one voice but the hope was belied.

Unwilling to hasten independence, the Raj cultivated the League, the princes, and opponents of Congress like Ambedkar. Linlithgow was candid in letters to London and also in some of his talks with Congress leaders. 'If Congress does not support me,' he told Patel in October, 'I'll have to take the Muslims' help' (*Patel*: 284). As we saw earlier, Linlithgow sought also 'to shepherd all the Muslims into the same fold' — the League.

By the end of November all Congress ministries were out of office. On 1 December Jinnah and Ambedkar jointly celebrated Deliverance Day. In March the following year the Muslim League passed its Pakistan resolution. A year later, at the League's session in Madras, Jinnah espoused a Dravidian nation in the south of the subcontinent, in addition to reiterating the Muslim homeland demand.

The war had come on top of several pulls and counterpulls. In 1939, Rajas and subjects were in conflict in Travancore and the Himalayan states. Socialists were asking Congress to turn left. The opening of Madura's famed Meenakshi temple to Harijans had sparked orthodox ire. Possessing a large following, Subhas complained that Congress was not combative enough towards Britain.

Sensing an ominous turn to the Hindu-Muslim question, Gandhi held discussions in July 1939 with Punjab's Premier, Sikandar Hyat Khan, who headed the province's pro-farmer Unionist party but was associated with the Muslim League at the all-India level. The Unionists had defeated both Congress and the League in the 1937 elections and sounded less nationalistic than either, but Gandhi knew they held vital cards. Gandhi praised Sikandar Hyat's 'solution' of the Hindu-Muslim tangle as 'the only proposal of a constructive character on behalf of the League,' while saying he could not fully agree with it (Letter of 17.7.39; 70:4). The talks were inconclusive and overtaken by the war.

Also in July 1939, in Abbottabad in the Frontier province, Gandhi addressed Muslims who had stood with him and Congress: 'If you could dissect my heart, you would find that the prayer and spiritual striving for the attainment of Hindu-Muslim unity goes on there unceasingly all the twenty-four hours without even a moment's interruption, whether I am awake or asleep.' We should note the fourfold underscoring. His striving, he claims, goes on all the 24 hours; it is unceasing; it is never interrupted; it is a night and day thing. Added Gandhi:

> Let no one imagine that because the Hindus constitute the majority community, they can win swaraj for India . . .

without the backing of the other communities . . . That
dream (of Hindu-Muslim unity) has filled my being since
my earliest childhood . . . I resign myself utterly to His
grace. Who knows, in spite of my incessant heartprayer,
I may not be found worthy for this great work . . . We do
not know when or on whom His choice may fall . . . Pray
for me that my dream may be fulfilled in my lifetime . . .
May our passion for independence prove a uniting bond
stronger than all the differences that divide us (70:22-4).

He bares and uses his heart; but his political instinct is also at work.
The League's Pakistan resolution is nine months away but Gandhi
has realized that he must bid for the Muslims of the Frontier and the
Punjab. They could bolt.

✳

But we should look at earlier history too. In 1916, Congress, formed
in 1885, and the League, born in 1906, had agreed in Lucknow to
strive jointly for 'early self-government' on the basis of direct elections, separate electorates for Muslims and Sikhs, and quotas for
religious minorities in provincial and central asemblies. Resentment at separate Muslim electorates that the Raj had announced in
1909 was laid aside by Congress for the sake of political unity.
Tilak and Annie Besant were the pact's architects on the Congress
side, and Jinnah and Fazlul Huq for the League. (But Jinnah was
also in the Congress, one of its leaders, in fact.) Having arrived in
1915 from South Africa, Gandhi attended the Lucknow deliberations, endorsed the pact and collected thousands of signatures in
Gujarat for a memorandum asking the Raj to implement it.

The First World War and the Balkan wars preceding it had created the climate for the accord. We have seen in previous chapters
that Muslims in India sympathized with Turkey, the world's premier Islamic state, its ruler the caliph or khalifa of Sunni Muslims
everywhere and the custodian of Islam's holy places. Turkey's humiliations in the Balkan wars had hurt India's Muslims and turned

them against the British, who were seen as anti-Turk. A member of Congress from 1906 and an ardent nationalist, Jinnah joined the League in 1913 because of the Turkey-related ferment. When Turkey aligned itself with Germany in the First World War, India's Muslims were reluctant to provide soldiers for the Empire, but did so when assured that Turkey would not be unfairly treated.

Among the champions of Turkey and the caliphate or Khilafat were the Ali brothers, Shaukat and Muhammad. The Raj detained them in 1915 and did not release them until the end of 1919, but Muhammad Ali was the League's president in absentia for its 1917 session in Calcutta.

This background is necessary for an understanding of the Gandhi-led noncooperation movement of 1920-22, which emphasized the Muslim demand for Khilafat's restoration. Until this juncture, Gandhi's agenda had seemed utterly secular or non-religious. He had defended the rights of railway passengers in Viramgam (Gujarat) in 1915, of indigo cultivators in Champaran (North Bihar) in 1917, of peasants in Gujarat's Kheda district in 1918, and of Ahmedabad's textile workers in 1918. In 1919 he had led a nationwide defence of free speech against curbs prescribed by the Rowlatt Act.

In 1920 Khilafat and Swaraj became the twin goals of the widespread Hindu-Muslim movement, led by Gandhi, of noncooperation with the Raj. India was astir as never before and the Empire was jolted, but after the February 1922 violence of Chauri Chaura Gandhi called off the movement, which was also hurt by Khilafat's decline and demise in Turkey.

The movement's suspension was followed by Hindu-Muslim violence and mistrust. There were Hindu charges that Muslims mouthed noncooperation but hung on to links with the Raj, and identical counter-charges. The suspicion that existed even during the struggle is indicated in a remark by Ikram, the Pakistani historian, about a fatwa in the Punjab asking Muslims to leave the Raj's police and army: 'The fatwa was widely hailed by the Hindu newspapers of the Punjab, who had complained of the Muslim preponderance in the police and the army, but it had no serious results, as very few soldiers and policemen obeyed it' (*UMM:* 101).

We should be able, more than seventy years later, to identify the lesson left by the controversial Khilafat movement. It has been diversely interpreted. In one view, Gandhi consciously egged the Muslims on because he wanted them injured in a clash with the Raj. In another, Gandhi appeased Muslim extremists. The fact that Jinnah left Congress at the end of December 1920 is cited to suggest that Gandhi encouraged communal Muslims against secular ones such as Jinnah, thereby estranging him, and the start of Pakistan is seen in Gandhi's endorsement of Khilafat.

There is no evidence, however, to suggest that Hindu-Muslim relations would have turned for the better if Gandhi, Congress and other Hindus had refrained from supporting Khilafat. No matter how strange or purposeless it may seem in hindsight, the Muslim passion over Turkey and Khilafat was a powerful reality owing nothing to Gandhi. It was a factor in Jinnah's 1913 decision to join the Muslim League, and in Tilak's 1916 decision to sponsor a pact that conceded separate electorates. Jinnah's 1920 difference with Gandhi was not over Khilafat. In September 1920 he spoke of 'the spoliation of the Ottoman empire and the Khilafat, a matter of life and death' (*UMM:* 133). He was not opposed, in principle, to non-cooperation either. What he was opposed to was the changing of Congress's goal from 'Swaraj within the Empire' to just 'Swaraj,' and to Gandhi's willingness to experiment with mass defiance of laws.

If there is no evidence that Congress or Hindu aloofness from Khilafat would have improved Hindu-Muslim relations, there is none either that the pre-Gandhian technique of lawful protest would have kept Hindu-Muslim relations on an even keel. Communal mistrust was neither created nor intensified by satyagraha or civil disobedience. Sayyid Ahmad Khan's sharp opposition to the 'constitutional' Congress and the bitterness over partitioning Bengal antedated satyagraha by years. The lesson, rather, is that a joint struggle against the British was an inadequate cement for the Hindu-Muslim relationship.

In the absence of trust, a struggle for freedom would have aroused suspicions irrespective of whether the struggle was lawful or defiant of laws, peaceful or violent, focussed on Khilafat, Jallianwala, land revenue, democratic rights, the salt tax or something else. Gandhi was wrong not in asking Congress and the Hindus to stand with India's Muslims over Khilafat (another freedom-loving Hindu leader might have done the same, and what Tilak said in 1920 and did in 1916 was not very different), but in thinking that 'passion for independence' could 'prove a uniting bond stronger than all the differences that divide us.'

In the years to follow, Gandhi would never regret his Khilafat role. And although many of Congress's Muslims allies of 1920-22 drifted away in succeeding years, including the Ali brothers, some key figures drawn by Congress's stand over Khilafat remained with it, including Hakim Ajmal Khan, Dr Mukhtar Ahmad Ansari and Maulana Abul Kalam Azad, serving the cause of Hindu-Muslim unity.

❈

Tension between the goals of independence and Hindu-Muslim unity was to dog every subsequent movement. In December 1928, Congress and the League had come close to an agreement on a constitution based on joint electorates and reserved seats for Muslims and Sikhs but were unable to bridge differences over Punjab and Bengal and the percentage of Muslim seats in a central assembly. Gandhi said that though in favour himself of meeting the Muslim demands, he was unable to persuade Hindus in Punjab and Bengal, and the Sikhs, to yield. Jinnah said he was personally willing to accept Congress's offer but helpless when other Muslims were not. By this time most Congressmen were athirst for a fight with the Raj, and Gandhi chose to design and lead that fight, shelving the Hindu-Muslim question. Jinnah spoke of December 1928 as 'the parting of the ways.'

Congress's 1930 fight against the Raj followed. Ansari, who had been Congress President in 1927, urged Gandhi to postpone it until Muslim anxieties were allayed, but the pull of independence was irresistible. Featuring the salt satyagraha, the 1930 fight was dramatic and nationwide. It impinged on the world's consciousness, but except in the Frontier province the Muslim qaum did not offer large numbers to it, a noteworthy item in the story of Partition.

Another crucial year was 1937, when, paradoxically or not, Congress's large electoral triumphs and the Muslim League's failures injured Indian unity. Congress obtained a clear majority in six out of eleven provinces and was the largest single party in three others. The Muslim League won only 109 of the 482 Muslim seats (its best performances being in Bengal, the U.P. and Bombay). Congress secured 26 Muslim seats, mostly in the N.W.F.P., where it formed a ministry. The League's display was particularly poor in the three provinces that had large Muslim majorities, the Punjab, where it won only a single seat, Sind, where it secured three, and the N.W.F.P. The farmer-based Unionist Party took most of the Punjab's Muslim seats and independents triumphed in Sind.

Defeats in the Punjab, Sind and the N.W.F.P. seemed to spur the League to champion, in those provinces, the Islamic card, to cultivate the Pirs, religious leaders with large rural followings, and to change its image of a purely urban party. In the eight provinces where Congress formed ministries, the League painted Congress as a Hindu force. Thanks to the League's skilful propaganda and Congress's blunders, Hindu Raj, which was neither India's reality nor Congress's wish, became the Muslim perception in 1937-9.

Gandhi was no longer a member of Congress. He had resigned in 1934 to encourage frankness in discussions which he felt his presence was inhibiting, and to enable Congress's conservative, socialist, Gandhiite and other factions to discover their separate strengths. Gandhi was willing to guide Congress if asked or in a contingency, but Congress's decisions were increasingly being taken without him. Nehru, Patel, Azad, Rajendra Prasad and Rajagopalachari were prominent among those making Congress's day-to-day decisions. Gandhi was not involved, for example, in the selection of Congress's candidates in the provincial elections of early 1937, or in the subsequent choice of Premiers and ministers. But he was instrumental in Congress's decision to form these ministries under the Government of India Act of 1935, hitherto denounced by Congress.

In strategic U.P., the League was willing to join a Congress-led government but the province's Congress leaders, backed by Nehru and Azad, stipulated unacceptable conditions. As Azad tells the story in his *India Wins Freedom,* Nehru, intervening unexpectedly, reduced an offer of two cabinet seats for the League to one. According to Khaliquzzaman, who was the League's president in the province, the deal collapsed because Azad wanted the League legislature party to dissolve itself and merge with Congress's group.

A partnership was also explored in Bombay. This was at the instance of Jinnah, who however had disapproved of the U.P. talks. The Bombay negotiations fell through because Patel insisted on a merger, whereas Jinnah demanded a coalition. K.M. Munshi, who became Minister for Law and Order in the Bombay ministry led by B.G. Kher, has written that League ministers in any coalition would have been 'at the disposal of Jinnah to obstruct, defy or sabotage' the ministry.[9] But this was not true of the U.P., where Khaliquzzaman, who had left the Raj's courts during the non-cooperation stir of 1920-22, and his colleague in the U.P. League, Nawab Ismail Khan, were willing to cooperate with Congress if their group's identity was protected, and if it received due representation in the cabinet.

To Muslims in the U.P., Congress's 1937 ministry seemed unrelievedly Hindu and strange. The historian Muhammad Mujeeb, who chose to remain in India after partition, has recalled his first impressions of the U.P. assembly:

> It was, I believe, the inaugural session. There were crowds of people in the visitors' galleries and the hall, but hardly a face that was known to me. I was simple-minded enough to ask a man standing next to me where the chief minister was, and I got in reply a reproachful look and the remark, 'Can't you see he is sitting there?' I felt extremely uncomfortable. I could not spot anyone dressed like me, the language spoken around me was not the Urdu which I thought was the language of Lucknow . . . I left the assembly building with a feeling of mingled panic and disgust.[10]

Gandhi's secretary and biographer, Pyarelal, has written that the exclusion of the League from Congress's 1937 ministries was 'a tactical error of the first magnitude' and a 'decision of the Congress High Command taken against Gandhiji's best judgment' (*Last Phase* 1:76). At this juncture the High Command comprised Nehru, the Congress President, and a three-man committee consisting of Patel (chairman), Azad and Rajendra Prasad. Each of the three was assigned provinces. The U.P. fell in the care of Azad, who was also given the task of choosing Muslim ministers in all provinces. Pant, who became the U.P. Premier, played a major role in the talks with the provincial League, which were also influenced by, among others, Purshottamdas Tandon, Speaker in the new legislature, who tended to champion Hindu interests.

There is a note of urgency in a letter dated 10 July 1937 from Gandhi to Nehru about Muslim ministers in the provinces. Also raising the question of Urdu, the letter reveals Gandhi's anxiety to address Muslim misgivings on that score (12.7.37; 65:380). Twelve days later Gandhi again writes to Nehru, this time mentioning a draft of an agreement between Congress and League members of the U.P. legislature that Azad had shown him: 'I thought it was a good draft. But he (Azad) told me that whilst you liked it, Tandonji did not. I have written to the latter about it . . . What is the objection?' (22.7.37; 65:427). The letter to Tandon does not seem to be available, and we do not know of anything more conveyed on the subject by Gandhi to the Congress High Command.

Penderel Moon, a member of the Indian Civil Service (ICS), mentions Congress's failure to cooperate with the League in 1937 as 'the prime cause of the creation of Pakistan,' and Frank Moraes has argued that 'Pakistan might have never come into being had Congress handled the League more tactfully' after the 1937 elections.[11] Gandhi seemed to concede something like this during a talk with Wavell in December 1945. According to the Viceroy:

> I said . . . that the increase in communal feeling was mainly
> due to the action of Congress Ministries in 1937-9 which
> had made the Muslims feel they could not get a square
> deal from Congress and had caused the rise of the Muslim
> League and the idea of Pakistan. He (Gandhi) defended

> the Congress Ministries at some length and said all
> Governors had admitted their fairness. I said there was
> no doubt about the psychological effect on the Muslims,
> whatever the facts may have been; and he admitted this
> (*Journal*: 193).

Soon after the start of the Second World War, in a remark related to the Hindu-Muslim question though not addressed to the 1937 U.P. talks, Gandhi had evidently admitted to Linlithgow too that Congress could have 'done better, and been wiser.'[12]

Any judgment of the 1937 events has to consider Jinnah and his reactions. Going by what he said in 1936-7 and later, Jinnah would have agreed only to a coalition of ministers from 'the Hindu Congress' and the Muslim League, with each set obedient to its High Command.[13] Such an arrangement of divided loyalties was as unacceptable to Congress as the insistence that Congress could only speak for Hindus. From its first day it was the Indian National Congress rather than a Hindu Congress. Muslims had often led it and belonged to it in large numbers. We have seen that in the 1937 elections, 26 Muslims had been elected to provincial assemblies on the Congress ticket. In the U.P., the League won 27 out of 64 Muslim seats and the Congress none, though two Congress Muslims were elected from general seats.

The Bombay League gave unquestioned obedience to Jinnah, but in 1937 his influence over the U.P. League was a good deal less. However, Congress squandered the opportunity for an accord that might have undermined separatism in the U.P. In the event the drive for Pakistan was fuelled by Muslims of the U.P. — by leaders left out of the ministry and by Muslims in the province unable to identify with it.

The coalition talks failed not because, as Azad alleges, Nehru halved Congress's offer from two seats to one. He seems to have done no such thing. In a letter he wrote to Rajendra Prasad on 21 July 1937, Nehru said: 'We came to the conclusion that we should offer stringent conditions to the U.P. Muslim League group and if they accepted them in toto then we would agree to two ministers from their group. Besides them one minister would be Rafi Ahmed Kidwai.'

The letter makes it clear that the 'we' meant Nehru, Azad, Pant, Kripalani, the U.P.-based general secretary of the all-India Congress, and Narendra Deva, the socialist. Other records, including Khaliquazzaman's autobiography, corroborate Nehru's statement in the letter that Congress asked for 'the winding up of the Muslim League group in the U.P. and its absorption in the Congress.' There is evidence that Azad too sought this 'winding up.'[14]

Moreover, Hindus in the U.P. Congress, forming its bulk, did not fancy three Muslims in a cabinet of six — two from the League and Congress's Kidwai. Congress Muslims, their loyalty proved in trying times, disliked being upstaged by the League. The Jamiat-ul-Ulema, a Muslim faction which had left the League for the Congress shortly before the Congress-League talks, also threw its weight against a deal with the League. So did U.P.'s leftist Muslims, who viewed the League as pro-feudal.

Narrow dislikes combined together and shortsightedness prevailed. For this outcome Gandhi must take his share of responsibility. We need not question Pyarelal's observation that Congress's leaders went against Gandhi's 'best judgment.' Yet Gandhi's inability to bring them round remains. In 1937, the attention he gave to the Hindu-Muslim equation did not match his concern with Congress's equation with the Raj. Because the League had no representation in Congress's ministries, the false charge that Congress was anti-Muslim was the more easily believed by the Muslim community.

Jinnah and the League pressed their allegations from the middle of 1937 until the resignation of Congress ministries: Muslims were being squeezed out of government jobs; Muslim children risked being Hinduized in state schools; Urdu was being sacrificed; it was the start of Hindu Raj; and so on. None of the Governors, who were all British, endorsed the allegations, which were exaggerated when they were not baseless, and Jinnah refused Congress's offer of a judicial inquiry. Linlithgow told Jinnah privately in October 1939 that there was no evidence of 'any positive instance of real repression.' Later, in January 1942, Linlithgow recalled the allegation and told Amery, the Secretary of State for India, that he 'never took these complaints seriously.'[15]

A secret Raj inquiry initiated by Linlithgow reached the following conclusion: 'As a rule the Ministries showed themselves ready to accept the Governor's advice and even to err on the side of generosity in the hope of disarming Muslim hostility, but some ministers had difficulty in overcoming an instinctive communal bias; and in some provinces the Hindu Congressmen in the countryside used all opportunities for arrogant behaviour.'[16]

This was close to an exoneration of Congress, but Linlithgow took care not to release the finding. The Raj had no stake in Hindu-Muslim unity, yet Congress, which did, was blinded by the power coming to it in 1937. The tone of the passage quoted from Nehru's July 1937 letter to Prasad reveals Congress's smugness. Backed by most Congressmen, Nehru, Patel, Azad and Pant seemed cool or opposed to an agreement with the League that preserved the latter's identity.

Gandhi could not override them, or defy the sentiment of Congress's supporters in the U.P., who were preponderantly Hindu.

❋

By the late 1930s, Gandhi's standing among the Muslims had fallen greatly from its level during the Khilafat stir, when Muhammad Ali had said: 'After the Prophet, on whom be peace, I consider it my duty to carry out the commands of Gandhiji' (*UMM*: 100). Now the focus was on Gandhi's Hinduness. That he was called a Mahatma, wore a Hindu's garment (even if that of a poor Hindu peasant), used the term Ram Rajya for an ideal future society, and drew on past Hindu models for steadfastness, constituted proof, it was alleged, of his alienness for Muslims. It was connected, in the League's propaganda, to the description by some Congress ministers of schools as 'temples' of learning, the singing, at government functions, of songs that were patriotic to Hindus but sounded Hindu to the Muslim ear, and the use by some ministers of Sanskritized Hindi. The package was presented as an early version of Hindu Raj.

Ainslee Embree, among others, has argued that Gandhi's 'use of a religious vocabulary — inevitably Hindu in origin' damaged the prospects of Indian unity. Yet in 1920-22 Gandhi's Hindu idiom seemed more of an asset than an obstacle: it helped ensure Hindu India's support for Khilafat. It was only when Gandhi lacked powerful Muslim allies that his Hindu idiom was noticed as divisive. William Shirer, the American journalist and author, argued with Gandhi that by 'inculcating so much Hindu religion in his Indian politics' Gandhi had 'kept the majority of Muslims out of his nationalist movement.' Revising his judgment, Shirer later wrote that Gandhi's Hindu idiom was 'the only way he could arouse the masses, at least the Hindu masses of India, which formed the great majority . . . Millenniums of adhering through thick and thin to Hinduism and its way of life had prepared them to follow a great religious leader, especially a saintly one who lived among them in their poverty and rags as one of them' (202-3).

Without his religious symbols Gandhi might not have touched the Hindu masses; yet after the Khilafat phase the symbols were seized upon to separate him from the Muslim masses. The deaths of Ajmal Khan (1927) and Dr Ansari (1936) removed links between Gandhi and the Muslim community that were not easy to replace. By the time Maulana Azad filled the vacuum, a distorted Gandhi had been sold to the community. Abdul Ghaffar Khan remained a valiant ally but with influence limited to the N.W.F.P.

Others before Gandhi had used Hindu symbols, notably Tilak in the late 1890s and Aurobindo Ghosh just thereafter. Tilak had invoked Ganpati and Aurobindo, Durga. Gandhi took greater care than Tilak or Aurobindo to assure Muslims that they had nothing to fear from his Hinduness. The last thing he wished to do was to frighten them, or to incite Hindus against them. Bringing Hindus and Muslims closer was one reason why he wanted to reach the Hindu heart, which his Hinduness enabled him to do. We have seen, too, that his satyagrahas from Champaran to Dandi had been for non-religious goals.

Gandhi took every chance to explain his Hinduness to Muslims, but he could not give it up without losing out on all fronts. He knew his India too well to think that her masses, Hindu or Muslim, could be stirred by men or movements divorced from their faiths or disdainful of their cultural and religious inheritance. This inheritance would need touchstones of ethics and commonsense, yet it could not be thrown overboard.

✵

If Congress's spell in provincial office had an unintended psychological effect on Muslims, its departure from office following the start of the war and subsequent campaigns against the Raj reduced the distance between the League and the British.

While Congress demanded a declaration of independence, Jinnah asked for a British assurance that no political step in India would be taken without the League's consent. In February 1940 he said that India was not one nation but two, and in March the League's 'Pakistan' resolution was passed in Lahore, though the word was not used. It asked for the demarcation of 'geographically contiguous units' into 'regions which should be so constituted, with such territorial adjustments as may be necessary, that the areas in which Muslims are numerically in a majority as in the North-Western and Eastern zones of India should be grouped to constitute "Independent States" in which the constituent units shall be autonomous and sovereign.'

Sikandar Hyat Khan, the Punjab Premier, who had affiliated the Unionist Muslims to the League in the latter part of 1937 (a significant index of Muslim feeling linked in part to the failure of Congress statesmanship in the U.P.), did not challenge the resolution in Lahore but spoke out a few months later in the Punjab Assembly: 'We do not ask for freedom, that there may be a Muslim raj here and Hindu raj elsewhere. If that is what Pakistan means I will have nothing to do with it.'[17]

Before the passage of the Lahore resolution, Sikandar had denounced the Pakistan idea to a British civilian, Penderel Moon, who had spoken favourably of it. His eyes 'blazing with indignation,' Sikandar had said: 'How can you talk like this? You have been long enough in Western Punjab to know the Muslims there. Surely you can see that Pakistan would be an invitation to them to cut the throat of every Hindu bania.'[18] Doubtless Sikandar knew that throat-cutting would not be a one-sided affair.

Gandhi joined issue at once with the Lahore resolution. He would not accept, he said, that a different religion meant a different nationality, or that 'Muslims, when it comes to a matter of actual decision, will ever want vivisection.' He added: 'Their good sense will prevent them. Their self-interest will deter them. Their religion will forbid the obvious suicide which the partition would mean . . . I make bold to say that [Jinnah] and those who think like him are rendering no service to Islam; they are misinterpreting the message inherent in the very word Islam.'

Calling the Pakistan idea 'an untruth,' Gandhi said 'there can be no compromise with it.' But he added that if all the Muslims desired it, Partition would come. 'Compelling the obedience of eight crores of Muslims to the will of the rest of India, however powerful a majority the rest may represent,' was not possible (*Harijan*, 6.4.40 and 4.5.40). He would oppose Partition and urge the Muslims to see its folly, but he ruled out coercion. It was not his or Congress's way; others might try it but he did not think it would work. 'The Muslims must have the same right of self-determination that the rest of India has. We are at present a joint family. Any member may claim a division.' But this could only happen after independence as an arrangement among Indians. It would be immoral for the League to demand Pakistan before independence or for the British to support it.

Six months earlier, when a Muslim correspondent claimed that India was not one and that Muslims were a separate nation, Gandhi had said:

> Why is India not one nation? Was it not one during, say, the Moghul period? Is India composed of two nations? If so, why only two? Are not Christians a third, Parsis a fourth, and so on? Are the Muslims of China a nation separate from the other Chinese? Are the Muslims of

England a different nation from the other English? How are the Muslims of the Punjab different from the Hindus and the Sikhs? Are they not all Punjabis, drinking the same water, breathing the same air and deriving sustenance from the same soil? . . . And what is to happen to the handful of Muslims living in the numerous villages where the population is predominantly Hindu, and conversely to Hindus where, as in the Frontier Province or Sind, they are a handful? The way suggested by the correspondent is the way of strife (*Harijan,* 28.10.39).

In September 1940 Gandhi was impassioned: 'To divide [India] into two is worse than anarchy. It is a vivisection which cannot be tolerated. I will say to them, "Vivisect me before you vivisect India. You will not do what even the Moghuls did not do" ' (*Harijan,* 22.9.40). Yet a few months earlier he had sounded less definite: 'If God so desires it, I may have to become a helpless victim to the undoing of my dream. But I do not believe that the Muslims want to dismember India' (*Harijan,* 4.5.40).

Though he did not say so, Gandhi knew that Britain could prevent partition by conceding Congress's demand for an assurance of independence. But Congress's stand against imperialism had not pleased the British establishment, and Gandhi's claim that there was an India beyond religions and castes that he represented had not gone down well either. Indian unity had its devotees in the Raj, but they thought it a British gift; an Indian assertion of unity independent of the British was presumptuous.

Some years after Indian independence, facing issues of decolonization in Africa, Britain came up with the principle of NIBMAR, or No Independence Before Majority Rule. If NIBMAR had been applied to India, partition would have been avoided; but for India HMG's principle was No Majority Rule Before An Indian Consensus.

Prime Minister from May 1940, Winston Churchill was determined, even in the thick of the war with Hitler, to show Gandhi and Congress their place. The so-called 'August Offer,' Britain's first formal response to the demands of Congress and the League, made it plain that a national government or an announcement of independence was not to be considered, but if Congress, the League and the princes all agreed, some politicians might be taken on the Executive Council of the Viceroy, who however would retain the last word. It declared also that HMG 'could not contemplate transfer of their present responsibilities for the peace and welfare of India to any system of government whose authority is denied by large and powerful elements in India's national life.'

To underscore what was meant, the new Secretary of State for India, Leopold Amery, told Parliament that 'foremost among [the powerful] elements stands the great Muslim community of ninety million, constituting a majority both in North-Western and North-Eastern India.' The veto that Jinnah had asked for had been provided.

The fall of France in the spring of 1940 had led to a temporary yet significant split between Gandhi and the Congress Working Committee. Arguing that the loss of France might make Britain more generous towards India, Rajagopalachari proposed support for the war effort in exchange for a national government in India, and won enough allies to carry the Working Committee. They included Abul Kalam Azad, who at Gandhi's suggestion, made in the light of the Muslim question, had become Congress President, but Patel was Rajagopalachari's 'greatest prize,' to use Gandhi's phrase.

Ahimsa had made Gandhi hesitant, but more decisive in his mind was his appraisal, after a three-hour talk with the Viceroy, that Britain was in no mood to act handsomely by Congress and in fact seemed to prefer an understanding with the Muslim League to foil it. Jawaharlal stayed on Gandhi's side, as did Ghaffar Khan and Kripalani, but a majority backed Rajagopalachari. After the 'August Offer,' Patel, Azad and the Working Committee returned to Gandhi. Patel said he would 'never again' desert Gandhi and added: 'Let power go to others today' (*Patel:* 295). However, his colleagues' 'secession,' as he called it, brief as it was, troubled Gandhi deeply. He lamented his failure to retain them, felt it suggested moral or spiritual weakness in himself, and noted his colleagues' interest in office. Their separation from him foreshadowed 1946 and 1947.

Subhas Bose, enjoying wide support despite his resignation from Congress, complained that Congress was doing nothing. While disagreeing on many issues with Bose, Jawaharlal also favoured defying the Raj. Yet, as Gandhi put it, defiance would hurt the British people 'at a time when it is a question of life and death for them' (72:20). Also, it would bring the Raj and the League closer to each other, and could spark off Hindu-Muslim violence.

Gandhi's solution was selective disobedience by disciplined and prominent satyagrahis. By the summer of 1941, nearly 15,000 were in prison as a result of this campaign of individual satyagraha. Most of them had been chosen by Gandhi himself. He saw to it that there was no violence and also that no satyagrahi troubled the Raj during the 1940-1 Christmas season. The skilful exercise dramatized India's wish for freedom but left the field unaltered.

Sikandar Hyat made a bid for an understanding between Congress and the League in the summer of 1941. His proposal was taken to Rajagopalachari, who was in a southern prison, by Kasturi Srinivasan, editor of *The Hindu*. Rajagopalachari responded favourably but, apparently influenced by British civil servants around him, Sikandar abandoned his initiative.[19] Linlithgow ticked off the Governor of Madras, Hope, for allowing Srinivasan to meet Rajagopalachari without a Raj functionary being present: 'Perhaps you would let me know,' the Viceroy wrote, 'whether Srinivasan was allowed to see Rajagopalachariar alone or whether anyone was present. I do not want to go too far in the direction of facilitating formulations of policy or of tactics . . . in jail.'[20] Especially when the goal was a Congress-League accord.

❋

Almost all the prisoners were out by 7 December 1941, when Japan attacked Pearl Harbor and began its sweep across the Pacific. Once more Rajagopalachari thought that the moment when Britain would want to settle with Congress had arrived. Once more he won the

Working Committee to his view, though Patel did not join him this time, and Nehru remained opposed to an approach to the Raj. Despite his disagreement with the Rajagopalachari line, Gandhi asked the AICC, meeting in Wardha in January 1942, to ratify the Working Committee's decision: 'That nothing is to be expected from the Government is probably too true . . . Only the resolution puts the Congress right with the expectant world. It is no longer open to the Government to say that Congress has banged the door to negotiation on the impossible ground of nonviolence' (*Harijan*, 25.1.42).

General Chiang Kai-shek, ruler of China, came to India in February 1942 and talked with Linlithgow, Gandhi and Nehru. Wanting an Indo-British accord for the sake of China's defence against Japan, for which India was a crucial theatre, he urged Churchill to make a move towards Gandhi. A stronger voice, that of Roosevelt, the American President, had been telling Churchill the same thing, but the British Premier was resistant. His hand was forced, however, by the fall of Britain's great eastern bastion, Singapore, on 15 February, and of Rangoon on 7 March.

On 11 March Churchill announced that his cabinet colleague and the leader of the House of Commons, Sir Stafford Cripps, would visit India with a proposal. In view of Roosevelt's promptings a package had to be offered to India, but Churchill was hopeful that Indian parties would quarrel over it. Even so he made sure that it was attractive to Congress's Indian foes. Since Cripps belonged to Labour's Left wing, was a friend of Nehru's and, like Gandhi, a vegetarian, and seemed capable, for these and other reasons, of going beyond his brief, Churchill also instructed the Viceroy, Linlithgow, and the Commander-in-Chief, Wavell, to keep him independently informed of Cripps's negotiations with the Indian leaders.

At first sight the package that Cripps carried was not without appeal. India was offered full dominion status, with the right to declare independence, at the end of the war; a post-war Constituent Assembly filled by nominees of provincial legislatures and of the princes; and, right away, a national government composed of representatives of the leading parties. But Gandhi rejected it at once, for the package also allowed each existing provincial legislature and prince to declare independence at the end of the war.

Though Gandhi left New Delhi for Wardha after a single meeting with Cripps, the Congress Working Committee held lengthy negotiations with him. The Working Committee members did not like the clause providing for the independence ('non-accession') of parts of India, but an immediate national government was unquestionably attractive, especially when Cripps indicated that it would function like a cabinet, with the Viceroy no more than a constitutional head. Later Cripps denied that he had conveyed this, but Azad and Nehru, Congress's principal negotiators, claimed that he had, and Wavell has recorded what Linlithgow told him in 1943: 'Cripps did not play straight over the question of the Viceroy's veto and cabinet responsibility and did make some offer to Congress' (*Journal*: 33).

Congress's talks with Cripps failed over the status of the proposed new government and also over the Defence portfolio. While conceding a British Defence Minister, Congress wanted an Indian to be associated with Defence as well. Cripps again seemed willing, but Churchill cabled him that he would accept no arrangement regarding Defence that did not have the full agreement, directly communicated to him, of Linlithgow and Wavell. The Viceroy and the C-in-C expressed opposition to Congress's proposal, and the Cripps mission ended.

Many an account quotes Gandhi as having described Cripps's offer as 'a postdated cheque on a crashing bank.' But the last four words were never uttered. 'I had of course said nothing of the kind,' Gandhi told Ghanshyam Das Birla when Birla confronted him with the words.[21] They emanated from an imaginative journalist.[22] All the same, this was an occasion when Gandhi and Churchill agreed. 'When Mr Churchill learned of the breakdown of the Delhi negotiations he put on an act of sham tears and sorrow before his guests at Chequers, not troubling to conceal his own pleasure.'[23]

The Congress Working Committee resolution rejecting the Cripps offer contained an implicit acceptance of Pakistan, even if not of the kind Jinnah may have had in mind. (Until September 1944, Jinnah did not spell out his Pakistan. Vagueness about it attracted all Muslims, including those in areas where they were in a minority.) After expressing disapproval of the provision for the non-accession of provinces and princely states, the Working Committee added:

'Nevertheless, the Committee cannot think in terms of compelling the people of any territorial unit to remain in an Indian Union against their declared and established will ... Acceptance of this principle inevitably involves that no changes should be made which would result in fresh problems being created and compulsion being exercised on other substantial groups within that area.'[24]

The first sentence concedes secession after an Indian Union has been formed. The second protects parts or portions of seceding provinces against compulsion; if these parts or portions do not wish to secede, their wishes too should be respected.

Gandhi was not present when the resolution was drafted, but we have seen that he had made similar observations when Pakistan was first demanded. Coercion was not an option he wished to retain, or concede.

HMG's suggestion, made to win Jinnah, that at the end of the war a province could opt for independence strengthened the League in the Punjab and other Muslim-majority provinces. Jinnah welcomed the provision as an implicit acceptance of Pakistan but, following Congress's rejection of the Cripps offer, turned down the package as well. He said the right of self-determination should have been given to 'the Muslim nation,' not to a province.

Comments that Gandhi made on the Pakistan demand after Cripps's departure revealed his difficulty. On 19 April he said: 'If the vast majority of Muslims regard themselves as a separate nation, no power on earth can compel them to think otherwise' (*Harijan*, 19.4.42). On 26 July, however, he said that no country would willingly consent to secession because the new 'sovereign state can conceivably go to war against the one of which it was but yesterday a part' (76:315). If coercion was a folly, secession was no different.

❋

Dilemmas of this kind produced Quit India. We have seen previously that Hitler's war and Japan's war as well as Jinnah, Subhas Bose and Churchill, and the forces they represented, drew Quit India out of Gandhi. In the process he reversed some important positions. Now he was willing to embarrass Britain, launch a mass defiance and risk violence. He would take care to limit the embarrassment, make clear (despite his nonviolence) that Allied forces would remain in India, enjoin nonviolence on all his supporters and make Hindu-Muslim unity a central theme, but no longer would he suppress his or India's passion for freedom. If it burst out with pure force, it would wash away the schemes for Pakistan. If not wholly pure, it would at least preserve both his vision and what in many ways was his creation, the Congress of the time, though it would also bring struggle and suffering to those who followed his call, and might provide space for the Muslim League.

If, said Gandhi, Britain was unwilling to hand over power to Congress, let the League receive it. Among those who endorsed the suggestion in 1942 was Patel, who said on 1 August: 'Let Britain only transfer power to Indian hands, whether it is to the Muslim League or any other party' (*Patel:* 314). Jinnah responded: 'If they (Congress) are sincere I should welcome it. If the British Government accepts the solemn declaration of Mr Gandhi and by an arrangement hands over the government of the country to the Muslim League, I am sure that under Muslim rule non-Muslims would be treated fairly, justly, nay generously; and further the British will be making full amends to the Muslims by restoring the government of India to them from whom they have taken it.'[25]

But he saw Quit India as 'blackmailing the British and coercing them to concede . . . a Hindu raj.'[26] Gandhi made a passionate refutation and reiterated the offer of a League government. He spoke, he said, for Indians, not for Hindus alone.

One wonders whether India has seen another Indian or 'all-Indian' like Gandhi. No one had more completely expelled smaller identities of language, province or caste. True, he often referred to himself as a staunch Hindu but never to distance himself from non-Hindus. Wherever and to whomsoever he spoke, he identified himself with them. When a Hindu leader of the N.W.F.P., Mehr Chand

Khanna, complained that Pathans were raising slogans for Islam's freedom, Gandhi replied: 'Surely you don't expect the Pathans living in the mountains to call for the freedom of the Jains of Gujarat.'[27]

Perceiving Gandhi's trait, Tagore had written in 1921: 'Who else has felt so many men of India to be of his own flesh and blood?' (*Modern Review*, Oct.1921).

As a result of Quit India and the wholesale arrests of Congressmen it invited, Jinnah was able to spread himself. The Raj did not come in his way. In November 1942 Churchill said in London that he had 'not become the King's First Minister in order to preside over the liquidation of the British Empire;' but cracks within India were permissible. In 1942 the League formed ministries in Sind and Assam, and a year later in Bengal and the N.W.F.P. Luck favoured Jinnah in another way: Sikandar Hyat, the Unionist Premier of Punjab, died in December 1942. The death removed a possible rival for the allegiance of the Muslims of the Punjab and perhaps beyond.

When, in February 1943, Gandhi fasted in detention in Pune, Rajagopalachari, who had opposed Quit India, resigned from Congress and remained out of prison, was able to meet him on the strength of being a relative. (His daughter Lakshmi was married to Gandhi's youngest son Devadas.) The two discussed Francis Thompson's 'Hound of Heaven' and also a formula that Rajagopalachari had conceived for a Congress-League accord. On Gandhi saying that he agreed with it, Rajagopalachari wrote it out. Gandhi read it and said he could support it.

Under the formula, Congress and the League would cooperate in the formation of a provisional national government by agreeing to the separation in the form of Pakistan of contiguous Muslim-majority districts in the North-West and East of India if a plebiscite in the areas held after a transfer of power from Britain went in favour of such a separation. In the event of separation, mutual agreements would be entered into for defence, commerce, communications and other essential subjects. Any transfer of population would be purely voluntary.

A month later, Rajagopalachari met Jinnah and told him that

Gandhi was flexible over Pakistan, whereupon Jinnah declared that he was open to an initiative from Gandhi. Gandhi read in detention in *Dawn*, the League mouthpiece, that Jinnah had asked why Gandhi was not approaching him for a settlement. Jinnah added that the Raj would not dare to block such an approach. Gandhi wrote to Jinnah expressing willingness to meet and said, 'I am in your hands.'[28] The implication was plain: if Jinnah wished to meet the imprisoned Gandhi, he, Jinnah, would have to obtain permission from the Raj. Despite what Jinnah had said, the Raj did not allow the letter to reach him. But it communicated its contents. Jinnah's response was to say that he would not be embroiled in a Congress-Raj quarrel and to ask why Gandhi had not signified acceptance of Pakistan.

A discouraged Rajagopalachari kept his formula and Gandhi's acceptance of it to himself for fourteen months. But in April 1944 he called on Jinnah in Delhi, showed him the formula and said that Gandhi had agreed to it. After studying it, Jinnah said, 'Your scheme does not satisfy me.' We may note here the information supplied by K.M.Munshi in his *Pilgrimage to Freedom* (84-5) that before Rajagopalachari's meeting with Jinnah some Hindu Mahasabha leaders, including Dr Shyama Prasad Mookerjee and Raja Maheshwar Dayal, had unsuccessfully explored a similar settlement with the League.

❋

In May 1944, a Gandhi thought to be dying was released by the Raj. He recovered (not, it may be said, to Churchill's great delight) and was joined by Rajagopalachari in the hill town of Panchgani in western India. Following consultations between the two, a wire went from Rajagopalachari to Jinnah asking if the latter would object to his telling the Press that Jinnah had rejected his formula, which he intended to release. Jinnah wired back saying that it was wrong to say he had rejected the scheme. If Gandhi dealt with him direct, Jinnah would refer the formula to the League.

Gandhi now wrote to Jinnah, proposing a meeting. Jinnah agreed and said they could meet in his house in Bombay. Because of Jinnah's poor health the talks at 10 Mount Pleasant Road commenced only on 9 September 1944 and continued until 27 September. The two met fourteen times. Newspapers printed pictures of the two smiling. Many in India prayed. Wavell, the Viceroy, wrote in his diary that he was 'sure that the G-J meeting will result in a demand for the release of the [Congress] working committee' (*Journal:* 87). 'The talks were so pregnant with possibilties,' observed Asoka Mehta and Kusum Nair, 'that every reporter waiting on Mr Jinnah's lawn began to feel himself a historical character.'[29]

But the talks failed. Jinnah described the Rajagopalachari formula that Gandhi put forward as 'a parody and a negation' of the League's Lahore resolution, offering 'a maimed, mutilated and moth-eaten Pakistan.' Jinnah said he had to have all of Bengal and the Punjab. Secondly, the 'bonds of alliance between Hindustan and Pakistan' that Gandhi and Rajagopalachari proposed in the treaty of separation seemed to Jinnah to clip Pakistan's sovereignty. Thirdly, while Jinnah wanted Pakistan before the British left and under British auspices, Gandhi envisaged it coming 'as soon as possible after India is free.' Fourthly, Jinnah objected to voting by non-Muslims in any plebiscite in Muslim-majority areas. Finally, Jinnah wanted Gandhi to agree that Hindus and Muslims were two separate nations.

Gandhi's offer was a spelling out of Congress's 1942 self-determination resolution, and he claimed that in substance it also met the call of the League's Pakistan resolution, which only referred to 'areas' where Muslims were in a majority and did not speak of the whole of the Punjab and Bengal. But the clause in Cripps's proposal of the non-accession of provinces had confirmed Jinnah in his conviction that the two provinces in their entirety belonged to Pakistan; and he wanted Pakistan before freedom because he did not trust Congress to allow separation once it controlled India.

Rajagopalachari pointed out that if a Congress-controlled India was capable of denying separation, it could also undo it after it occurred, for the British were unlikely to leave behind an army to sustain partition. There was therefore no 'material difference arising out of the order in which the two events, withdrawal of British domination and partition, take place' (*Rajaji* 2:103). But both Jinnah and Gandhi thought the difference significant, Jinnah because of his mistrust of Congress, and Gandhi because of his national pride, wanting Indians, and not the British, to decide India's future. By agreeing to separation before independence Gandhi would not have tangibly hurt his position, and he might have disarmed Jinnah's suspicion; yet such a concession might not have been ratified by Congress and its national following.

In a letter to Jinnah sent during the course of the talks, Gandhi described what he could concede: 'India is not to be regarded as two or more nations but as one family consisting of many members of whom the Muslims living in . . . Baluchistan, Sind, the N.W.F.P. and that part of the Punjab where they are in absolute majority over all the other elements, and in parts of Bengal and Assam where they are in absolute majority, desire to live in separation from the rest of India' (24.9.44).

Gandhi also proposed that a 'third party' arbitrate between them if they failed to reach an agreement, and asked for an opportunity to defend his offer before the League's executive. Though drawing upon his entire stock of patience and skill, Gandhi failed to budge Jinnah. The formula, arbitration and the request to be heard by the League executive were all turned down.

Hearing of the Gandhi-Jinnah talks in their prison, Nehru, Patel and Azad felt that by calling repeatedly on Jinnah Gandhi had helped strengthen the League leader's standing among the Muslim masses. Yet that standing had been pretty solid, and growing steadily, ever since 1937; and Gandhi might not have been forgiven by himself, others and history if he had not attempted a settlement with Jinnah, or rejected a widespread and not unreasonable demand for a face-to-face encounter between him and Jinnah. It was voiced in particular by Muslims torn between Congress and the League and by politically nonaligned non-Muslims — groups that Gandhi sought to win.

Also, it was necessary to know with precision what Jinnah wanted and with what keenness he wanted it. No one knew until the Bombay talks. 'I went to him to know his mind,' Gandhi would say after another meeting with Jinnah in May 1947 (87: 433). It was one of the purposes also of his 1944 visits. Though willing, Gandhi did not always look forward to a meeting with the astute, dedicated and touchy League leader. 'I cannot crack a joke [with Jinnah] without exposing myself to being misunderstood,' he said to Tej Bahadur Sapru in 1941 (73:297).

In 1944, Gandhi saw for himself the intensity of Jinnah's passion. His Pakistan vision seemed to possess Jinnah, and Gandhi felt that the once-secular Jinnah who in the past had opposed separate electorates for Muslims as 'dividing the nation against itself'[30] and had initiated the 1916 Congress-League accord now thought of himself as 'the saviour of Islam' (85:514). To the press, Gandhi said: 'We have parted as friends. These days have not been wasted. I am convinced that Mr Jinnah is a good man. I hope we shall meet again. I am a man of prayer and I shall pray for understanding' (*Rajaji* 2:105).

The Pakistan that Jinnah secured three years later was in area almost exactly what Gandhi had offered, and he had rejected, in 1944. In his *Pathway to Pakistan*, published in 1961, Khaliquzzaman questioned the wisdom of Jinnah's rejection. Commenting on one of Jinnah's 1944 conditions, Khaliquzzaman said: 'The right of self-determination by Muslim votes alone . . . formed a demand without parallel in world history' (278).

The virtual identity between the Pakistan discussed by Gandhi and Jinnah in 1944 and the one reluctantly accepted by all concerned in 1947 suggests that a partition in peace and concord, so different from the historical, was a possibility. If, for what was not averted, Britain and the League are unlikely to be spared by the historian's finger, that finger may point elsewhere too. By ruling out a role for Britain in a Congress-League settlement, Gandhi and the freedom movement created and embodied by him incurred some responsibility for the tragedy that accompanied the joy of 1947.

❋

'I think the failure of the Gandhi-Jinnah talks has created a favourable moment for a move by His Majesty's Government.' So wrote Wavell to Churchill in October 1944. Wanting to 'capture the Indian imagination,' Wavell proposed the release of the Congress Working Committee and talks towards a provisional political government. He told Churchill that the wish to sever the British connection had large backing in India and that British soldiers would not want to stay in India in large numbers after the war to hold the country down. Churchill sat on the proposal for eight months. When Wavell went to London to see him, Churchill, in the Viceroy's words, 'launched into a long jeremiad about India which lasted for about 40 minutes' and seemed to 'favour partition into Pakistan, Hindustan and Princestan etc.'

Finally extracting Churchill's approval, Wavell declared in June 1945, after the war in Europe had ended, that he would invite Indian leaders to Simla for talks about a new Exeutive Council representative of organized political opinion and composed, apart from the Viceroy and the C-in-C, entirely of Indians. For the first time, Home, Finance and Foreign Affairs would be in Indian hands. One of the Council's main tasks would be to bring the war against Japan to a successful conclusion, but its Members would also consider how to reach a new constitution for India. Wavell also announced that the Working Committee members were being released.

After a detention that had lasted 34 months and six days, Azad, Nehru, Patel and their colleagues were released amidst joy and hope. But the Simla Conference of June-July 1945, attended by Gandhi, Jinnah, Azad, Nehru and some others, failed. Congress accepted the Viceroy's proposal of a new Council with an equal number of caste Hindus and Muslims, a Hindu Scheduled Caste Member and representatives of other minorities. Congress nodded, too, when urged not to harbour undue fears regarding the Viceroy's veto. It was Wavell's intention to include Congress Hindus as well as one from outside Congress, and League Muslims as well as a Unionist Muslim. But Jinnah insisted that all Muslim members had to come from the League. As Wavell put it:

> He refused even to discuss names unless he could be given
> the absolute right to select all Muslims and some guarantee

that any decision which the Muslims opposed in Council could only be passed by a two-thirds majority — in fact a kind of communal veto. I said that these conditions were entirely unacceptable and the interview ended (*Journal:* 154).

Some Governors advised Wavell to proceed with a new Council comprising Congress and other members, keeping vacant seats for Jinnah to fill if he changed his mind, but the Viceroy rejected this option, for it would have meant a Council dominated by Congress. What the 1942 movement had done to the war effort when Wavell was C-in-C was a recollection that the Viceroy 'could never rid [his] mind of,' as he admitted in a letter to the King a year later (*Journal*: 494). He preferred to announce the conference's failure.

'Lord Wavell had in effect capitulated to Mr Jinnah.' This verdict of H.V. Hodson, who had been the Raj's Reforms Commissioner in 1941-2, seems valid.[31] Equally of interest is the instruction the Viceroy received from London to refrain from stating that Jinnah's intransigence had killed the talks.[32] Adds Hodson:

Mr Jinnah's control of the Muslim League was at that time far from complete. The Unionist Party was still strong, and Mr Liaqat Ali Khan favoured a settlement. There were still many uncommitted Muslims in the country. It is arguable that if the Viceroy had been as adamant as Mr Jinnah, the latter would have been obliged to give in; that the destruction of the Unionist Party, which paved the way for partition of the Punjab, would have been averted.[33]

However, Wavell's stand was the price of Quit India. To expect the British to remain friendly and unbiased despite being asked to clear out was not realistic. It was natural for Churchill to be sympathetic towards the enemy's enemy, and for Wavell to remember 1942.

Within two weeks of the Simla failure, Churchill and his fellow Tories were unseated by the British electorate. In August the atom bombs fell on Japan and the war was over. Summoned to London by the new government, Wavell was authorized to announce that elections to provincial legislatures and the Central Assembly would be held in early 1946. The Viceroy called on Churchill, now the leader of the opposition, whose 'final remark' was: 'Keep a bit of India' (*Journal*: 168).

The Indian elections showed that except in the N.W.F.P. the League commanded the Muslim vote. All 30 Muslim seats in the Central Assembly and 427 of the 507 Muslim seats in the provinces were bagged by the League. In the Punjab most Muslim Unionists were humbled by the League, which had avenged the 1937 results. Performing equally impressively in all General seats, Congress formed eight provincial ministries, including in the N.W.F.P., and shared office in the Punjab with the Unionists and Akalis. Led by the Unionist Khizr Hyat Khan and sustained almost wholly by Hindu and Sikh members, the Punjab ministry was successfully depicted as anti-Muslim by the League. In Bengal and Sind, the League headed coalition ministries.

Prime Minister Clement Attlee told the House of Commons on 15 March that Britain had indeed decided to quit India. 'If India elects for independence,' he said, 'she has a right to do so.' What Attlee said next also gladdened Congress hearts: 'We are very mindful of the rights of minorities. On the other hand, we cannot allow a minority to place a veto on the advance of the majority.'

Nine days later, three members of the British Cabinet, Lord Pethick Lawrence, Secretary of State for India, Sir Stafford Cripps, President of the Board of Trade, and A.V. Alexander, First Lord of the Admiralty, arrived in India in a bid to see how and to whom power was to be transferred.

The three Ministers stayed in India for over three months, conferred interminably with a range of Indian leaders, failed to obtain a consensus, and announced awards both for an immediate national government and for the long term. The latter was given out first, in the Statement of 16 May. On 16 June a proposal for a government was announced.

The May award, or 16 May, as we may call it, pleased Congress by rejecting Pakistan. 'Neither a larger nor a smaller sovereign state of Pakistan would provide an acceptable solution,' the statement said. It also rejected Jinnah's demand for Hindu-Muslim equality or parity in a central assembly, and provided for a Union dealing with Foreign Affairs, Defence and Communications. All other subjects and residuary powers were vested with the provinces. Existing provincial legislatures and rulers of princely states would send representatives to a Constituent Assembly, the former in Hindu-Muslim ratios reflecting the composition of their populations.

However, 16 May was capable of contradictory interpretations. The ambiguity was deliberate. Anxious to announce a solution and to install an Indian government, the first an understandable and the second a laudable wish, the Cabinet Mission, as it was described, made 16 May 'purposely vague,' to quote Cripps's later word to the House of Commons, in order to obtain the signatures of both Congress and the League, clearly a dubious recourse.[34]

In initial negotiations the Mission pursued the idea of a 'large' Pakistan within a loose Indian Union, to be reached by grouping together, in the Northwest, the Punjab, Sind, Baluchistan and the N.W.F.P., and, in the East, Bengal and Assam, and enabling the two Muslim-majority groups to act as one. Jinnah indicated that he would agree if the Union was either nominal or gave parity to Hindus and Muslims, and if the groups could secede. Congress said it would agree if provinces had the right to stay out of a group as well as the right to secede from it. To simplify we can say that Jinnah wanted the Union, and Congress the Groups, to be optional.

At this stage the Mission did not do what it might have. It did not say to Congress that the League had to have a large area if it was to agree to a Union, or to the League that it had to agree to a Union if it wanted a large area. A sacrifice of territory had to match a sacrifice of sovereignty. Instead of saying this, the Mission sacrificed clarity and consistency. 'Purposely' it drafted an award which Congress could interpret as recommending optional grouping ('Provinces should be free to form groups,' Paragraph 15 of 16 May said) and the League as prescribing compulsory grouping (Paragraph 19, referring to the Constituent Assembly that was proposed, said that members from each Muslim-majority Group, meeting separately, 'shall proceed to settle' provincial and group constitutions). A reconsideration of the Union and Group constitutions ten years after their being framed was also provided for. The League saw room in this provision for a Group's secession.

If the League's was the right interpretation of 16 May, Assam (which had a non-Muslim majority) would be absorbed into the eastern Muslim-majority Group, and the N.W.F.P. (which had a Congress ministry following an election in which the League had made Pakistan the issue) into the Northwestern Group. If Congress's was the right reading, Assam, the N.W.F.P., Sind and Baluchistan all had the right to stay out of the Muslim-majority Groups. The Groups could vanish if Britain helped enforce Congress's view; a Greater Pakistan might come into being if the League's version was upheld and if the Muslim Groups managed to secede.

Gandhi said he could accept 16 May if it meant optional grouping. On 25 May the Cabinet Mission said that such an interpretation did not accord with its 'intentions.' But it accorded, Gandhi argued, with 16 May's language. An award or a law, he claimed, had to be understood from its text, not from the supposed intentions of its authors. Later, on 24 June, Cripps and Pethick Lawrence gave Gandhi the assurance on grouping that he had asked for. (This is documented in more than one book, including in Wavell's *Journal*, Sudhir Ghosh's *Gandhi's Emissary*, and in my *Patel*.)

But the assurance to Gandhi was not wholehearted. It could not be, for Jinnah had to be offered a contrary assurance. In fact Jinnah was advised by Woodrow Wyatt, an aide to the Mission and afterwards an MP, that though Pakistan had been turned down the League could accept 16 May 'as the first step on the road to Pakistan.' 'At this proposition,' Wyatt noted, Jinnah 'was delighted' (On 24.5.46. See *TOP* 6: 684-7).'That's it, you've got it,' he told Wyatt.

Armed with assurances he had been given, not all recorded here (they can be found elsewhere, including in *Patel*), Jinnah 'accepted' the 16 May plan on 6 June. Reiterating that 'complete sovereign Pakistan' remained 'its unalterable objective,' the League claimed that 'the foundation of Pakistan' was 'inherent' in what it saw as the plan for 'compulsory grouping' and asserted that the plan 'by implication' gave the Muslim Groups 'the opportunity and the right of secession.'[35]

On 16 June came the plan for a national government. Fourteen individuals were invited to join it: 6 Congress Hindus (Nehru, Patel, Prasad, Rajagopalachari, Mahtab and Jagijivan Ram), 5 League Muslims including Jinnah, a Sikh (Baldev Singh), a Parsi (N.P.Engineer), and a Christian (John Matthai). Clause 8 of the 16 June Statement said that if the proposed government was unacceptable to Congress or the League of to both, then the Viceroy would 'proceed with the formation of an Interim Government which will be as representative as possible of those willing to accept the Statement of May 16th.'

In view of the controversial use that Congress would make of this clause, we should consider its origin and meaning. According to Wavell, 'This clause was put in, perhaps rashly, because we felt that Mr Jinnah, who had already accepted the Statement of May 16, should not be put at a disadvantage with the Congress, who had not; and in furtherance of our pledge that we would go ahead as far as possible with anyone who accepted the statement of May 16' (*Journal*: 304). Its meaning was that those accepting May 16, such as the League, could renegotiate their representation in the new government if they were dissatisfied with the 16 June list, a right not available to those rejecting 16 May.

In Congress eyes, the 16 June list was flawed: the absence of a non-League Muslim suggested that Congress was for Hindus only and also that only the League could represent Muslims. More flaws were revealed when Wavell confirmed that he had promised to consult Jinnah if those on the list who were neither Muslim nor caste Hindu — Jagijivan Ram, Baldav Singh, Matthai and Engineer, or any of them — were unwilling or unable to join, and substitution was needed. The Viceroy also agreed, in a letter to Jinnah, that Congress would not have the right to substitute a Muslim for one of the Congress Hindus invited, and that on a communal issue the League could have a veto. Keen as they were on office, the Working Committee members felt unable, in the light of all this, to accept the 16 June plan.

On his part Gandhi had advised rejection. He could not agree that Congress was only for Hindus, or that power and influence should be equally divided between Congress and the League. During negotiations before the British awards were announced, Gandhi had written to Cripps (on 8 May) that parity between 'nine crores of the [Muslim] population against nineteen crores' of Hindus was 'really worse than Pakistan.' If, added Gandhi, it was 'considered unfair' to frame the government and the Constituent Assembly 'on the population basis,' then 'an impartial non-British tribunal should award on this as on any other matter otherwise incapable of adjustment' (*TOP* 7:465-6). Cripps replied that he could appreciate Gandhi's difficulty with 'equality at the centre' but 'not that it would be worse than Pakistan' (9.5.46; *TOP* 7:466). As for arbitration, Cripps said it would be fine if Congress and the League both asked for it.

To return to the 16 June statement, Cripps and Pethick Lawrence convinced Patel, and through Patel others including Nehru, Azad and Rajagopalachari, that Clause 8 of the statement provided the way out. If Congress accepted 16 May, it could reject 16 June and still, courtesy of Clause 8, obtain the right to a team of its choice in the new government. The attractive advice was accepted. Congress announced that it was rejecting 16 June but accepting 16 May with its own interpretation of the grouping provision. And the British Delegation (the Cabinet Mission and the Viceroy) accepted Congress's 'acceptance,' providing Congress with the freedom to choose its representatives in the new government.

When Cripps and Pethick Lawrence were giving Gandhi their 'assurance' on grouping, Wavell had interjected to say that 'grouping was essential.' Though Pethick Lawrence asked the Viceroy 'not to press the point,' Gandhi was troubled. He told the Working Committee: 'I cannot advise you to accept the May 16 proposition . . . But you should follow my intuition only if it appeals to your reason . . . I shall now leave with your permission.' At this point Azad, who was presiding, said: 'What do you desire? Is there any need to detain Bapu further?' No one said a thing, and Gandhi got up and left.[36]

In interaction with the Cabinet Mission and eagerness for high office, the Working Committee members had found their independence from Gandhi. The 'secession' of 1940 had been repeated, this time not to be withdrawn, for power was at hand. The League had to be prevented from running off with the government now, even if, according to Jinnah, 16 May supplied the League with the possibility of running off later with Greater Pakistan.

As soon as he heard that Congress was rejecting 16 June but accepting 16 May, Jinnah conveyed his acceptance of 16 June to the Viceroy, demanding at the same time that Congress's 'insincere' acceptance of 16 May be turned down. He was, in fact, asking for and fully expecting a Jinnah-led government. When he found that the British Delegation had accepted Congress's acceptance, scrapped the 16 June list and invited Congress names for a new government, he was furious.

Accusing Congress of dishonesty, Cripps and Pethick Lawrence of treachery, and Wavell of betrayal, he claimed that 'a fantastic and dishonest construction' had been placed on Clause 8. This was not so. Though introduced to protect him, and this explained part of Jinnah's anger, Clause 8 was available to Congress as well.

Where Jinnah was right was in his charge of insincere acceptance. Once Congress knew (on 25 May) that the Mission intended compulsory grouping, it should have rejected 16 May or accepted compulsory grouping. It did neither. Equally, once Jinnah saw that 16 May had rejected Pakistan, he should have either said no to 16 May or shelved Pakistan. He did neither. His acceptance was as conditional as Congress's.

Normally the historian has little difficulty in conceding that the conditional yes is the essence of politics. It is different, however, when the subject is Gandhi, who insisted that Hindu-Muslim unity was what he lived for. He was entitled to oppose compulsory grouping and on solid ground in claiming that Paragraph 15 ruled it out.

Yet since he knew, as he put it, that grouping was a device 'which the Congress interprets in one way, the League in another and the Cabinet Mission in a third way,'[37] he could have insisted on a new and unmistakable award from the Raj, or on a rejection by Congress.

After he heard of Jinnah's reaction following the Raj's acceptance of Congress's acceptance, Gandhi seems to have said that Jinnah, 'a great Indian and the recognized leader of a great organization,' should not have been dealt with 'in a legalistic manner.'[38] Yet, as we have seen, he was legalistic himself when it came to interpreting 16 May, and though he told the Working Committee that he could not favour the plan, he stopped short of asking for its rejection. Later he advised the AICC to endorse what the Working Committee had done. Seeing the ambiguity of 16 May, sensing the insincerity of the assurance given to him by Cripps and Pethick Lawrence, and anxious that Jinnah be treated right, Gandhi was yet keen to see Nehru, Patel and company in power.

They were like sons or younger brothers. He had put much into them and received much from them. Moreover, he could not be certain that they were in the wrong and he in the right. Years earlier, in August 1939, well before the 1940 'secession,' he had described the basis of his teamwork with them: 'I have not felt called upon to sever the moral tie with the old colleagues. I do not arrogate to myself any superiority over them. It has been a privilege to work with them. They are as good and faithful servants of the nation as I claim to be myself. I cling to them because I have the hope that one day they will be converted to my point of view or . . . I to theirs' (*Harijan*, 12.8.39; 70:67).

Also worth noting is the firmness of Gandhi's opposition to Greater Pakistan as well as to any bar on a Congress Muslim. Though a Muslim was free to leave the Indian joint family, he had no right to take a Hindu with him, or restrict the role of a Muslim willing to stay. On these propositions Gandhi was unyielding.

In July, thanks to Gandhi's intervention, Nehru took over from Azad as Congress President. Why Gandhi intervened to this effect, choosing Nehru over Patel, who was the choice of a majority of

Congress's provincial committees, will be discussed in the next chapter. Nehru's elevation meant that he rather than Azad or Patel was invited by the Viceroy to submit names for the Interim Government and become its Vice-President, with Wavell as the President.

In his first Press Conference as the new Congress President, Nehru said that Congress would be 'completely unfettered by agreements,' adding that the grouping scheme would probably never come to fruition, the Union would be much stronger than what the Mission seemed to envisage, and the Constituent Assembly would have the power to alter the Mission's plan. An enraged Jinnah demanded the annulment of the Raj's invitation to Congress. The Raj not obliging, Jinnah had the League rescind its acceptance of 16 May. Charging that the British had surrendered to the 'fascist, caste-Hindu Congress,' Jinnah said that, 'bidding goodbye to constitutional methods,' the League would resort to Direct Action to achieve Pakistan. So far, said Jinnah, the British had held the pistol of authority and Congress the pistol of mass struggle, but 'today we have also forged a pistol, and are in a position to use it.'

Nehru's indiscreet remarks had given the League leader a handle. 'We have to work within the limits of the State Paper (the 16 May Plan),' Gandhi told Jawaharlal, adding, 'If we cannot admit even this much . . . it will justify the accusation of Jinnah Saheb.'[39] However, the League's Direct Action and its consequences cannot be ascribed solely to Nehru's mistake. In letters to Attlee and Churchill written on 6 July, four days before Nehru's rash observations, Jinnah had spoken of Congress's 'aggressive and dictatorial attitude, pistol in hand,' and said that he trusted that the British Government would still 'avoid compelling the Muslims to shed their blood' (*TOP* 8:106-7). It was Congress's arrival at the threshold of power despite its 'defiant' interpretation of grouping that had incurred Jinnah's wrath.

The threat of Direct Action did not go down well with the Raj. On 8 August a formal offer was sent to Nehru, who gave twelve names to Wavell: seven Congressmen (Nehru, Patel, Prasad, Rajagopalachari, Sarat Bose, Asaf Ali and Jagjivan Ram), two non-Congress Muslims (Ali Zaheer and Shafaat Ahmed Khan), a Sikh (Baldev Singh), a Christian (John Matthai), and a Parsi

(C.H.Bhabha). The list was accepted.

Direct Action Day, fixed for 16 August, led to the Great Calcutta Killing of 16-20 August, 1946. About 4,000 lost their lives; 11,000 were injured. A League rally had touched it off, and the Bengal ministry headed by the League leader Suhrawardy seemed unwilling or unable to suppress the rioting at its start. In later rounds Hindu groups obtained the upper hand; in a letter to Rajagopalachari, Patel spoke of 'a good lesson for the League' (*Patel*: 376). Nehru said that 'our programme will certainly not be upset because a few persons misbehave in Calcutta,' and on his part Jinnah described the Calcutta incidents as 'an organized plot to discredit the Muslim League on the part of the Hindus.' Gandhi exclaimed: 'Would that the violence of Calcutta were sterilized, and did not become a signal for its spread all over.'[40]

❈

The Great Calcutta Killing influenced Wavell. Inviting Gandhi and Nehru to meet him on August 27, the Viceroy asked them to sign a statement he had drafted to the effect that Congress accepted compulsory grouping, adding that he would not summon the Constituent Assembly until 'this point was settled.' We have looked at this encounter earlier. Here we may note that after the interview Gandhi wrote asking Wavell to withdraw the invitation to Congress and 'form another ministry enjoying your fullest confidence' (*Journal*: 342-3). Wavell did not accept the challenge. And despite his threat he summoned the Constituent Assembly. But he made up his mind to bring the League into the Interim Government.

When on 2 September the new government was installed, Gandhi was joyous. Vallabhbhai, Prasad, Sarat Bose and Jagjivan Ram came for his blessings to the Valmiki Colony, the settlement of the 'untouchable' scavengers where Gandhi had made his home in New Delhi. 'I have been thinking of you since the morning,' he said. He asked them to recall the salt march, abolish the salt tax, remove untouchability and work for Hindu-Muslim unity. The ex-residents of the Raj's prisons were moving into the spacious lawn-surrounded houses used by India's rulers and getting them tidied and cleaned. Gandhi asked the new Ministers to see as well to the cleaning of the servants' quarters on the grounds of their new houses.

But the Ministers' priorities were different. On 22 September Gandhi recorded the divergence and his unhappiness: 'The inwardness of the spinning-wheel seems to have been forgotten. I was angry . . . My heart-searching continues' (Diary entry, 22.9.46; 85:355). The spinning-wheel stood for a spectrum of ignored values. Troubled as much by his reaction as by his colleagues' attitudes, he said to an unnamed friend: 'I am filled with agitation; why could not I suffer this inner anguish with unruffled calmness of spirit?' (85:370). Long periods of silence was the remedy he prescribed for himself, an addition to his old practice of treating Mondays as days of silence.

As keen as Wavell for the League's entry into the government but through an Indian rather than a British initiative, Gandhi underlined recent examples from Bombay and Ahmedabad of Hindu and Muslim youths dying while attempting to put out communal violence. He also encouraged the Nawab of Bhopal's effort for a Congress-Jinnah accord to facilitate the League's entry. Jinnah conceded Congress's right (by now accepted by the Raj) to send any member including a Muslim into the government in exchange for an acknowledgment that Gandhi made of the League's preeminent right to speak for India's Muslims. But Jinnah would not agree to Gandhi's proposal that Congress-League differences be resolved without involving the Viceroy.

When Wavell sought Nehru's reaction to bringing the League into the Council, the answer the Viceroy first got was that it was up to Congress to try and persuade Jinnah. Later, however, Jawaharlal said to Wavell: 'If you want to see Jinnah, I can't prevent you' (*Journal*: 349). Jinnah responded positively to Wavell's approach. He would not join the government himself, for that would mean being ranked below Nehru. But he would not deprive the League of a share in power, and the League would come in without accepting May 16. Wavell did not make an issue of this with Jinnah. He told himself that the 'acceptance' through which Congress had gained power had also been dishonest, even if, 'out-talked by Cripps and Pethick Lawrence,' he had been party to it himself (*Journal*: 305).

❋

Jinnah produced another card from his sleeve. Authorized to name Ministers, he included J.N. Mandal, a Hindu Scheduled Caste leader from Bengal, in his list. If Congress could nominate Asaf Ali, a Muslim, he would retaliate by sponsoring a Hindu 'untouchable.' If Muslims and Hindu 'untouchables' joined hands in eastern and northeastern India, the League's influence in the region would become unassailable.

News of anti-Hindu violence and rape in Noakhali in revenge for Muslim losses in the Calcutta Killing came at about the same time as the League's nomination of Mandal. Both were factors in Gandhi's decision to go to East Bengal. If a Congress-League accord at summit-level was elusive, he would strive for peace on the ground in Noakhali, and for courage in East Bengal's Hindus, especially Hindu women. And he would counter Jinnah's Mandal move with a bid to unite Bengal's Hindus and Muslims.

He was disappointed with the mildness of Nehru's and Patel's reaction to the Mandal card, to him proof that the League's 'whole mode of entering into the Cabinet had not been straight' (*Last Phase* 1:287). He would have liked the Congress Ministers to resign on the issue. They rejected the idea. The independence of his colleagues was undoubtedly another factor in Gandhi's departure from Delhi. They no longer needed him.

Gandhi himself spoke of an irresistible urge to go to Noakhali when 'a very esteemed friend' whose name we are not given tried hard 'to dissuade him from setting out on such a long journey.' Said Gandhi: 'I do not know what I shall be able to do there. All I know is that I won't be at peace with myself unless I go there. There are two kinds of thoughts — idle and active . . . Myriads of the former swarming in one's brain . . . do not count. But one pure, active thought proceeding from the depth and endowed with all the undivided intensity of one's being becomes dynamic and works like a fertilized ovum' (*Harijan*, 10.11.46; 86:52).

Hearing, en route to Noakhali, of anti-Muslim riots in Bihar sparked by the arrival of Hindu refugees from Noakhali, Gandhi cut down on his diet and declared in Calcutta that he would go on a complete fast if the Bihar violence continued. Even if half of what he had heard was true, it meant that Bihar had 'forgotten humanity.' On 4 November he appeared to think that he would have to fast and probably die as a result. Several letters he wrote that day (to colleagues in the Sevagram Ashram, Jawaharlal, Vallabhbhai, and several others) seemed to contain 'deathbed' instructions. The last was a stirring 'Letter to Bihar,' published in the press.

Nehru, Patel, Liaqat Ali and Abdur Rab Nishtar (the last two were among the new League Ministers) reached Bihar to help put down the violence, which was soon controlled, but the Bihar toll much exceeded that of Noakhali, and Gandhi was urged by Bengal's Muslims to go to Bihar. Replying that he had played a part by threatening a fast and pointing to Nehru's energy in dealing with the Bihar violence, Gandhi said he would not alter his destination. Firefighting was not his only goal. Unlike Bihar, Bengal was being claimed for Pakistan and east Bengal had a large Muslim majority. There he would make a bid to save Indian unity.

Establishing a relationship with Suhrawardy, the Chief Minister who had failed to arrest the Calcutta Killing, Gandhi reminded him of their meeting in 1924 when Suhrawardy had claimed that he thought of Gandhi as a father. Though Suhrawardy had been one of those urging Gandhi to go to Bihar, he on the whole backed Gandhi's Noakhali mission and assigned security for Gandhi and his small party. From Noakhali's villages and small towns Gandhi kept in steady touch with Suhrawardy and with other Ministers and officials of Bengal, reporting to them the difficulties being faced by the people he was meeting and their needs for relief and rehabilitation. Suhrawardy's rival, Fazlul Huq, the mover of the League's Pakistan resolution in 1940, met Gandhi in Haimchar on 27 February, and explained that a remark by him that he would push Gandhi into the water if he came to Huq's town was not meant to be taken seriously. But the remark reflected the Muslim hostility that Gandhi encountered and to a fair extent overcame in Noakhali.

✻

We should look at his Noakhali discourse, public and private. He asked the area's Hindus to stay and fight, and said that it would have been manlier for the Hindus in Bihar who had attacked innocent Muslims in that province to come to Noakhali and take on its Muslim assailants. To a Muslim-majority audience of 15,000 he said on 7 November: 'I have not come to excite the Hindus to fight the Muslims. I have no enemies. I have fought the British all my life. Yet they are my friends. I have never wished them ill.' He criticized forcible conversions, forcible feeding of beef, forced marriages, abductions and the destruction of idols.

His teaching was down-to-earth and his language a mix of the religious and the secular. Hindus and Muslims 'were nourished by food grown from the same soil, quenched their thirst from the waters of the same river and finally laid themselves to rest in the same earth. If they feared God they would fear no one else' (86:214). His directness is striking. Asked in the village of Paniala whether he did not think that Muslim neighbours had saved Hindu lives and property in Noakhali, Gandhi answered on 22 January that what was wanted was 'repentance that there were enough Muslims found in Noakhali who lost their heads' and committed terrible crimes. 'If more mischief was not done, God alone was to be thanked, not man.' However, he would freely concede that, 'be it said to their honour, there were Muslims who afforded protection to Hindus' (86:382-3).

He asked Muslims to test him by hosting him in their villages. Many did. To give courage to the Hindus he split up his party, in which most were Hindus, getting them to live singly, each in a different village. If they were fearful, or bore illwill towards Muslims, they could leave Noakhali, Gandhi said. When Muslims blamed the violence on goondas, he replied, 'No one is a goonda, or all are goondas.' When a transfer of population was suggested, he said it would lead to apartheid in every part of India. He told Sarat Bose and other Congress leaders calling on him that the Namashudras of Noakhali had been more courageous than caste Hindus.

The Harijans were constantly on his mind. Frequently a Harijan was his host. 'I am really happy I am staying with a Harijan weaver,' he said on 27 January (86:399). 'He looks after me with such love and care! A palace where love is not is a prison; and a hut where love abides is more than a palace.' On another occasion he said that Hindu touch-me-notism had been a factor in the Hindu-Muslim divide.

To G.D.Birla he wrote: 'My voice carries no weight in the Working Committee.' Still, Nehru and Patel were advised by him that they, Azad, Rajagopalachari, Prasad and Kripalani should go into the Constituent Assembly. There was no sulking, and he poured out all he had into Noakhali. In Srirampur he held his prayer meeting on the ground where sixty-three Hindu houses had been gutted. On Christmas day he had Paul's epistle on love read out. To a Muslim critic, a Parliamentary Secretary in Suhrawardy's government, he sent a detailed, painstaking reply. When Hindus asked how they could forgive or forget, he replied, 'Remember Bihar.'

He complained to the Bihar Chief Minister, Shri Krishna Sinha, that no one from Bihar had come to inform him in detail about the violence, and asked Sinha to hold an inquiry into it.

Daily he did his Bengali lessons, subscribing to the view that a man should live thinking he might die tomorrow but learn as if he would live forever. At times in Noakhali he cooked for himself and gave himself a massage, chores that for years others had performed for him. Though the path from village to village was sometimes thorny or on occasion deliberately soiled with excreta by Muslims resentful of his arrival, he made light of his barefoot trek. 'The earth of Noakhali was like velvet and the green grass was a magnificent carpet to walk on,' reminding him of 'soft English grass,' he said on 6 February (86:440).

When Amtus Salaam, one of his co-workers, fasted because Muslims in the village that she had taken on, Sirandi, had not surrendered a dagger used against Hindus, Gandhi wrote her a letter a day, and sometimes two letters daily, during her 25-day fast. From the remoteness of Noakhali he wrote to someone in Baluchistan: he had a stake there as well.

Now and again a poetic or memorable utterance would emerge, the issue of his wrestling soul. On 18 December he said: 'Truth is greater than the sun; some day or the other it will come to light.' To riot victims in a ruined house he said on 2 February: 'My heart weeps to God not to man.' Courage more than solace was what he wanted to instil.

To Mira Behn he wrote on 6 February: 'The way to truth is paved with skeletons over which we dare to walk' (86:437). We can see this sentence in several ways. It is, for a start, a literal if condensed description of his Noakhali trek. But it also suggests guilt at a hurried walk over, or past, grief. Again, it is the skeletons alone that know the truth of what happened. The living conceal or lie. Finally, perhaps, there is a hint that India's way to freedom was paved with death and yet could not be abandoned.

Many of Noakhali's Hindus returned to the homes they had abandoned. Overcoming fear of Muslim neighbours, many found courage to sing Ram Dhun at Gandhi's prayer sessions. Hindu women wore vermillion and bangles again. In a gesture of goodwill, eleven Muslims and an Englishman together sent 200 pairs of conchshell bangles, a pound of vermillion and Rs 850. In the presence of Muslims who had earlier broken it, an idol was reinstalled in the village of Bhatialpur. Joining Gandhi while he walked in Bhatialpur, 'a number of Muslim youths expressed gratification at his work in Noakhali' and assured him, according to the *Amrita Bazar Patrika* of 19 January, that 'they would stand guarantee' against a repetition of what had happened. When the young men raised Pakistan with him, Gandhi said, 'Once freedom is secured for the country as a whole, then we can decide about Pakistan or Hindustan.' In his view, 'to reverse the process was to invite foreign (British) help' (86:354-5).

❉

In Delhi, meanwhile, the League had announced a boycott of the first session of the Constituent Assembly. With Congress telling the Viceroy that the League had to accept a Union and the League answering that Congress had to accept compulsory grouping, HMG invited Nehru and Jinnah for talks in London. After fruitless discussions in which Cripps and Pethick Lawrence seemed to support the Congress viewpoint and Wavell and Alexander that of the League, HMG gave its verdict, which vindicated the League. Provinces had to join their Groups and abide by the constitutions the Groups framed for them. Attlee's decisive voice had gone in the verdict's favour.

In a letter to Cripps, Patel charged Britain with betrayal: 'You know when Gandhiji was strongly against our settlement, I threw my weight in favour of it . . . [HMG's] interpretation means that Bengal Muslims can draw up the constitution of Assam . . . Do you think that such a monstrous proposition can be accepted by the Hindus of Assam?' But to Gandhi, Patel said, 'From the start their (the Raj's) interpretation was different' (*Patel*: 381).

Accompanied by Kripalani, who had replaced Nehru as Congress President, Jawaharlal came to Noakhali to consult Gandhi, whose advice was that the British award had to be accepted by Congress. However, if Assam wanted to stay out of the Muslim Group, it could act on its own, seceding if need be from Congress. Likewise, if the Sikhs did not want to remain in the Muslim Group to which they had been assigned, they too could act on their own.

In a note that he scribbled for Jawaharlal at 3 a.m. on 30 Deember, shortly before Nehru's departure from Noakhali, Gandhi recalled the misgivings about the 16 May Plan that he had conveyed in June to the Working Committee but added that 'this does not mean that what was done by the Working Committee should not have been done.' He felt it appropriate, however, to ask Nehru to meet him whenever necessary or send an emissary if 'you cannot come' or if it was not 'seemly that you should often run to me.' The note's last sentence said: 'So, I suggest frequent consultations with an old, tried servant of the nation.' That he had to say this showed his distance in 1946-7 from Nehru, Patel and company. That he said it showed his sense of duty.

Earlier, when leaders of the Assam Congress had called on Gandhi, they were advised to rebel against Congress if the latter accepted the HMG award. Wavell described Gandhi's advice as 'mischievous' (*Journal:* 409) and Jinnah denounced Congress when the advice was carried out. Was it proper for a Mahatma to ask a political body to accept an award and a provincial unit of that body to rebel against that award? The exercise was the inescapable corollary of the conditional acceptance of a 'purposely vague' Plan.

We should recognize that while he strove with all his being for Hindu-Muslim peace at the grassroots, Gandhi's bid for a Congress-League rapprochement was spasmodic. He had concluded that a political accord was impossible as long as British power remained in India. It was in the prevention of Greater Pakistan that much of his zeal was spent. His doings and sayings in Noakhali suggest that his political aims at this juncture were to show that Hindus and Muslims could live together, to keep all of Bengal if possible out of Pakistan, and to ensure that Assam and West Bengal were not absorbed, through strategies such as a Muslim-Harijan alliance, into any future Pakistan.

At the end of February he was asked in Haimchar whether Bengal's partition was not desirable. His answer was that he preferred a single India and a single Bengal, yet just as India's Hindu majority did not have the right 'to keep everyone united by means of compulsion,' Bengal's Muslim majority did not have the right to compel the province's Hindus. Gandhi said he was 'as much against forced partition as against forced unity' (87:30).

❋

It was a message sent by Syed Mahmud, a Minister in Bihar, that brought Gandhi to Bihar on 5 March. At his last prayer meeting in East Bengal, Gandhi told an audience of about 30,000 in Chandpur that so far 'he had turned a deaf ear to pressing requests made to him by the Bengal Premier and Mr Fazlul Huq to go to Bihar' and thought that he would 'affect the Bihar Hindus from my place in Bengal,' but Mahmud's letter brought by his secretary had persuaded him (87:35).

By now Attlee had announced that Britain would quit India by June 1948, handing over 'to some form of central government or in some areas to the existing provincial governments' or 'in such other way as may seem most reasonable.' The word of departure was thus laced with a clear hint of partition. 'This may lead to Pakistan for those provinces or portions which may want it,' Gandhi wrote to Nehru. Attlee also said that Wavell was being replaced by Mountbatten.

The departure deadline and the possibility of power going directly to provincial governments triggered a struggle for their control. The League was in charge of the ministries of Bengal and Sind and could count on Baluchistan. But a coalition of the League's foes governed the Punjab, and Congress was in power in the N.W.F.P. and Assam, provinces also claimed for Pakistan. In these three provinces the League launched anti-ministry movements. Its bid in Assam was wholly unsuccessful, but in the Frontier province the cry of Islam-in-danger found receptive ears, and in the Punjab the Unionist Premier, Khizr Hyat Khan, was dubbed a stooge of Islam's enemies.

India was polarizing, a process decisively aided by the violence in Calcutta, Noakhali and Bihar. In the Punjab, Muslims, Sikhs and Hindus raised private armies. Defying restrictions, crowds of Muslims, including women and students, picketed government buildings in the Punjab, hoisted the League's flag over them, and stopped the movement of trains.

On 2 March, Khizr gave in and resigned. Next day the Raj asked the League leader, the Khan of Mamdot, to form a new ministry. To the Sikhs this seemed the start of oppression. In the riots that ensued, different private armies went into action. At least a thousand, and perhaps several times that number, were killed within a few days in half a dozen cities and numerous villages of the Punjab. The Mamdot ministry, which in any case lacked a majority, was dismissed, and the Governor, Evan Jenkins, assumed direct power, but the Punjab's unity was dead.

In Bihar, Mahmud's ministerial colleagues attacked him for urging Gandhi's visit without consulting them, but Gandhi defended

Mahmud and made Mahmud's Patna house his residence in Bihar. The loss of life and property in Bihar greatly exceeded the Noakhali levels but neither the Ministry nor the provincial Congress committee seemed sufficiently resolved to restore normalcy. There was evidence to suggest that some Congressmen had connived at the violence.

However, what Bihar's Hindus told Gandhi was the mirror image of what he had heard from Noakhali's Muslims. Goondas, not Hindus, had misbehaved; Muslims had supplied provocation; many Hindus had gone to the aid of Muslims; 'innocent' Hindus were being harassed by the police; and so on. Gandhi's response was as candid as it had been in Noakhali. During a discussion with Congress workers he said on 19 March:

> Is it or isn't it a fact that quite a large number of Congressmen took part in the disturbances? How many of the 132 members of your committee were involved? . . . I have also worked in the Congress. Today I am not even a four-anna member. But there was a time when I was . . . virtually all in all. Hence I know the Congress inside out.
>
> I wish to ask you, how could you live to see an old woman of 110 years being butchered before your eyes? . . . I will not rest nor let others rest. I will wander all over on foot and ask the skeletons lying about how all this had happened . . . If I find that my comrades are deceiving me, I will be furious and I shall walk barefoot on and on through hail or storm. I will throw away the soft seat and other amenities which you have offered me (87:118-9).

Then Gandhi reminded the Congress leaders that in 1917 he had defied the British authorities' order to him to quit Champaran. 'It is difficult to force me out of Bihar.' But compared with Champaran in 1917 'the work in Bihar this time is far more difficult and significant.' He would 'strive to the utmost to prove that Hinduism and Islam can exist side by side.' One of the leaders admitted that 'we have become vicious, the whole atmosphere has been vitiated' and that some Congressmen were 'carried away by the tide.' Gandhi said they should 'either achieve success' in restoring amity 'or die in the attempt' (87:118-21).

Earlier, Gandhi had told Bihar's Congress leaders and Ministers that from what he had heard 'the Bihar massacre was like the Jallianwala Bagh massacre.' 'Give us orders,' said Rajendra Prasad, President of the Constituent Assembly and Gandhi's colleague from Champaran days. Gandhi replied: 'In Champaran nobody ordered anybody. It was spontaneous loyalty. You saw the miracle.' Thirty years later, Congress's leaders were still prepared to obey Gandhi, but their hearts leapt at other hopes. They were human. Gandhi understood this and backed them, but he also wanted them to be heroic.

✳

Bihar's skeletons, and those of Noakhali, spoke to Gandhi. Facing their evidence, looking at ruined homes, at pieces of flesh sticking to crumbling walls and into the shattered eyes of women and orphans, Gandhi seemed to weaken in his resistance to partition before independence. An indication was his willingness to see Bihar's Muslim refugees settle in villages with substantial Muslim populations instead of returning to the scenes of their suffering. Earlier he had been opposed to the creation of such Muslim 'pockets.'

Another indication, indirect but meaningful, was a statement by him before Bihar's leading Congressmen: 'He wondered whether his earlier determination to stay on in Noakhali was not "sheer obstinacy" on his part' (87: 59). If conviction about persevering in Noakhali now appeared as obstinacy, his beliefs about partition too may have been assailed by doubt, especially since preventing partition was one of his principal Noakhali aims.

Warmth was interwoven with directness in his Bihar discourse. Quoting 'the English saying "The greater the sin, the greater the saint"' to a prayer meeting audience of over 100,000 on 5 March, Gandhi asked for 'honest reparations greater in magnitude than their crimes.' If these were forthcoming, Bihar would 'hold her head high' again. Abducted women, stolen goods and illegal weapons should be surrendered — to the police if possible or, if necessary, to him, Prasad or Mahmud (87:43-6). When a Hindu beggar gave four annas for the Muslim relief fund that he had initiated, Gandhi told Manu, 'This is true charity! These are the people of Bihar!' (87:51). Patting the beggar on his back, Gandhi asked him to give up begging and work — at spinning at least.

He invited Ghaffar Khan to join him in Bihar — to reach the province's Muslims more effectively and also to discuss the future of the N.W.F.P. As in Noakhali, he went to affected villages. As in Noakhali, he taught through prayer meetings. In Bihar these were at times attended by tens or even hundreds of thousands. On 11 March he explained the dynamics and folly of retaliation:

> If I am starving and you feed me, the contentment in my eyes will brighten your face too. But suppose I am starving and demand food from you by abusing you. You will drive me away, saying, 'Go and starve yourself to death.' My abuses will not get me food. They will, however, make me feel that I am a brave man. Again, if you ask your gatekeeper to beat me up for my abuses, that will sow the seeds of hatred against you in my heart . . . The next day I shall gather a few friends and retaliate. If you manage to kill me, it will create among my relations and friends a feeling of revenge against you . . . .The world has reached the stage of atomic warfare in returning violence for violence (87:70).

We may note that in this parable Gandhi casts himself in a beggar's role.

Biharis were proud of their role in 1942. Acknowledging it, Gandhi contended that its violent component had aided the communal violence of 1946-7. 'Once the evil spirit of violence is unleashed, by its inherent nature it cannot be checked or even kept within any prescribed limits. All violence inevitably tends to run to excess'

(87:424). To those who thought their own hands were clean, Gandhi said: 'Everyone of us is equally guilty of what anyone of us has done' (87:55).

Hindu men gave money and Hindu women their jewels for Gandhi's fund for Muslims. In the village of Siparah, Gandhi was given a purse, a letter of apology, and an assurance that returning Muslims would be protected. Many Hindus wrote to him confessing their guilt. Fifty persons wanted in connection with the riots surrendered themselves in Masaurhi the day after Gandhi's arrival there. He told Bihar's Ministers that if he succeeded in Bihar, 'India would be saved, the situation in the Punjab would be controlled, and the Frontier Province, Sind and Baluchistan would come into their own.' Preventing partition was still his desire.

But the Ministers dragged their feet over the inquiry into the violence that Gandhi (and Bihar's Muslim League) had been asking for. Gandhi had demanded a similar inquiry into the Bengal riots. Bihar's British Governor, Hugh Dow, and the Home Member in New Delhi, Gandhi's own Vallabhbhai Patel, supported the Ministers in their opinion that an inquiry would worsen the atmosphere instead of improving it. Neither Congress nor the Raj was interested at this stage in bids to restore Hindu-Muslim trust.

❁

On 8 March, well before Mountbatten's arrival, the Congress Working Committee took a decisive step by asking that Punjab's 'predominantly Muslim portion . . . be separated from the predominantly non-Muslim portion.' Though Bengal was not mentioned, the Working Committee clearly implied support for that province's division as well. The partition of India as a whole seemed a corollary. Gandhi was neither consulted nor informed in advance about this move, and this despite the reply he telegraphed on 3 March to a wire from Kripalani, the Congress President, urging Gandhi to attend the Working Committee deliberations. In his wire Gandhi said: 'Regret inability. Send messenger Bihar' (87:38).

No messenger seems to have been sent. On 22 March Gandhi

wrote to Patel: 'If you can explain your Punjab resolution to me, please do so. I do not understand it.' Patel answered: 'It is difficult, in a letter, to explain the Punjab resolution. It was arrived at after a great deal of reflection, not in haste or without thought' (*Patel*: 390). There was a similar exchange between Gandhi and Nehru. Gandhi's message to Vallabhbhai conveys unhappiness. However, the fact that he sent it on 22 March, fourteen days after the resolution was passed, suggests either an unwillingness to clash with Patel and Nehru, or an uncertainty about what he himself felt, or both. As mentioned before, the skeletons of Bihar and Noakhali had softened Gandhi's resistance to Pakistan before independence; he was aware that West Bengal's Hindus wanted Bengal's partition (87:282); and he was opposed to coercion against Muslims who wanted to separate from India, or against non-Muslims in the Punjab and Bengal wanting to separate from the Muslims of their provinces.

Gandhi was opposed to a Greater Pakistan even if 'linked' to India. He did not think that Jinnah would retain any links, and he did not want non-Muslim areas detached. He knew that Jinnah was opposed to Smaller Pakistan, even if conceded before independence. Reflecting on these two 'givens,' and influenced also by his view that government by one party was preferable to a coalition about which neither party was in earnest, Gandhi came up with the solution that he proposed in New Delhi on 1 April in a private talk with Mountbatten, the new Viceroy:

> Let Jinnah head an Indian government of his choice, comprising League members alone or including others as well; unless Mountbatten ruled that a League measure was not in the national interest, Congress would back the Jinnah government in the Central Assembly; and let Muslim Groups too be formed within India, but without Assam, the Frontier province, East Punjab and West Bengal, unless, as a result of the League's persuasiveness, any or all of these areas opted to join them.

This was the gist of Gandhi's proposal. Its last item was that in the event of refusal by Jinnah, the offer, *mutatis mutandis*, should go to Congress. Gandhi's preference for a cohesive government had been made known from 1945. In June 1946, when Wavell was attempting to put together a coalition, Gandhi had written to him: 'You are a great soldier — a daring soldier. Dare to do the right. You must make your choice of one horse or the other . . . Choose the names submitted either by Congress or the League. For God's sake do not make an incompatible mixture and in trying to do so produce a fearful explosion' (*Journal:* 293).

Gandhi was thus offering Jinnah the Prime Ministership of India, and within India a truncated Pakistan, with scope for expansion. This was his alternative both to a sovereign truncated Pakistan and to a Greater Pakistan loosely connected to India. Also, and this too was evidence of the skeletons' influence, he was offering Mountbatten, the British Viceroy, a crucial role, a veto in fact, swallowing his principle of a purely Indian solution. This is the more interesting when we realize that Gandhi had started the interview by telling the Viceroy that Britain had ruled India by using Hindu-Muslim differences even if she did not create them. Gandhi sweetened the dose for himself by clarifying that Mountbatten would act 'as a man and not in his representative capacity.'

Gandhi's proposal staggered Mountbatten who first accused Gandhi of suggesting a League government but designing a Congress one, for surely Gandhi expected Jinnah to reject the offer? When Gandhi said that he would offer all his services to Mountbatten to 'get the Jinnah government through, first by exercising his influence with Congress to accept it and secondly by touring the length and breadth of the country getting all the peoples of India to accept the decision,' the Viceroy replied that he was convinced of Gandhi's sincerity (*TOP* 10:84).

Mountbatten's immediate, and seemingly positive, reaction to the plan did not survive his consultations with his staff. Though assuring Gandhi that he would examine his scheme, and privately telling his staff that 'it would not be very easy for Mr Jinnah to refuse Mr Gandhi's offer' and that 'basically Mr Gandhi's objective was to retain the unity of India and basically he was right in this,' the Viceroy sought ways to kill the proposal.

That Gandhi mentioned his plan to Mountbatten before discussing it with his Congress colleagues is one of the ironies of the freedom movement. Aware of his declining sway in Congress, Gandhi hoped to use Mountbatten (the chief of 'the third party' that Gandhi normally wanted to keep out) for obtaining his colleagues' acceptance. Nehru and Patel, on their part, were already conferring much more with the Viceroy than with Gandhi. Mountbatten and Patel had discussed their opposition to Gandhi's wish for an inquiry in Bihar, and Nehru had told the Viceroy, with reference to Gandhi's work in Bihar, that Gandhi 'was going round with ointment trying to heal one sore spot after another on the body of India, instead of diagnosing the cause of this eruption of sores and participating in the treatment of the body as a whole' (*TOP* 10:71).

At the Gandhi-Mountbatten discussion the Bihar inquiry had come up. The Viceroy said that he, Patel and the Bihar Governor were opposed to an inquiry. According to Mountbatten's record, Gandhi 'flatly disagreed' and said that it was 'essential that the Congress government in Bihar should in all events show good faith.' At this point the Viceroy asked Gandhi to 'discuss the matter with the Home Member, Sardar Patel' (*TOP* 10:83). We are not told whether Gandhi showed a reaction but the viceregal confidence about the Sardar's support must have humiliated Gandhi.

While Gandhi hoped to enlist Mountbatten in his approach to Congress colleagues, he was of course bound to talk to them on his own and had told the Viceroy that he would. That Gandhi might bring round the Working Committee to his plan was a thought that seemed to trouble the Viceroy's staff and Mountbatten himself. After the possibility was discussed by Mountbatten and his staff on 5 April, the Viceroy, so the Mountbatten Papers tell us, 'decided to talk to Pandit Nehru that afternoon about Mr Gandhi's scheme' (*TOP* 10:128).

No student of this episode can fail to be struck by the exertions in the Viceroy's office against the scheme. The staff, and the Viceroy too, seemed to resist a solution emanating from Gandhi, an encroachment on their prerogative by an unrepentant foe of the Raj. As active as the rest was V.P. Menon, who had worked under Wavell as Reforms Commissioner and was retained by Mountbatten as Secretary (Reforms). He prepared a note: 'Tactics to be adopted with Gandhi as regards his scheme.' Menon had established a close relationship with Patel, who was opposed to any idea of a Jinnah government (see *Last Phase* 2:80) and by now a convert to Partition. The Gandhi-Mountbatten meeting had taken place on the morning of 1 April. At 2.30 that afternoon Menon called on Patel. Later in the day Patel and Mountbatten met. The Viceroy's record of this interview contains no mention of Gandhi's scheme, but Mountbatten took care to reiterate his opposition to a Bihar inquiry (*TOP* 10:73).

As for Nehru, the Viceroy's office turned to his close friend, Krishna Menon, for supplementing Mountbatten's direct effort. After the Viceroy and Krishna Menon had lunched together on 5 April, Lord Ismay, chief of Mountbatten's staff, had 'a prolonged talk about Gandhi's proposals' with Krishna Menon, who then went to work on Nehru.[41]

On 9 April Mountbatten tested the waters by saying to Jinnah that 'it was a daydream of mine to be able to put the Central Government under the Prime Ministership of Mr Jinnah himself.' Mountbatten's record of the interview, at which, among other things, Jinnah 'once more appealed' against 'a moth-eaten Pakistan,' goes on to say:

> Some 35 minutes later, Mr Jinnah, who had not referred previously to my personal remark about him, suddenly made a reference out of the blue to the fact that I had wanted him to be the Prime Minister. There is no doubt that it had greatly tickled his vanity, and that he had kept turning over the proposition in his mind. Mr Gandhi's famous scheme may yet go through on the pure vanity of Mr Jinnah! (*TOP* 10:104).

Azad also surprised the Viceroy by telling him that Gandhi's was 'a perfectly feasible' plan and that there was a chance that Jinnah might accept it. However, Mountbatten elicited Azad's agreement to the view that other solutions might be more practical (*TOP* 10:86).

The Viceroy's anxiety did not last long. On 11 April Gandhi wrote to him: 'I had several short talks with Pandit Nehru and [last night] an hour's talk with him alone, and then with several members of the Working Committee . . . about the formula I had sketched before you . . . I am sorry to say that I failed to carry any of them with me except Badshah Khan . . . Thus I have to ask you to omit me from your consideration. Congressmen who are in the Interim Government are stalwarts, seasoned servants of the nation, and, therefore, so far as the Congress viewpoint is concerned, they will be complete advisers' (87: 254-5). (They included Nehru, Patel, Azad, Prasad and Rajagopalachari.) Gandhi ended by saying that he was returning to Bihar.

The letter suggests that despite the opinion that Azad held even he did not back the proposal during the discussions to which Gandhi refers. Rajagopalachari noted in his diary that Gandhi's 'ill-conceived plan of solving the present difficulties' was 'objected to by everybody and scotched.'[42] An immediate and complete separation of Smaller Pakistan was by now the Congress leaders' agreed if still unspelt solution. The Interim Government was a house at war; the League seemed to block all roads before the Congress leaders; they wanted to get on with governing even if the India they governed excluded Smaller Pakistan.

Personal elements played a role in Mountbatten's worry about the possibility of Gandhi's plan succeeding and in the Congress leaders' view of it as 'ill-conceived.' In a conversation on 8 April, Gandhi said: 'Who cares for the nation today? Everyone wants to realize his ambition . . .' (87:233). That an interest in power was not the only consideration with the Congress leaders was, however, freely acknowledged by Gandhi, who wrote to Patel, from his train to Patna, on 13 April: 'There is a wide and frequent divergence of views between us . . . Is it desirable that I should see the Viceroy even in my individual capacity? . . . It is possible that in the course of administering the affairs of the millions you can see what I cannot. Perhaps I too would act and speak as you do if I were in your place' (*Patel*: 393). Yet the letter was also a confession of defeat.

Gandhi was admitting that Patel, representing Congress, and Mountbatten, representing the Raj, had isolated him.

In any case, Gandhi's proposal was never put to Jinnah. V.P. Menon thought at the time that the League leader would not have accepted it, a view supported by some future Pakistani scholars. However, one of Jinnah's biographers felt that Gandhi's plan 'might just have worked; surely this was a King Solomon solution.'[43] That Jinnah's acceptance was not to be entirely ruled out is suggested by the League leader's comment on a similar proposal in 1942. We have seen it previously: 'If the British government accepts the solemn declaration of Mr Gandhi and by an arrangement hands over the government of the country to the Muslim League, I am sure that under Muslim rule non-Muslims would be treated fairly, justly, nay generously . . .'

Gandhi's mood of disappointment and anxiety (and, for all that, ultimate faith) can be seen in what he said to visitors from South Africa, Yusuf Dadoo and G.M. Naicker, on the day before he left for Bihar: 'India is now on the threshold of independence. But . . . to my mind it will be no independence if India is partitioned and the minorities do not enjoy security, protection and equal treatment . . . If what is happening today is an earnest of things to come after independence, it bodes no good for the future . . . I therefore feel ill at ease. But I am content to leave the future in God's good hands' (87:257).

Before leaving for Bihar, Gandhi signed, along with Jinnah, a joint appeal for peace. This had been a Mountbatten suggestion. Gandhi had thought that Kripalani, who was the Congress President, should sign in addition to, or instead of, himself. To be confined, even by implication, to Hindus or the Congress was not to Gandhi's liking. But Jinnah said he would not sign if Kripalani signed, and Mountbatten pressed Gandhi, whose way out was to sign his name in Hindi, English — and Urdu. By signing in Urdu he was asserting his right to address Muslims as well. The joint appeal said:

> We deeply deplore the recent acts of lawlessness and violence that have brought the utmost disgrace on the fair name of India and the greatest misery to innocent people, irrespective of who were the aggressors and who were the victims. We denounce for all time the use of force to achieve political ends, and we call upon all the communities of India . . . not only to refrain from all acts of violence and disorder, but also to avoid both in speech and writing any words which might be construed as an incitement to such acts (87:261).

The Punjab was the latest scene of violence, and Gandhi had wondered in Delhi whether he should not go there instead of returning to Bihar. On 7 April he said: 'Today a Hindu from Rawalpindi narrated the tragic events . . . there. Fifty-eight of his companions were killed just because they were Hindus. He and his son alone could survive . . . No matter how provocative had been the language of Hindus and Sikhs in the Punjab, that was no excuse for the barbarity and cruelty perpetrated on non-Muslims by Muslims in the areas where they were in a majority.' But he felt he lacked a clear call to the Punjab. 'Whether I go to the Punjab or not, I shall certainly work for it,' he said (87:259).

He ruled Delhi out. Nehru and Patel were in charge there. Staying on there 'is for me fraught with danger,' he said on 11 April (87:258-9). Yet he took care to refute an item 'in a leading paper with a large circulation' alleging that Gandhi was leaving Delhi because he had 'fallen out' with the Working Committee. This was 'sheer nonsense,' Gandhi said in his post-prayer speech of 12 April, just before his departure for Patna. He pointed out that Azad, Rajaji, the Sardar, Nehru and Kripalani had seen him earlier in the day. 'We have our differences,' Gandhi admitted, adding, however, that he had told Patel that he 'would be back the moment I heard his summons.' 'Would I talk that way,' Gandhi went on, 'if we had quarrelled? If I choose to be a rebel I can be a pretty tough one'

(87:264-5). His resolve not to allow the sharpest difference to cause a break is a clear, continuous thread in the story of Gandhi's relationship with Nehru, Patel, Azad, Prasad, Rajagopalachari and Kripalani.

Gandhi spent April and May 1947 in Bihar, Calcutta and Delhi. In Calcutta, Suhrawardy, Bengal's League Chief Minister, was attempting to keep his province united. Sarat Bose made a similar effort for a single, independent Bengal. Though he warmed to the concept, Gandhi wanted an assurance that Bengal and its Hindus were not being tricked into joining a Greater Pakistan; he had smelled such a danger when the League named Mandal to the Interim Government. Jinnah's fear, we may note, was of the opposite kind. He thought that a united Bengal and its Muslims might be lured into joining 'Hindu' India. On the other hand, Shyama Prasad Mookerjee's championship of the province's partition was drawing a strong response from West Bengal's Hindus.

The record suggests that it was to weigh the option of backing the United Bengal movement that Gandhi made his May visit to Calcutta. He probed Suhrawardy and his colleagues at lengthy meetings and finally made a remarkable offer:

> I recognize the seriousness of the position in Bengal in the matter of the partition. If you are absolutely sincere in your professions and would disabuse me of all the suspicion against you, and if you would retain Bengal for the Bengalis — Hindus and Muslims — I am quite willing to act as your honorary private secretary and live under your roof till Hindus and Muslims begin to live as the brothers that they are (87:460).

Thus Gandhi wanted to test, trust and affect Suhrawardy. We will see before long that this 'mad offer,' as Suhrawardy called it, of 13 May, conveyed by Gandhi in writing, was accepted but only after India's and Bengal's partition had become facts. In May it was ignored, a reaction that must have contributed to Gandhi's unwillingness to throw his weight behind the United Bengal movement.

Earlier in May Gandhi was once more in Delhi, at Nehru's request. On 6 May he and Jinnah had a long talk in the latter's home on Aurangzeb Road, their last encounter. Patel and others had opposed the meeting, but Gandhi said he would go to Jinnah 'seventy times seven' if necessary. 'I claim to have his friendship,' Gandhi said after the meeting. 'After all he also belongs to India. Whatever happens, I have to spend my life with him' (87:433). A statement about their discussion drafted by Jinnah and agreed to by Gandhi said that while in Gandhi's opinion partition was neither desirable nor inevitable, Jinnah thought the contrary. It added that the two would do their best to ensure that their April 12 appeal for peace was heeded.

A 20 April speech by Nehru had conceded Smaller Pakistan: 'The Muslim League can have Pakistan, if they wish to have it, but on the condition that they do not take away other parts of India which do not wish to join Pakistan.' On 29 April Prasad told the Constituent Assembly of the likelihood of 'not only a division of India, but a division of some provinces' (*Patel*: 396-7). 'But I for one cannot agree to Pakistan on any account,' said Gandhi on 7 May (87:432). His dissent was clear and constant, but it was also clear that it would take the form of dissociation and not of disruption or defiance. 'When I say that I cannot bear it, I mean that I do not wish to be a party to it,' he said (87:433).

He tested the ground for signs that Partition could be foiled. The Calcutta probe was an instance of this exercise. Another was a talk with two prominent socialists, Aruna Asaf Ali and Asoka Mehta, on 6 May. 'Tell me how many of you are with me?' he asked them. 'Is Aruna with me? Are Asoka and Achyut (Patwardhan) with me? No, you are not. The Congress is not. So I am left to plough my lonely furrow . . .' Aruna and Asoka did not challenge his statements (87:423).

To many Partition seemed to offer an end to the chain of killings and also to the League's obstructions. It also, by now, seemed unavoidable. Yet it was helped, too, by the inability of those opposed to it to find common ground. The socialists critical of Partition were not willing to abjure violence and class war, which was Gandhi's stipulation to them; nationalist Muslims in the U.P. and Bihar who were fearful of Partition's implications had little affinity with staunch Hindus resenting the Pakistan demand such as the U.P.'s Purshottamdas Tandon or the Hindu Mahasabha leaders, or with Hindu minorities, anxious about the future, in Sind, the Frontier and West Punjab.

Gandhi was unable, amidst this reality, to envision, let alone forge, an alliance for defying Partition. As he put it, he saw 'nothing in common between me and those who want me to oppose Pakistan except that we are both opposed to the division. How can love and enmity go together?' (88:118). The opposition of most of the others, of the fervent Hindu in the Indian heartland and of nervous Muslim or Hindu minorities was based on distrust and fear, his on trust.

In defence of his non-defiance, Gandhi also claimed, not without truth, that a majority of the people of India seemed to favour Partition. He noted that 'the Hindus and the Sikhs all say that they would live in their own homelands, not in the Muslims' . . . The Khalsa as also the Hindus desired it (division)' (88:75). On 9 June he said:

> Lately I have been receiving a number of letters attacking me. A friend points out how ineffective were my words when I said that vivisection of the country would be the vivisection of my own body . . . But when the popular opinion is contrary to mine, should I force my own view on the people? . . . I can say with confidence that if all the non-Muslims were with me, I would not let India be divided. But I must admit that today the general opinion is not with me, and I must step aside and stay back (88: 117-8).

Ready himself not to 'worry about anarchy' and saying 'I am after all a gambler,' he noticed no groundswell of support. 'Who would listen to me?' he said on 4 June. 'You (the Hindus) do not listen to me. The Muslims have given me up. Nor can I fully convince the Congress of my point of view' (88:75). He was in agony. 'I feel as if I was thrown into a fire-pit and my heart is burning,' he said on June 5, but to die by self-immolation 'in order to prove that I alone was right' would be 'mad' (88:84).

If he saw no popular will against Partition, he saw no alternative to the leadership of Nehru, Patel, Azad, Prasad and Rajagopalachari. The five were not the only leaders and not equally influential: Nehru and Patel were in a category of their own. Yet the five were the core of a team that was hard to replace and thus dangerous, even if simple, to dislodge. Though the five did not agree on everything, they were as one on many crucial things. It was difficult to contemplate an alternative team approaching the five in strength, cohesion and prestige.

This became a decisive consideration for Gandhi because in 1947 the Partition that the League was demanding was not the only threat to the order and unity of India. There was every likelihood that the British would permit each of the 500-odd princely states to declare independence, turning India, as Gandhi said on 8 April, into a ground for numerous battles (87:233). If he defied the storm, he knew he might hit an iceberg — and lack a trusty crew.

Then there was his attachment to this crew. Kripalani would afterwards speak of 'the emotional attachment' between Gandhi and Nehru. This was real and never denied, but it also existed between Gandhi and the four others, and between Gandhi and Kripalani, and in Gandhi's relationship with several other Congress leaders. (We can think of Ghaffar Khan, Pant, Kher, Sarojini Naidu, Pattabhi Sitaramayya, Prafulla Ghosh and Shankarrao Deo, among others, confining ourselves to one generation.) The bonds built over thirty years of sharing exertions, joys, sorrows, hopes and disappointments were not inconsequential.

'I have to do many things out of the love that binds me to Jawahar and Sardar,' Gandhi said on 22 July. 'They have tied me up with the chains of their love' (88:394). Severe as he could be, Gandhi never forgot the sacrifices that Jawaharlal, Vallabhbhai and others had made because of him. On 22 July he said: 'Jawahar and his colleagues appear old. The struggles of satyagraha and frequent incarcerations have reduced their expectation of life by 20 to 25 years' (88: 398). Aware of their yearning for power, he yet refused to obstruct while they encashed their costly and faithful toil of three decades. Time and again he conveyed (e.g., to Patel on 13 April, Nehru on 9 June, and Rajagopalachari on 25 May) his unhappiness at the gulf he felt with them. The letter to Patel we have seen. To Nehru he spoke of the 'differences in outlook and opinion between the members of the W.C. and me' (88:113). To Rajagopalachari he said: 'I see no place for myself in what is happening around us today. You know I have given up the hope of living for 125 years. I might last a year or two more' (88:4). But despite this sense of isolation and rejection he would not readily break with, or unseat, the persons whose growth he had watched over and helped, and who, as far as he could see, comprised India's best material. Admitting that a revolt by him was 'not inconceivable under all circumstances' (88:63), he ruled it out in the conditions of the summer of 1947.

His response to Partition contained four elements: dissociation, a bid to make Partition an Indian rather than a British process, vigilance in regard to the princely states, and an effort for a Hindu-Muslim rapprochement that might overcome the blow of political division. An instance of the second element was his statement on 7 July:

> [The division] should be taken as final, no more open to discussion now. But if ten representatives of either party sit together in a mud hut and resolve that they will not leave the hut till they have arrived at an understanding, then I can say than the decision that they will arrive at will be a thousand times better than the present Bill before the British Parliament . . . which envisages the setting up of two Dominions.

His hurt pride was a factor in this reaction. The Viceroy was 're-proved' (Mountbatten's word) by Gandhi on 9 July for referring to the two 'nations' being created and was advised to use 'States or Countries instead' (88:490). Gandhi's dislike of the theory extended to the sound. As a proud Indian that he never ceased to be, he also hated the division under British auspices. We see this in an account he gave of a talk with Mountbatten on 6 June: 'He said that the British could not leave at once because even dividing the effects of a small house took time and here it was the question of dividing a whole country. But I asked the Viceroy to relax. It would be better that we should attend to the task of division ourselves' (88:92).

But commonsense too was involved. Since Hindus and Muslims had no escape from living right next to one another, arrangements they devised among themselves had more meaning than those arbitrated by a departing power. And if the two sides could not work things out on their own? Gandhi was prophetic in the future he painted:

> The army is going to be divided — the army which so far had one single purpose, whatever that purpose might have been. This division of the army certainly fills the heart of every patriot with fear and misgivings. Why are two armies being created? Are they to defend the country against foreign aggression or are they to fight each other and prove to the world that we are good only for fighting and killing each other? (88:297)

On 4 June, after Congress had in writing accepted Partition, Gandhi said: 'I would like to request Jinnah Saheb, implore him, to have direct talks with us at least now. Whatever has happened is all right, but now let us sit together and decide about the future. Let him forget all about the Viceroy now, and let him invite us to come to any understanding he wishes to have, so that it is in the interest of all of us' (88:76).

When Mountbatten charged Congress with withholding cooperation in working out the division of assets and liabilities and hinted that Britain's departure might be delayed as a result, Gandhi wrote one of his toughest letters to the Viceroy. We have seen it before in another context. He spoke of defying 'the atom bomb . . . what to say of a fleet of Dreadnoughts.' It is a classic document, brilliant in its summary of the nationalist answer to the Empire's claim that threatened minorities required its presence in India (June 27-8; 88:225-7).

The princely states featured strongly in his dealings with the Viceroy and in public utterances. The author, when freedom was distant, of Congress's policy of leaving the princes alone (he did not want to push them into an alliance with the Raj), Gandhi now told the Maharajas and the Nawabs that their interest lay in accepting the sovereignty of their people. They should not toy with independence; it was risky. The Raj was going but the people were coming into their own. The rulers should do what their subjects wanted, and join either India or Pakistan. From April 1947, if not earlier, Kashmir, Junagadh and Hyderabad appeared in his letters and talks, and on 13 June he warned Sir C.P. Ramaswami Aiyar, the Dewan of Travancore, who had said on 11 June that Travancore would 'set itself up as an independent and sovereign state,' and the Nizam of Hyderabad, on whose behalf a similar declaration was made on 12 June, that 'the Princes . . . should be the servants of their people; they can be masters no more' (88:146-8).

We should look, finally, at his bid to defeat the division on the map with a unity of hearts. 'All my activities revolve round the unity of India,' he said on 29 July (88: 457). Part of his strategy was a defence of Hindustani written in either Nagari or Urdu as the subcontinent's common language. In the polarization of 1947, he lost this battle too, and Hindi in the Nagari script was chosen in India, and Urdu in Pakistan.

The fact that Hindi and Urdu were essentially the same when spoken was refused recognition, and the champions of Hindi and Urdu devoted themselves to the expurgation in one case of 'Islamic' influences, which meant words of Persian or Arabic origin, and in the other of 'Hindu' links betrayed by phrases descending from Sanskrit. Thus Savarkar had said: 'Hindustani must be ruthlessly suppressed . . . It is our bounden duty to oust out . . . all unnecessary alien words whether Arabic or English from every Hindu tongue, whether provincial or dialectical. Nagari script along with the Hindi language must be made a compulsory subject in every school in the case of Hindu students.'[44]

Yet habit and convenience were to prove hard to overthrow, and decades later a great many people in North India and Pakistan would continue to speak a language that Gandhi had espoused but lawmakers had rejected on both sides of the emerging border. Though he felt that ground reality was on his side, Gandhi was much hurt by the dismissal of Hindustani and the antagonism to 'their' script, whether Nagari or Urdu.

To Kulsum Sayani, a Muslim co-worker in Bombay, he said: 'Whatever is decided by the C.A. (Constituent Assembly), Hindustani with the two scripts remains for you and me' (88:393). On 25 July he wrote: '[Neither] Hindi, highly Sanskritized, written in the Nagari characters, nor Urdu, highly Persianized, written in the Urdu characters, can ever be the link between two or more communities in India. It can only be a fusion of the two forms robbed of their artificial character and written either in the Nagari or the Urdu characters' (88: 420). Yet in 1947 fusion was not the popular wish, and the artificial seemed natural. (We may look, however, at a 1994 assessment: 'It is closer to the truth to say that Urdu and Hindi are one great language divided by a script and a lot of politics.')[45]

Gandhi's strategy included a refusal to limit himself to one of the two new countries. 'Both India and Pakistan are my country,' he said on 2 July. 'I am not going to take out a passport for going to Pakistan' (88:265). He saw value in declarations of his faith and hoped to infect others with it. To Bhimsen Sachar, the Punjab Congress leader, he said on 29 June: 'I shall be happy if you and your family do not leave Pakistan . . . All of you are my fellow soldiers. The strength of an army depends more on the soldiers than on the captain . . . But I am sorry to say that the local leaders who have some influence are trying at any cost to transfer their property and family to safety. When this is happening, with what face can I advise the poor not to run away . . . ?' (88:236).

He strove, too, in himself and others, to put disappointment to use and find meaning in it. To Hindu refugees from the Punjab he said on 24 June: 'If we learn a lesson from the misery that has overtaken us and make our lives successful, then that misery is not misery but happiness.' Using the *Ramayana* story, he added: 'Had Rama been crowned a king, he would have spent his days in luxury and the world would hardly have heard of him . . . But the day he was to be crowned, he had to put on bark clothing and go into exile. Isn't it the limit of unhappiness? But Rama and Sita turned that sorrow into joy' (88:203). It was a hard lesson in the summer of 1947 but one illumined by the courage of many a refugee — Sikh, Hindu and Muslim.

Goodwill towards the Pakistan-to-be was another element. 'Let the people in Pakistan go ahead of the Congress in their efforts to bring progress to their land,' he said on 7 June (88:99). More than once he acknowledged Jinnah's feat in obtaining his Pakistan. 'Mr Jinnah is doing something very big. Nobody had ever dreamt that in this day and age Pakistan would become a possibility,' he said on 11 June (88:134). 'It is Mr Jinnah who created Pakistan,' he said six days later, adding, 'with the help of the British,' and also, 'he is a brave man' (88:168). 'What the Qaid-e-Azam used to say has come to pass,' he said on 5 July. 'I think one can say that he has won complete victory' (88:281). This was not Jinnah's view. He had hoped for Greater Pakistan.

A challenge to Pakistan was joined to Gandhi's goodwill: 'The real test . . . will be the way it treats the nationalist Muslims, Christians, Sikhs and Hindus in Pakistan. Then there are Shias and Sunnis and other [Muslim sects]. It is to be seen how these various sects are treated' (88:282). On 7 June he 'appealed to Jinnah to build a Pakistan where the Gita could be recited side by side with the Koran, and the temple and the gurdwara would be given the same respect as the mosque, so that those who had been opposing Pakistan till now would be sorry for their mistake and would only sing praises of Pakistan' (88:99-100).

As a concluding element in Gandhi's strategy for unity despite Partition, we may mention his post-prayer speeches and also his response to the frequent objections to the recitation at his prayers of verses from the Koran. To those objecting that the Koran contained hard words for infidels, he said, 'The Koran says that an infidel would be answerable to God. But God would demand an explanation from everyone, even from a Muslim. And He would not question you about your words but your deeds.' He added, 'Why, our Manusmriti talks of pouring molten lead into the ears of the untouchables' (88:42).

He read out the abuse mailed to him and answered it. Of those Hindus who seemed to hate his stand he said, 'What pricks them most is that I keep calling upon them to lay down their lives instead of rousing them to kill. They want me to call upon the Hindus to avenge violence by violence, arson by arson. But I cannot deny my whole life . . .' (88:37). He could understand and even defend a fight with arms against attackers but 'what do you gain by taking an eye for an eye' from the innocent? (88:359-60). Hindu rulers like Maharana Ranjit Singh and Chhatrapati Shivaji had respected Islam, Gandhi said, adding that after defeating Muslim aggressors Maharana Kumbha had inscribed the name of Allah on the victory pillar at Chittor, next to Brahma, Vishnu and Mahesh (88:117).

In 1941 Ambedkar had written that to Hindus and Muslims 'Divinity is divided' and added: 'With the division of Divinity, humanity is divided and with the division of humanity they must remain divided.'[46] This view had its supporters among both Hindus and Muslims but Gandhi insisted on the unity of Divinity:

> When God is here, there and everywhere, God must be one. . . That is why I [ask] whether those calling God Rahim would have to leave Hindustan, and whether in the part described as Pakistan Rama as the name of God would be forbidden. Would someone who called God Krishna be turned out of Pakistan? . . . We shall worship God both as Krishna and Karim and show the world that we refuse to go mad (88:144).

To get more of a flavour of how he was tackling anger and hate, we can look at this excerpt from his post-prayer speech of 28 May: 'Yesterday somebody asked what we should do with a mad dog, whether we should not kill it. He should have actually asked what should be done when a man went mad . . .

'When I was about ten, a brother of mine had gone mad. Afterwards he was cured. He is no more. But I remember him well. In a fit of madness he would rush out and strike everyone. But what could I do? Could I beat him? Or could my mother or father beat him? A *vaidya* was called in and he was asked to treat my brother in every possible manner except by beating him. He was my blood-brother. But now I make no such distinctions. Now all of you are like my blood-brothers. If all of you lose your sanity and I happen to have an army at my disposal, do you think I should have you shot?' (88:28-9). But one who thought of Hindus *and* Muslims as blood-brothers was not popular in 1947.

As for those objecting to the Koran verses, he ensured that they were heard and treated with respect. If they presented their case soberly, he praised them. If the others were courteous towards an objector, he praised the others. Sometimes he cancelled his prayers if there was an objector. At other times he proceeded with them, requesting objectors to be content with their say. So the prayer ground became also a class in tolerance. It always also was a platform for addressing a Churchill, a Jinnah, a Mountbatten or a Nehru.

❉

To sum up, Congress turned towards the Partition option after HMG gave its 8 December 1946 award in the League's favour. The violence in the Punjab in early March 1947 produced the resolution in favour of the province's division. In April Nehru and Patel informed Mountbatten that Congress would concede Smaller Pakistan. At 0030 hours on 3 June, a letter signed by Kripalani, the Congress President, accepting Partition on the Working Committee's behalf was placed in the Viceroy's hands.

Invited to the Working Committee meeting on 2 June to discuss the Mountbatten Plan for Partition, Gandhi had said that 'though he did not agree with the decisions of the Working Committee regarding the division of India, he did not want to take any step which would stand in [their] way' (88: 61). He met Mountbatten, too, on 2 June, but it was his day of silence, so he was spared the embar-

rassment of repeating his dissent from colleagues as well as the
humiliation of conceding Partition before the Empire's Viceroy. On
the back of envelopes he scribbled some sentences: 'I am sorry I
can't speak . . . But I know you do not want me to break the silence.'
Mountbatten saved the envelopes 'as a document of some historic
importance' (88:60).

When, on 14 June, the AICC met to consider the Working
Committee's decision, Gandhi stuck, in a short speech that yet covered the ground, to his position of dissociation without defiance. He
pointed out that the AICC was constitutionally empowered to throw
out the decision and the leadership, which had not only accepted the
Plan before them but had helped, along with the League and the
Raj, to prepare it. Added Gandhi:

> You have a perfect right to [revolt], if you feel that you
> have the strength. But I do not find that strength in us
> today. If you had it I should also be with you and if I felt
> strong enough I would, alone, take up the flag of revolt.
> But today I do not see the conditions for doing so . . .
>
> I criticize them (the leadership), of course, but
> afterwards what? Shall I assume the burdens that they
> are carrying? Shall I become a Nehru or a Sardar or a
> Rajendra Prasad?
>
> We have to draw something good out of this bad thing
> . . . The world is watching us. In the three-quarters of the
> country that has fallen to our share Hinduism is going to
> be tested. If you show the true generosity of Hinduism,
> you will pass . . . If not, you will have proved Mr Jinnah's
> thesis that Muslims and Hindus are two separate nations,
> . . . that the two will never unite, and that the Gods of the
> two are different . . .

Going deeper and wider, and revealing an old view of his, Gandhi
suggested to the AICC that India's misfortunes, of which Partition
was the latest, were linked to the sin of untouchability. He asked:
'And what about the untouchables? It is said that Islam has risen to

abolish untouchability. If you say that untouchables are nothing, the Adivasis are nothing, then you are not going to survive . . . But if you do away with the distinction of *savarna* and *avarna*, if you treat the Shudras, the untouchables and the Adivasis as equals then something good will have come out of a bad thing . . . But if we oppress them and oppress those following other faiths then it will mean that we do not want India to survive.'

Referring, in the end, to the Princes, Gandhi said: 'They must concede that all men are created equal . . . They must recognize the paramountcy of the people as they recognized the paramountcy of the British Government. Then they can freely carry on' (88:153-7).

The official resolution was opposed by Purshottamdas Tandon, Choithram Gidwani of Sind, who spoke of 'the ultimate sacrifice' of the Hindus in Muslim-majority areas, Maulana Hifzur Rahman, and Dr Saifuddin Kitchlew, who alleged a surrender to communalism. In the voting 157 backed the Working Committee, 29 raised their hands against it, and 32 were neutral.

Some days later, Gandhi recalled the offer he had made to Jinnah in 1944, 'when I trudged my way in the sun on eighteen successive days (actually he had gone 14 times) to the Qaid-e-Azam's house.' He added: 'I did not seek to appease the Qaid-e-Azam. Had he accepted what I went to offer him all this blood that has now been shed would never have been shed . . . My talks with Mr Jinnah were friendly' (88:313). As mentioned before, the Pakistan that Jinnah secured in 1947 was in area no bigger than what Gandhi had conceded in 1944.

We should dispose of an erroneous story bequeathed by Mountbatten about Gandhi's acceptance of Partition. In an Addendum dated June 1947 to Item 69 in Volume Eleven of *The Transfer of Power* series, Mountbatten claims that following a letter to him from Krishna Menon stating that Gandhi was in an unhappy mood and likely to denounce the Partition Plan, he, the Viceroy, invited Gandhi over and succeeded in calming him by presenting the Mountbatten Plan as nothing except a version of what Gandhi had been prescribing. It was, so Mountbatten claims he said, a Gandhi Plan, whereafter, so the story continues, an 'impressed and mollified' Gandhi told his prayer meeting that the Viceroy and the Partition Plan could not be blamed.[47]

Some of the flaws in the story are these. One, whereas the *Transfer of Power* (*TOP*) series gives 4 June as the date of the interview, the papers evidently released by the Mountbatten Archives to the *Collected Works of Mahatma Gandhi* state that the alleged interview took place on 6 June. The equivocation over the date may suggest difficulty in reconciling the Addendum with available evidence. Two, the letter from Krishna Menon to which the Addendum refers and which is on record, dated 4 June and printed as Item 58 in *TOP* 11, does not bear the meaning Mountbatten ascribes to it in the Addendum. Three, there is no mention, direct or indirect, of the supposed conversation either in Mountbatten's letter of 5 June to the Secretary of State (Item 90 in *TOP* 11), or in his eight-page Personal Report (Item 91), or in the Report of his Meeting with his Staff (Item 70) which took place immediately after the alleged conversation. Considering the significance of the Addendum's claim, the absence of any reference to it in the three Items, all dealing with the details of political developments and discussions, is intriguing, not to say revealing.

Four, Gandhi's post-prayer speeches of 4 June and 6 June, which are on record and in fact quoted from in the foregoing, do not contain what the Addendum claims he said. In both speeches, Gandhi proposed a Congress-League agreement without the Viceroy. Five, as the foregoing shows, Gandhi had conceded Partition and rejected the option of defiance well before the alleged conversation of 4 June (or 6), and had done so clearly and often. Finally, we must wonder about the insertion into a record that proceeds from day to day, indeed hour to hour, of an Addendum about an 'old' discussion. The clue may lie in the 'Note' added by Mountbatten to the Addendum. The Viceroy says in the 'Note' that Krishna Menon and V.P. Menon had told him that 'the line I had taken had been remarkably successful' with Gandhi. Neither Menon was close to Gandhi, but imparting 'information' of Mountbatten's success with Gandhi may have suited their equation with the Viceroy. Receiving reports of his 'triumph,' Mountbatten may have been tempted into inserting a 'record' of how he achieved it.

Edwina Mountbatten, the Vicereine of India, called on Gandhi on 5 July in his room in the sweepers' colony. 'Where would you like to sit,' he asked her, 'on the floor or in a chair?' She chose the floor, which is where he sat, and accepted his offer of a cup of tea. He took orange juice (Brij Krishna 3:197).

❈

As his talk to the AICC showed, Gandhi was as 'all-Indian' as ever, and seeking to include all Indians in his family. When, at the end of May, Chakrayya, a young Harijan member of the Sevagram Ashram in whom Gandhi had hopes, died, Gandhi said: 'I feel like crying over his death, but I cannot cry. For whom should I cry and for whom should I refrain from crying?' (88:47) Recalling his friendship with Sindhis, he said, 'I used to call myself a Sindhi' (88:20). 'Bengal is dear to me,' he said in June (88:137). 'You are my children,' he told a group of Communists who called on him on 8 June (88:107). 'I am also a Punjabi,' he said on 10 June (88:125). And he claimed on 16 June, referring to his mail from different corners of the country, 'I have information from all over India' (88:163). 'I love you socialists,' he said on 2 July (88:261). When, as happened at times, soldiers and officers called on him, he sought to befriend them.

Two youths belonging to the Hindu Mahasabha came to him on the morning of 10 June and told him that he was no Mahatma. He said: 'I repudiated the title of Mahatma long before you questioned it. But maybe out of your concern for me you feel it necessary to put me on my guard.' After returning the withering reply, he warmed towards the young men. Saying, 'We, old leaders, are like autumn leaves,' he asked them to 'throw yourselves into constructive work with all your heart and soul.' He related the conversation to Rajendra Prasad, who joined him after the young men left, and added: 'We ought to take warning from this . . . Before we pass away, we should . . . train younger people . . . [for] building the India of our dreams just as we trained them before as nonviolent soldiers of the freedom struggle . . . [For this] at least a portion of the top-ranking leaders [must] remain outside the Government' (88: 122-3).

The movement he had led from 1920 had ended and others, principally Nehru and Patel, were now in charge of the India that his movement had helped to shape, but he who had said, 'Action is my domain,' was not going to retire. He would educate, counsel, analyze, comment. If *Harijan* remained a channel, so did the press as a whole, publishing all he said at his prayer meetings or elsewhere. And now All India Radio, overseen by Patel, was broadcasting the post-prayer talks. After an initial hesitation during which he cited the inability of most Indians to own radios, he agreed to the broadcasts.

He advised Nehru and Patel to include non-Congress experts in legislatures and the government, warned that controls would hurt not help food distribution, admonished a Chief Minister on the state of refugee camps in his province and told another Chief Minister, Prafulla Ghosh, who had taken over the West Bengal government from Suhrawardy, that instead of attending meetings of the Working Committee in Delhi he should resign from the Committee and look after Calcutta.

When the press reported that a Bombay Congress leader, S.K. Patil, had warned of reprisals after 15 August by Congress in India if Hindus were harmed in Pakistan, Gandhi wrote to Patil and warned him: 'You are enunciating the doctrine of an eye for an eye and a tooth for a tooth . . . Only you will wait till the 15th August . . . Who can control the people if they go mad and launch on a course of retaliation?' (88:318).

He said he hoped that a Harijan like Chakrayya or a worthy Harijan woman would become India's first President. Nehru and other Ministers would serve such a President, he added. The range of his teaching was wide. Sadhus should work, he said (88:131). Poets should fight superstition (88: 172). Students may criticize leaders but should learn a sense of proportion from Europeans and

Americans (88:78). To a group of socialists he offered a diagnosis for the splits and divisions in India:

> As soon as we differ from somebody ever so slightly, or a misunderstanding arises, instead of meeting the person concerned and trying to find a solution, we take him to task publicly. This creates . . . antagonism. Parties and isms are only results of such differences. One fruit of this poison we have seen in the coming . . . of Pakistan (88:96).

'The judicious use of earth, sun, ether, light and water' for 'attending to bodily ailments' (85:125) remained of interest to him, as did the condition of the earth's denizens. He brought to India's attention Britain's Green Cross Society, dedicated to 'the wild life heritage,' and the Society's proposal for a World National Park, under UN auspices, 'in the immense mountains encircling Tibet' (86:66-7).

'The true function of the medical profession,' he said on 28 May, 'is not to prescribe cures, whether foreign or indigenous, but to prevent illness by teaching the people to observe the rules of health' (88:24). As for growing more food, he preferred, he said, 'proper methods of tillage and the use of organic manure' to artificial fertilizers (88:62). He was afraid that 'the land will lose its fertility' if cattle was not kept and only tractors were used (88:221). Encouraging tree-planting, he recalled how in South Africa rainfall had increased after trees were grown. 'The foliage in a forest attracts precipitation from clouds like milk from the udder of a cow,' he said three weeks before independence (88:425).

Militarization, of which he saw signs in India, worried him. 'The spinning wheel has almost been forgotten,' he told Rajagopalachari on 25 May. 'There is all this talk of militarization' (88:4). Six weeks before Partition he warned against an arms race between India and Pakistan: 'If one country increases the army, the other will do the same . . . The result will be war . . . Shall we spend our resources on the education of our children or on gunpowder and guns?' (88:287). 'Whenever there is some incident,' he noted, 'we at once ask for the army . . . In Noakhali, Bihar, the Punjab and the N.W.F.P., wherever there were riots, there was only one demand, that the army be sent' (88:344). If the tendency persisted, it was 'quite possible that a military regime will take over' (88:357).

'Sometimes I wonder,' he said on 8 July to a deputation of Hindus from Quetta in Baluchistan, 'whether during the last thirty years I had not taken the country in the wrong direction . . . Our struggle was based on the nonviolence of the weak. Even then a great power had to leave the country' (88: 300). He thought Indians had accepted his remedy because a violent alternative was not visible.

'No one at the time showed us how to make the atom bomb,' he said on 16 June. 'Had we known how to make it, we would have considered annihilating the English with it' (88:163). 'There was violence in the name of nonviolence and now we are tasting its bitter fruit,' he said on 21 July in response to a letter from Swami Sivananda (88:388). This, as we have seen in a previous chapter, was his explanation for the violence around him, which had been horrible enough by July, but worse was to come. On 24 July he elaborated his diagnosis and issued a sombre warning:

> We became rebels and dislodged [foreign] rule. Outwardly we followed truth and nonviolence. But inwardly there was violence in us . . . As a result we have to suffer the pain of mutual strife. Even today we are nurturing attitudes that will result in war and if this drift is not stopped we shall find ourselves in a conflict much more sanguinary than the Mutiny of 1857 . . . God forbid that (88:416).

He feared that Indian violence might invite foreign intervention. However, if each Indian looked after himself, 'all the three (England, America and Russia) together cannot destroy us,' he said on 25 May (88:8). But if there was Hindu-Muslim or India-Pakistan strife, he said on 24 July, 'England, Russia, America or China — any of these countries may attack and enslave us.' He asked: 'Do you, on the fifteenth of August, want to witness the spectacle of

Hindus fighting Muslims and the Sikhs being crushed between the belligerents?' An earthquake that crushed everybody including himself would be better, he said (88:416-7).

Then there were the 'heaps of letters' he was receiving from freedom fighters asking for posts in the new India (88: 190) and other letters complaining that 'so-called eminent leaders are making money through their sons' (88:191-2). 'If someone has been to jail,' Gandhi asked at his prayer meeting on 12 July, 'has he done a favour to India?'

❋

His spirit uncrushed by disillusionment, anguish, and isolation, he told Manu on 1 June: 'Today I find myself all alone. [Even the Sardar and Jawaharlal] think that my reading of the situation is wrong and peace is sure to return if Partition is agreed upon. They did not like my telling the Viceroy that even if there was to be Partition, it should not be through British intervention or under British rule.' Added Gandhi:

> But somehow in spite of my being all alone, in my thoughts
> I am experiencing an ineffable inner joy and freshness of
> mind. I feel as if God Himself was lighting my path before
> me . . . and am able to fight on single-handed (88: 50-1).

And though Partition was coming and more violence seemed likely, Independence too was coming. To a friend Gandhi wrote on 10 June: 'For sixty years we have been in the thick of the fight, and now we have ushered the goddess of liberty into our courtyard.' This would give, if Gandhi's memory was not deceiving him, 1887 as the start of his fight for political freedom, and confirm that the humiliation of alien rule had gone deep into Mohan's soul in Rajkot. In this 10 June letter Gandhi also said, 'I remain happy and cheerful' (88:121).

Three days later, in his post-prayer speech, he recalled the woman who had attracted him in 1920, and her husband: 'I had a Punjabi friend, Rambhaj Dutt Chowdhary, who is now no more. Sometimes he composed poems. When he came out of jail he brought along a poem he had composed, and since he himself could not sing he asked his wife Sarla to sing it. In her melodious voice Sarla sang: "Never admit defeat even if you should lose your life." And I told myself that I would never accept defeat' (88:145). Evidently Gandhi felt forgiven for the brush with desire about which he had been ashamed and which no more clouded his memory of Sarla, who had died in 1945, and her husband.

Something of Gandhi's character in the summer of 1947 is also suggested by these lines he wrote on 2 July to a friend: 'God is humbling my pride. I am being severely tested. But still my heart is full of joy' (88:259). And also by his answer to Manu who wanted to know why, despite seeking 'the steadfast mind' recommended by the Gita, he still turned sad: 'If I did not feel unhappy, I would be a person with a heart of stone' (88:159).

If many were now attacking him, many continued to praise him, some out of love, others from flattery. To one who sent 'a loving letter' and wanted a great one's blessings for a newborn son, Gandhi wrote on 13 June: 'I am a sinner like others. However, may God protect you and your son. You should bring him up . . . to serve the poor of India' (88:143). The immense crowds that he drew in Bihar had not deceived him. 'People are always eager to see me,' he said, referring to them. 'They wonder what Gandhi looks like. They want to see if he is a creature with a tail and horns' (88:5).

He was expecting to be killed, and ready. 'I will die smiling with the name of Rama on my lips,' he said on 25 May (88:6). 'I shall consider myself brave if I am killed and if I still pray for my assassin,' he said on 16 June (88:164). Four days later he said:

> Whom are we afraid of? The Muslims? If they become devils let us become men. Then they will also become men. When I, a poor Bania, am not frightened, why should you be? The worst they can do is to kill me. Let them kill me. Will they drink my blood? Let them do so. That will save some food and I shall consider that I have been of

some service. But who am I to render service? It would
be more appropriate to say that it is God who has used me
for service (88:184).

His death would make no difference, he declared on 7 August. 'I
shall be alive in the grave and, what is more, speaking from it'
(89:16). That he was likely to be killed was, we know, an old belief
of his, yet we need not assume that waiting for the inevitable, final
blow was easy for him, or deduce from his incessant references to
death an extinction of his love of life.

His opinion that one who had mastered his passions could live
until 125 and his assertions that he was striving for that span testify
to his interest in living. As with others sentenced by terminal illness or by a judge, the closing in of death intensified his life, and if
in some this intensity shows itself in a relationship or in art, in
Gandhi's case it was revealed in his passion for communicating his
truths.

❋

On 19 July Aung San, the Burmese leader, and several of his colleagues were assassinated. Aung San had 'brought Burma to the
gates of freedom,' Gandhi said. The Burmese killings brought to
Gandhi's mind his talks in London forty years earlier with Indian
terrorists, who 'did not accept my advice' and, like the killers of
Aung San, regarded their 'victims as criminals' and 'never regarded themselves as criminals' (88:381 and 390).

Led by Z.A. Phizo, a Naga delegation met him on the day of the
Burmese killings and spoke of their people's wish for independence.
Gandhi said they could experience independence right away if they
wanted to, adding, 'I was independent when the whole of India was
under the British heel . . . Personally, I believe you all belong to me,
to India. But if you say you don't, no one can force you' (88:373-
4).

A pain and a guilt was the abandonment by Congress of their
allies in the N.W.F.P. — Ghaffar Khan, his brother Dr Khan Sahib,

who was the Chief Minister, and their followers. The Partition Plan proposed a referendum for the Frontier province to choose between India and Pakistan. Though in the early 1946 elections the Frontier had chosen a pro-Congress ministry, in the climate of mid-1947 the referendum was bound to be turned into a vote for or against Islam. On 2 June Ghaffar Khan asked the Working Committee to strive for a third option of independence for his province. Gandhi backed him but to little effect. In his meetings with the Viceroy, Nehru had agreed to the choice of India or Pakistan, and Patel too was opposed to pushing the Raj over the Frontier.

Autonomy within Pakistan was the solution that Gandhi and Ghaffar Khan now sought, and Gandhi said to his valiant colleague who had disproved the two-nation theory that India would not be a silent spectator if the N.W.F.P. was oppressed in Pakistan. He also tried to mediate a settlement between Jinnah and Ghaffar Khan but failed. Jinnah's condition was that Congress should retire from the N.W.F.P., which Gandhi saw as an unacceptable prescription for *harakiri*.

The Khan brothers and their supporters boycotted the referendum, which was held in July. Pakistan secured 289,244 votes, India 2,874. Of the roughly 280,000 who did not vote, a large number were loyal to the Khan brothers. Ghaffar Khan, better known as Badshah or Bacha Khan or the Frontier Gandhi, would spend as many years in prison after Partition as during the struggle against the British, and die in 1988 at the age of ninety-eight, his friendship for Hindus and India, belief in nonviolence and commitment to the Frontier's autonomy unimpaired.

The N.W.F.P.'s neighbour to the east was Jammu and Kashmir (or J & K or, simply, Kashmir), which had a Muslim majority but was ruled by a Hindu prince, Hari Singh, who had placed the state's popular leader, Sheikh Abdullah, under arrest. Abdullah had close links with Nehru, whose origins lay in Kashmir, and seemed in favour of the state's merger with India. Since there was also a sentiment in favour of Pakistan, Hari Singh saw prospects of independence. Nehru, who felt that Abdullah's detention called for a visit by him to Kashmir, was confirmed in the wish when he heard that Hari

Singh was against his entry.

Yet, since a visit by Nehru could trigger friction, he and Gandhi agreed that the latter should go to Kashmir. From 31 July to 6 August, accordingly, Gandhi was in Kashmir and, en route, in the Punjab. He wrote to a friend on 30 July: 'I am going to Kashmir . . . to see for myself the condition of the people. In any case I shall have a glimpse of the Himalayas. Who knows if I am going there for the first and the last time?' (88:463). When his train stopped at Amritsar station, angry young Hindus shouted slogans against him, but he valued his visits in the Punjab to Lahore, Rawalpindi, Wah, where large numbers of Sikhs and Hindus were camping for safety, and the Punja Sahib Gurdwara. He left Sushila Nayar at Wah to assist the campers.

In Kashmir, where huge crowds came to Gandhi's prayer meetings, he met Hari Singh and his wife, Hari Singh's Premier Ramchandra Kak, and Begum Abdullah, the detained leader's wife. From Hari Singh and his wife he elicited the admission that with the lapse of British paramountcy the paramountcy of the people should commence. It was Gandhi's view that 'the people of Kashmir should be asked whether they want to join Pakistan or India' (88:461).

Following the visit, in remarks in Wah in the Punjab that revealed a guardian's eye, Gandhi said that Kashmir 'had the greatest strategic value, perhaps, in all India' (89:6). In a note to Nehru and Patel, he said, 'In my opinion the situation in Kashmir can be saved.' He quoted the assessment of Abdullah's colleague, Bakshi Ghulam Mohammad, that if Abdullah and his co-prisoners were released, all bans were removed and Premier Kak was replaced, 'the result of the free vote of the people . . . would be in favour' of Kashmir joining India (89:5-8). The Gandhi who visited Kashmir in the first week of August was thus both a votary of the popular will and an emissary of India.

❋

He had decided to spend 15 August in Noakhali. Looking at the strife around him and at 'the seeds of future conflict between India and Pakistan,' he was not inclined to 'light the lamps' on 15 August (88:380). To him Swaraj did not 'mean only that the British rule should end' (88:418). He would fast that day, remember Mahadev Desai, who had died on that date, and spin and pray more than his daily portion, for India faced a food shortage. But he agreed that 'we should not mourn' (88:462).

By spending 15 August in Noakhali, he would signal that there was a unity beyond Partition. Claiming that 'both Hindustan and Pakistan were my homelands,' he added that 'similar was the case with Jinnah Saheb' (89:18). On 6 August he left Lahore by train for Patna, en route for Calcutta and Noakhali. There were big crowds at every stop on the way. It rained, the roof of his compartment leaked, and the guard suggested that Gandhi should shift to another compartment. *Gandhi*: 'What will happen to this one?' *Guard*: 'The passengers from the other compartment will occupy it.' *Gandhi*: 'If it is good enough for them, it should be good enough for me' (89:11).

When, on 9 August, he arrived in Calcutta to proceed to Noakhali, the retiring Governor of Bengal, Frederick Burrows, and Muslim leaders pressed Gandhi to delay his departure by a few days. There was trouble in the city, Gandhi was told. He tarried, therefore, in Calcutta, hoping to 'pour a pot of water over the raging fire' (89:20) in what he described as 'the premier city of India' (89:22). As a condition of his staying on in Calcutta, he had its Muslim leaders send telegrams and emissaries to Noakhali to prevent violence against the Hindus there.

On 11 August a BBC correspondent sent Gandhi a request for a message to be broadcast on Independence Day. 'I have nothing to say,' replied Gandhi via Nirmal Bose. 'It will be broadcast in various languages,' the correspondent pleaded. 'I must not yield to the temptation,' Gandhi scribbled on a piece of paper for Bose. 'They must forget that I know English' (89:23).

That night Gandhi renewed to Suhrawardy the offer the latter had rejected in May, that the two should live under the same roof and restore peace to the city. 'Go home and consult your daughter,' Gandhi added. 'The old Suhrawardy will have to die' (89:28). The next day Suhrawardy, whose Premiership of Bengal was coming to an end, sent word that he would accept the offer.

Hydari Manzil, 'an old abandoned Muslim house' in a squalid Hindu-majority locality in Beliaghata, where Muslims had been victims, now became Gandhi's latest ashram, and Suhrawardy his latest fellow-ashramite. Addressing a prayer meeting on 12 August, Gandhi said that he had been 'warned that Shaheed Saheb was not to be relied upon.' But Muslims had been similarly warned about himself, Gandhi added. He was supposed to be 'a consummate hypocrite.' He had decided to trust as he expected to be trusted. 'Both would live under the same roof and have no secrets from each other. They would together see all the visitors (Hindu and Muslim)' (89:31).

'Young blood is boiling,' Gandhi said on 13 August in a letter to Pyarelal, who was in Noakhali (89:35). Attacking Gandhi for protecting Muslims rather than Hindus, a group of Hindu youths asked Gandhi to leave Beliaghata. Gandhi had two sessions with them, the second in Suhrawardy's presence. If Beliaghata's Hindus invited their Muslim neighbours to return, he said to them, he and Suhrawardy would next live in a predominantly Muslim locality until Hindus were invited to return there. The youths were 'completely won over.' Another group of angry young Hindus was pacified when Suhrawardy admitted his responsibility for the Great Killing a year earlier (89:42-3).

So Gandhi opened his eyes in free India in a Muslim house in one of Calcutta's poorest quarters. Whatever he may have felt about lighting lamps, Calcutta had been lit all night by fireworks. On the fifteenth there was a stream of visitors to Hydari Manzil: Hindus, Muslims, the new West Bengal Ministry headed by Prafulla Ghosh, Rajagopalachari, who had taken over as West Bengal's Governor, Communists, students. Gandhi saw that 'the joy of fraternization' seemed to be 'leaping up from hour to hour.' One of his letters that day was written to Agatha Harrison, his Quaker friend in England: 'You know, my way of celebrating great events, such as today's, is to thank God . . . and therefore to pray. This prayer must be accompanied by a fast, and then, as a mark of identification with the poor . . . there must be [extra] spinning . . . My love to all your friends'

(89:43-4). The foe of their country's rule was thus able to express his love to Britons on Independence Day.

His Independence Day advice to West Bengal's ministers calling on him was given in short sentences: 'Be humble. Be forbearing . . . Now you will be tested through and through. Beware of power; power corrupts . . . Do not let yourselves be entrapped by its pomp and pageantry. Remember, you are in office to serve the poor in India's villages' (89:45).

A large crowd of Hindus and Muslims came to his prayer meeting on the fifteenth. He congratulated Calcutta, hoped that the city would remain free from the communal virus, and made an appeal for aid to Chittagong, now in East Pakistan, which had been hit by floods. After the meeting Gandhi made an unusual request: he asked to be driven anonymously round the city. He wanted to see more of the day's joy with his eyes, and to see whether it was 'Miracle or Accident,' his title for an article he wrote the next day for *Harijan*. In the article he referred to the credit given to him for what had happened in Calcutta and said:

> All the credit . . . is quite undeserved. Nor can it be said to be deserved by Shaheed Saheb (Suhrawardy). This sudden upheaval is not the work of one or two men. We are toys in the hands of God. He makes us dance to his tune . . . In the present exuberance one hears also the cry of "Long Live Hindustan and Pakistan" from the joint throats of the Hindus and the Muslims. I think it is quite proper (89:49).

But by now, in the Punjab, terrifying cries were being raised.

❋

Now that we have arrived at that bittersweet milestone where India is free, divided and blood-spattered, we should ask, in broad terms, how Gandhi might have done differently on the journey to the milestone, and whether unity and lives could have been saved.

Our survey has shown that one Indian's freedom was another's fear. Congress-League coalitions in the provinces in 1937 and sincere power-sharing at the Centre in 1946 might have preempted Muslim anxieties but we have seen that though Gandhi came out with some bold and dramatic plans, he did not make a settlement with the League his priority. Behind this attitude lay Gandhi's belief that the Hindu-Muslim equation could only be sorted out once the British left, and also his awareness of Jinnah's extreme terms. Yet his insistence on Britain's departure as the first step could not but fuel Muslim suspicion.

Alien rule was personally humiliating to Gandhi and widely resented by all Indians, yet Gandhi and the Indian people may not have lost tangibly by recognizing, and talking to, 'the third party' at an Indian negotiating table. Gandhi participated in many an Indo-British encounter, some on the battlefield and some at a table, and in several Congress-League encounters, but he disliked the three-sided negotiation. British involvement in what he saw as the problems of the Indian family was unacceptable to him.

Yet by virtue of its power Britain sat at the table anyway, and the eventual outcome of freedom-in-partition was settled in a three-sided negotiation. India's unchecked slide in 1946-7 towards strife and Partition drives us to ask whether Gandhi was entirely right in his thesis that a Congress-League accord was impossible without Britain's exit, with the implication that such an exit would result in an accord, and whether Gandhi could not have employed 'the third party' in aid rather than rejecting it as irredeemably divisive. We have seen that at least twice, in 1944 and 1946, Gandhi was ready for arbitration, but not at British hands.

If the sole difference between what Gandhi offered Jinnah in 1944 and what, no matter how reluctantly, both accepted in 1947 was that Britain oversaw the 1947 division, whereas in 1944 Gandhi wanted separation under a free India's auspices, then we must wonder whether Gandhi should not have accepted a British role in 1944. If such a concession had resulted in an agreement with Jinnah, then lives would certainly have been saved, though not unity. There is no evidence that with this concession Jinnah would have accepted truncated Pakistan in 1944, but Muslim suspicion of Gandhi would have been allayed, and Britain too would have become less distrustful of Gandhi. Such gains might have forestalled some of the bitter clouds that were soon to fill India's skies.

Any suggestion that he or Congress might renege after independence on assurances to Muslims outraged Gandhi and drew spirited responses from him. We have seen some of them, and the Constitution that Gandhi's followers framed for the new India was the final reply. Yet he was not always prepared to extend to the British the trust he wished from Muslims. Perhaps it was more nationalist pride than mistrust, but he tried to prevent a British role in India's division.

No doubt Gandhi had to ensure that he was not lending credence to an influential British line, voiced by Churchill among others, that Indian divisions would be permanent and require a permanent British presence. If their presence was temporary, and they were in fact going to leave, then they should let go, and allow Indians to learn to live with one another without outside help. While sound in this attitude, Gandhi could have been more flexible in his stand that Indians alone should decide on division.

He was ambivalent about the history of Britain's role in Indian divisions. In *Hind Swaraj* (1909) he wrote: 'The Hindus and the Mahomedans were at daggers drawn. This, too, gave the [East India] Company its opportunity' (Ch. 7). In 1931, however, he said in London that the Hindu-Muslim quarrel was 'not old . . . but coeval with the British advent' (*UMM* 315). In April 1947 he told Mountbatten that the Raj had used Indian divisions but not created them. In July 1947 he paid a tribute:

> The British carried on their rule in India for 150 years and . . . accepted the fact that politically India was one nation. They also tried to develop it as a nation and to some extent succeeded also. Before them the Moghuls had made a similar effort but they were less successful. Having first unified the country, it is not a very becoming thing for them to divide it (88:281).

We should not forget Gandhi's 1918 bid to recruit soldiers for the Empire or his September 1939 reaction in Britain's favour. A wary steersman, he had an instinctive appreciation of the influence of India's rulers and no wish to annoy them unduly. But there was a limit to the friendship he could offer if he wished to represent the Indian people, who had little sympathy for their alien rulers. If Gandhi drew his strength from the Indian people, he was also limited, in his strategic options, by their sentiments. Likewise there was a limit to his offers to the League, which strained the loyalty of his Hindu following.

Apart from ruling out Britain as a legitimate 'third party,' Gandhi at times played a partisan role when he might have been more effective as an 'outsider' or an umpire. Thus in 1946 he could have advised Congress to reject the Cabinet Mission Plan which had contradiction and a capacity for mischief built into it. He criticized the Plan's inconsistency, and a year later noted that the Mountbatten Plan, whatever its faults, at least did not have 'any ambiguity or ... a language which can bear different interpretations' (88:281). Yet in 1946 he allowed Congress to use the inconsistency in the Cabinet Mission Plan to gain power. Congress was doubtless entitled to power but the means it adopted in 1946 were open to question. In *Hind Swaraj* Gandhi had said that means govern ends even as a seed decides the tree. In conformity with this truth, a poisonous creeper grew quickly in 1946-7, and many an Indian ate its leaves.

This is not to suggest that in 1946 the British or the League were more virtuous than Congress. For as long as was possible, British representatives offered opposite interpretations to Congress and the League, and Jinnah said in the same breath that he would and would not accept something less than full sovereign Pakistan. Britain should have asked Congress and the League, in each other's presence, to choose between a sovereign truncated Pakistan and compulsory grouping in a united India, and, in the absence of agreement, announced a clear award for one or the other. Yet a plain compromise of this sort was not spelt out by the British or anyone else. Gandhi must take his share of responsibility for the failure.

A third failure, over coalition-building, has already been alluded to. We have seen his definite preference for a Congress or a League government over a coalition at the Centre, as well as his inability in 1937 to get Congress to accept a coalition with the League in the U.P., but we should also note his failure to forge an alliance with the Unionists of the Punjab. An accord of Congress with the Unionists and another with non-League and non-Congress Muslim forces in Bengal might have isolated the League, but Congress lacked the flexibility to attract the supposedly pro-British and pro-landlord Unionists. In Bengal, curiously enough, it was the anti-landlord flavour of many non-League Muslims that deterred the often pro-landlord Bengal Congress from an alliance.

We have seen that in the late thirties and the early forties Gandhi tried to promote an understanding with the Unionists, and that, as far as Bengal was concerned, he wooed Suhrawardy and Fazlul Huq in 1946-7. Yet his efforts do not cancel his and Congress's failures. In part at least they are attributable to complacency and rigidity in Congress, weaknesses that Gandhi was unable to rectify. Success would have detached major Muslim constituencies from Jinnah's influence.

In short, we can say that on crucial occasions when the two goals were in conflict, Gandhi's passion for freedom from the alien power took precedence over his passion for Hindu-Muslim unity, and also that at times he mistakenly equated power for Congress with Indian freedom. His legacy on the Hindu-Muslim relationship is thus not without flaws. But it is compelling and of rare richness.

❀

Before leaving this chapter we may consider the revisionist thesis that Congress desired Partition more than the League,[48] and a related argument that Partition was 'a victory for Hindu civilization' ending 'the stalemate between Hindus and Muslims in favour of Hindus in three-fourths of India.'[49]

When the League's Pakistan resolution was passed in 1940, Gandhi said that the Muslims' good sense and self-interest would deter them from supporting it. They would see, and reject, its suicidal implications, he said. He used the last phrase advisedly, aware as he was of Islam's abhorrence of suicide. He was proved wrong, but the support given to the Pakistan idea in 1946-7 by the Muslims of Hindu-majority provinces is one of the stranger facts of this century's history. Pakistan might confer blessings on *its* Muslims but what could it bring to Muslims in the U.P., in Delhi, in Bombay, in Bhopal, in Madras? Only, surely, the resentment of the vastly more numerous Hindus they were living amidst.

If Congress rule caused Muslims in the U.P. to feel threatened or left out, how was Pakistan hundreds of miles away an answer? An exodus of all Muslims in Hindu-majority provinces was unthinkable, and the argument that Muslims in India would be safe because Pakistan also had minorities 'in hostage' could not bear scrutiny. When aroused, anger against Muslims in India was incapable of being checked by warnings of what might happen to Hindus in Pakistan. Equally, anger against Hindus and Sikhs in Pakistan would not be curbed by reminders of the vulnerability of Muslims in India. Frenzy against the visible 'enemy' would be stronger than love for the invisible 'brother.'

Jinnah may have sensed this. In any case, Hindu-Muslim parity in a Union government plus a large Pakistan zone, inclusive of East Punjab, West Bengal and Assam, comprised his first preference. If there was no parity in the Union, he would still take the large Pakistan zone provided the Union was nominal and the zone could secede from the Union after a few years. The Smaller Pakistan he obtained was his third preference. His doings reveal this hierarchy of goals; as a player he was too careful to spell them out.

We have seen that to Gandhi the combination of Hindu-Muslim parity, separate electorates and a Pakistan zone was 'worse than Pakistan.' It was Pakistan plus two nations everywhere in India. Sovereign Pakistan would be better, provided Hindu-majority areas were not absorbed. This, on all sides, was the least objectionable solution. But to proceed from this to argue that Pakistan is what Congress forced on the League is to deny history's facts.

From 1940 Jinnah steadfastly maintained that he wanted Pakistan. He said so to Gandhi in each of their 1944 and subsequent talks, to Wavell, Cripps, Mountbatten and other British representatives, to the League executive and to his Muslim constituency. That he concealed his true objective from each and everyone is more than can be accepted. His first and second preferences, noted above, were extensions, not an exclusion, of the Pakistan he obtained.

It is a fact, nonetheless, that the Muslims of the India that remained after Partition were its worst victims. To say this is not to underestimate the insecurities of the Hindus remaining in Bangladesh, or in Pakistan, where they are mostly to be found in Sind, nor to imply that the terror and trauma of 1947 can be divided into Hindu and Muslim portions.

Yet it remains true that the Muslims of post-1947 India, several times more numerous than the Hindus of what became Pakistan, lost the political influence, separate electorates, reserved legislature seats and share in government jobs that they used to enjoy. The new Constitution gave them equality but could not compensate for the smallness of their share in India's vast numbers. It is also true that the Congress leadership was well aware of this consequence of Partition. All this may translate into a 'victory for Hindu civilization' if Hindu means a tribe or race, and a civilization's victory means getting the upper hand, but for Gandhi the phrases held other meanings.

Chapter 10

Sons and Heirs

WHEN GANDHI FIRST sensed that Jawaharlal Nehru might be his successor for steering India is not entirely clear. It may have happened in 1920, when, against his father Motilal's preference and at Gandhi's call, Jawaharlal tossed away a career at the bar that held the promise of riches and embraced a life different from the one he had been used to, and likely to involve hardships, including imprisonment.

The sense was not confirmed until much later, and Gandhi was also considering others. In 1927 he said in Karaikudi that Rajagopalachari was his 'only possible successor' (35: 32). But by the end of 1929 Jawaharlal was a strong candidate. By this time Vallabhbhai Patel's remarkable success at the head of the 1928 satyagraha of the Bardoli peasants had brought him to centre-stage, and the charisma of Subhas Bose had been displayed at the end-1928 Calcutta Congress, where, designated 'commander of Congress's volunteer force,' Bose wore a military uniform.

Expecting a new and crucial round of battle against the Raj, most Congressmen in 1929 wanted Gandhi to head Congress personally and formally, and he was in fact declared President. He not only withdrew but asked Patel, the second choice of Congress committees, to withdraw as well, and arranged Nehru's installation.

Patel was named a General Secretary under Nehru, but in 1931 Vallabhbhai, by Gandhi's choice, became Congress President, with Jawaharlal as one of the General Secretaries. Later in 1931, when

Gandhi was chosen as Congress's sole representative to the Round Table Conference in London, he wrote to Rajagopalachari:

> There are two men whom I would like by my side in London, you and Jawaharlal. But I feel that even if both of you were available I must not have you by me. You will both help me like the others by being here (4.7.31; *Rajaji* 1: 225).

Though Patel is the President, it is the presence with him in London of Jawaharlal and Rajagopalachari that Gandhi wishes for but 'must not have.' We can fairly take this to mean that he is consciously or subconsiously thinking of the two as candidates for the 'succession' and limiting the choice to them.

In 1934 Gandhi retired from Congress. He listed his reasons in a long letter to Vallabhbhai Patel, whose presidency, interrupted by struggles and prison terms, continued until October 1934, when Rajendra Prásad took over. Gandhi wanted to release Congress from the 'stifling effect' of his personality. Many in Congress concealed their lack of sympathy for the spinning wheel or his struggle against untouchability. Gandhi felt they ought to declare their views. Secondly, he wanted Congress's different factions, centrist, conservative and socialist, to find their different levels. Thirdly, his departure might facilitate a Congress-Raj rapprochement.

But he was not running away. To Rajagopalachari, who protested the withdrawal, Gandhi wrote: 'I do not retire to a cave. I hold myself at everybody's disposal.' A relieved Rajagopalachari explained to a puzzled Englishwoman, Monica Whately, that Gandhi's step was more 'a judicial separation' than 'a divorce' (*Rajaji* 1:268-9). In fact the separation was judicious.

Yet we should also see the 'retirement' as a responsible step of one of advancing age (Gandhi was now sixty-five). Entrusted with a vital movement and a large organization, he had to safeguard the future by handing over while he was fit. As for the present, he would be available for any emergency or for fresh rounds of struggle.

Prison sentences awarded to Gandhi and thousands of others in

Congress, leaders and activists, had barely concluded when Gandhi wrote his letter of withdrawal to Patel. Among the few still in gaol was Nehru. Gandhi's letter contained a sentence about him that was virtually a decree: 'I miss at this juncture the association and advice of Jawaharlal who is bound to be the rightful helmsman of the organisation in the near future' (*Patel*: 247).

❋

Should Gandhi have named an heir, as he did, like a king? Is it not an immodest, an arrogant, even an undemocratic thing to do? Yet a wise ruler must, and a wise helmsman or general also must. Gandhi was in some ways all of these. While always ready and even keen to humble himself, he did not flinch from a kingly duty and never felt that his calling was minor. Also, the work of his father and grand-father with rulers in Kathiawad had cured Gandhi of any awe of princes. We may note Gandhi's 1907 evaluation, offered to Joseph Doke, of Rana Vikmatji, under whom both Uttamchand and Karamchand Gandhi had served as Prime Ministers: 'Keen-sighted, often cruel, so independent that he quarrelled with the political agent, so stubborn that he raised a civil war, so niggardly that his dependents almost starved, and yet with compensating chracteristics . . .' (Doke: 18).

He wore a peasant's clothes when invited to tea by George V in 1931 but saw an equal, not a superior, in the King and looked him calmly in the eye. The first large group of people for whom he fought, the indentured Indians in South Africa, called him Gandhi Raja. It was a title he repudiated as clearly as, later, he did the 'Mahatma.' While knowing himself as made of common clay, he could decree like a king or deny himself like a Mahatma.

In his satyagraha campaigns, too, Gandhi always drew up a list of commanders in order of succession so that if one was arrested or rendered out of action, all knew who would lead next, including the commander concerned. He may not have quoted the saying, 'Leave nothing to chance and then leave everything to God,' but seemed to act by it, even in the matter of the future of the organizations, large or small, with which he was connected. Who, in the event of his arrest or death, should edit his journals, conduct his ashrams or guide his movement were questions he straightforwardly and at times publicly tackled.

Some hesitate to nominate out of a fear that rivals would physically or politically destroy the one named. Gandhi's assumption that an heir named by him would be accepted as such by the rest, including rivals, was vindicated by events, a tribute to Gandhi's authority, to the quality of the movement that he had created, to the gifts of the one he named, and to the character of the ones excluded.

Dynastic rulers don't nominate; the matter is settled by rules of succession, though to help or deny someone a ruler may try to amend the rules. In any case Gandhi was a captain who seemed to rule out a major role by any of his own sons in the Indian boat.

We need not assume that rejecting kith-and-kin claims and considerations cost Gandhi nothing. He told Doke in 1907 that 'the Gandhi clan were . . . of considerable importance in the political life of Porbandar' and added: 'One of my earliest memories is connected with the learning and repetition, as a child, of the family pedigree, with all its ramifications and offshoots, away there in the old home within the walls of the White City' (Doke: 19). The Gandhi we know, severe with his sons, had started out as a child in whom pride in the family line had been carefully instilled.

He was proud when his eldest son, Harilal, courted imprisonment in South Africa, a fact he conveyed to Tolstoy among others. Much later, in the mid-forties, his second son Manilal's fight for justice and nonviolence in South Africa cheered him greatly. In 1928 he choked when, while blessing his third son Ramdas and his bride Nirmala on their marriage, he anticipated a life of hardship for them. He wrote to Devadas in 1918 of his high expectations from his youngest son.

His sons, however, had to be a good deal abler than others to qualify for praise or a place, and if it was a question between one of his sons and someone else equally qualified, the latter was invariably preferred. Harilal accused him of sacrificing his sons at the altar of ambition, but perhaps it was also, or more, the price that a commander in action, and his nearest, have to pay. When all in the boat have to be saved, the helmsman's children cannot be the first to receive lifejackets.

It may only have been a coincidence, but after Devadas informed his father that he wished to marry Rajagopalachari's daughter Lakshmi, Gandhi ceased to refer to Rajagopalachari as a successor. A letter that he wrote in June 1947 to a relative named Narmada Gandhi seeking a favour on the ground of kinship reveals Gandhi's dilemma and decision:

> I have many sons, some of whom bear the name Gandhi and some bear other names. A man who has risen above caste or community . . . — if you can count how many crores of sons, and therefore daughters-in-law, such a man is likely to have, please do the total yourself (88:64).

On the other hand, a 1928 article entitled 'My Best Comrade Gone' on Maganlal Gandhi showed that relatives were not wholly barred, though it could only have confirmed the opinion of those like Harilal who thought that Gandhi favoured remotely-related nephews over sons:

> He whom I had singled out as heir to my all is no more. Maganlal K. Gandhi, a grandson of an uncle of mine, had been with me in my work since 1904 . . . He responded to my sudden call to self-imposed poverty, joined the Phoenix settlement and never once faltered or failed after so joining me. If he had not so dedicated himself, . . . his undoubted abilities and indefatigable industry would have made him a merchant prince . . . .
>
> When satyagraha was born he was in the forefront . . . On our return to India, it was he again who made it possible to found the Ashram . . . Let not the reader imagine that he knew nothing of politics. He did, but he chose the path of silent, selfless constructive service . . .
>
> He was my hands, my feet, and my eyes . . . But for a

> living faith in God, I should become a raving maniac for the loss of one who was dearer to me than my own sons . . . Maganlal is dead, but he lives in his works whose imprints he who runs may read on every particle of dust in the Ashram (*Young India*, 26.4.28).

The Mahabharata contains a conversation between the sage Markandeya and the Pandava chief Yudhishthir in which, speaking of 'the eternal rules of righteous conduct by which are guided kings, women, and saints,' the sage says: 'He that hath no feeling of kindness for relatives cannot be free from sin, even if his body be pure. That hardheartedness of his is the enemy of his asceticism' (Vana Parva, verses 190-9). Gandhi was not devoid of kindness for relatives, but he suppressed it for the sake of his larger family.

❀

To return to Gandhi's thoughts about a successor for guiding India, the field in the 1920-48 period seemed limited to (listing them by age) Patel, born in 1875, Rajagopalachari (1878), Rajendra Prasad (1883), Abul Kalam Azad (1888), Jawaharlal (1889), and Subhas Bose (1895). These were the individuals Gandhi strengthened with doses of private encouragement and public praise. India knew — was made to know — that they were close to Gandhi and trusted or well regarded by him.

Of these Subhas was in a class of his own. He publicly broke with Gandhi in 1933 and, after a reconciliation that led to his installation, at Gandhi's initiative, as Congress President in 1938, was publicly disowned by Gandhi in 1939 following his re-election as President in the teeth of Gandhi's opposition. Bose saw Gandhi, at times, as an obstacle to progress, and himself as an alternative, views never entertained by the other five. On his part Gandhi was not sure of Subhas's commitment to democracy. Bose seemed to admire Mussolini and had also been in contact, in the late 1930s, with the German Consul in Calcutta. The Raj's Director of Central Intelligence had given the information to K.M.Munshi, Law Minister in

Bombay in 1937-9, who passed it on to Gandhi.[1]

After his dramatic disappearance from house arrest in Calcutta in January 1941, leadership of the Indian National Army (INA), and alliance with Japan, Subhas called Gandhi 'the father of the nation' in a broadcast to India. Word of Bose's death in a 1945 plane crash and of Hindu-Sikh-Muslim partnership in the INA moved Gandhi, who often lauded Subhas in his post-1945 utterances, but the bare facts given above show that Subhas, the youngest of the six, was not likely to be named as his heir by Gandhi.

The difference between Bose's attitude to Gandhi and Nehru's can be seen in their reaction to Gandhi's 1922 suspension of the campaign against the Raj following the Chauri Chaura violence. Though Jawaharlal felt dismayed and angry when, as a prisoner of the Raj, he learnt of the suspension, he soon revised his opinion. 'All organization and discipline was disappearing,' he wrote. 'Gandhiji's decision was right. He had to stop the rot and build anew' (*Patel*: 104). Bose's comment in his *The Indian Struggle* was: 'To have sounded the bugle for retreat at a time when the enemy was on its knees was nothing short of a national disaster' (108).

We may note that Patel and Prasad were the only ones not to criticize the suspension when it occurred. In his prison Rajagopalachari noted: 'In spite of my tenderest and most complete attachment to my master and the ideal he stands for, I fail to see why there should be a call for stopping our struggle for birthrights [because of] every distant and unconnected outburst.' Four months later, Rajagopalachari, like Nehru, changed his assessment: 'When the probability of violence stared us in the face ... in spite of every temptation that urged us to advance and fully realising all the losses and risks which sudden halt involved, we deliberately chose to stop ...' (*Rajaji* 1:111-2).

The five (or six) were not, of course, the only ones that Gandhi buttressed. He created openings for the Congress Socialists in the mid-thirties, and in the forties three of them, Jayaprakash Narayan, Narendra Deva, and Rammanohar Lohia, were publicly defended, commended, or recommended by Gandhi. When Kripalani resigned as Congress President at the end of 1947, Gandhi wanted J.P. or Narendra Deva to succeed him, but Patel was opposed to the move and Nehru unenthusiastic, and Prasad filled the vacancy.

'Jayaprakash is like a son to me,' Gandhi said in July 1947 (88:263). Nine months earlier, when Lohia was injured at the hands of Goa's Portuguese authorities, Gandhi wrote in *Harijan*: 'Dr Lohia is not a little man . . . The injury done to him is injury done to our countrymen in Goa and through them to the whole of India' (85:457). Gandhi seemed to see Deva, J.P. and Lohia as part of India's leadership in a not distant future, but he warned the socialists against splitting Congress or 'banding themselves' into a separate group (88: 396).

Kripalani himself was another colleague whom Gandhi prized. He had met Gandhi in 1915, ahead of any of the others named in this chapter, and hosted him in Muzaffarpur just before the Champaran satyagraha. When Nehru and Kripalani visited Gandhi in Noakhali in the winter of 1946-7, one heading a government and the other a party, Gandhi acknowledged them equally at his prayer meeting. But Kripalani did not appear to Gandhi as a likely leader of his successors. Difficulty in working with colleagues was one of Kripalani's handicaps.

Three of the five, Rajagopalachari, Prasad and Azad, eliminated themselves, the first because, despite Gandhi's repeated urgings, he did not master Hindi. One unable to communicate with India's Hindi heartland could not guide it. Had Gandhi not prodded him, Rajagopalachari might have also neglected Tamil, the language to which he was born.

> *G. to R., 1924:* I had a chat with your son last night. Incidentally I asked him whether he wrote to you and you to him in English or Tamil. When he told me it was English, the information cut me to pieces . . . You are my greatest hope. Why this, as it seems to me, grave defect? If the salt loses its savour, etc. What are the Tamil masses to do if her best sons neglect her? (*Rajaji* 1:148).

Rajagopalachari became a force in Tamil literature but Hindi eluded him. So did the Congress presidency and the Gandhi succession.

Rajendra Prasad was in Gandhi's sights from 1917, when he joined the Champaran struggle. A brilliant student and able advocate, Prasad was introduced by Gandhi to a Gujarat audience in 1918 as follows: 'My own brothers are dead; but we have here Shri Rajendra Babu, on seeing whom I forget their loss. He has given me love such as I can never forget.' The Congress President in 1934, 1939-40 (after Subhas was obliged to leave), and 1947-8, Prasad was a staunch Gandhi ally who, unlike Rajagopalachari and Nehru, refrained from questioning Gandhi. Mildness and an appearance that was even milder were his weaknesses. Liked everywhere and, in his native Bihar, followed by fair numbers, Prasad did not however sparkle or crackle.

If Prasad was too gentle, Azad was too aloof. A striking appearance, eloquence in Urdu, an independent and learned mind and an unflinching commitment to Hindu-Muslim unity were his assets, but society and crowds taxed his patience, though there were few more compelling orators. In 1923, at the age of thirty-five, he presided at a special Congress session. Early in 1939, well before the League's demand for a Muslim homeland, Gandhi 'instinctively felt' that Azad should head Congress again, but the Maulana, a resident of Calcutta, thought that a contest with Subhas, Bengal's favourite son, would be 'inelegant and even distasteful' (Sitaramayya 2:105).

Bose defeated Pattabhi Sitaramayya of the Telugu country, despite the backing that Pattabhi received from Gandhi, but in 1940 Azad became Congress President, taking over from Prasad who, we saw, had replaced Subhas. Congress's wartime involvements preventing a change, Azad continued as President until the summer of 1946. However, that Gandhi never quite saw Azad as his heir is revealed by what he told the AICC early in 1942:

> I have said for some years and say it now that not Rajaji, not Sardar Vallabhbhai, but Jawaharlal will be my successor. You cannot divide water by repeatedly striking it with a stick. It is just as difficult to divide us . . . When I am gone, he will speak my language (75:224).

Hearing the remark, Nehru, hitherto cross-legged on the ground with a bolster behind his back, 'sprang from his seat' and sat on top of the bolster.[2]

To see why Gandhi named Nehru rather than Patel, we should retrace our steps and return to 1929, when ten provincial Congress committees proposed Gandhi's name for Congress's chair, five Patel's, and three Jawaharlal's. As noted earlier, Gandhi was in fact declared chosen, but he withdrew and also obtained Patel's withdrawal. Informing the public of some of his reasons, Gandhi said he wished to rally India's young men and women and wanted a young leader. Jawaharlal might be thought impetuous, but Gandhi was sure that 'responsibility' would 'mellow and sober' him. He had had sharp differences with Jawaharlal in 1928 but could count on his loyalty. 'His being in the chair is as good as my being in it.'

Gandhi clarified, too, that 'a President of the Congress is not an autocrat . . . He can no more impose his views on the people than the English King' (*Young India*, 1.8.29). If he was grooming a possible successor, Gandhi was also establishing conventions against a concentration of powers in an individual.

Before going into the other reasons, we should look at the Gandhi-Nehru differences of 1928. Raising the issue of Dominion Status versus Independence, a radical wing led by Jawaharlal and Subhas had secured, at the end of 1927, a commitment by Congress to Complete Independence.

To Gandhi, who had not attended the session, the resolution was no more than brave talk when teeth were needed. He wrote in *Young India* that it reminded him of 'prisoners in chains spitting frothy oaths only to provide mirth for their gaolers.' Also, the resolution needlessly ruled out what might be a useful option. 'Dominion Status can easily become more than Independence, if we have the sanction to back it. Independence can easily become a farce, if it lacks sanction. What is in a name if we have the reality? A rose smells just as sweet . . .' (*Young India*, 12.1. and 6.9.28).

In letters to Gandhi, Nehru defended his stand strongly but he declined the challenge when Gandhi asked him to announce a parting of the ways. 'Am I not your child in politics,' Jawaharlal wrote to Gandhi, 'though perhaps a truant and errant child?'[3] At Congress's next session, held in Calcutta in December 1928, Motilal Nehru, the President, said he could not forgo Dominion Status. His son Jawaharlal and Subhas first said they would not touch it but agreed to support Gandhi's compromise proposal of giving Britain a year for granting Dominion Status. If Congress's demand was not conceded in a year, it would fight; and in that case Complete Independence would be its goal. Bose issued a press statement that he would not oppose Gandhi's compromise.

But at Congress's open session, Subhas moved an amendment opposing the compromise, and Jawaharlal spoke supporting the amendment. They invited scathing words from Gandhi: 'You may take the name of independence on your lips but all your muttering will be an empty formula if there is no honour behind it. If you are not prepared to stand by your words, where will independence be?' (Tendulkar 2: 441). Bose's amendment was defeated but only by 1,350 votes to 973.

In 1929 Gandhi was readying himself for another round of struggle — for the nationwide satyagraha of 1930 which would be remembered as the Salt March. Without Jawaharlal and Subhas, or at least one of them, he would find it difficult to carry India's youth. There was, too, the Muslim question. It was at the end of 1928 that Jinnah and Muhammad Ali had announced their rejection of Congress's approaches, and even a nationalist like Mukhtar Ahmad Ansari was cautioning Gandhi against launching an anti-Raj struggle before Muslim fears were allayed. Jawaharlal was more likely than Vallabhbhai to attract or re-attract Muslims.

Another unstated reason was Jawaharlal's appeal to India's growing leftist element, which saw Patel as a conservative. Gandhi hoped that young radicals tempted by Communist ideas would remain with Congress if Nehru became President, and also that the move might help 'to wean Nehru himself from the drift to the far left,' as Nehru's biographer, Michael Brecher, has put it.[4] Kerala's Communist Chief Minister in 1957-9 and 1967-9, E.M.S.Namboodiripad, makes the same point when he says that

Gandhi sought to 'tame' radical forces by installing 'a widely accepted young leader who was also a devoted disciple of Gandhi.' In Namboodiripad's assessment, the move ensured that Jawaharlal 'did not cross the bounds.'[5]

At the end of 1929, then, Jawaharlal took over, in Lahore, from his father, Motilal. (We might as well note that in 1928, stating that Bardoli had made Vallabhbhai 'the hero of the hour,' Motilal had proposed to Gandhi that Patel be made President. 'Failing him,' added Motilal, 'I think that under all the circumstances, Jawahar would be the best choice.'[6] Wanting then to check youthful exuberance, Gandhi had asked Motilal to accept the honour.)

Presiding at Lahore, Jawaharlal declared that he was 'a republican and no believer in kings and princes,' but the succession from father to son seemed to send Jawaharlal's mother Swaruprani into 'a sort of ecstasy,' and there were admiring references to 'a king passing on the sceptre of the throne to his logical successor.'[7] Gandhi, champion of the rights of the halt and the lame, the last and the least, had unwittingly launched a dynasty.

In 1929-30 it was still only a question of who should be Congress President, not of Gandhi's heir. We have seen that Vallabhbhai followed Jawaharlal to the chair, and that Jawaharlal followed Vallabhbhai as General Secretary. Yet we should also note what Patel said as President in Congress's March 1931 session in Karachi. He was addressing young radicals impatient with what in the spring of 1931 seemed to be Congress's moderation: 'Gandhiji is now almost 63 years old. I am 56. Should we, the old, be anxious for independence, or you, the young? We are interested in seeing India independent before we die. We are far more in a hurry than you' (*Patel*: 205).

In 1931 Vallabhbhai thinks of himself as old, and he brackets himself, in age-group, with Gandhi. He can be a member of Gandhi's team, or the captain of a team that Gandhi appoints in his lifetime, but not quite Gandhi's heir. Three weeks earlier, Gandhi had touched on the question at a Press Conference in Delhi, after signing his Pact with Irwin, the Viceroy. *Reporter*: 'Do you expect to achieve Purna Swaraj (Complete Independence) in your lifetime?' *Gandhi*:

'I do look for it most decidedly. I still consider myself a young man of 62.' ... *R:* 'Would you agree to become the Prime Minister of the future Government?' *G:* 'No. It will be reserved for younger minds and stouter hands' (Sitaramayya 1:755-63).

In 1932-3, following another round of battle, Gandhi, Vallabhbhai and Mahadev Desai spent many months in Pune's Yeravda prison. Desai's diary describes their life together. In this diary, Desai is a Boswell for two Johnsons. Vallabhbhai's services for Gandhi are matched by a wit that spares nothing of Gandhi. The two pledge themselves not to die before winning independence. The implication that they are allowed to die once independence is attained is another hint that Patel cannot be Gandhi's heir.

Patel was making envelopes in the prison one day when he was unexpectedly asked by Gandhi: 'Which portfolio in the Swaraj cabinet would you like reserved for you?' 'I will take the beggar's bowl,' was the instant reply. Gandhi rejoined: '[C.R.] Das (who died in 1925) and Motilal (who died in 1931) used to discuss what posts they would occupy. Muhammad Ali thought he should become Education Minister and Shaukat Ali wanted to become Commander-in-Chief. Well, Swaraj is still to come' (*Patel*: 224).

So in May 1932, when this talk took place, Vallabhbhai could guess that if India became free in his and Gandhi's lifetime, a portfolio rather than the Premiership was in store for him. If the slightest doubt remained, it was removed by Gandhi's 1934 statement, which we have seen, communicated to none other than Patel, that Jawaharlal was 'bound to become the rightful helmsman in the near future.'

That statement was followed by steps that Gandhi took that made Jawaharlal the Congress President in 1936 and again in 1937. In 1936, following his wife Kamala's death and the reluctance of Rajagopalachari to accept 'the crown of thorns,' Nehru was almost everyone's choice. Gandhi informed Vallabhbhai, who had been keen on Rajagopalachari, that he had 'asked Jawaharlal with Rajaji's consent' (*Patel*: 253). Nehru agreed, but Gandhi also asked him to consult Patel and Prasad before naming his Working Committee. Vallabhbhai, Rajagopalachari and Prasad led a ten-strong 'old guard' in the new team, which also included three socialists, Jayaprakash, Narendra Deva and Achyut Patwardhan. According to Patwardhan, the socialists 'owed their appointment not to Jawaharlal but to Gandhi.'[8]

A remark by Nehru that he had accepted the Committee's composition 'against his better judgment' was among the factors that caused Patel, Rajagopalachari, Prasad and three others to send in their resignations. On his part Nehru also threatened to resign, but Gandhi obtained the withdrawal of all resignations and offers to resign. 'I look upon the whole affair as a tragicomedy,' he told Nehru, asking him not to compel the AICC to choose between him and his colleagues. 'If they are guilty of intolerance,' Gandhi added, coaching the future helmsman in teamwork, 'you have more than your share of it. The country should not be made to suffer for your mutual intolerance' (*Rajaji* 1:282).

Six weeks later, the Committee and its President produced an agreed manifesto for the provincial elections due early in 1937. Patel wrote to Gandhi: 'We have been getting on beautifully this time ... I cannot speak too highly of Jawaharlal. We found not the slightest difficulty in cooperating with him' (*Patel*: 255).

A hitch, however, arose when, at the end of 1936, Jawaharlal declared his willingness to be reelected. Though enthusiastic about electioneering, Nehru had expressed his opposition to Congress accepting power under the Raj's constitution. In a letter to Mahadev Desai, Vallabhbhai, whose election was desired by many Congressmen, bitingly referred to Nehru as 'a decked-up prince ready at one stroke to marry as many girls as he can find.' (*Patel*: 256). A remark by Nehru that those considering him for another term should 'bear in mind' that he was a socialist further aggravated Patel. Kripalani has left an account of what happened next:

> Jawaharlal approached Gandhiji and told him that he felt that one term of 8 months was not sufficient for him to revitalise Congress. He would like a second term of office ... Gandhiji remained thoughtful for some time. Then he said, 'I shall see what can be done.' I was present

when the conversation between Gandhiji and Jawaharlal took place. In pursuance of [this] talk, . . . Gandhiji asked Sardar to withdraw, which he did.[9]

The 1929 exercise was repeated. It was agreed, however, that Vallabhbhai would continue as the chairman of Congress's Parliamentary Board, conduct the elections and guide the selection of Congress candidates. It was also understood that, Nehru's declarations notwithstanding, his reelection would not mean that Congress had endorsed socialism or was committed to reject provincial power. In addition, it was agreed that the Congress President could not override his Committee.

It is worth marking that these were all Gandhi's terms. Some of them were spelt out in the statement in which Patel announced that he was standing down. It was Gandhi who had drafted it.

Gandhi to Patel, 24.11.36: 'If you do not like the draft, write out another, and if you think it your duty to enter into competition, do so. You may change the draft where you think it necessary.'

There is no evidence that Vallabhbhai altered a comma in the Gandhi draft. Here we may usefully note that some of Vallabhbhai's key pronouncements during the 1928 Bardoli struggle had also been drafted by Gandhi. To do as Gandhi asked was, until 1945, Patel's commitment to himself. (We have seen in a previous chapter that in 1940, believing that a Britain involved in the war would accept an offer from Congress, he had gone against Gandhi's advice; but the offer was rejected, and saying, 'Never again,' Vallabhbhai had reverted to the commitment.) The November 1936 statement read as follows:

After consultations with friends, I have come to the conclusion that I must withdraw from the contest . . . At this critical juncture, a unanimous election is most desirable.

> My withdrawal should not be taken to mean that I
> endorse all the views Jawaharlalji stands for . . . For
> instance, I do not believe in the inevitability of class war.
> [Also], I can visualise the occasion when the acceptance
> of office may be desirable to achieve the common purpose.
> There may then be a sharp division of opinion between
> Jawaharlalji and myself.
>
> We know Jawaharlalji to be too loyal to the Congress
> to disregard the decision of the majority. The Congress
> President has no dictatorial powers . . . The Congress
> does not part with its ample powers by electing an
> individual no matter who he is (*Patel:* 257-8).

Let us remember, too, as we absorb this statement, that Nehru would
have known who authored it. Acknowledging the terms, he clarified that 'it would be absurd to treat this presidential election as a
vote for socialism or against office-aceptance' (*Patel:* 258). 'Nehru
to attract the masses and secure their votes, and Patel to control the
ministries after winning the elections — such was the division of
labour inside the Congress.'[10] This summing up by Namboodiripad
is justified. Despite their clashes, Nehru and Patel were willing to
play complementary roles in a larger design, enabling Gandhi to say
in December: 'I have cast all my cares on the broad shoulders of
Jawaharlal and the Sardar' (64:170).

Jawaharlal 'shot through the country like an arrow,' as his biographer, Brecher, puts it, and played the largest part in Congress's
electoral successes, but Patel and Rajagopalachari, who were for
office-acceptance, successfully pushed it through.

Gandhi's keenness about Nehru and Patel and their partnership
comes through in a letter written in September 1937 to Patel, who
had invited Nehru to Gujarat and presented a handsome contribution for a hospital in the U.P. in Kamala Nehru's name:

> What really surprises me is that you did not break down
> during this strenuous tour lasting five days. When two
> hard-working types get together, they wear each other out.

> Weak and thin people generally manage quite well in each
> other's company. A strong man has some consideration
> for a feeble companion. But when you two got together,
> there was no telling which of you was tougher. Your tour
> must have been remarkable (26.9.37).

For Patel, however, it was not easy to acknowledge the younger
partner's apparent edge over him. Gandhi warned Vallabhbhai not
to sulk or withdraw. To Patel's lasting credit, he rejected many a
strong temptation to do so.

Gandhi to Patel, 14.10.39: 'Kishorelal (Mashruwala, editor of
some of Gandhi's journals) was telling me yesterday that you had
said, "Bapu has placed us in Jawaharlal's charge, so we must go on
doing as he says." I hope this was only a joke. I have not handed
you over to anyone . . . It will not do if all of you do not exercise
your independent judgment.'

We can look at another letter from Gandhi to Patel. This one was
written on 31 October, 1941: 'Bhai Vallabhbhai, I hear it is your
birthday today . . . Remember we are not to go until we have attained Swaraj.' Less than three months later, on 15 January 1942,
Gandhi made the statement we saw earlier that 'not Rajaji, not
Sardar Vallabhbhai, but Jawaharlal will be my successor.'

Four years later, in the summer of 1946, after Quit India and
long and bitter spells in prison for Gandhi, Vallabhbhai, Nehru,
Azad, Prasad, and tens of thousands of others (Rajagopalachari
had disagreed with Quit India and was not arrested), it was time to
choose a Congress President again. Extended by several years because of Congress's rebellion against the Raj, Azad's term, begun
in March 1940, had ended.

Who would follow Azad? The question was of more than usual
interest because Premier Clement Attlee of Britain had declared that
Britain was quitting India and sent three Cabinet Ministers to arrange the withdrawal, which meant that Azad's successor was likely
to become India's first Prime Minister. Azad desired reelection, a
fact that agonized his close friend Jawaharlal, who had his hopes
and claims. Vallabhbhai also was involved, for twelve of the fifteen

provincial Congress committees had proposed his name. The names of Kripalani and Pattabhi, too, had been suggested.

The twenty-ninth of April, 1946, had been fixed as the last date for receiving nominations. On 20 April, Gandhi wrote Azad as follows, enclosing a newspaper report that claimed that Azad was willing to serve again but Gandhi was against the idea:

> Please go through the enclosed cutting . . . When one or two Working Committee members asked me for my opinion, I said that it would not be right for the President to continue for another term . . . If you are of the same opinion, you may issue a statement about the cutting and say that you have no intention to become President again. It is but proper that another person should now be the President.
>
> If asked, I would prefer Jawaharlal in today's circumstances. I have reasons for this. Why go into them?[11]

The trouble was that no provincial committee had proposed Nehru's name. Learning of Gandhi's wishes, Kripalani 'sent a paper round' on 25 April, proposing Nehru's name and obtained the signatures of several Working Committee colleagues and also of some Delhi members of the AICC. Fifteen valid signatures sufficed for Nehru's nomination; in deference to Gandhi's wishes, Patel, Kripalani and Pattabhi withdrew; and Jawaharlal was duly elected President.

A small but important incident was, however, part of the exercise. Before signing his statement of withdrawal, Vallabhbhai handed it to Gandhi, who showed it to Jawaharlal, saying, 'No PCC has put forward your name, only the Working Committee has.' Nehru, it seems, responded with 'complete silence.' Returning the paper to Patel, Gandhi asked him to sign it. Vallabhbhai signed it at once.[12]

Why did Gandhi show the sheet to Nehru and say what he did? Was he giving Jawaharlal an opportunity to withdraw? A more likely reason is that Gandhi wanted Nehru to recognize Patel's strength in the party and the dimension of his sacrifice. As in 1936,

Gandhi wanted Nehru to understand that his election and weightage for Patel went together.

Writing in the 1970s, Kripalani said that Gandhi's preference for Jawaharlal was 'personal rather than political,' and that 'the two were emotionally attached to each other, deny it though they may.'[13] Another possible explanation, added Kripalani, was that 'like the good shepherd' Gandhi 'left the many going straight and ran after the one going astray.'

Kripalani's long experience of Gandhi gives his assessment weight, but it should be noted that, contrary to what he suggests, Gandhi never denied his 'emotional attachment' for Nehru. He spoke and wrote freely of it, yet we have seen that this attachment did not prevent Gandhi from chastising Nehru on several occasions or, as over Quit India, from declaring that he would go ahead with or without Nehru. Moreover, we have seen evidence of Gandhi's 'emotional attachment' for Vallabhbhai, Rajagopalachari and Prasad as well.

In support of Kripalani's view we may cite Patel's occasional remarks to the effect that Gandhi was partial towards one of his two 'sons.'[14] The remarks were made with a twinkle but they reflected Vallabhbhai's bruised heart. The truth, however, seems better brought out in Kishorelal Mashruwala's summing-up: 'I would describe the Gandhi-Patel relationship as that of brothers, Gandhi being the senior brother, and Gandhi-Nehru as that of father and son' (*Patel*: 183).

In August 1928, Gandhi had told the Bardoli peasants: 'I admit I am Vallabhbhai's elder brother, but in public life . . . whether one is the father or the older brother of the man under whom one serves, one must obey his instructions' (*Patel*: 167). Gandhi's letters to Patel began with 'Bhai (brother) Vallabhbhai,' but his prefix for Jawaharlal was 'Chi.,' short for 'Chiranjiv,' the traditional blessing to a son or one like a son, and we have seen that Jawaharlal told Gandhi that he was his 'child.'

The pattern was governed by the ages of the three. Vallabhbhai was only six years younger than Gandhi but Jawaharlal was twenty years younger. Unfortunately for Vallabhbhai, though Gandhi thought of him as a younger brother, he not only called Gandhi 'Bapu' but saw him as a father. Two months before his death, and two-and-a-half years after Gandhi's assassination, Patel would say, 'amid sobs and great emotion':

> Today I see before me the whole picture of life ever since I joined Bapu's army. The love which Ba bore me I never experienced from my own mother. Whatever parental love fell to my lot, I got from Bapu and Ba.
>
> We were all soldiers in their camp. I have been referred to as the Deputy Prime Minister. I never think of myself in these terms. Jawaharlal Nehru is my leader. Bapu appointed him as his successor and had even proclaimed him as such.
>
> It is the duty of all Bapu's soldiers to carry out his bequest. Whoever does not do so from the heart in the proper spirit will be a sinner before God. I am not a disloyal soldier. I never think of the place I am occupying. I know only this much, and am satisfied, that I am where Bapu posted me (*Patel:* 527-8).

If the words show the nobility in Gandhi's ally, the emotion in which they were immersed reveals the warmth given and received in the Gandhi-Vallabhbhai relationship, and also perhaps the hurts exchanged. To return, however, to the triangular relationship, we should note that while the younger brother may be taken for granted, a son is fussed over though he may also, at times, be threatened with disinheritance. A younger brother may serve as a regent but the son will be the heir. The prestige and influence of a younger brother matter to a ruler, and we have seen that Gandhi frequently intervened to protect Patel's standing.

But the son and successor was Jawaharlal. As Mashruwala put it and as we have discovered, 'Bapu began early to look upon Jawaharlal as the destined leader of India after him' (*Patel:* 124). In preferring the younger one over the older, Gandhi brushed aside the hoary principle of seniority.

Another factor, almost a decisive one, was of health. Cancer of the rectum was suspected in Patel when he was in prison in 1941 but soon ruled out. However, he was quite unwell in January 1942 when Gandhi made his 'not Rajaji, not Sardar, but Jawaharlal' announcement. In June that year, two months before the launch of Quit India, Lumley, the Governor of Bombay, forwarded to the Viceroy a report that Patel 'is believed to be dying' (*TOP* 2:186).

Gandhi may have been influenced too by an impression that while Nehru's selection would not deprive India of Patel's services, 'Jawahar will not take second place.'[15] This view was evidently held by Vallabhbhai as well, who seems to have told his daughter that whereas Prime Ministership had moderated Nehru, rejection would have driven him into opposition, leading to a split in Congress and a bitter division across India.[16] We have seen that a Nehru-Patel partnership was what Gandhi envisaged: 'They will be like two oxen yoked to the governmental cart. One will need the other and both will pull together.'[17]

In the division of work that Gandhi had in mind, the tricky question of the princely states was Patel's responsibility. We do not know whether it was at Gandhi's initiative that Vallabhbhai had assumed charge of the States department at the end of June 1947, but when portfolios in free India's first cabinet were being considered, Gandhi wrote to Vallabhbhai: 'The problem of the States is so difficult that you alone can solve it' (11.8.47).

That Patel led Congress's 'Hindu' Right while Nehru, though identified with the 'secular' Left, seemed more of a bridge between factions, and that taming the Left might be easier than moderating the Right were additional considerations.[18] Alive to the Indian state's potential for oppressing the weak, Gandhi probably felt that Nehru was more likely than Patel to restrain the state.

Another factor was spelt out by Gandhi on 2 June 1947: 'Jawaharlal cannot be replaced today when the Englishmen are withdrawing their authority . . . He who was educated at Harrow and Cambridge and became a barrister is greatly needed to carry on the negotiations with the Englishmen' (88: 62).

We thus find the author of *Hind Swaraj* asking for a Harrow and a Cambridge student as free India's first Premier. This Gandhi is well aware that Jawaharlal admires Western civilization. A manifesto for the freedom campaign and the governance of modern India were two different things. A day earlier, addressing the Indian people, Gandhi had said: 'Your real king is Jawaharlal. He is a king who wants to serve not only India, but through it the whole world. He has acquainted himself with the peoples of all lands and is adept at dealing with diplomats from all countries' (88:53).

In the winter of 1941-2, after announcing his support for Rajagopalachari's line as against Gandhi's at an AICC meeting, Jawaharlal had added that Congress was Gandhi's 'creation and child and nothing can break the bond.' He seemed to mean, or include, himself when he said Congress, and Gandhi remarked that Nehru's 'love for and confidence in me peep out of every sentence referring to me' (*Harijan,* 25.1.42).

Five years later, Gandhi gave Jawaharlal high praise in a comment to Manu: 'He has the heart of a child. And yet he has the intellect, learning and power that only the greatest among intellectuals could boast of. He can renounce things as easily as a snake its slough. His tireless energy would put even a youth to shame' (88:150). Shortly before, he had said in Calcutta, referring to Nehru, 'In many ways, he has surpassed me.' This was to companions on a walk, one of whom, Gaganvihari Mehta, recorded the remark.[19]

A month before independence, speaking about nonviolence to a group of foreigners, Gandhi said: 'My co-worker Jawahar, who is like a son to me, is working hard to make my dream come true' (88:398). However, he also said that 'if Jawaharlal's words and actions differ, I shall shun him' (88:368).

Often, though not always, his praise for Nehru was accompanied by praise for Patel. In the previous chapter we noted his remark that he did many things 'out of the love that binds me to Jawahar and Sardar' (88:394), and the comment to Manu quoted above was preceded by the observation, 'I am at Jawahar's and Sardar's orders.' On 18 July 1947, asking a rhetorical question, 'To whom shall we go for help?' he added: 'To Jawaharlal Nehru? Or Sardar Patel? For they have today become the rulers' (88:366).

On other, and rarer occasions, others too were named. Thus on 28 May he spoke of Nehru as 'a very big man,' Patel as 'the hero of Bardoli,' Prasad as 'a great scholar' and Rajagopalachari as one with a 'great intellect.' He added, however: 'These are not the only persons in the Congress. All of you belong to it' (88:31).

Again, he took care to defend Vallabhbhai. On 10 July 1947, when Arthur Moore, former editor of *The Statesman*, said that Patel's attitude towards Muslims was 'bellicose,' Gandhi said, 'You do not know the Sardar. He is not vindictive or communal' (88:311).

In short, Gandhi loved Nehru, named him as his heir and ensured free India's Premiership for him, yet he also saw to it that Vallabhbhai, in particular, and others like Prasad and Rajagopalachari, who too were colleagues he loved, were in positions of influence. And while he used regal language and spoke of kings and rulers, he seemed to make all his successors, whether 'younger brothers' or 'sons,' subservient to democratic and ethical norms.

If Gandhi had not intervened over the Congress Presidency in the summer of 1946, would Patel have become free India's first Premier? As party chief he would no doubt have received the invitation from the Viceroy and become Vice-President of the Executive Council, or the de facto Premier of the Interim Government, the position that Nehru occupied from September 1946. But the question of the Premiership on 15 August 1947 would have come up afresh, and we cannot be certain that Indian public opinion would have retained Vallabhbhai. The assessment of one of Patel's closest Congress allies in 1946-7, Dwarka Prasad Mishra of the Central Provinces, is of interest:

When we . . . preferred him (Patel) to Nehru as Congress President, we had no intention of depriving Nehru of future Premiership. The younger man had already been raised to the office of Congress President thrice, and we therefore thought it just and proper that Patel, the older man, should have at least a second chance. As regards the Premiership of free India, we had always a vague idea that having been declared as his successor by the Mahatma, Nehru was bound to occupy that exalted office at the dawn of freedom.[20]

In one important respect, the Gandhi of 1946-7 was different from the initiator of Quit India. In 1942, Gandhi was ready to go ahead without his 'brothers' and 'sons,' and had accordingly informed Azad, President at the time, and Nehru. Patel had fallen in at once with Quit India, but Gandhi would have gone ahead without him as well. But on the eve of freedom, an older Gandhi surrounded by violence but not by a younger set of leaders, was loth to defy Patel, Nehru, Prasad and Rajagopalachari. They had taken over not long after prison doors opened in the summer of 1945.

This can be documented in, for instance, the Gandhi-Patel relationship in 1945-6. Gandhi advised Vallabhbhai against approaching businessmen for funds for the elections of December 1945, but Patel felt he had no choice. The Working Committee and the President, Azad, had asked him to, and he felt himself that money was needed. 'It must be understood between us,' he wrote to Azad, 'that no seats should be lost for want of money' (*Patel*: 348).

Sensing Vallabhbhai's independence, Gandhi said in a letter to him: 'You are after all the Sardar of Bardoli and, as it happens, of India.' Two months earlier, on Patel's birthday, Gandhi had said, 'Sardar is as dear as a son to me' (*Patel*: 350). We have noted the significant difference between a son and a younger brother. Now, for the first time, Gandhi was calling Vallabhbhai 'Chi.' rather than 'Bhai' in letters.

We have also seen, earlier in this work, how at a crucial Working Committee meeting in the summer of 1946 Azad asked if it was necessary to detain Gandhi, and everyone, including Gandhi, interpreted the silence that followed as a verdict in favour of his leaving. The successors had taken over, and Gandhi was willing to hand over.

Awareness of his differences with them imparted pain to the succession, but it had taken place. In his letters we can read the pain as well as Gandhi's acceptance of the change.

To Patel, 13.4.47: 'I notice that there are frequent differences between your approach and mine. Such being the case, would it be advisable for me to meet the Viceroy even as an individual? Please think over this objectively . . . Please do not see the slightest suggestion of a complaint from me in this' (87:271).

To Nehru, 7.6.47: 'The oftener we meet the more convinced I am becoming that the gulf between us in the thought world is deeper than I had feared . . . I had told the Badshah (Ghaffar Khan) that if I do not carry you with me, I shall retire at least from the Frontier consultation and let you guide him' (88:94-5).

On 10 September Gandhi spoke to Brij Krishna Chandiwala, his faithful friend and helper in Delhi, about his successors: 'I know [Vallabhbhai's] heart better than anyone else. His heart and mind were with me. Now he goes on another line. He thinks it is the right one. If I were to order him he would leave it, but that is not my way. Jawaharlal listens to me and he concedes that I have some sense. But he is unable to do what I tell him. Rajendra Babu has also changed. Maulana and I have differences' (Brij Krishna 3:282).

Nehru told an interviewer that if Gandhi had insisted on rejecting the Mountbatten Plan, he and the others would have obeyed Gandhi. We need not question this statement, which corresponds with Gandhi's observation to Brij Krishna that Patel would heed Gandhi's injunctions. But the time for injunctions had passed, and rightly so, as far as Gandhi was concerned. His successors were on the throne, not he. He would neither order nor undermine them. When in April 1947 a newspaper reported that there was a 'quarrel' between Gandhi and the successors, notably Patel, Gandhi instantly repudiated the report as 'sheer nonsense' (87:265).

Not he but the people of India were now the masters of the successors. On 1 June 1947, he referred to 'Rajaji, Rajendra Babu, Jawaharlalji' and others in the Interim Government and said that if despite cooperation from the public and traders, 'India cannot have enough food and clothing and there is no progress in the country,' then the people 'can remove them from office' (88:56).

Also relevant is Gandhi's emphasis on the successors' need for support from outside Congress. We have referred previously to Gandhi's role in the inclusion of Ambedkar and Shyama Prasad

Mookerjee in the Cabinet that took over on 15 August 1947, and seen Gandhi's remark: 'Jawahar, freedom has come to the country, not to Congress.' He said to Rajendra Prasad in June: 'Congressmen know how to give a fight [and] fill jails but they lack the art of government . . . Because Congressmen have gone to prison, it does not mean that they should now hold all administrative jobs . . . On the contrary . . . we should freely make use of . . . talent and experience wherever it is to be found, even outside the Congress ranks' (88:72).

Gandhi played a part, too, in the presence in the Constituent Assembly of some of its ablest non-Congress members. B. Shiva Rao has recalled a talk in the summer of 1946:

> I sought an interview late one evening . . . 'What is it about?' he asked me with a smile as I met him in front of his hut. I explained that it was the composition of the Constituent Assembly I was interested in: Congress leaders who had been to prison several times could not be expected to have specialised in constitution-making. There were fifteen persons outside the Congress, I took the liberty of adding, who could contribute . . . Gandhiji readily agreed.
>
> 'But have you a list?' he asked. I promptly pulled out a sheet of paper . . . At the top of the list were Sir Tej Bahadur Sapru, Mr N. Gopalaswami Iyengar, Dr M.R. Jayakar and Sir Alladi Krishnaswami Aiyar. 'They are all good names,' Gandhiji said, 'but show the list to Maulana Azad, who is the Congress President, and to Jawaharlalji. You may tell them it has my approval.' . . . The list went through the Working Committee, with one or two changes.[21]

To return, however, to the Nehru-Patel question, we should look at what Rajagopalachari wrote in 1971, more than seven years after Nehru's death. Subhas, Patel, Azad and Prasad had died before Nehru, but Kripalani would survive Rajagopalachari:

> When the independence of India was coming close upon

us and Gandhiji was the silent master of our affairs, he had come to the decision that Jawaharlal, who among the Congress leaders was most familiar with foreign affairs, should be the Prime Minister of free India, although he knew Vallabhbhai would be the best administrator among them all . . .

Undoubtedly it would have been better . . . if Nehru had been asked to be the foreign minister and Patel made the Prime Minister. I too fell into the error of believing that Jawaharlal was the more enlightened person of the two and therefore it would be best that he was Premier . . . A myth had grown about Patel that he would be harsh towards Muslims. This was a wrong notion but it was the prevailing prejudice (*Swarajya*, 27.11.71).

Later Jayaprakash quoted this 'confession' by Rajagopalachari and said he agreed with it. While considering it, we should not perhaps forget that Rajagopalachari's clashes with Jawaharlal's daughter, Indira, who had become Prime Minister in early 1966, formed its context, or that Jayaprakash too was opposed to Indira's attitudes and policies. In other words, their assessment of the choice of Nehru was also influenced by their reaction to his daughter's performance.

A ploughboy with a chip on the shoulder who became watchman, welder and policeman to India, Vallabhbhai understood the soil of India and the peasants who tilled it. He fought with tenacity, delegated with ease, and stood by his supporters. He was also a great tactician who knew when to be silent and when blunt. In these qualities he scored over Nehru, who spoke oftener and more emotionally but also less clearly.

When, in the 1920s, Jawaharlal was in charge of the Allahabad municipality, 'memoranda flowed from his pen on issues great and small — education, sanitation, prostitution, the removing of billboards which disfigured the city, and the like.'[22] Vallabhbhai, who ran the Ahmedabad municipality at about the same time, preferred to send a councillor or municipal officer to the spot that had a problem, and make the representative responsible for tackling it.

Socialist and Marxian literature stirred Nehru's heart but failed to impress Vallabhbhai's brain. A vision of an India modernized by dams and steel plants likewise influenced Jawaharlal, whereas the bias of Patel was for agriculture, dairying and rural industry. And though Nehru was Congress's undoubted expert on foreign affairs, Patel had an instinctive grasp of the impact on India of events around her and beyond, revealed, for instance, in his well known exchanges with Nehru over Tibet and China in 1949-50 (*Patel*: 510-3).

If Vallabhbhai was abler or sounder than Nehru in some crucial areas, does it follow that Gandhi could or should have named Patel as the rightful future helmsman in the thirties, or installed him at the head of the government in 1946-7? To picture Gandhi as one who could have imposed his preferences on India may be to misread the India of his time. Certainly he did not read India that way. He said to Nirmal Bose in August 1947 that his gift lay not in 'creating a new situation' but in sensing and 'giving shape' to 'what is stirring in the heart of the masses.'[23] And there seems no doubt that in the thirties and the forties the Indian people entertained a fondness for Jawaharlal in a degree not extended to Patel.

His youth, handsome appearance, light skin, physical courage, daring demeanour and record of sacrifice, including long years in prison, had made Jawaharlal a darling of the masses; his gift for outlining an appealing vision of the future stirred students and intellectuals; and he was seen as holding his own, admired by important foreigners, on the international stage. If to represent India in her encounters with the world the choice was between Nehru and Patel, Indians were for Jawaharlal. Even on the Indian stage, Jawaharlal was the more arresting communicator. Vallabhbhai could be a biting orator in Gujarati but his writing and speaking skills, whether in Hindi or English, could not compare with Nehru's.

Perceptions alter over time. Joined to other circumstances including the warmth and trust he received from Gandhi, Jawaharlal's birth as the only son of the rich and powerful advocate and Congress leader, Motilal Nehru, in a Brahmin family in Hindi-speaking North India, gave him advantages that in the thirties and the forties could not be matched by Vallabhbhai, the fourth son in a family of impoverished peasant proprietors in the interior of Gujarat. The U.P. was seen as India's heartland, Hindi as the national language, and to be a Brahmin was prestigious. Gujarat, on the other hand, was small and over to one side.

Today Vallabhbhai's peasant and middle-caste background would give him a nationwide standing that could not be cultivated fifty or sixty years ago, though the intermediate castes were as large a population percentage then as they are now. Socialism, centralized planning and the Soviet model have lost much of their appeal, and in many minds Patel's image as a staunch defender of Hindu interests contrasts favourably with a Nehru perceived as more secular than necessary. However, we should remember that the Nehru years saw respect for the Constitution and for many democratic institutions — for a free press, the judiciary, state chief ministers and legislatures. They were years of tolerance.

In any case, the India of Gandhi, Patel and Nehru was different from the India that today debates the question of Nehru versus Patel. Its sentiments and moods were different. In 'nominating' Jawaharlal, Gandhi did not override public opinion. Neither can it be said that he allowed personal considerations to override national ones. For representing and uniting Indians of all ages, classes and religions, Jawaharlal seemed more suitable than Vallabhbhai.

We should also note the unreality of much of the debate. As we have seen, it was the Nehru-Patel duo rather than Jawaharlal that Gandhi installed, and even that duo was part, we saw, of a larger pool of successors, extending beyond Congressmen. Again, students of the so-called Nehru-Patel duumvirate, a period that began in September 1946 and ended with Patel's death in December 1950, have found that complementarity between the two far outweighed their conflicts. Each was more useful to the other, and more aware of the other's usefulness to him, than is allowed by the champions of either.

Also, the debate focusses too narrowly on the choice of the Congress President in the summer of 1946, overlooking that the succession in Nehru's favour had been settled and announced much earlier, and more than once. It also overlooks the crucial age factor as well as Patel's own sense of the soundness of Gandhi's decision. In November 1948 he had said: 'Mahatma Gandhi named Pandit Nehru as his heir and successor. Since Gandhiji's death we have realized that our leader's judgment was correct' (*Patel*: 490). Human as he was, and undoubtedly hurt by Gandhi's preference, Vallabhbhai was yet big enough to speak in such terms, and also to say to the American journalist Vincent Sheean, with reference to a huge crowd that had surrounded him and Nehru in Bombay: 'They come for Jawahar, not for me' (*Patel*: 490).

However, Gandhi was probably more effusive than was good for Jawaharlal in his praise of him. Also, the spectacle of the Congress crown passing in 1929-30 from Motilal to Jawaharlal, for which Gandhi was responsible, and Gandhi's references to Jawaharlal as 'your king' in his talks to the people of India, contributed to the creation of the dynasty that governed India from 1947 to 1989, except for eighteen months in 1964-6 and about three years in 1977-80.

If, in relation to his offspring, Gandhi was not generous enough, Jawaharlal, in relation to his daughter, was perhaps overgenerous in assenting in 1958, when he was Prime Minister, to her elevation as Congress President when her talents were unproven and her experience limited. Those happy with the romance of many in India with Jawaharlal and his descendants will not regret Gandhi's role in helping to kindle it; those regretting the romance are bound to lay some blame at Gandhi's door.

Chapter 11

The Last Lap

'I WILL NEVER be able to forget the scene I have witnessed today,' Gandhi said on 18 August 1947 in Calcutta, where independence had found him living in Hydari Manzil, a Muslim home in the neglected quarter of Beliaghata. It was the day of Id, and he was looking at about half a million Hindus and Muslims who had gathered in friendship on the grounds of the Mohammedan Sporting Club for his prayer meeting, their orderliness ensured by Congress and League volunteers working in unison. 'However,' added Gandhi, 'I want this unity to be everlasting' (89:60).

That day he was asked by Congress workers of Khulna, which the Boundary Commission had assigned to Pakistan, about the Union flag they had hoisted on 15 August. The reply scribbled by Gandhi, who was observing silence, was pure precision: 'The Union flag *must* go. Pakistan's must be hoisted without demur, with joy if possible. Award is award, good or bad' (89:59).

Some days later he wrote out, for an unknown friend or visitor, the 'answer to doubt' that was to become famous. Though written in English, it was signed in Hindi and also in Bengali:

> I will give you a talisman. Whenever you are in doubt, or
> when the self becomes too much with you, apply the
> following test. Recall the face of the poorest and the
> weakest man whom you may have seen, and ask yourself

> if the step you contemplate is going to be of any use to
> him. Will he gain anything by it? Will it restore him to a
> control over his own life and destiny? In other words,
> will it lead to swaraj for the hungry and spiritually starving
> milions? Then you will find your doubts and yourself
> melting away (89: 125).

But he was having difficulty himself in deciding when to go to the
Punjab and tackle the violence there. Telegrams and letters pressed
him to go there, and Calcutta's Punjabis urged him likewise, but
Gandhi seemed torn between a wish to 'rush to the Punjab and if
necessary break myself in the attempt to stop the warring elements
from committing suicide' (to Nehru, 89:117) and a desire to await a
clear call. It seemed plain, too, that horror was common to West
and East Punjab, and it was not easy to choose the half to confront
first. In a letter to Vallabhbhai, Gandhi said he felt 'totally lost,'
adding, 'I pin my hopes on you two,' Nehru being the other (89:127).
The uncertainty about the Punjab was matched by a sense that Bengal, including its Pakistani part, and Bihar continued to need him.
The view of Nehru, consulted several times, was that Gandhi should
go to the Punjab but 'not yet.'

He was all set, in the circumstances, to proceed to Noakhali when
a violent demonstration at Hydari Manzil by a group of Hindus on
the night of 31 August changed his mind. A lathi and brick aimed at
Gandhi, who had come out to meet the demonstrators, missed him.
There were killings elsewhere in Calcutta later that night and the
next day. Fifty lost their lives and nearly five hundred were injured.
Visiting the affected areas, Gandhi saw, as he told the press, 'two
dead bodies of very poor Muslims,' victims of a grenade attack on a
truck in which they were fleeing.

Asking himself whether Calcutta's amity had been 'a mere sham,'
Gandhi announced a fast by him, to 'end only if and when sanity
returns to Calcutta.' He would drink water during the fast, said
Gandhi, with, if necessary, salt, soda bicarb or sour lime. By now
Jawaharlal had concluded that Gandhi should visit the Punjab 'as
early as possible,' but Gandhi thought that 'if the fury (in Calcutta)

did not abate, my going to the Punjab would be of no avail.' If Calcutta responded to his fast, he would go to the Punjab with confidence. Meanwhile, the fast might speak to the Punjab also, to both parts of it.

To Patel Gandhi wrote that Rajagopalachari, from 15 August the Governor of West Bengal, had 'admonished me a lot, tried hard to persuade me not to go on a fast,' but 'I saw my duty clearly before me.' When Gandhi told Rajagopalachari that his trust was in God alone, his old friend pointed to the reference to sour lime, whereupon Gandhi said he would forgo that nutrient. 'Can you fast against the goondas?' Rajagopalachari asked. Gandhi's reply was that his fast could 'touch the hearts of those behind the goondas,' without whose 'sympathy and passive support the goondas would have no legs to stand upon.'

The fast began at 8.15 p.m. on 1 September and at once triggered action. Hindus and Muslims marched for peace. About 500 members of the North Calcutta police force, including Britons and Anglo-Indians, went themselves on a 24-hour sympathy fast while remaining on duty. The Shanti Sena, or Peace Brigade, was born, comprising young men willing, at jeopardy to their lives, to intervene in a clash.

'University students would come up to us,' a professor would later recall, 'and ask to be excused from attending their classes [as] they felt disturbed [because] if anybody had to suffer for the continued killing and betrayal in the city, it was not Gandhiji.' Added Amiya Chakravarty:

> Some even gathered weapons from streets and homes at great personal risk and returned them to Gandhiji. Men would come back from their offices in the evening and find food prepared by their family ready for them; but soon it would be revealed that the women of the home had not eaten during the whole day . . . They could not understand how they could go on when Gandhiji was dying for their own crimes.[1]

Rammanohar Lohia, the Socialist leader, brought to Gandhi a body of Hindu youths who admitted complicity in violence and surrendered a small arsenal of arms. A gang of goondas followed and asked for 'whatever penalty you may impose.' Only 'you should now end your fast.' Gandhi asked them to go 'immediately among the Muslims and assure them full protection' (89:151).

Leading the Forward Bloc, Subhas Bose's older brother Sarat called on Gandhi and offered his assistance. So did Shyama Prasad Mookerjee of the Hindu Mahasabha. The Forward Bloc and the Mahasabha had accused each other of inciting the disturbances. 'I am not here to judge,' Gandhi said to Sarat. 'My fast is an appeal to everybody to search his heart.' Wanting to affect more than Calcutta, Gandhi sent a letter via Pyarelal to Khwaja Nazimuddin, the chief minister of East Bengal, telling him that he was being asked to visit 'both parts of the Punjab,' which had gone 'utterly mad,' but Calcutta had held him, and asking Nazimuddin, meanwhile, 'to tell me all about Noakhali' (89:147).

At 6 p.m. on 4 September Suhrawardy escorted a deputation of Hindu Mahasabha, Muslim League and Sikh leaders to Gandhi's bedside. When they pleaded that he end the fast, Gandhi asked them if they would risk their lives to prevent a recurrence of communal killings. The deputation withdrew to another room, conferred, and returned with a pledge. After reminding them that 'above all, there is God, our witness,' Gandhi broke his fast, which had lasted seventy-three hours.[2] Communal violence would not return to Calcutta for years.

'Gandhiji has achieved many things,' Rajagopalachari said on 5 September, 'but in my considered opinion there has been nothing, not even independence, which is so truly wonderful as his victory over evil in Calcutta' (*The Statesman*, 6.9.47). 'My life is my message,' Gandhi wrote in Bengali on 5 September, when Devtosh Das Gupta, secretary of the Shanti Sena Dal, sought a message (89:156).

Thanking the people of Calcutta and acknowledging the martyrdom of two young men, Sachin Mitra, who was killed on 1 September while defending Muslims, and Smritish Banerjee, who lost his life on 3 September while protecting a peace procession, Gandhi boarded, on 7 September, three weeks after Independence, a train for Delhi, en route, as he informed Jawaharlal in a wire, to the Punjab.

❊

And when he was come near, he beheld the city, and wept over it, saying, If thou hadst known . . . the things which belong unto thy peace! but now they are hid from thine eyes (Luke 19:41-2).

Delhi detained Gandhi. 'The city was under curfew. Thousands had been killed. There was looting and firing. All bazars were closed. People's rations were exhausted . . . Localities like Karol Bagh, Sabzimandi and Paharganj were being emptied of Muslims' (Brij Krishna 3: 278). To Gandhi's disappointment, Vallabhbhai, who met him at Shahdara station, took him not to the sweepers' colony, where he had stayed in June and July and during the previous summer, but to Birla House. Refugees from Pakistan had taken the space available at the sweepers' place. Also, Patel thought it would be impossible to protect Gandhi's life there.

Vallabhbhai, Gandhi noticed, was without a smile. Police officers also looked sad. 'The city of Delhi, which always appeared gay, [seemed] turned into a city of the dead.' After 'listening the whole day long to the tale of woe that is Delhi today,' Gandhi decided that he could not go to the Punjab until Delhi 'regained its former self' (89:166-7). To an old associate, Valji Desai, Gandhi wrote, 'My cart has got stuck in a wood' (89:179).

Within twenty-four hours of his arrival in the capital, Gandhi had visited the camp near Humayun's Tomb where Muslim Meos from Alwar and Bharatpur had taken refuge, the Jamia Millia, where many of Delhi's Muslims were huddled, and camps filled with Hindu and Sikh refugees from West Punjab at Diwan Hall, Wavell Canteen and Kingsway.

Angry faces and shouts of 'Go Back!' greeted Gandhi in almost all the camps, Muslim and non-Muslim, but the anger of the latter seemed greater. He was told that he was for the Muslims, that his heart was of stone. He had not suffered the way they had, his near and dear ones had not been killed, he did not have to beg for his food. Gandhi said later to his companion and aide Brij Krishna that he was happy the refugees could lighten their sorrows by abusing him.

It was the kind of comment his aides would hear whenever they questioned the time he devoted to answering correspondents who attacked him. Those criticizing him to his face were 'a thousand times better than those who . . . applaud me but at the same time commit murders and disregard what I say.' Through their candour, the critics' 'anger is spent and their hearts are cleansed,' and they would 'work wonders' if his attention and answers managed to convince them (89:367). To the refugees, Gandhi offered the strong truth that God who gave life also took it; all were to die one day, and the only remedy was to live right while one lived.

Delhi's place in the life and history of India seemed burned into him by her travails, and he sought to remind her citizens of it: 'It is said that in the Mahabharata period the Pandavas used to stay in this Purana Qila. Whether you call it Indraprastha or Delhi, the Hindus and the Muslims have grown here together. It was the capital of the Moghuls. Now it is the capital of India. The Moghuls came from outside [but] identified themselves with the manners and customs of Delhi. In such a Delhi of yours the Hindus and the Muslims used to live together peacefully . . . They would fight for a short while and then be united again . . . This is your Delhi' (89:181).

Apart from being the capital, Delhi was 'the heart of India' (90:419). 'If peace is not established here, the whole of Hindustan will be on fire' (89:237). 'Ultimately, Delhi will decide the destiny of the whole country' (89:465). His own heart, too, was intertwined with Delhi. He recalled his previous visits and the friends he had there, many no longer living: Swami Shraddhananad, who in 1919 had been invited to speak in Delhi's greatest mosque, the Jama Masjid; Hakim Ajmal Khan, in 1915 the leader, as Gandhi had discovered, of Delhi's Hindus as well as its Muslims; Dr Mukhtar Ahmad Ansari, Gandhi's faithful ally who died in 1935; Charlie Andrews, who at the turn of the century had learnt from aged Delhi residents of the Hindu-Muslim friendship they knew in their youth; Principal S.K.Rudra of St. Stephen's College, Gandhi's first Delhi host, a Christian through whom Gandhi had met Ajmal Khan and Ansari; and others.

Delhi was where he had fasted for twenty-one days in 1924 in the home of the Ali brothers, where, in 1927, his grandson Rasik, son of Harilal, had died, where he had addressed the Raj in Hindustani in 1918, stood up thereafter to a series of Viceroys, and signed his pact with Irwin in 1931. If people continued to be killed in Delhi, 'I would also wish to die here' (89:187). This grew into a clear conviction: 'I have to do or die here. If heart unity is not restored in Delhi, I can see flames raging all over India' (90:61).

Yet he would shiver when, in September, it rained, and then as winter approached — he would shiver thinking of the uprooted and unprotected ones, Hindu, Sikh and Muslim, in Delhi's camps. People sought out and killed in a hospital, a man stabbed in a train and thrown into a river, another killed while he was opening the little shop where he repaired spectacles, trainloads of refugees stopped and butchered, all because they belonged to the Other religion and none because of any offence committed, all before approving or silent onlookers — such were the incidents related to Gandhi, often by those directly bereaved.

'There is a constant stream of visitors,' he wrote to a friend in November. 'How can I refuse to listen to their sorrows? Very often my own grief becomes overwhelming' (89: 510). Shame joined pain. 'I do not wish to be a witness to these things. I do not wish to see such a downfall' (89: 271). And guilt too, for he identified with the attacker as well as the victim. 'When someone commits a crime anywhere, I feel I am the culprit' (90:133). 'So I pray to God day and night that He should take me away, or He should give me the power to extinguish this fire' (89:272). The desperate tides of the sorrow, shame and guilt of India and Pakistan seemed forced through the channels of his heart.

Agony drove him to greater toil. 'I can't interrupt [my] work. If my life ebbs away in the process, I would feel happy' (89:148). His duty was to 'take care of the immediate task before him, whether great or small, with all the care and freedom from bias or mental worries which he could bring to bear upon it' (89:143).

So he wrote for *Harijan*, composed his post-prayer utterances, practised his Bengali lessons, scribbled or dictated letters, made writing pads out of the envelopes he received, and gave his ears to the flow of visitors. If he laboured as intensively as ever, it was not at the cost of circumspection. 'Whatever I say in my prayer meetings or in my writings is done after due deliberation,' he observed towards the end of August (89:67). The record shows that despite the emotions involved, he was seldom carried away or trapped into indiscretion.

He held on to his truth. 'I have endless work here,' he wrote in November. 'I get utterly exhausted by the end of the day . . . Still, I retain my faith, [and] derive solace from the dictum that adversity is the mother of progress' (89:510). The wish to live for 125 years left him, he hoped to do or die, and prayed to be taken away rather than remain 'a helpless witness of the butchery by man become savage,' but in the end he was content to 'dance as Rama wills,' to 'cry "Not my will but Thine alone shall prevail"' (89:286 and 90:295).

He likened his state to Draupadi's when, in the *Mahabharata*, the Kauravas had tried to disrobe her in a public chamber. To a friend he wrote in November:

> I saw your letter only now, after listening to the sweet and sad bhajan containing Draupadi's prayer . . . Draupadi had mighty Bhima and Arjuna and the truthful Yudhishthira as husbands; she was the daughter-in-law of men like Dronacharya, Bhishma and Vidura, and yet amidst an assembly of people it appeared she was in a terrible plight. At that hour she did not lose faith and prayed to God from her heart. And God did protect her honour.
>
> Today I also am seated in a palatial house surrounded by loving friends. Still, I am in a sad plight. Yet there is God's help, as I find each day (89:464-5).

Ready for anything, he expected to be killed. On 16 September he told Brij Krishna and Sushila Nayar that he was reminded of the

French Revolution, adding, 'I would not be surprised if some of us
. . . go the way of the leaders of the French Revolution' (89:195; and
Brij Krishna 3:297). In October he said to a group of Muslims,
including several old friends, who called on him on the day of Bakr-
Id: 'It is my constant prayer to God that He may give me the strength
to intercede even for my assassin. And it should be your prayer too
that your faithful servant may be given that strength to forgive'
(89:411).

However, any assassins would need to put in their work. Gandhi
was continuing to take care of his health and limbs. They were in
good shape, though on 24 September he wrote to Kalelkar, 'I have
often confessed that my memory is not what it used to be' (89:228).
A Czech visitor in 1947, Jiri Nehnevasja, recorded: 'My hand rests
in his for a while. It is a small wrinkled hand with a white palm and
pale fingers. The handshake is firm, manlike.'[3] In November he told
visitors from Indonesia: 'I look after my health with care . . . I have
decided to live cheerfully even in this atmosphere of darkness and
inhumanity' (89:494-5).

When a car door slammed by Brij Krishna injured his finger and
his son Ramdas wrote expressing concern, Gandhi answered: 'It is
true that I crushed my finger . . . It was nothing to worry about . . .
I am no doubt careful but even a careful person does meet with such
accidents' (90:279-80).

Persisting with his enthusiasms and concerns, and finding new
ones, he was involved in sanitation, prohibition, Hindustani, attacks
on leprosy and on untouchability, the co-workers he had left behind
in Noakhali and Bihar, the Shanti Sena that had been born in Calcutta,
removal of controls on the movement and pricing of foodgrains, the
Sevagram Ashram, khadi and other village industries, nature
cure . . .

A letter he wrote to Jivanji Desai, the Ahmedabad-based printer
of his journals, brings out the practical Gandhi and also one who is
short of help: 'I am very sorry to learn that you got the articles on
Wednesday . . . I take the utmost care to see that you get all the
material on Monday evening. With that aim, I send the material by
airmail on Sunday . . . But I have no paid employee . . . Do you send

anybody to the airport when the plane arrives on Mondays?' (89:65).

And we wonder whether the one obliged to author the following humble, if also eminently practical, piece, under the heading, 'Is *Harijan* wanted?', was the same person at whose call India's streets used to be emptied and her prisons filled: 'My life has become, if possible, more tempestuous than before. Nor can I at present claim any place as a permanent habitation. The columns are predominantly filled by my after-prayer speeches. In the original I contribute, on an average, only one and a half columns per week. This is hardly satisfactory. I would like, therefore, the readers . . . to give me their frank opinion as to whether they really need their *Harijan* weekly to satisfy their political or spiritual hunger. They should send their answer to the Editor of the *Harijan,* Ahmedabad . . . In the left hand upper corner of the envelope, the writer should state: "About *Harijan*"' (89:82-3).

A large number replied in the affirmative and *Harijan* continued to appear. We should here remember that an important reason for Gandhi's sense of isolation over *Harijan* was the withdrawal, linked to Gandhi's testing of his chastity, of Kishorelal Mashruwala, who used to edit the journals and was known as one of Gandhi's ablest interpreters.

Also among Gandhi's interests in what were to be the final six months of his life were an English-Hindustani dictionary, the biography of Gandhi that D.G.Tendulkar was writing (according to Tendulkar, Gandhi discussed 'the smallest details' with him, including the format, the typeface, and standardization of spellings),[4] and the creation of new cities: 'I feel that all professional and non-professional, rich and poor, refugees should live together and build ideal cities just as the rich people of Lahore made Lahore an ideal city which the Hindus and Sikhs had perforce to give up' (90:84).

More than causes or institutions, people continued to fill Gandhi's life. Those physically around him in the final six months were Manu and Abha, Brij Krishna, Shivbalak Bisen (whose duties included opening Gandhi's mail and posting his letters), and, for shorter spells, Pyarelal, his sister Sushila Nayar, and Mirabehn. Jawaharlal was often in, and, less frequently, Vallabhbhai.

Almost every night, Devadas spent a few minutes with his father before he went off to sleep. The sight of Devadas's two-year-old son Gopal, Gandhi's youngest grandchild, seemed to give joy to the grandfather, who would make faces at the youngster and on occasion tell Devadas that Gopal was missed more than him if they did not turn up.

'Bapuji,' one of his younger helpers said to him on 2 October, his last birthday, when, opposite where he sat, Mirabehn had laid out flowers that spelt Rama and the sacred syllable Om in Hindi and made a Cross, 'on our birthdays, we touch others' feet and take their blessings, but in your case it is the other way about. Is it fair?' Gandhi laughed: 'The ways of Mahatmas are different! It is not my fault. You made me Mahatma, so you must pay the penalty' (89:524).

Perhaps the young person's freedom with him reminded Gandhi of Sonja Schlesin, who was seventeen when about four decades earlier she joined Gandhi as a secretary in South Africa. 'She seemed to mind neither age nor experience,' Gandhi had written about her in his autobiography. 'Her impetuosity often landed me in difficulties, but her open and guilelesss temperament removed them as soon as they were created.' In October 1947 she wrote a letter that must have moved the 78-year-old man:

> Far from losing your desire to live until you are 125,
> increasing knowledge of the world's lovelessness and
> consequent misery should cause you rather to determine
> to live longer still . . . You said in a letter to me some time
> ago that everyone ought to wish to attain the age of 125,
> you can't go back on that (89:449).

To Lilavati Asar, who was about to become a doctor in Bombay and had written of a severe supervisor, Gandhi wrote in December 1947: 'If a doctor makes a mistake, the patient has to pay for it — at times with his life. One should therefore look for a teacher who does not condone mistakes . . . Ponder and digest what you read. The student given to cramming is considered to be a fool of the first water' (90:272).

Then there was Sharda Chokhawala, daughter of Chimanlal Shah, manager of the Sevagram Ashram, who had fallen seriously ill and written that she might die. To her Gandhi replied: 'But how can you die before I do? The very thought is unbearable to me' (90:285). This was on 23 December. He wrote to her again on 30 December, 31 December, and 12 January.

Prema Kantak was older than Lilavati or Sharda and a faithful associate. Her father died in September. Gandhi wrote to her: 'You have lost your father, but . . . all who are our seniors in age should be as fathers to us . . . or mothers. Those who are our equals in age are our brothers and sisters, and our juniors are our sons and daughters. Then the world will never die for us . . . Death, moreover, is man's true friend. Why then should we be unhappy when our dear ones meet their dearest friend?' (89:249-50). The warmth in Gandhi that made him write the letter probably meant as much to the grieving Prema as the truth in it.

Another loyal associate, Dilkhush Diwanji of Karadi in Gujarat, lost his mother and sent Gandhi yarn she had spun. 'I shall use it lovingly,' Gandhi wrote to Diwanji. 'Her blessings, I know, are ever with me. What if her mortal frame is no more?' (89:326).

At the end of October he spoke of his associate from 1916, Vinoba Bhave, who had dissented from Gandhi's celibacy experiments, as 'a very great man indeed' for, among other things, inspiring the service of leprosy victims near Wardha (89:394). After Vallabhbhai had called on Gandhi on his (Patel's) birthday, Gandhi wrote: 'You came and saw me yesterday but I did not then remember it was your birthday. Therefore I could not give you my best wishes on the spot. Such is the sorry plight I am in' (*Patel*: 433)

Those used to seeking counsel from him were increasingly urged to find it within themselves. *To Rameshwari Nehru, 19.9.47:* 'In the end, follow the promptings of your heart.' *To Amtus Salaam, whose relatives had to flee Patiala, 16.10.47 and 1.11.47:* 'All are safe but they had to leave Patiala for good! . . . Look into your heart and do as it bids' (89:203, 341 and 451).

Kailas Nath Katju, the Governor of Orissa, had sent articles in Gandhi's praise for publication in *Harijan*, and referred to his

(Katju's) high blood pressure. Returning the articles, Gandhi added: 'I asked Dr Jivraj about your blood pressure. He suggests that you should take *sarpagandha*. The extract is available at the Tropical Medicine School in Calcutta. Would you like me to send it from my stock?' (89: 282).

Richard Gregg, the Quaker who had explained nonviolence and village industries to America, sent a piece dissenting from Gandhi's explanation of Indian violence and asking Gandhi not to be discouraged. This one was published. To Gregg Gandhi wrote: 'By the way, has vegetarianism a real foothold in America or is it merely a fad of cranks like you and me? . . . How are you getting on yourself? . . . What are you doing for earning? Or are you living on past savings?' (90:3-4).

The Iftikharuddins of Lahore were among the Pakistanis he was in touch with. Mian Iftikharuddin, once president of the Punjab Congress, had joined the Muslim League in 1946. *To his wife Ismat Iftikharuddin, who was ill, 9.12.47:* 'You should get quite well quickly, so as to do the very necessary work of reclaiming the poor abducted women in both the parts of the Punjab. Tell Iftikhar it was naughty of him to cease to write to me after his transfer of loyalty' (90:198).

Gandhi planted a mango tree inside Delhi Jail before holding a prayer meeting with the prisoners on 25 October; along with other trees and structures, this mango tree was uprooted some years later, with no trace left, when the jail was moved and a college built on the site.

In November he asked Mountbatten, who had been retained as India's Governor-General, to carry to London a tablecloth 'made out of doubled yarn of my own spinning' and give it as Gandhi's wedding present to Princess Elizabeth and her bridegroom, Prince Philip, 'with my blessings [and] the wish that they would have a long and happy life of service' (89: 507).

The following month he recalled Kasturba's saris for an artist, Bapsy Pavry, who wanted to do a portrait of Kasturba: 'The ground of Kasturba's sari always used to be white. Occasionally it had lines or dots in colour. The hem and the borders used to be coloured.

There was no particular choice in the colours.' (90:150) Elsewhere, he said: 'Don't you know that I was a barrister and Ba was almost illiterate? And yet, whatever progress I have been able to make in my life today is all due to my wife' (89:485).

※

We should note some of his post-independence pronouncements (All quotes from *CWMG* volumes 89 and 90).

> *On religion and the state*: The state should undoubtedly be secular. It could never promote denominational education out of public funds. Everyone living in it should be entitled to profess his religion without let or hindrance (Aug.16).

> *To the Press*: Let the past be buried. Do not rake it up. Think of the future. Analyse things. Do not hesitate to point out defects if they are detected. Do not exaggerate (Aug.20).

> *On prayer*: In the course of our lives we talk quite a bit in 24 hours, we commit crimes and run madly after money; so let us at least offer some prayer (Sept.23).

> *On ticketless travelling*: Had I been a railway manager or a railway minister . . . the train just would not move till the passengers paid the fare . . . I have heard that in Pakistan too people travel in trains without tickets just as here. And why should they not do so? After all we were all born in the same environment, have eaten the same salt (Oct.28).

> *On the condition of widows*: In no other country are widows insulted as much as they are in our country . . . The rigidity of social customs and conventions must be broken (Nov.14).

> *On jobs in the villages*: Everyone will remember this old man one day when it is realized that India has no alternative

except to develop village industries. Any government formed by any party — Congress, Socialist or Communist — will be forced to accept this truth . . . We shall realize it after we stumble in our attempts to compete with America or Russia (Nov.17).

On militarization: Our statesmen have for over two generations declaimed against the heavy expenditure on armaments under the British regime, but now that freedom from political serfdom has come, our military expenditure has increased . . . and of this we are proud! There is not a voice raised against it in our legislatures . . . However, the hope lingers in me and many others that India shall survive this death dance and occupy the moral height . . . (Nov.29)

To Burmese visitors led by Premier U Nu: We must admit with shame that today we have brought [India's] culture into disrepute. You must not remember our disgrace . . . You must ignore our lapses and see our virtues and make them your own. (Dec. 4).

❋

Picking up his pen seemed to liberate him from painful surroundings, and writing seemed to provide relief. We can sense it in some of his words. *To Mirabehn, obliged, for health reasons, to abandon cattle-rearing in the Himalayas, 20.8.47:* 'Have no irons in the fire till your body is like true steel.'

When a Hindu reader of *Harijan* warned him against sheltering 'frozen Muslim snakes' who would bite on revival, Gandhi wrote:

To liken a human being . . . to a snake to justify inhuman treatment is surely a degrading performance . . . I have known rabidly fanatical Muslims to use the very analogy in respect of Hindus . . . Lastly, let me, for the sake of snakekind, correct a common error [and point out] that eighty snakes out of every hundred are perfectly harmless and render useful service in nature (Oct.3; 89:276).

A friend having written that independence had enthused him, Gandhi answered: 'I am now an old man; and maybe the country is experiencing, in your sense, the surge of freedom. I do not see the joy of it on any face. It may be that since I myself feel no joy my eyes cannot see any. Does not a jaundiced person see only yellow?' (90:265-5).

But the lighter touch was the exception, and other passages better convey his mood in 1947-8. On Diwali, falling on 12 November, he said: 'Today is Diwali and I congratulate all of you . . . But alas! . . . We must kindle the light of love within. Today thousands are in acute distress. Can you, everyone of you, lay your hand on your heart and say that every sufferer, whether Hindu, Sikh or Muslim, is your own brother or sister?' (90:18). *On banishing fear, 24.9.47*: 'I have just a handful of bones in my body. But my heart belongs to me. So do your hearts belong to you' (89:231).

Few things affected him more than the abduction of women in both parts of the Punjab:

> The number could be in hundreds or even thousands . . . Muslims have abducted Hindu and Sikh girls . . . I have received a long list of girls abducted from Patiala. Some of them come from very well-to-do Muslim families. When they are recovered it will not be difficult for them to be returned to their parents.
>
> As regards Hindu girls it is still doubtful whether they will be accepted by their families. This is very bad . . . If my daughter has been violated by a rascal and made pregnant, must I cast her and her child away? Some girls say that they do not want to come back . . . [for] the parents will tell them to go away, so will the husbands. A sort of home should be established for such girls which should take up the responsibility for their food, shelter and education, so they can stand on their own feet. These girls are innocent (90: 301-2).

✳

The conscience that had disturbed him in childhood was still robust, and Gandhi had not ceased scrutinizing himself in public. In October, his response to the stream of birthday greetings and urgings against depression he received was to publish one of the messages and his reply. The writer had described the violence in India as 'the final attempt of the forces of evil to foil the divine plan of India's contribution to the solution of the world's distress by way of non-violence,' and asked Gandhi to remember that he was 'the only instrument to further the divine purpose.' Replied Gandhi:

> This is a telegram sent more out of personal affection than knowledge . . . I am not vain enough to think that the divine purpose can only be fulfilled through me. It is as likely that a fitter instrument will be used to carry it out . . . May it not be that a man purer, more courageous, more farseeing is wanted? (89:285).

He told a British journalist in September that 'it was not true that he was never off his balance.' He was not immune, he added, from irritation; but he had learnt to keep it 'within very narrow bounds' (89:143). In October he said to his prayer audience: 'I myself do not quite know how wicked or good I may be. God alone knows it' (89:412). In November he wrote to Mathuradas Trikumji: 'I myself cannot see the traces of ego and impatience that may be lurking within me. Only other people can observe them to some extent' (90:34).

Also in November, he wrote to a friend that he had just given Manu 'a long lecture.' Lecturing people, he added, had become his profession, and he wondered whether he would prove wise only in advising others. While Manu seemed to have a wise head on young shoulders, 'it occurs to me how dense I was at the age of 18' (90:61-2).

However, when Manu and Abha burst out laughing at the wrong note in which they had sung a bhajan during his prayers one day, Gandhi wanted, he told them later, to weep. If they were to 'behave like hired singers, it [was] as good as kiling me.' The apology they read out the next day was drafted by Gandhi: 'We two girls were guilty of a grievous error . . . We knew that it was wrong to laugh but we could not control ourselves. We knew that even though his eyes were closed, Bapu would know and would be much hurt, and that is what happened. We sought his forgiveness and he has forgiven us' (89:217-8).

Periods and days of silence helped his introspections. At times he was awake in the middle of the night, reflecting and praying while his companions slept. Normally it was Bisen who rose first, before three in the morning, and woke everyone else, including Gandhi, but it was a chore that Gandhi also often performed.

Perhaps it is to such solitary or silent moments that we owe letters of the sort he sent to C.P. Ramaswami Aiyar, the Dewan of Travancore, whose vain bid for the state's independence Gandhi had criticized. In August, some days after press reports of an assault on Aiyar at a public meeting, Gandhi learnt that Aiyar had indeed been injured.

> *To Aiyar,* 27.8.47: You will forgive me for this belated solicitude. I was perplexed about your attitude on Travancore . . . When I heard about the attack on you, I regarded it as of no consequence. 'It must have been a mere scratch, probably a made-up affair.' But Krishna Hutheesing and Manibehn opened my eyes to the serious attack . . . I am amazed at my unbelief. Pardon me for it (89:96).

Let us return to Gandhi's arrival in Delhi on 9 September. The following morning a Sikh taxi driver told Brij Krishna: 'If Gandhiji had waited some more days before coming to Delhi, all the Muslims here would have been eliminated' (Brij Krishna 3: 282). Among the first things Gandhi did was to confront the RSS chief, M.S.Golwalkar, with the reports he had received of the body's hand in the Delhi violence. Golwalkar, who called at Birla House on the morning of 12 September, assured Gandhi that 'this was untrue.'

When Golwalkar affirmed that the RSS did not stand for the killing of Muslims, Gandhi asked him to issue a statement to that effect. Golwalkar said Gandhi could quote him. This Gandhi did in his prayer speech that evening, but he told Golwalkar that the statement ought to come from him, and he said later to Nehru that he did not find Golwalkar convincing.[5]

Four days later he met, at his own initiative, a number of the RSS cadres. His message to them is of interest. He told them that while he had been impressed years earlier by the discipline, simplicity and absence of untouchability he had noticed in an RSS camp in Wardha, 'sacrifice without purity of motive and true knowledge has been known to prove ruinous to society.' (In a retort to Birla, who had once spoken of someone as 'a great renouncer,' Gandhi had said: 'Ravana was a renouncer too — he placed all his ten heads at the feet of Siva.')[6] Hinduism would be destroyed, Gandhji added to the RSS gathering, if Muslims in India were treated as slaves; and Islam would be finished if Hindus in Pakistan were enslaved. He did not know if the allegations he had heard against the RSS were true, but they had to disprove them by their 'uniform behaviour.'

Asked by one of the cadres if Hinduism permitted killing of an evildoer, Gandhi answered: 'How could a sinner claim the right to judge or execute another sinner?' Only a properly constituted government could exercise the right of punishing an evildoer. Finally, he spoke of Nehru and Patel as a united pair: 'They have been colleagues for years and have the same aim.' 'Do not think you can succeed,' he seemed to imply, 'in playing Patel against Nehru.' His parting words were: 'Both the Sardar and Pandit Nehru will be rendered powerless if you become judge and executioner in one. They are tried servants of the nation . . . Do not sabotage their efforts by taking the law into your own hands' (89:177 and 193-5; and Brij Krishna 3: 294-7).

He repeated that last thought on his birthday: 'I would appeal to the people not to take the law into their hands but leave it to the Government to decide' (89:275). This rather than nonviolence was his emphasis in the final six months, though he continued to recall nonviolence as the ideal. Excerpts from his prayer speech of 12

September give a fuller picture of what he was trying to say and how he said it:

> The very first thing I want to tell you is that I have received disturbing news from the Frontier Province . . . I am amazed that the Hindus and Sikhs there cannot live . . . in peace . . . What I think to myself I may as well convey to you, that is, we should not get angry. We can, of course, feel the pain. We ought to feel sympathy.
>
> It is natural to feel, 'Why not kill the Muslims because our brothers have been killed.' But I for one cannot kill even the actual murderers of my brothers. Should I then prepare myself to kill other innocent people?
>
> I have seen the terrible plight of the Hindus and Sikhs of Pakistan. I have lived in Lahore. Do you think I am not pained? I claim that my pain is not less than that of any Punjabi. If any Hindu or Sikh from the Punjab comes and tells me that his anguish is greater than mine because he has lost his brother or daughter or father, I would say that his brother is my brother, his mother is my mother, and I have the same anguish in my heart as he has.
>
> I am also a human being and feel enraged but I swallow my anger. That gives me strength . . . How should I take revenge so that they feel repentant for their crimes?
>
> The people of Pakistan resorted to ways of barbarism, and so did the Hindus and the Sikhs . . . He who does good to one who has been good to him is a mere Bania and a pseudo-Bania at that . . . A true human being is one who does a good turn for evil. I learnt this in my childhood. I still believe in the rightness of this. I would like you to return evil with good.
>
> The Government needs arms, what has the citizen got to do with them? . . . I would like the Muslims to surrender all the arms in their possession to the Government. The Hindus too should surrender all their arms.
>
> You must create such conditions here that Jawaharlal

Nehru and Sardar Patel should be able to say Delhi had lost its senses for a few days but now it has become sane . . . After all, so much of business in Delhi, such wonderful buildings, this culture of Delhi, belong both to the Hindus and Muslims and not exclusively to either (89:173-7).

Told that Muslims would feel securer if he lived in one of Delhi's Muslim localities, Gandhi was considering a shift from Birla House until someone pointed to the calamity that would fall on Muslims if Gandhi was hit even accidentally by a bullet from one of their settlements. He was frank about what the city's Muslims needed to do. They should not run away. Any arms with them should be handed over but they should demand protection from the government, and they should demand humane treatment for Pakistan's Sikhs and Hindus.

That all Muslims were secretly-armed fifth-columnists was a line persistently thrown at Gandhi. He dealt with it by asking if Pakistan would be justified in treating every Hindu and Sikh as a traitor, and by predicting that 'if there is aggression from the Muslims outside India or from any other power or from Pakistan,' India's Muslims would be loyal to the country (89:210-1).

Even as he recalled a nobler past and envisioned a better future, Gandhi smelt evil. 'I do not know who they (the mischief-makers) are, but they are definitely there, and are working to carry out pre-planned murders, arson and forcible occupation of buildings' (89:271).

Jamnadas Dwarkadas of Bombay met Gandhi on 20 September and reported on a visit he had made to Karachi. He could not see Jinnah, who was ill, but gathered from Ghazanfar Ali Khan, a member of the Pakistan cabinet, that 'if Sikhs can be kept aside they would be perfectly happy to let the Hindus stay.' The Pakistanis seemed to want Hindu traders, and Ghazanfar had apparently proposed a conference in Lahore, hoping that Gandhi, Mountbatten, Nehru and Patel would take part.

'This would create a new quarrel,' Gandhi observed. 'Separating Sikhs from Hindus — I can never accept that,' he added (Brij Krishna 3:304-5). The hint of a Muslim-Hindu pact leaving out the Sikhs was repeated later by others returning from Karachi. Gandhi commented on it in *Harijan*: 'I know the vicious suggestion that the Hindus would be all right if they would sacrifice the Sikhs who would never be tolerated in Pakistan. I can never be a party to any such fratricidal bargain. There can be no rest for this unhappy land unless every Hindu and Sikh returns with honour and in safety to West Punjab, and every Muslim refugee to the Union' (90:98-9).

But Gandhi spoke, too, of Sikh excesses and of the misuse of the *kirpan*, and stood his ground when warned by a Sikh politician that he 'should be cautious about what he says about the Sikhs.' Said Gandhi: 'I speak freely and frankly (to the Sikhs) because I am their true friend. I make bold to say that many a time the Sikh situation was saved because the Sikhs in general chose to follow my advice . . . A sacred thing has to be used on sacred and lawful occasions. A *kirpan* is undoubtedly a symbol of strength, which adorns the possessor only if he exercises amazing restraint over himself and uses it against enormous odds' (90:97-8).

Lahore featured often in his remarks: 'It is the city built up by the Hindus where I saw the big mansions of the Hindus and so many educational institutions' (89:185). 'All those who have their properties in Lahore should get them back. They have to be returned the houses which have been confiscated. What wonderful buildings I have seen there! And what about all those educational institutions for girls? . . . Where is that Lahore today? . . . The people of the Punjab come from a sturdy stock. They are business-minded and produce wealth. There are great bankers there who know how to spend money as well as earn it. I have seen all that with my own eyes . . . All those colleges for men and women, and then all those grand hospitals . . .' (89:271).

If Delhi found peace again, he would go to Pakistan, he said. 'When I go to Pakistan, I will not spare them. I shall die for the Hindus and the Sikhs there. I shall be really glad to die there. I shall be glad to die here too. If I cannot do what I want to do here, I have got to die.' The news of many Hindu and Sikh women in West

Punjab who chose death over dishonour stirred him:

> They have gone with courage. They have not sold away
> their honour. Not that their lives were not dear to them,
> but they felt it was better to die with courage rather than
> be forcibly converted to Islam by the Muslims and allow
> them to assault their bodies. And so those women died.
> They were not just a handful, but quite a few (89:202).

But revenge against India's Muslims was folly. If all of them were
driven out, which was not possible, the Hindus would fight one
another. 'This is inevitable. Once one has a taste of killing, one
can't resist the temptation' (89:386).

In November and December he made an unsuccessful bid to persuade Muslims in Panipat, 60 miles north of Delhi, not to migrate to
Pakistan. Though at first willing to stay on, they changed their
minds when Hindu and Sikh refugees who had come from West
Punjab to Panipat demonstrated against their presence. Gandhi went
twice to Panipat and met with the Muslims and with the non-Muslim refugees. In a hospital where Muslims injured in communal violence were being treated, he 'spent a few minutes with every patient,
occasionally covering a patient properly with the sheet' (89:517).
To the Muslims he said on 2 December: 'Gandhi can only tell you
that you should stay, for India is your home. And if your brethren
should kill you, you should bravely meet death . . . Still, if you are
resolved to go . . . there is nothing further I can say to you . . .
Having heard you and seen you, my heart weeps. Do as God guides
you.'

Their decision to leave was a bitter disappointment, but Gandhi
drew a little solace from the attitude of some of the Sikh and Hindu
leaders who joined him in Panipat. In his prayer speech in Delhi
later that evening, he recounted what Swaran Singh, a Minister in
the East Punjab government and a future Foreign Minister of India,
had said in Panipat to the Hindu and Sikh refugees, adding that he
liked the remarks. Swaran Singh had said that Muslims and mosques
would be protected in East Punjab, and Muslims forcibly converted

to Hinduism or Sikhism would be regarded as Muslims.

Gandhi also reported his encounter in Panipat with a boy from West Punjab: 'Today a small boy confronted me. He was wearing a sweater. He took it off and stood glaring at me as if he would eat me up . . . "You say that you have come to protect us," he said, "but my father has been killed. Get me my father back." . . . I can imagine that if I had been of his age and in his position, perhaps I would have done the same' (90:153-61).

That some of his closest Hindu friends in Sind chose to come to India also saddened him, the more so since a large number of poorer Hindus and numerous Harijans were unable to get away. 'Look at what happened in Sind,' he said in a letter to a friend. 'All the leaders managed to come away and the innocent people are being killed . . . It makes me shudder' (90: 83).

In the last week of September, he asked his trusty co-worker Thakkar Bapa to take a letter from him to two ship-owning friends in Bombay, requesting vessels for moving the Harijans of Sind to any port in Kathiawad (89:235-7). Later he was involved in lengthy correspondence with the Nawab of Bahawalpur, a state bordering the Punjab that had acceded to Pakistan, about the state's Hindus and Sikhs. Gandhi tried to assist the non-Muslims of Bahawalpur to stay where they were if they could, or leave in safety for India, and sent his doctor and aide Sushila Nayar, along with Leslie Cross of the Quakers' Friends Unit, to them.

Thanks to Gandhi's exertions, a bid to send the Muslim Meos of Bharatpur and Alwar to Pakistan was abandoned. 'How shameful it is for us,' Gandhi had exclaimed at an AICC meeting in November, 'that we should force them to trudge three hundred miles on foot!' (90:42).

December seemed to bring some good news. A group of U.P. Muslims who had twice visited Lahore with Gandhi's approval claimed that the West Punjab government wanted the non-Muslims residing there to remain, and those who had migrated to India to return. The group added that they would accompany any Hindus and Sikhs willing to return to West Punjab, and 'protect them at the cost of our own lives.' In a prayer speech, Gandhi referred to the initiative as 'a very promising development' but added that he did not know the extent of any improvement in West Punjab (90:213).

✵

We may note some other elements of Gandhi's 1947-8 discourse on communal violence (All quotes from *CWMG* 89 and 90):

> [If people take the law into their own hands,] the world will ridicule Delhi . . . And then the European powers, be it Russia, France or Britain, as well as America will laugh at us and say that we are not capable of preserving our freedom. We are only capable of being slaves (Sept.14).

> *To the citizen*: Who are you to punish the wicked for their wrong deeds? (Sept.14).

> This is the time to remember Khuda, Allah, Ishwar, Rama. He helps us without fail . . . The blood of these three communities (Hindu, Sikh and Muslim) is one . . . To prove this I would cry myself hoarse and shed tears before God. I do not shed tears before man, but I can do so before God (Sept.20).

> You may behave as you like, but I shall continue to warn you, so long as I am alive (Sept.21).

> The trains coming from Pakistan these days do not bring Muslims. Hindus and Sikhs are brought on those trains. Some get killed on the train. And the people who go from here are Muslims who are killed on the way. I am told that I should count the figures . . . What will I do knowing the figures? (Sept. 24).

> I have been a fighter for many, many years, more than 60 years. But I fight not with the sword, but with the weapons of truth and nonviolence (Sept.25).

> Arjun Dev (the Sikhs' fifth Guru) was a great Guru and a

great poet. He said: One may recite Ramanama or Khuda's praise, one may serve Gosain or Allah (Sept.27).

We kept their (the untouchables') food separate and declared that they could not live in our midst. We decided to treat them as our slaves. Later they turned to Islam (Sept. 30).

Who would determine how much goodness and how much wickedness exists here and there? And what would we gain by it? (Oct.9).

To a Muslim of nationalist views who had been attacked in Jullundur by non-Muslims who in 1946 had organized pro-independence processions along with him: Is it not the lot of us mortals that the innocent suffer for the guilty? (Oct.13).

To students from West Punjab and the Frontier province at the Aligarh Muslim University who wanted to collect blankets for Hindu and Sikh refugees: [Your] intention is good and the refugees need them too. But really speaking, [you] should go to Pakistan and ask the Muslims [there] why the Hindus and Sikhs have to leave their homes at all (Oct.28).

A wonderful thing I learnt about Lahore is that a Muslim gentleman has kept a Sikh in his own house . . . The Muslim kept an open copy of the Guru Granth Saheb in one of the rooms of the house with due respect. He has saved that Sikh because he happens to be his friend. This makes me very happy (Nov.2).

I was pleased most by the speeches of Zafrullah Khan (Pakistan's Foreign Minister) and Ispahani (Pakistan's ambassador to America) which appeared in the newspapers today. At the United Nations, they said in plain words that Indians in South Africa were not given the same treatment as the whites . . . If the Hindus and the Muslims can speak unitedly outside India, they can certainly do so here as well (Nov. 16).

I am told that . . . in a village called Kanhai which is 25 miles away from Delhi . . . the Roman Catholics were threatened that they would suffer if they did not leave the village . . . The freedom we have achieved does not imply the rule of Hindus in the Indian Union or that of the Muslims in Pakistan (Nov. 21).

It is a matter of shame for us that . . . in Rohtak district . . . there are Jats and perhaps Ahirs too [who] felt that the Harijans were their slaves . . . They may be given water and food but they can get nothing by right . . . We feel that we can even intimidate a judge if we are brought before him . . . The result is that the Harijans are ruined (Nov. 23).

It should not be our fate to be eternal enemies of each other (Dec. 19).

On a couplet in an Urdu magazine asking for 'a new Ghaznavi to avenge the renovation of the Somnath temple': It is painful to think that such a thing can issue from the pen of a Muslim . . . [But] I cannot return evil for evil . . . [Hindus] must not remember the wrong that Ghaznavi did. Muslims must realize and admit the wrongs perpetrated under the Islamic rule (Dec.25).

He wanted to go to Pakistan. On 23 September he had said: 'I want to go to the Punjab. I want to go to Lahore . . . I want to go to Rawalpindi . . . Let me tell you that once peace descends on Delhi, I shall not stay here even a day longer' (89:225).

Through Suhrawardy, who was shuttling between India and Pakistan, and sometimes directly he sent messages to Jinnah. The burden was that both countries should protect minorities and ask those who had fled to return. In September he acknowledged Jinnah's qualities in *Harijan*. He was 'an able President (of the League) whom neither riches nor titles could buy. He was a front-rank Barrister . . . Being the son of a merchant he knew how to multiply his earnings as a lawyer by wise investments' (89:98).

Yet he held Jinnah responsible for embittering Hindu-Muslim relations. To Suhrawardy he wrote on 27 October: 'Muslims never shall be slaves of Hindus nor Hindus of Muslims. Hence you and I have to die in the attempt to make them live together as friends and brothers, which they are . . . I cannot escape the conclusion that the mischief commenced with Qaid-e-Azam . . . This I say more to make myself clear to you than to correct you' (89:418).

Earlier in October Suhrawardy had told Gandhi, 'Jinnah says I have allowed myself to be taken in by you.' *G*: 'There cannot be a worse libel on me.' *S*: 'Jinnah speaks very highly of Nehru.' *G*: 'Maybe. He has never done so in public. But that is neither here nor there. Neither Pandit Nehru nor the Sardar cares for praise or blame. If only you could get Jinnah to do the right thing . . .' *S*: 'Jinnah says he has never asked the Hindus to go out of Pakistan.' *G*: 'You surprise me.' *S*: 'You do not know how unpopular with the masses the Pakistan government has become. Some are even abusing Jinnah and Liaqat Ali.' *G*: 'That is neither my concern nor yours. Your [task in] Karachi was . . . to put the facts as you know them before Jinnah' (89:307).

Refusing to allow Nehru to be split from him, Gandhi is also quick to bring Patel into the picture. Jinnah should not imagine, even as the RSS should not, that Gandhi or Nehru or Patel could be dealt with singly and separately. As long as he could help it, there would be a Gandhi-Nehru-Patel front.

In what was to prove his last letter to Jinnah, who was Pakistan's Governor-General as well as President of the Muslim League, Gandhi wrote to him on 11 October endorsing Suhrawardy's efforts towards an Indo-Pak accord and urging a commitment that 'each State will induce the refugees to return and occupy their respective homes' (89:318). On 27 October Gandhi said in a note to Suhrawardy: 'I am at a loss to understand what Pakistan really wants to do — whether they want the Hindus to stay there or not . . . I know what is happening to the minorities in the Punjab, in Sind and in the Frontier province' (89:417).

A month later Liaqat, the Pakistani Premier, visited Delhi. Gandhi met him and said in a prayer speech: 'We talked at length . . . I found that Liaqat Ali was not only ill but also confined to bed. He was having pain in the chest and palpitations. He is better now, but has gone very weak. He is staying at the Viceregal Lodge, hence I went and looked him up' (90:115). His nursing instincts would never leave Gandhi.

In this prayer speech Gandhi also referred to allegations in two newspapers in Pakistan, *Dawn* and *Pakistan Times*, that Muslims were being harassed in Kathiawad. Said Gandhi: 'Both these are prominent dailies of Pakistan. When something appears in *Dawn* or the *Pakistan Times* we cannot dismiss it. That way the people of Pakistan can dismiss the reports in the *Hindustan Times* and the *Bombay Chronicle*, can't they?' (90: 117). Gandhi followed up by asking a range of people in Kathiawad about the allegations and sending a group of Parsi friends to Kathiawad to see if they were true.

Recounting the 'evil deeds of Pakistan . . . won't help the Hindu or the Sikh sufferers,' he said on 24 November. 'Pakistan has to bear the burden of its sins, which I know are terrible enough. It should be enough for everybody to know my opinion (in so far as it has any value) that the beginning was made by the Muslim League long before the 15th of August . . . This statement of mine can't help you . . . The [non-Muslims] copied the sins and thus became fellow-sinners. Odds became even. Shall we now awake from the trance?' (90:99). So he gives, and devalues, his view of 'Who started it?' but says the question about the past was redundant.

But the future of Pakistan and the honour of Islam were relevant questions. 'Pakistan or Islam cannot mean that non-Muslims cannot live there. The Muslim empire has spread far and wide; but nowhere was it laid down that non-Muslims cannot live there' (89:206). If India's Muslims thought that non-Muslims in Pakistan were not getting a fair deal, they should say so, and add 'unequivocally that this was a disgrace to Pakistan and a stigma on Islam' (90:204). On 30 December he asked whether Pakistan had 'become

Islamistan where no non-Muslim may live or where he can only live as a slave' (90: 327).

Kashmir engaged him from the last week of October, when raiders from Pakistan's Frontier region entered the state and the Maharaja acceded to India, ending his indecision. We have seen earlier in the study that Gandhi, in his own words, gave 'tacit consent' to the dispatch of Indian soldiers to Kashmir. Neither Sheikh Abdullah the acknowledged leader of the Kashmiris, nor the Indian government shared his belief in nonviolence, and armed defence was any day better than surrender.

Abdullah's trust in India and success in enlisting many of Kashmir's Hindus and Sikhs to his side gladdened Gandhi, who hoped that the people of the state would disprove the two-nation theory. In Gandhi's view, the future of the state was for them to decide, just as it was for the people in the states of Hyderabad and Junagadh to determine where they should go. On 11 November he said:

> Neither the Maharaja of Kashmir nor the Nizam of Hyderabad has any authority to accede to either Union without the consent of his people . . . If it had been only the Maharaja who had wanted to accede to the Indian Union, I could never support such an act. The Union Government agreed to the accession for the time being because both the Maharaja and Sheikh Abdullah, who is the representative of the people . . . wanted it (90:8-9).

On 26 October he had said: 'It makes no difference to me whether is the question of Kashmir or Hyderabad or Junagadh. Let no one be forced into anything. Let there be no coercion . . . Real rulers of the states are [their] people. If the people of Kashmir are in favour of opting for Pakistan, no power on earth can stop them from doing so. But they should be left free to decide for themselves . . . If the people of Kashmir, in spite of its Muslim majority, wish to accede to India, no one can stop them' (89:413-4).

In Junagadh, Samaldas Gandhi, a cousin's son, had led a popular movement that undid the wish of the Junagadh Nawab to accede to Pakistan. The Nawab fled to Pakistan, but Gandhi thought that Samaldas could have claimed 'real victory' only if the Nawab had 'handed over power voluntarily.' He noted, too, that the installation of popular rule in Junagadh had been aided by the stationing of Indian security forces at its borders (90:101-2 and 111).

We may note two other pronouncements by Gandhi on Kashmir: 'I shall advise Pakistan and India to sit together and decide the matter. If the two are interested in the settlement of the dispute, where is the need for an arbitrator? . . . Let India and Pakistan deliberate over the matter. Sheikh Abdullah will of course be there. If they want an arbitrator, they can appoint one from among themselves, but it should certainly not be a third power' (Dec.25; 90:298).

'Mistakes were made on both sides. Of this I have no doubt . . . Therefore the two Dominions should come together with God as witness and find a settlement. The matter is now before the U.N.O. It cannot be withdrawn from there. But if India and Pakistan come to a settlement the big powers in the U.N.O. will have to endorse that settlement' (Jan.4, 1948; 90:357).

❈

The future of Congress troubled him. In 1942 Nehru had said that Congress was Gandhi's 'creation and child and nothing can break the bond.'[7] The statement was literally true for the Congress shaped in 1920. Gandhi had written its constitution, designed its multi-layered democratic structure from village level up to a central All India Congress Committee, with a Working Committee as its executive arm, sought to miniaturize India into it, infused it with a purpose, and honed it into a fighting instrument. Congress was his life in one sense, and could be its extension. Weaknesses Congress always had, including rivalries, fictitious names on membership rolls, and incompetent account-keeping. Now, after independence, it was afflicted with uncertainty about its ideals, strained relationships at the top, corruption in the middle layers and dryness at the grassroots.

Though helmsman no longer, Gandhi could not cut his ties to

Congress or its government. It was not easy, however, to know what his relationship should be. He had expressed his dilemma in Calcutta on 30 August after receiving a message from Nehru that though 'the time has not come for you to visit the Punjab . . . your presence in Delhi [is] very desirable so as to . . . advise us' (89:108). Replied Gandhi: 'If I am not going to the Punjab, would I be of much use in Delhi as an adviser or consultant? I fancy I am not built that way. My advice has value only when I am actually working at a particular thing. I can only disturb when I give academic advice . . . (89:117).

He had said the same thing to Patel: 'I do not see what I could do in Delhi if I went there. I feel I would only be intruding' (26.8.47; 89:91). Preferring a hands-on task to consultancy or intrusion, he felt presented with one, the restoration of communal amity, on arrival in Delhi. Discharging this duty, he felt less uncomfortable about offering advice.

It was not always heeded. Nehru and Patel were at one in their dissatisfaction with Kripalani as the Congress President, who on his part felt excluded from decision-making. As was inevitable, the relationship between the Party President and a Congress Prime Minister and Deputy Prime Minister became an issue. Gandhi supported Kripalani's resignation. His reasons for doing so, spelt out to the AICC, are worth noting: 'Your President Kripalani desires to hand over the responsibility of his office to other hands. You should accede to his request . . . He feels he is unable to discharge his functions effectively . . . It is beyond his power to create conditions where not a single Muslim's life will be unsafe in India' (90:39).

Patel and Nehru stalled, however, when Gandhi proposed the socialists Narendra Deva or Jayaprakash Narayan for the succession. Gandhi was looking ahead and wanted a younger person, and he expected Deva or Narayan, if chosen, to 'follow the Congress policy' rather than press socialism. 'When a person who has opposed the official policies from outside becomes the leader of the whole country, he would . . . give up his opposition,' Gandhi said, referring to the possibility of Jayaprakash as President. 'This is not a rule laid down by me, but the common rule in a democracy' (90:43).

We can infer that he also thought that Narayan or Deva might do more than Kripalani for restoring a sense of security to the minorities.

But Patel's resistance and Nehru's lack of enthusiasm killed the idea. Gandhi did not persist with it. We can speculate on the course that India's politics might have taken if either J.P. or Narendra Deva had followed Kripalani as Congress President at the end of 1947. In either case, the Congress Presidency could have led to candidacy for the Prime Ministerial succession after Nehru. In the event, it was Rajendra Prasad who took over from Kripalani.

Learning that 'now there are even some Congressmen who think that Muslims should not live [in India],' Gandhi insisted on a clear statement of Congress's position. In November he spent long hours on the question with the Working Committee and the AICC (90:65). We can gauge the extent of Gandhi's involvement from remarks in a letter: 'These days we are busy with the AICC meeting. There is great pressure of work. I hardly have time to breathe' (90:57).

His speech to the AICC was quite impassioned. They represented, he told the members, 'the vast ocean of Indian humanity.' India's honour was in their keeping. Were they going to be 'true to the basic character of the Congress, and make Hindus and Muslims one?' Added Gandhi:

I am an Indian to the last. Ever since I returned from South Africa I have tried to serve the Congress in every way and have done nothing else. I have tried to understand Indians from different walks of life, have lived with them, eaten with them, and loved them . . .

There are many places today where a Muslim cannot live in security. There are miscreants who will kill him or throw him out of a running train for no reason other than that he is a Muslim . . . I am ashamed of what is happening today; such things should never happen in India . . .

We would be betraying the Hindu religion if we did evil because others had done it . . . The wicked sink under the weight of their own evil. Must we also sink with

> them? . . . You must be humane and civilized, irrespective
> of what Pakistan does. If you do what is right, Pakistan
> will sooner or later be obliged to follow suit.

This would prove to be his last speech to the AICC. In the course of
it he took care to remind Congress of Jawaharlal's value. He was
'respected outside India as one of the world's greatest statesmen,'
even by 'those who have fabulous wealth, vast armies and the atom
bomb.' The strong defence of Nehru was part of his fight for the
reputation of Congress and also of Hinduism:

> I know what some people are saying. 'The Congress has
> surrendered its soul to the Muslims. Gandhi? Let him
> rave as he will. He is a washout. Jawaharlal is no better.
> As regards Sardar Patel, there is something in him. A
> portion of him is sound Hindu, but he too is after all a
> Congressman.' [But] violent rowdyism will not save either
> Hinduism or Sikhism . . . Hinduism cannot be saved by
> orgies of murder (90: 37-43).

The effort with Congress gave Gandhi some satisfaction. 'The more
I look within the more I feel that God is with me,' he said in a letter
to a friend on 15 November, adding, 'These days the Working Committee meeting is going on and I am doing some plain speaking . . .
We shall perish if we become cowards, that is, the Congress will
die' (90:37). Two weeks later he wrote to Pyarelal: 'The six resolutions of the AICC this time were practically mine . . . It now remains to be seen how they are implemented' (90:145).

By the first resolution, Congress committed itself to 'develop this
great country as a democratic secular state where all citizens enjoy
full rights . . . irrespective of the religion to which they belong.'
Coercing minorities to leave India or Pakistan was condemned in
the second resolution, which also called for efforts to enable refugees 'ultimately to return to their homes and to their original occupations under conditions of safety and security.' Another resolution
sought governmental action against private armies maintained by

communal organizations (90:537-42).

There was friction between Nehru and Patel, and at the end of September Gandhi thought that for cohesion one or the other should leave the government (89:520). Soon, however, he changed his opinion. 'The two make an inseparable pair,' he said on 2 December. 'Neither can do without the other' (90:157). Yet he was pained that he did 'not see amity even between these two' (Dec.17; 90:248).

Two ir...idents occurring in December, one of which concerned Kashmir, widened the breach. Patel offered to resign, and so did Nehru. The offers and a defence of their positions were contained in letters the two separately wrote to Gandhi, who was requested to arbitrate. At the end of December, Gandhi said to Patel: 'Either you should run things or Jawaharlal should.' Vallabhbhai replied: 'I do not have the physical strength. He is younger. Let him run the show. I will assist to the extent possible from outside' (*Patel*: 458).

Gandhi was wrestling with this question when a letter arrived that he found 'too shocking for words' (90:405). It was from Konda Venkatappayya of the Telugu country, a veteran freedom fighter described by Gandhi as an 'aged friend.' Stating that he was 'old, decrepit, with a broken leg, slowly limping on crutches within the walls of my house' and had no axe to grind, Venkatappayya referred to 'the moral degradation' of Congress legislators who were 'making money by the use of influence' and 'obstructing the administration of justice in the criminal courts.' His last sentence was stinging: 'The people have begun to say that the British government was much better . . .' (90:410).

Venkatappayya's letter and similar complaints from other parts of the country played a role in triggering a thought of another fast in Gandhi's mind, and another thought about Congress. Gandhi wondered whether, its role fulfilled with political independence, Congress as a political body should not now dissolve itself and 'flower into' an association for gaining 'social, moral and economic independence' (90:526-8).

The new organization would tackle illiteracy, ill-health, unemployment, untouchability and communal intolerance in every village in the land. Parties old and new and from the Left to the Right would fill the political vacuum left by Congress's departure and accommodate those in Congress unable to live without politics. For several hours on the evening before his assassination and before dawn on the following day, the author of Congress's 1920 constitution would work on a proposal for changing the body's goal and character.

❋

On 8 January he wrote: 'It was with the greatest of difficulty that I could find time to talk to [Kalelkar] . . . Innumerable people — men and women — visit me during the day. There is a huge pile of letters to be attended to. The work connected with *Harijan* has to be done. There is not a moment to spare. Usually Manu shaves me, but today I am lying in the bath, plying the razor and dictating this letter to her' (90:383).

'To give and not to count the cost; to fight and not to heed the wounds; to toil and not to seek for rest.' Living out Ignatius's lines, Gandhi was yet thirsty for a deeper satisfaction which he found on the morning of 12 January when, after 'brooding over it for three days,' the 'conclusion flashed upon' him that he must fast and not resume eating until and unless he was satisfied that there was 'a reunion of hearts of all communities.'

He claimed God sent the fast, that 'the peremptory call of conscience and duty' required it, that it came 'out of felt agony.' We know the events that caused the agony: a bid by Hindu and Sikh refugees on 4 January to eject Muslims from their homes in North Delhi and take over the homes; a 6 January attack on a gurdwara in Karachi where Sikhs from upper Sind had taken refuge, resulting in 120 dead; the Nehru-Patel friction; the letter we have seen from the Andhra veteran; a request on 11 January for 'a passage to England' from a group of Muslims who were opposed to Pakistan but felt unsafe in Delhi; and a decision by the Government of India, linked to the conflict in Kashmir, to withhold payment of the Rs 55 crores owed to Pakistan under an agreement signed in November for sharing the assets and liabilities of undivided India.

To Mira he wrote that this was his 'greatest fast.' 'Don't rush here because I am fasting,' he added. 'Trust God and be where you are.' On the fifth day he said: 'This fast has brought me higher happiness than hitherto.' His strength lay in weakness, his triumph in his vulnerability. All he had was his life. It was precious to him. But he would offer it.

Until the decision to fast, a feeling of impotence had been gnawing at him; he had no answer for Muslims requesting a passage to England, or for the people quoted by Venkatappayya who thought that 'British rule was much better.' Now he could face them. On the second day of the fast he told the Delhi Muslims: 'Do you not feel ashamed of asking to be sent to England? . . . How dare you, who claim to be patriots and nationalists, utter such words?'

He wrote out his announcement and explanation of the fast on 12 January, which was a Monday, his day of silence. Jawaharlal and Vallabhbhai came to see him that day but received no inkling. The shock was delivered in the prayer speech read out on Gandhi's behalf in the evening. 'The loss of her soul by India,' Gandhi said, 'will mean the loss of the hope of the aching, storm-tossed and hungry world.' He added:

> Death for me would be a glorious deliverance rather than that I should be a helpless witness of the destruction of India, Hinduism, Sikhism and Islam . . . Only then Islam dies in the two Indias, not in the world. But Hinduism and Sikhism have no world outside India.
>
> I would beg of all friends not to rush to Birla House nor try to dissuade me or be anxious about me. I am in God's hands. Rather, they should turn the searchlight inwards.

Not many sought to dissuade Gandhi. Devadas was among those who tried. Telling his son, 'I cannot accept your counsel,' Gandhi urged Devadas to join him in the prayer that 'the temptation to live may not lead me into a hasty or premature termination of the fast.' Rajagopalachari said in Calcutta: 'I have wrangled with Gandhiji on similar occasions in the past. But this time I confess I am not inclined to wrangle.' Added Rajagopalachari: 'The only sane man today is Gandhiji.'

Ghazanfar Ali Khan said in Lahore that 'the fast should open people's eyes not only in India but also in Pakistan to the shame that they had brought upon themselves.'

After a meeting with two of Gandhi's friends, Jehangir Patel and Dinshaw Mehta, who, with Gandhi's consent, had gone to Karachi to explore the possibility of Gandhi visiting Pakistan, Jinnah sent a message urging Gandhi to 'live and work for the cause of Hindu-Muslim unity in the two Dominions.' Sent via Sri Prakasa, the Indian High Commissioner in Karachi, Jinnah's message, an indirect appeal against the fast, was also conveyed to Gandhi by Zahid Hussain, Pakistan's High Commissioner in New Delhi.[8]

Again and again Gandhi was asked who he was fasting against. To a Sikh friend who repeated the question, Gandhi said: 'My fast is against no party, group or individual exclusively and yet it excludes nobody. It is addressed to the conscience of all, even the majority community in the other Dominion. If all or any one of the groups respond fully, I know the miracle will be achieved. For instance, if the Sikhs respond to my appeal as one man, I shall be wholly satisfied.'

Repudiating a suggestion that the fast was aimed at Vallabhbhai, Gandhi said that Patel's critics were wrong to isolate him, 'a lifelong and faithful comrade,' from 'Jawaharlal Nehru and me, whom they gratuitously raise to the sky.' Vallabhbhai's language was blunt and could hurt, but he had to be judged by his actions. As for his fast, Gandhi said it was in aid of the minorities in both India and Pakistan.

It began on the morning of 13 January. On the fourteenth morning, Vallabhbhai argued with Gandhi against the release of the Rs 55 crores to Pakistan. The money would be used for bullets in Kashmir, Patel said. Tears running down his face, Gandhi said a promise was a promise. Nehru, who had been party to the decision to withhold the sum, now felt unhappy with it. He, Vallabhbhai and the rest of the Cabinet had looked at the question from the Indian or, in some cases, the Hindu point of view. Gandhi looked at it also with Pakistani eyes. Later that afternoon, Patel broke down and wept but went along when the Cabinet agreed to part with the money, rescinding the earlier decision.

Gandhi hailed the step but said he could not end the fast until he saw commitments for harmony in Delhi. Though acetone was found in his urine, he was cheerful and active, answering letters, receiving some callers, and writing out articles and statements. In one *Harijan* article he addressed the people of Gujarat, asking them to realize the importance of Delhi which was India's 'eternal city' from which no Indian could be excluded, and placing before them a vision of a democratic India where women, untouchables, toilers, the humblest and the lowliest would feel themselves the rulers of India along with the tallest in the land.

When Sushila Nayar spoke to him of her concern about the acetone bodies, he said their presence showed that his faith in God was inadequate. 'But acetone is a chemical,' the young doctor protested. 'Where does faith in God come in?' 'So your science knows everything, Sushila?' observed Gandhi, his voice low, his words slow, and his eyes distant. 'Do you remember the last verse in the tenth chapter of the Gita? A fragment of God upholds the universe.'

Mridula Sarabhai wired from Lahore that Pakistanis were asking how they could help. They too should turn the searchlight inwards, Gandhi replied. Enquiries from Pakistan heartened him, but a gruesome attack in West Punjab on 13 January on a train filled with Hindu and Sikh refugees threatened to undo the effects of Gandhi's fast. 'If this kind of thing continues in Pakistan,' said Gandhi on the fourteenth, 'how long will the people of India tolerate it? Even if a hundred men like me fasted, they would not be able to stop the tragedy that may follow.'

Decades earlier, said Gandhi, he had read outside the Red Fort the verse, 'If there is paradise on earth, it is here.' He did not find the Fort to be paradise. 'But,' Gandhi added. 'I should love to see that verse with justice inscribed on the gates of Pakistan at all the entrances.' Again he painted a picture of an ideal India and Pakistan and said:

> I hope everyone who listens to me or reads these lines will forgive me if stretched on my bed and basking in the sun, inhaling lifegiving sunshine, I allow myself to indulge in this ecstasy . . .
>
> When I was young [and] never even read the newspapers, could read English with difficulty and my Gujarati was not satisfactory, I had the dream that if the Hindus, Sikhs, Parsis, Christians and Muslims could live in amity not only in Rajkot but in the whole of India, they would all have a very happy life.
>
> If that dream could be realized even now when I am an old man on the verge of death, my heart would dance. Children would then frolic in joy (Jan.14).

The intense pain written on the face of one surviving on water and sunshine was belied by such words, but they were as true as the suffering that showed itself. On the sixteenth Gandhi referred to the Indian government's decision on the Rs 55 crores: 'It ought to lead to an honourable settlement not only of the Kashmir question but of all the differences between the two Dominions . . . In the name of our people, our Government have taken a liberal step without counting the cost. What will be Pakistan's counter-gesture?'

Delhi, meanwhile, was stirring. Rajendra Prasad, the Congress President, and Maulana Azad mobilized citizens, officials and organizations. In sympathy with Gandhi, a number of Hindu and Sikh refugees cut down on their food. So did Nehru, as also a British journalist and former editor of *The Statesman*, Arthur Moore. When Azad and Prasad asked Gandhi what he wanted in Delhi, they received clear answers: 'Muslims should be allowed to hold their annual fair at the mausoleum of Khwaja Qutbuddin. Mosques converted into temples and gurdwaras should be returned. Muslims should be ensured safety in their homes and on trains. The economic boycott imposed against Muslims in some Delhi localities should be lifted.'

Groups of Delhi's Hindus, Sikhs and Muslims called on Gandhi and assured acceptance of his demands. A peace pledge was signed by more than 200,000 people. On the eighteenth, the sixth day of the fast, a large delegation of citizens, politicians and officials led by Prasad called on a Gandhi looking frail and shrivelled and described a shift in the city's mood. In their company, which included representatives of the Hindu Mahasabha and the RSS, sat Zahid Hussain, Pakistan's High Commissioner.

Prasad said to Gandhi: 'We take the pledge that we shall protect the life, property and faith of the Muslims and that the incidents which have taken place in Delhi will not happen again.' 'You have given me all that I have asked for,' replied Gandhi. He said he would end the fast but added that he would not 'shirk another fast should he afterwards discover that he had deceived himself into breaking it prematurely.'

According to Brij Krishna, Gandhi's lined and shrunken face was radiant. Prayers, Hindu, Muslim, Sikh, Christian and Buddhist, were recited or sung in Gandhi's room in Birla House, and silence reigned while Gandhi extended his long and bony hand at 12.25 p.m. to hold the glass of orange juice handed to him by Maulana Azad and drank from it. Then, amid noises of joy and congratulation, all present, at Gandhi's instance, partook of fruit.[9]

It was the anniversary of Guru Gobind Singh's birth. Gandhi dictated a message for the Sikhs: they had shown true bravery by swallowing their anger. About a hundred Muslim women who had come to Birla House to persuade Gandhi to end his fast met him. 'You veil yourselves before me?' Gandhi protested. At once the veils were removed. Later in the day Gandhi spent some time with Arthur Moore. 'He was lightsome and gay,' Moore would recall afterwards, 'and his interest while we talked was not in himself but in me, whom he plied with probing questions.'

Brij Krishna thought Gandhi had coped better than expected with the fast, putting in lots of work and walking when it was thought he would need to be carried. Dropped during the fast, spinning was restored to Gandhi's routine. The ending of the fast seemed to affect his sense of peace. 'From calm I have entered storm,' he wrote to Rajagopalachari.

His duty by Delhi done, Pakistan seemed Gandhi's next arena of action, though he felt he would need first to visit Wardha and see about the future of his institutions there. He thought he would be strong enough to travel to Wardha on 2 February. Hoping that the Pakistan government would 'tell me that I can go and carry on my work there,' he said: 'Even if any one of the provincial governments of Pakistan invites me, I shall go' (90:494).

> *To Ismat Iftikharuddin*, 22.1.48: Your services are required much more than ever before. Therefore be up and doing. I assure you I am eager to go to Lahore as soon as my convalescence is finished and the way is open for me to go to Lahore (90:475).

Seven men in a conspiracy to kill Gandhi joined his prayer meeting on 20 January. As planned, one man, Madanlal Pahwa, set off a bomb behind Gandhi, which was to be the cue for another conspirator, Digambar Badge, to throw a grenade at Gandhi's face, but Badge lost his nerve. The courage of a woman named Sulochana Devi led to Pahwa's apprehension but the other six slipped away.

Gandhi, who was speaking when the blast occurred and assumed that the sound came from an army unit testing its firepower, continued with his speech. He said the next day: 'I displayed no bravery. I thought it was part of army practice somewhere. I only came to know later that it was a bomb and it might have killed me if God had not willed it that I should live.' He added:

> You should not have any kind of hate against the person who was responsible for this. He had taken it for granted that I was an enemy of Hinduism. Is it not said in Chapter 4 of the Gita that whenever the wicked become too powerful and harm dharma, God sends someone to destroy them? The man who exploded the bomb obviously thinks that he has been sent by God to destroy me.
>
> But . . . if we do not like a man, does it mean that he is

wicked? . . . If then someone kills me, taking me for a
wicked man, will he not have to answer before God? . . .
When he says he was doing the bidding of God, he is only
making God an accomplice in a wicked deed . . . Those
who are behind him or whose tool he is should know that
this sort of thing will not save Hinduism. If Hinduism has
to be saved it will be saved through such work as I am
doing.

Some Sikhs came to me and asked me if I suspected
that a Sikh was implicated. I know he was not a Sikh.
But what even if he was? What does it matter if he was a
Hindu or a Muslim? May God bless him with good sense
(90:472-3).

Someone suggested that by referring to the possibility of being killed
Gandhi had prejudiced the courts against Pahwa, who might be no
more than a prankster. Gandhi smiled and said: 'Can't you see that
there is a conspiracy?' (Brij Krishna 3:548). He had been told of
Pahwa's revelations to the police, which confirmed the message of
his instincts.

Pahwa threw some light on his fellow-conspirators and security
at Birla House was strengthened a little. Ghanshyam Das Birla did
not like having policemen in his house and asked Gandhi about it. 'I
do not find this as shocking as you do,' Gandhi replied. Barring the
police would only add to the burden that Patel and Nehru were carrying. But Gandhi refused permission sought by Patel for frisking
prayer-meeting participants (90:469).

Jehangir Patel and Dinshaw Mehta had meanwhile returned from
Karachi. The two Parsis were accompanied by a third, the khadi-
wearing Karachi-based helper of refugees of all backgrounds,
Jamshed Mehta, of whom Jinnah had once wryly said, 'I know he is
a Gandhian at heart but I cannot do without him.'[10]

As long as he did not ask for reunion, Pakistan would welcome
him, Gandhi was told; but he would have to accept protection by
Pakistan's police. Gandhi resisted the second condition but yielded
when pressed by Jamshed Mehta. By 27 January the three Parsis

were back in Karachi and talking with Pakistan's leaders. Gandhi's arrival in Pakistan was tentatively fixed for 8 or 9 February.

On 23 January he remembered Subhas Bose, whose birthday it was. On 26 January he remembered India's 'lowliest villager.' The needs of Mysore, Meerut, Ajmer, Gwalior and Madras elicited his involvement, as did the suspense of the Hindus and Sikhs of Bahawalpur, and the continuing struggles of Indians in South Africa and Harijans in India. Gandhi gave of himself to the callers continuing to stream in: Vincent Sheean (Jan.27-8) asking about life in the modern world, Kingsley Martin (Jan.27) about the violence in Gandhi's India, Margaret Bourke-White (Jan.29) about nonviolence under the atom bomb . . .

When an influential Sikh leader, Giani Kartar Singh, spoke of cruelties against Sikhs in Pakistan and added, 'Afflicted men cannot be balanced men [and] everybody cannot be a Mahatma Gandhi,' he received this reply: 'Mahatma Gandhi is neither an angel nor a devil. He is a man like you' (90: 471).

Reflection during the fast had settled one important question on his mind. Despite their differences, Nehru and Patel had to stay together. He would talk to the two separately and later, if need be, to both together.

On 27 January he attended the annual fair at the twelfth century tomb in Mehrauli of Khwaja Qutbuddin and asked for a vow 'at this holy place' by Hindus, Sikhs and Muslims that they would not allow strife again. Until Gandhi's fast, Delhi's Muslims had thought that they would no longer be allowed to hold the fair. At 4.30 a.m. on 29 January he wrote assuring a scholarship to Vijaya Walji Sodawala, a Harijan girl in the final year of a medical course in Bombay.

There were other precious contacts. His eldest grandson, Harilal's son Kanti, sent a letter that Gandhi used in *Harijan*. 'Your letter is beautiful,' Gandhi said to Kanti (90:483). Manu's progress was shown in the record she was keeping of Gandhi's conversations. To her father Gandhi conveyed the summit of praise: 'She takes great interest in writing notes and when I see them, Mahadev's face appears before my eyes' (90:488).

Pyarelal's presence was a strength, too. Gandhi had missed him but rejoiced in Pyarelal's work in Noakhali. Now he was good company and a valuable sounding board. 'I am taking Pyarelal home for dinner,' Devadas said to his father one evening. 'Go ahead, but do you ever think of inviting me?' said Gandhi with a great laugh that crackled with the energy of a lifetime's self-denial.

On the morning of 29 January he wrote a warm letter to Kishorelal Mashruwala, who had withdrawn from *Harijan*. Later that day about forty Hindus from Bannu in the Frontier province saw Gandhi. They bore wounds on their bodies and in their spirits and took out some of their resentment on Gandhi, who recounted their discussion in his prayer speech in the evening:

> One of them said I had done enough harm already and that I should stop and disappear from the scene . . . I asked him where he wanted me to go. He said that I might go to the Himalayas . . . I asked why I should go merely because he wished it . . . I can only do as God bids . . . God is the help of the afflicted, but an afflicted person is not God . . . God will do what He wills. He may take me away . . . My Himalayas are here. (90: 524-5).

But to his companions Gandhi said: 'You can take that as notice served on me . . . We should accept curses from a sorrow-laden heart like that as the voice of God' (Brij Krishna 3: 571).

'What news?' he said from his bed on the floor when at 9.30 pm on the twenty-ninth Devadas and his wife Lakshmi appeared. Devadas, who had no news to impart, asked, 'How does the ship of state fare?' Replied Gandhi, referring to Nehru and Patel: 'I am sure the little differences will vanish. But things may have to await my return from Wardha. That won't be long. I am sure they must hold together.' After more conversation on the same lines, Devadas, preparing to leave, said, 'Bapu, will you sleep now?'

'No, there is no hurry . . . Talk for some time longer.'

The legion of sons and daughters filling his heart could not crowd out Kasturba's sons, the flesh of his flesh.

❋

Gandhi was up as usual at 3.30 on the morning of Friday, 30 January. At 3.45 he and his companions said the morning prayers on the cold verandah next to the Birla House guest rooms lent to them: 'Forgive, O Merciful and Loving God of Gods, all my sins, of hand or foot, body or speech, eye or ear, of commission or omission ... I ask neither for a kingdom nor for heaven nor for liberation but only for an end to the pain of the suffering ones ...'

Until six, aided by a hot drink of lemon and honey and a glass of sweet lime juice supplied by Abha and Manu, he worked on the proposal for Congress's future that he had commenced drafting the previous evening. At seven he talked with Rajen Nehru, who was leaving for America, and gave his limbs some exercise by walking inside his room. Shortly before eight he gave his draft on Congress to Pyarelal, saying, 'Go through it with care. Fill in any gaps ... I wrote it under a heavy strain.'

Also, he asked Pyarelal to prepare a note, in the light of his Noakhali experience, for a rice crisis threatening the province of Madras. 'The Food Ministry is feeling nervous,' said Gandhi, but if its resources were husbanded, he added, Madras with its 'coconut, palm, groundnut, bananas, roots and tubers of all kinds and fish' would not starve.

Brij Krishna gave him an oil rub at eight. After a bath he had a brunch of goat's milk, boiled vegetables, tomato, radish, and orange juice. The fast having strained his heart, doctors had advised against bread. Over the meal he discussed Noakhali with Pyarelal: 'You have shed the fear of death and established yourself in the hearts and affections of the people ... You know, I need you here, the burden is so heavy. And there is a lot I would like to share with the world which I cannot do now that you are away. But I have steeled myself to it; the work you are doing is more important.'

Rustom Sorabji, an old associate of his South African days, called with his family. After a nap and another drink of lemon and honey, Gandhi talked with the group of Delhi Muslims who visited daily. 'I can't go away to Wardha without your consent,' he told them. They encouraged him to leave, and one of them, Maulana Hifzur Rahman, said, 'We will find out what Delhi is like in your absence.'

Mahadev Desai was in his thoughts. When someone mentioned the diaries that Desai had maintained from 1917 to 1942, Gandhi said they should be 'edited well and compiled'; but by whom? Narhari Parikh, who had joined Gandhi in 1917 along with Desai, was the ideal candidate but his health, Gandhi pointed out, did 'not permit any work.' Mashruwala, who would have been as good, 'has dissociated himself from all my activities.' 'How can it be said,' added Gandhi, 'that he has done so without full understanding?'

'If Chandrashanker (Shukla) shoulders this responsibility, he will exhibit his talents as well. What similarity between the handwriting of the two! I shall write to him.'

Sudhir Ghosh and Pyarelal then discussed with Gandhi an editorial in the London *Times* about the alleged rift between Nehru and Patel. Gandhi said he would raise the question with Patel, who was coming at four that afternoon, and with Nehru, who was due at seven, and also in his prayer speech.

He spent the early afternoon stretched out in the sun, receiving visitors to whom, on his behalf, Brij Krishna had given time. On his head was the large Noakhali straw hat, on his stomach a mudpack. Jat leaders from East Punjab came after P.B.Chandwani of Sind had read for Gandhi from the day's newspapers; with the Jats Gandhi discussed the condition of their province's Harijans.

To a deputation of Hindus from Sind, Gandhi said 'in an exceedingly tender voice' that while 'outwardly he seemed light and happy,' his 'heart was smitten with grief.' He recalled for them the advice he had received the previous day from the refugee from Bannu to retire to the Himalayas. Chuckling, Gandhi said that nothing would be better; he would become a double Mahatma and attract bigger crowds. But he did not want vainglory or ease. He would face 'the prevailing darkness and misery.'

De Silva from Sri Lanka arrived with his daughter, who obtained the last autograph that Gandhi would sign. Professor Radha Kumud Mookerjee came at 3 p.m., presented a book he had written, and said that Gandhi's message had been taught during the time of the

Buddha. A French photographer who offered a book of his pictures was followed by a delegation from the Punjab states and another of Sikhs, who were organizing a large gathering in Delhi and wondered who should preside. Gandhi suggested Rajendra Prasad, the Congress President.

Manu mentioned that U.N. Dhebar and Rasiklal Parikh of Kathiawad had turned up, hoping to see him. 'Tell them I shall talk with them during my walk after the prayers, if I am alive,' said Gandhi.

At 4 p.m. he walked back to his room, an arm resting on Brij Krishna's shoulder. Brij Krishna was told to arrange the journey to Wardha the next day, in consultation with Patel. 'Ask Bisen to pack Prof. Mookerjee's book with my things,' Gandhi added.

Vallabhbhai had arrived, accompanied by his daughter Maniben. Gandhi's talk with him commenced at 4.15. During the conversation Gandhi ate his evening meal, served by Abha, of goat's milk, boiled vegetables and three oranges, and plied his spinning wheel. Gandhi said that although he had earlier thought that either Patel or Nehru should withdraw from the Cabinet, he had now 'come to the firm conclusion that the presence there of both of them was indispensable.' Any breach in their ranks at this stage would be disastrous. He would say so, Gandhi added, in his speech after the prayers that were to start at five, and to Nehru at seven.

Patel, too, had things to say, and spoke until after five. Aware of Gandhi's fussiness about starting the prayers on time, Abha fidgeted but dared not interrupt. Finally she picked up Gandhi's pocket watch and held it before him. But Gandhi was focussed on Vallabhbhai, and it was 5.10 when, thanks to a tactful intervention by Manibehn, the talk ended.

❋

Gandhi stood up to go to the southern end of the Birla House grounds where he had held prayers every evening since his arrival in Delhi the previous September. Hurrying his feet into his chappals, he placed his hands on the shoulders of Abha, who was on his right, and Manu, to his left, and advanced for the prayers about 170 yards away.

'Your watch must feel very neglected. You would not look at it,' Abha said to Gandhi as he quickened their pace. 'Why should I when I have two timekeepers?' he replied. 'But you don't look at the timekeepers either,' said one of the girls. Gandhi laughed but said, 'It is your fault that I am ten minutes late. It is the duty of nurses to carry on their work even if God himself should be present there. If it is time to give medicine to a patient and you hesitate, the poor patient may die. I hate it if I am late for prayers even by a minute.'

With this the three and those walking behind them fell into complete silence, for they had reached the five curved steps that gently led up to the open prayer ground. It was Gandhi's stipulation that small talk and laughter had to cease, and all thoughts turn to their sacred purpose, before they put their feet on the prayer site.

Behind their backs the winter sun was setting. A 32-yard path lay between the steps and the platform where Gandhi used to sit for the prayers. The women and men who had come for the prayers lined the path on both sides. Removing his hands from the shoulders of the girls, Gandhi brought them together to acknowledge the greetings of the congregation.

From the side to the left of Gandhi, Nathuram Godse of Pune roughly elbowed his way towards him. Godse had been on the scene ten days earlier for the abortive attempt to kill Gandhi, had slipped away, travelled to Bombay, and returned with a fresh plan of assassination. Thinking that Godse intended to touch Gandhi's feet, Manu asked Godse not to interrupt Gandhi, added that they were late already, and tried to thrust back Godse's hand.

Godse violently pushed Manu aside, causing the Book of Ashram Prayer Songs and Gandhi's rosary that she was carrying to fall to the ground. As she bent down to pick the things up, Godse planted himself in front of Gandhi, pulled out a pistol and fired three shots in rapid succession, one into Gandhi's stomach and two into his chest.

The sound 'Rama' escaped twice from Gandhi's throat, crimson spread across his white clothes, the hands raised in the gesture of greeting which was also the gesture of prayer and of goodwill dropped down, and the limp body sank softly to the ground. As he fell, Abha caught Gandhi's head in her hands and sat down with it.

Always a sharp observer and well aware, as we have seen, of a conspiracy aimed at his life, Gandhi may have perceived Godse's intention before seeing the pistol in his hand. We will never know for certain whether he forgave Godse before life left him, but his mind was on prayer when he was shot and he had prayed earlier to be able to forgive his assassin.

Brij Krishna, following behind Gandhi, had run forward on hearing the shots, and seen Gandhi first standing, blood streaming down his body, and then collapsing into Abha's lap. 'Handled by us with a tenderness greater than we would extend to flowers, prepared to be trampled under it rather than see it bruised in any way, we saw that gentle body of his lying lifeless on the grass and moist mud.'

A haste to pray. A hush on entering holy ground. A sense of the Eternal. Lines of fellow-worshippers. A gesture of goodwill. Rude elbows. A smell of attack. The ring of three bullets. 'God! God!' Possibly a silent, 'God! Forgive them.' Loving hands underneath. Earth, moisture, grass. The open sky. Rays from the dipping sun. A perfect death.[11]

Chapter 12

In Perspective

MUCH OF GANDHI was inevitably missing from the preceding pages, and some interesting but poorly known parts of him were only fleetingly present. In these final pages we will focus on a few of these and, thereafter, take some broad views.

We should mark, for instance, Gandhi the alert observer. 'I saw everything that happened there,' he said two months before his death, referring to Porbandar and Rajkot, where he spent the first seventeen years of his life (90:141). In the second chapter we saw that his articles in the magazine of the London Vegetarian Society contained descriptions of peasants that suggested a youth who studied the people around him. His ear too must have been attentive, for he showed a facility throughout his life for buttressing his points with a Gujarati verse or proverb picked up in boyhood.

> His dress was simple, a dhoti and shirt, an angarkhun and a turban of mixed silk and cotton yarn. I do not remember that these garments used to be strikingly clean or carefully ironed . . . He used to walk slowly, and the passer-by could see that he was absorbed in thought even while walking. There was a strange power in his eyes; they were extremely bright, and free from any sign of impatience or anxiety . . . The face was round, the lips thin, the nose neither pointed nor flat and the body of light build and medium size. The skin was dark.

This was Gandhi's recollection of his view as a twenty-two-year-old of the Jain poet Rajchandra.[1] His autobiography, *My Experiments with Truth,* written when Gandhi was fifty-seven, has the following memory of Narayan Hemchandra, a Gujarati befriended by a twenty-year-old Gandhi in London:

> His dress was queer — a clumsy pair of trousers, a wrinkled, dirty, brown coat, after the Parsi fashion, no necktie or collar, and a tasselled woollen cap. He grew a long beard. He was lightly built and short of stature. His round face was scarred with small-pox . . . With his hand he was constantly turning over his beard.

About his friend Joseph Doke of South Africa, Gandhi would recall a 'frail body,' 'a mind of adamant' and 'jaws [that] showed the determination of the owner' (*Indian Opinion*, 23.8.13). We saw that in 1931 he distrusted Mussolini's eyes.[2] Referring, in 1947, to an associate who was probing him, Gandhi said, 'I did not like the manner of [his] questions and the grin on his face' (87:98).

He similariy studied the faces and limbs of the refugees visiting him, some with wounds. In the last chapter we saw his picture of the angry boy confronting him in Panipat. Earlier, in 1940, he had said to the AICC in Ramgarh: 'Fifty years of public life have given me the capacity to read your faces' (71:349).

None of this, of course, makes Gandhi a phrenologist or novelist, and we should note that people's appearances are but rarely sketched in his writings. Since he wrote for a political, social or spiritual purpose, and therefore left out much of what he observed, not many are aware that the seeker of truth and defender of India's honour was also a watcher and reader of people.

Also, and contrary to a common impression, Gandhi took history seriously. Green's view (197) that Gandhi 'repudiates history as a criterion of wisdom' has been expressed by others as well, but in fact Gandhi was drawing lessons from history all the time. 'History teaches us,' he said to Mahadev Desai in 1918, referring to the possibility of Hindu-Muslim and Indo-British cooperation, 'that these things have happened the world over.'[3] 'Look at the history of the British Empire and the British nation,' he had said at Benares in 1916. 'It will not . . . give freedom to a people who will not take it themselves' (13:216).

To those arguing in 1921 that a fight for freedom would lead to civil war, Gandhi again cited history: 'The English carried on internecine warfare for 21 years before they settled down to peaceful work. The French fought among themselves with a savage ferocity hardly excelled during modern times. The Americans did nothing better before they evolved their commonwealth. Let us not hug our unmanliness for fear of fighting amongst ourselves' (21:319).

A few months earlier he had said, 'It is quite possible that I am doing an injustice to the British, that I have misread history' (20:48). But misreading history is different from rejecting its relevance; and fighting the trends of an age need not be inconsistent with a respect for history. Certainly Gandhi questioned the belief that 'what has not occurred in history will not occur at all' (*Hind Swaraj*, Ch.14), and in 1915 he invited the history professor, J.B. Kripalani, to make and not just teach history. We are entitled to ask for grounds for his audacity but not perhaps to see in it a disdain of history.

In *Hind Swaraj* he examines India's history and gives a convincing explanation of the start of British rule. He calls his account of the satyagraha in South Africa a 'history,' and in one of his prison terms begins, even if he cannot complete it, a 'history' of his ashrams. Recalling, as he often did, the legend of Harishchandra, 'who sacrificed his all at the altar of Truth,' he asks, in a 1921 article, 'What must be the position about untouchability in those early days?' (*Navajivan*, 20.11.21). Whether or not the Bhagavad Gita was independent of and an interpolation into the Mahabharata is a historical question that interests him.

He refers to the carnage of 1857 as an event of history to learn from (88:416). He is distressed that Gujaratis possessing 'ancient manuscripts concealed in their clothes cupboards' are likely to ruin them.[4] He tries, in detention in Pune, to write a history of Indian nonviolence but gives up when he confronts Indian violence. In 1947 he reminds Mountbatten of the history of Britain's exploitation of Indian divisions. During the violence of 1946-7 it is the French Revolution that springs to his mind; and it is the history of Delhi that he summons in aid of his bid for peace. This man who hoped to alter history was also mindful of it, yet surely he was entitled to dispute a history that was no more than 'a record of the wars of the world.' He added in *Hind Swaraj*: 'How kings played, how they became enemies of one another, how they murdered one another, is found accurately recorded in history, and if this were all the history of the world, it would have been ended long ago . . . Not a man would have been found alive today.' In this perspective, peace was not news, so that history became 'really a record of every interruption of the even working of the force of love or the soul.' Gandhi's bid to provide new evidence of the power of love and nonviolence was a repudiation of prevalent wisdom but not of history.

Also insufficiently understood is Gandhi's love of life. The man who again and again spoke to himself and others of Death as a wonderful friend, inspired large numbers to offer their lives, and frequently put his own life on the chopping block, could yet love life in general and his own in particular. In 1897 he walked into the crowd in Durban that threatened to lynch him; but the same day he also acted on the advice of Alexander, the police chief, to escape in disguise from his friend Rustomji's house, which was surrounded by a mob bent on mischief, in order, as Alexander put it, 'to save your friend's house and property and also your family.'

Gandhi has recorded the incident in his autobiography. 'As suggested by the superintendent, I put on an Indian constable's uniform and wore on my head a Madrasi scarf wrapped round a plate to serve as a helmet . . . and escaped by (a side) gate.' Adds Gandhi: 'Who can say whether I did so because my life was in jeopardy, or because I did not want to put my friend's life and property or the lives of my wife and children in danger?'

More than fifty years later, he again referred to love of his own life in the reply he sent to Devadas's entreaty against his father's last fast: 'I have only one prayer: "O Rama, give me strength during the fast so that desire to live may not tempt me into premature termination of my fast.' "

In the twenty-one-day protest fast that he undertook in 1943 as a prisoner of the Raj, Gandhi survived a crisis on the thirteenth day when, with his permission, sweet lime juice was added to the water that he was unable to swallow by itself. This was a right or latitude that Gandhi had reserved beforehand, for he knew from experience the mounting difficulty in swallowing water during a fast; yet he felt some guilt and joked to Candy, the Raj's prison chief, 'Where is my fast now?' To B.C. Roy, West Bengal's future Chief Minister and the doctor allowed by the Raj to examine him, Gandhi said: 'To drink water with juice added and live, or die — this was the choice before me. I preferred to live.'[5]

He survived a critical illness in 1918 by drinking goat's milk despite an earlier vow to abjure milk. Doctors had said he would not live without milk or eggs, and Kasturba argued that only cow's milk was in Gandhi's mind when he made the vow. 'I succumbed,' Gandhi wrote in the autobiography. 'The will to live proved stronger than the devotion to truth . . . The memory of this action even now rankles in my breast.'

Not long after Kasturba's intervention, however, Gandhi had spoken almost positively of it to Millie Polak, who was visiting India. According to Polak, he said, 'You women are very persistent and clever,' with 'a twinkle in his eye and an intonation in the voice as though he almost admired Mrs Gandhi for the subtle distinction' that restored his health.[6]

Revealed, too, in his desire, until the 1947 killings, to live to an age of 125 years, in the wishes of long life he extended to many of his correspondents, and in his lifelong inclination towards nursing, Gandhi's love of life included a love of stars and sunsets, of music and literature, of laughter, of the taste of food, of interesting places, of the children of his flesh and the children of his spirit. Thus on 29 October 1947, he spoke of 'the melodious voice' of Dilip Kumar Roy, who had just sung a bhajan, adding, 'I would even say that very few in the world have a voice like his' (89: 431). In December that year, two months before his death, he similarly referred to M.S.Subbulakshmi: 'You heard the bhajan and the Ramdhun sung by Subbulakshmi . . . Today you must have realized why people are so keen to hear her' [90:187].

Writing to Mira during his last fast, he said it had commenced with songs and hymns, including, he added, 'When I survey,' often rendered in the past, in prayers conducted by him, by Mira. 'It was well sung by Sushila,' he said (90: 430). On her part Mira thought well of Gandhi's voice, and recalled a pre-dawn moment in Sabarmati: 'He was the first to arrive for the morning prayer and as it was time had started chanting it. His voice was beautiful.'[7]

Kalelkar has written of moments while he travelled with Gandhi in South India, Lanka and Orissa: 'At times Gandhiji drew my attention to nature's beautiful scenes, especially to the glories of dawn and the dipping sun. I can never forget how he shared with me his joy at the sunrise and sunset in Itamati and Charbatia in Orissa.' Referring to voyages with Gandhi from Bombay to Tuticorin and Tuticorin to Colombo in 1927, Kalelkar says: 'We talked about the sea's changing hues, the flares on the horizon, the shapes of the clouds, the stars in the sky.'

In 1932, acceding to a request by Gandhi during another of his prison terms, the Raj installed in Pune's jail a telescope belonging to Gandhi's friend Lady Premlila Thackersey. Studying the night-sky, Gandhi also loved it, and spoke of the 'holy companionship' offered by the stars.[8] Five years earlier, visiting the large incongruous houses, choked with ornate furniture, of the Chettiars of Chettinad in the Tamil country, who gave gold and silver for his Harijan work, he told his hosts that he could design and furnish their homes better.

While loving life, Gandhi had a horror of indulgence as well as a sense of the importance of each fleeting moment for his national and spiritual undertakings, and also of the power of self-denial. From early manhood, he said in 1932, 'my life . . . was not one of enjoyment but of duty discharged from day to day.'[9] The horror, commitment and self-denial severely constrained but could not crush his love of life. Believing in 'the less I have, the more I am,' he yet cherished Noakhali's 'velvet-like' grass, the sun that nourished him during his fast in Delhi's winter, the sounds of music, the happiness on the faces of children, including the children of his sons . . .

Hidden from many who only saw the ascetic leader and revolutionary, the Gandhi with longings, humour and hurts, of flesh, blood and vulnerability, was known to those around him, to Kasturba and her sons, to Henry and Millie Polak and Hermann Kallenbach, Joseph Doke and Sonja Schlesin, to Charlie Andrews, to Nehru, Patel, Rajagopalachari and Prasad, to Vinoba and Kalelkar, Mahadev and Pyarelal, Jamnalal Bajaj and Ghanshyam Das Birla, Nirmal Kumar Bose, Mira, Sushila, Amtus Salaam, Manu, Abha and Brij Krishna, and many others.

His writings, Gandhi told Bose towards the end of 1946, were misleading. They 'showed him at his best' and 'presented a picture of his aspirations, and not of his achievements.' In his answer Bose quoted Tagore, who had said that a man should be 'judged by the best moments of life, by his loftiest creations, rather than by the smallnesses of everyday life.' Gandhi replied: 'Yes, that is true of the Poet; for he has to bring down the light of the stars upon the earth. But for men like me, you have to measure them not by the rare moments of greatness in their lives, but by the amount of dust which they collect on their feet in the course of life's journey.'[10]

Bose, who saw in East Bengal, Calcutta and Bihar that Gandhi's 'tenderness which he exercised on men soothed them and lifted them above their sorrows,' felt that it was Gandhi's 'questioning attitude about his own perfection' that brought him close to ordinary men and women.[11]

❊

His sagacity, too, seems underrated. Gandhi could prevent neither Partition nor a carnage but the independence of India, the unity of the India that survived the Partition, and the rooting of the new India in democracy, tolerance and a concern for the underdog are part of the history of our world. No one played a greater role than Gandhi in creating this portion of history. He was helped by his commitment and astuteness both.

'In his superb sense of timing,' says George Woodcock, 'in his quick intuitive grasp of the balance of forces, in his instinct for effective symbolic action and in his grasp of the strategy of struggle, Gandhi was one of the most able politicians of his time.' Seeking to liberate and unite Indians across formidable divides of religion, caste, class, and untouchability, Gandhi succeeded in greater measure than seemed possible. While he was gifted with an instinctive political skill, which neither adversity nor advancing age seemed to blunt, and an equally valuable ability to bounce back from the isolation into which he was forced from time to time, a more effective weapon was his passion to identify with all Indians. As Tagore said, no one else had conveyed this identity.

Feeling that they and Gandhi belonged to one another, most Indians were also moved by, and proud of, Gandhi's moral sense. His scrutiny of himself and of his ventures was conducted with a frankness that amazed and inspired the Indian people, even if it also at times embarrassed them. He was always examining the rights and wrongs of a personal or political step, a social or economic practice. His reflections were ethical; and the people of India, who had access to them, derived dignity and confidence therefrom.

After referring to his mother, whom he said he 'deeply revered,' and to Maulana Abdul Bari, his 'religious guide,' whose 'loving kindness,' he added, held him 'in bondage,' Muhammad Ali said in 1923: 'But in spite of all this I make bold to say that I have not yet found any person who in actual character is entitled to a higher place than Mahatma Gandhi' (*UMM*: 109).

With Gandhi at their head, the Indian people could look the Raj, Britain and the West in the eye and challenge the assumption of the East's moral degeneracy; and their gratification was greater on finding that astuteness plus an identification with all Indians were allied to Gandhi's character. 'He was a friend and lover of all the men and women he met,' said Rajagopalachari soon after Gandhi's death. Nine years earlier, he had spoken of 'an old but big and good boat piloted by Mahatma Gandhi,' adding: 'We have tried Mahatma Gandhi for 20 years — to our satisfaction. What he says he means. He promises the minimum but performs the maximum' (*Rajaji* 2:37).

The Hind Swaraj manifesto (1909), the Khilafat-Swaraj campaign (1920-2), and Quit India (1942) were the strokes of a political master. In *Hind Swaraj* Gandhi bracketed nonviolence and spirituality with Indian culture, contrasting them with materialism, violence and Western civilization, the three being lumped together. With the message of *Hind Swaraj* he removed the platform of Indian civilization from under the feet of the advocates of the bomb, and convinced India that he was the most authentic Indian and Hindu of them all.

Though the Hindu-Muslim alliance forged by the Khilafat-Swaraj struggle proved of short duration, that struggle delivered a blow to divide-and-rule from which the Raj could never recover.. Hindus and Muslims alike had forever rejected British rule, even if, later, they also rejected one another. To divide India remained an option for Britain, but not to remain in India. Britain divided India and quit.

Quit India took a heavy toll. Thousands were bereaved or separated from loved ones, or cut off from education or jobs. The transfer of Congress from legislatures and secretariats to prisons or the underground gave new life to the Muslim League. Yet, without Quit India, Congress would have lost the confidence of the Indian people. Since there was no national alternative to Congress, a scramble for the Raj that was being vacated by the British might have led to a fragmentation of India. So while Quit India strengthened the League, it also, by bonding Congress afresh with the Indian people, gave to India minus its seceding parts a linking and uniting mechanism.

A fourth masterstroke, the salt satyagraha of 1930, has been largely left out of this study. It was the greatest, perhaps, of the Gandhi-led campaigns. Unlike the Khilafat-Swaraj battle, the salt marches did not underscore the Hinduness or Muslimness of Indians. Quit India, too, was a purely secular struggle; but some Indians found it awkward to defy a Britain that was fighting Nazi Germany and Militarist Japan. In contrast, the salt campaign was uncontaminated. Moreover, it spoke directly to India's poor, who were burdened by the tax on salt, the sea's free gift.

The salt campaign's greatest strength was its simplicity. All that a salt satyagrahi had to do was to walk to the sea and scoop up some salt, an illegal act — or to buy or sell salt illegally scooped up. The satyagrahi also, of course, had to be willing to be arrested or beaten. Tens of thousands along the coast and in the hinterland were found to be so willing; the defiance was open, contagious and dramatic, and showed Gandhi's skill with symbolism and as a strategist.

If the ordinary Indian found the salt satyagraha perfectly simple to grasp, that satyagraha was also calculated to make an almost irresistible impact on the British mind. In the letter to the Viceroy, Lord Irwin, in which Gandhi announced the satyagraha — sent, again with deadly symbolism, by the hand of an English supporter, Reginald Reynolds — he revealed his intention of affecting British opinion. 'My ambition is no less,' Gandhi said, 'than to convert the British people through nonviolence and thus make them see the wrong they have done to India' (43:6).

The results of the salt satyagraha vindicated Gandhi's confidence. And if we recall that Gandhi's restiveness against the salt tax was first uttered when he was a student in London and repeated several times before it found expression in 1930, then we are struck once more by the early start of the future man.

But that Gandhi the strategist was more than merely shrewd is confirmed by his exertions for the future beyond victory over the Raj. We have seen that in the course of the struggle for that victory and in the months before and after 15 August 1947, he made crucial interventions designed to support the weak against the strong, and the citizen against the state. His strategies were not confined to the immediate.

Salt, indigo, the cotton cloth, the spinning wheel, the blanket for the refugee, the journalist's pen, a loaf of bread, a walking stick, a pair of glasses, a pocket watch, nursing hands — it is worth observing that these secular items are the religious Gandhi's lasting symbols. These, plus the oneness of Ishwar, Allah and God.

❋

We should distinguish, of course, between the Gandhi of his place and time — the father who failed with his eldest son, the Empire's avenger, the restorer of the self-respect of Indians, Asians and the coloured, the man who could not, for all his opposition, prevent either Partition or a bloodbath, the architect of a secular, democratic, and pro-poor India, a spirited iconoclast in the Temples of Size, Modern Civilization and War whose rejection sometimes went too far — and the Gandhi for all, and for all seasons.

This latter Gandhi is the one who saw equal value in all human lives, asked ethical questions and sought ethical answers, preferred winning his opponents to eliminating them, welcomed hardship as an inevitable part of the spiritual or religious life, gave his utmost for the truths he saw, made implications for the weak the touchstone for public policy, and held that 'self-government is not an end but only a means to good government' (90:325).

We should distinguish between the Gandhi who from 1919 to 1947 led India's historic battle against the British Empire and the Gandhi who, in his own life and around him, also fought the eternal battle between the noble and the base. Exhilarating as it was to most Indians of his time, Gandhi's nationalism may mean less to the future, which is bound to accord greater value to what human beings do to one another, including what Indians do to other Indians, than to what 'they,' the British, did or failed to do to 'us,' the Indians of Gandhi's time.

Let us look again at the letter that Gandhi wrote to Nehru at the end of August 1947: 'If I am not going to the Punjab, would I be of much use in Delhi as an adviser or consultant? I fancy I am not built that way. My advice has value only when I am actually working at a particular thing. I can only disturb when I give academic advice as on food, clothing, the use of the military . . .' (90:117).

It is legitimate, I think, to see in this letter an admission that the advice to fight nonviolently that he gave to the Jews, the British and the other Europeans attacked by Hitler was 'academic' or theoretical. He was not 'working at' their defence. When, in 1947-8, he was in Delhi and fully involved, at the side of Nehru and Patel, in the defence of peace in the capital and its neighbourhood, he did not plead for disarming the police or the military; and while he raised the possibility of nonviolent defence when an incursion took place in Kashmir, he gave 'tacit consent,' to use his own words, to an armed defence.

As the discoverer or rediscoverer of satyagraha, Gandhi would not, in theory, concede any weakness in nonviolence; but in practice he acquiesced in or associated himself with some exercises of violence. Violence was better than cowardice, he would say; and though nonviolence was unquestionably better than violence, it could not always be summoned or mobilized. This was Gandhi's explanation for the violence he condoned but he did not offer it for the violence employed against Hitler. It was an inconsistency born of nationalism that hurt some of the closest of his associates, including Polak, Kallenbach and Andrews. If Gandhi's life was his message, then it follows that he would have offered battle, nonviolently if possible and in other ways if necessary, had he been a Pole, Czech, Jew, Dane, Norwegian, Russian, Frenchman or Briton facing Hitler.

Gandhi's nationalism was a truth for Britain and the West, for it bared the greed and vainglory that had masqueraded as the white man's burden. For India, however, nationalism was in the end a drug. It blinded Indians to the cruelties they were capable of perpetrating on one another, to the smaller nationalisms it seemed inexorably to breed, and also to the advantages that association with the West could bring. Gandhi made sure of equality in any future association; and two months before his death he envisioned 'a new and robust India, not warlike . . . learning the best that the West has to give and becoming the hope not only of Asia and Africa, but of the whole of the aching world' (90:130). This is the voice of Gandhi freed from nationalism's magnetic field; but the magnet continues to hold many Indians in its thrall, and while he had reservations about nationalism, no one infused more power into that magnet than Gandhi.

We should distinguish between the Gandhi who stared the West down and the one who looked at Indians, Asians, Africans and Westerners as individuals, God's children all, each with needs and gifts; between the Gandhi who stood up to others, taking their and his measure, and the one who took their hand and reassured them. The first Gandhi, encountering Ollivant, Smuts, Churchill, Linlithgow, and Wavell, thrilled the East, taught the West and indeed loved many in both East and West; yet he also saw the world in two, the brother's and the other's, while insisting that the divide was temporary. The second Gandhi, the one encountered by Andrews, Kallenbach, Vincent Sheean, William Shirer and Louis Fischer, among others, saw different persons but one people.

For Gandhi himself the two were chicken and egg. Each grew out of the other. 'My national service,' he claimed in 1924, 'is part of my training for freeing my soul from the bondage of flesh . . . My patriotism is for me a stage in my journey to the land of eternal freedom and peace' (*Young India*, 3.4.24). But we understand him better if we see the two separately.

Here is a man who more than once told William Shirer that he would win India's independence in his lifetime and who said in 1930, 'I was born to destroy this evil government'; in 1932 (in jail), 'Just as a pregnant woman takes care of her health for the sake of the baby in her womb, I take care of myself for the sake of the swaraj that is supposed to be in my womb,' and in 1936, 'Out of my ashes a thousand Gandhis will arise.' However, the same man declared in 1926: 'We cannot love one another if we hate Englishmen. We cannot love the Japanese and hate Englishmen. We must either let the Law of Love rule us through and through or not at all. Love among ourselves based on hatred of others breaks down under the slightest pressure.'[12]

When in 1929 John Mott asked him what weighed most on his mind, Gandhi spoke not of alien rule but of 'our apathy and hardness of heart, if I may use the Biblical phrase . . . towards the masses and their poverty' (*Young India*, 21.3.29).

Both Gandhis had a role in conceiving the masterstrokes referred to. His truth never quite left the nationalist alone; moreover, the politician in Gandhi knew the practical value of decency, and also that his nationalism needed his God, for some of the forces he was releasing were unpredictable and uncontrollable.

'This evening's is the most important meeting of his life,' Mahadev Desai said to Kalelkar in Bombay on 8 August 1942, Quit India's eve. 'He has decided to pray before setting forth.' *Vaishnava Janato* was sung in the company of eight or ten, and Kalelkar thought that Gandhi's face during the singing 'shone with the pure radiance of trust in God, a firm resolve and gentleness.' Kalelkar has also recorded Gandhi's practice of re-reading and pondering the Sermon on the Mount before any important encounter with a British functionary.[13]

Misgivings always knocked on the doors of Gandhi's nationalism, which he sought to soften and purify. In that 1930 letter to Irwin announcing the salt satyagraha, Gandhi had said: 'If I have equal love for your people with mine, it will not long remain hidden.' On occasion a blithe remark revealed his uncertainty, as when he said: 'My narrow nationalism rebels against the hat, my secret internationalism regards the sola hat as one of the few boons from Europe.'[14]

Yet the nationalism never wholly left his system, so that his masterstrokes had some unwholesome fallouts as well. We have seen in this study that they afforded scope for violence, Partition and an outlook of blame, but we can recall also the unease caused by the burning of foreign cloth in 1921 and 1930. Tagore and Andrews were troubled; in the sacrifice they saw hate as well as the destruction of useful and beautiful objects.

As we saw, Gandhi's answer was that using cloth made in foreign mills destroyed the Indian destitute's chance to spin, weave and survive, and also that he was deflecting hate from people to things. Offering a similar answer, Martin Luther King Jr. would say: 'Many . . . wince at a distinction between property and persons . . . My views are not so rigid. A life is sacred. Property is part of the earth man walks on; it is not man.'[15] Yet sadness is undoubtedly one of our emotions on reading a recollection of the sacrifice of both objects and lives in the battles led by Gandhi.

To the fires the celibate Vinoba, who had embraced a simplicity severer than Gandhi's, offered a scarf left by his mother which he had kept under his pillow for years. Vallabhbhai's seventeen-year-old daughter Mani, who also remained single throughout her life, wrapped all her jewels in a bundle of cloth that she gave to Gandhi for the sinews of struggle. A pair of gold bangles given by an aunt, a gold wristwatch brought for her from England by her uncle Vithalbhai, and a pair of earrings, all went into the campaign for Indian liberty.

Thousands of others gave similarly of their precious hoards and, in addition, heaped foreign cloth into bonfires. Lives were given; freedom was dearly bought. Moved by the sacrifice and proud of it, we also, in one part of us, regret it. And we ask if its alien origin can suffice to trash an object, and whether such trashing is not bound to harm a people's outlook.

※

All human beings are several in one and partake of one another. We have separated the nationalist Gandhi from the one seeking union with Truth; in him we have seen the soul of a proud East, the voice of ancient peoples, and a defier of Western civilization. We may even concede the similarity Fatima Meer perceives between Gandhi and the late Ayatollah Khomeini of Iran in 'resurrecting the indigenous intellect and the indigenous spirit.'[16] However, the value Gandhi gave to individual freedom, and to goodwill across boundaries, separates him from Khomeini. We know there were other Gandhis too: the nurse and servant; the doctor prescribing 'pure air, clean water and clean earth'; the earth-lover who wanted humans to restrict their assaults on the planet; the life-artist expressing something 'through the tidiness with which he conversed with others, did his work, washed his face, chopped vegetables, folded clothes . . .'; the potter from whose wheel and hands men and women emerged with enhanced devotion, courage and confidence[17]; the teacher who in November 1947 responded as follows to a comment by Manu on his 'funny appearance' in the Noakhali hat that protected him from the sun:

> We will be saved a lot of bother if we cease to think of how we appear to others and concentrate on what is beneficial to us . . . If I care for appearances, I will have

> to face the sun and damage my health for no reason . . .
> Well, I have taught you a good lesson after many days. If
> we analyse it minutely, our barbaric behaviour and Hindu-
> Muslim tension are also due to our preoccupation with
> how we appear to others [89:512].

When Kalelkar once spoke about an old man they both knew who talked normally in company but strangely when alone, Gandhi the student of human nature observed: 'But aren't all of us like that? You and all of us speak soberly in society but are wild and reckless when alone with our thoughts. The only difference is that that poor old man comes out with what may be flying within our minds.'[18]

A king, too, was in Gandhi. As Jawaharlal said, 'In spite of his loincloth and bare body, there was a royalty and kingliness in him.' 'Bapu,' as many called him, was how a ruler was addressed in Kathiawad, and we have seen that Gandhi was at ease in royal company. He partakes of rulers across the ages, and in Chapter 6 we looked at Erikson's discovery of a similarity, in the context of Gandhi's chastity experiments, between Gandhi and David, the Biblical king.

We may never fully or precisely know whether these chastity experiments were solely that, or constituted a yearning in Gandhi for a power to change the world around him, or whether, from close human contact, he wanted assurance when in old age violence and hate seemed to shatter his dreams, or wanted to be mothered and to mother (there was, as he always claimed, a woman too in him, and we saw that he had no qualms in likening himself to a pregnant woman), or whether all these or other motivations were at work. We can, however, see in this older Gandhi one struggling to hold on to or regain his confidence. The sure General and the desperate struggler both inhabit our Gandhi.

Like David, Gandhi was aware of enemies plotting to kill him. Towards the end of their lives, both prayed from their depths, David for deliverance from his foes, Gandhi for the ability to do or die and for goodwill towards his killers. The name of God, Rama in Gandhi's case, meant much to both. David sang with burning sincerity —

'David's psalms transport you to raptures,' Gandhi wrote in 1926 (*Young India*, 15.4.26). With equal earnestness, morning and evening, Gandhi joined in the prayer songs with his heart, palms and sometimes his lips.

If he partook of David, he also, as Rajagopalachari and D.P. Mishra, among others, have said, partook of Krishna. 'He was a friend and lover of all the men and women he met,' said Rajagopalachari, adding, 'Indeed he was like Krishna [who] died when a hunter's arrow pierced and sucked his life away. So also our Krishna has died' (*Rajaji* 2: 156). He had something of the Rama of the epic too, who was sent into exile in the forests when he should have been crowned. As the freedom he had pledged to win approached, Gandhi, on his part, walked in the desolation of Noakhali and the baking soil of Bihar.

If all of us partake of one another and are many people in one, it follows that our reading of another is influenced by the parts of us and the other person that are in interaction. Thus the part of Wavell that seemed allergic to powerful individuals and even more to foes of the Empire wrestled with the nationalist in Gandhi and the outcome was an assessment that Gandhi was 'malevolent.' A meeting of other parts of Gandhi and Wavell might have produced a different comment. Influenced by the chemistry between them, other Europeans described Gandhi as one of the century's most Christlike individuals. In a similar comment, Tagore said in 1921 that Gandhi 'has what is known as the Christ spirit.'[19]

The faithful helmsman brought the good ship India to freedom's shore, though many of the travellers remained in the portion of the boat that was sawed off messily and precariously in midstream and taken separately to the shore under a different skipper (who once had hoped to steer the whole ship). During the long voyage the boatman had served and taught the people on board, spotted talent, trained a crew, and installed successors.

He was making an internal journey as well, towards God, which he felt could only be undertaken while he safeguarded India on her voyage towards freedom.

He hoped that both journeys, India's to freedom and his to God, would have something to say to the world. We have seen that the misadventures on India's voyage were linked to the nationalism he shared with almost all Indians — to a pride that hated the foreign presence, assumed a unity among Indians that did not quite exist and also assumed an unproved and perhaps unprovable superiority in civilization over the West. This pride sought purely Indian solutions and ignored the possibility of employing the British presence, while it lasted, in aid of Indian unity. As he had told Desai in 1918, 'a feeling deep down' in him cautioned him against haste in extinguishing the humiliating 'British connection,' but Gandhi was unable to tame the impatience he had helped engender.

On his personal journey he may have asked too much of himself in wanting to be perfect, to be womanlike, to be Godlike, to be capable, through a flaming purity, of moulding his world. Scrutinized and cross-examined without pause by others, especially by orthodox Hindus such as Ranchhoddas Patwari whose eighty-eight questions he patiently, truthfully and skilfully answered, yet by none more than by himself, Gandhi allowed his imperfections to vex him more perhaps than was warranted. When surrender might have sufficed, he aspired for perfection, and blamed himself when he could not attain it.

An excessive self-reliance was his fault, not vanity. He was more tolerant and understanding of a God in repose than of idle human beings. We have seen that he entertained no delusion of perfection or Godliness and constantly likened himself to everyone else; yet one feels he could have put a little more on God's shoulders than he did, and somewhat less on his own, and could have afforded to be less appalled than he usually was by human weaknesses, including his own.

If we learn from his errors, we profit, too, from the truths he illumined. His warnings against violence were necessary and prophetic — we can recall the 1908 statement: 'The bomb now thrown at Englishmen will be aimed at Indians after the English are there no longer.'

Secondly, through his great campaigns and 'little' interactions with individuals, he left behind persuasive answers to the difficult yet everyday questions of our relationship with one another, and the relationship of 'our' group with another group. That human lives have equal value; that individuals and groups should extend freedom and respect to one another, and be willing to suffer unto death in struggles against their denial but unwilling to cause death — these are truths to which his life gave new life.

When, as in our times, hates between castes, tribes, races, sects or nations threaten to erupt in violent conflict, these truths have obvious relevance, and not merely for high and low castes, or Hindus and Muslims, or India and Pakistan.

Thirdly, bringing home the evil of high and low, and the ordeals of the deprived, he taught us that the condition of others, especially the weak, is as important as, and vital to, our own material or spiritual state; that God, or happiness, lies not in gold, learning or holy ritual, but in compassion.

Another legacy is constituted by the norms he demanded and often obtained from his colleagues in public service. These norms were seen in the humble estate of many fighters for India's independence despite the power they secured towards the end of their lives, and in the conventions observed in the early years of self-government. Thus, to add to the instances given already, when, after being elected Speaker of the U.P. Assembly in 1937, Purshottam Das Tandon hesitated to resign from Congress, citing a widespread trust in his impartiality, Gandhi persuaded Tandon to sever the party tie; while character made an individual trustworthy, only conventions imparted trust to a system.[20]

A fifth legacy is Gandhi's attitude to women, which was reflected in the reply he sent three months before his death to a woman who had sought his blessings for a son born after three daughters: 'Should even a woman like you make a distinction between a son and a daughter?... Can even a wise woman like you have such an antipathy towards womankind? Of course all your children have my blessings' (89:471). Cultivating, as we saw, a woman in himself, Gandhi strove for a greater womanliness in the India and world around him, even while insisting that the emasculation of India was one of the most tragic consequences of British rule. He knew that masculinity to machismo to violence was a quick journey. At his call, women broke out of seclusion and faced imprisonment, but to relieve women he also ensured that the evening meals in his ashrams ended before dusk, and that men joined the women to cook, serve and clean.

Finally, he enriches our understanding of the relationship between humans and God by stressing the importance of the role of the human being. God and prayers to Him meant much to Gandhi. When, on one occasion in 1927, fatigue at the end of a gruelling day sent him to sleep before he had said his evening prayers, he sweated and shivered in remorse at 2.30 a.m. the following morning and begged God's pardon.[21]

God's grace was necessary and had to be sought, but the lesson of Gandhi's life, even if he stressed it to excess, was human effort. Starting as 'Everyman,' he grew, says Bhabani Bhattacharya, to 'an extraordinary, towering height' through a process that 'involved Gandhi in the most sustained and most agonizing struggle for self-transformation that any man in the world has ever experienced. Knife in hand, he slashed off every element of weakness, every tangled web of contrariness, in the depths of his being. He moulded himself with all the intense passion and all the superb patience of an artist working with his chisel bit by bit on rough stone.'[22]

Working tirelessly on himself, Gandhi hoped that others would work on themselves. For others he would be neither guru nor godman; none except God would be his guru. Others, too, should make God or conscience their guru. Human beings could share experiences and insights with one another, and stimulate or even inspire one another, but none was worthy of being a complete guide to someone else. Some might steer a people to political liberty, but there was only one Boatman for the voyage through and beyond life, who however relied on exertions and exercises from every traveller.

On meeting him, many felt Gandhi's power but others became aware of their own. 'What was his secret?' asked Upton Close, adding: 'I think my wife discovered it. She said: "In his presence I felt a new capability and power in myself rather than a consciousness of his power. I felt equal, confident, good for anything — an assurance I had never known before, as if some consciousness within me had newly awakened." '23

Strange yet wise, hard with many, hardest with himself, and yet twinkling, drawn instinctively to truth and persevering in love, his life a fuel for lighting up human suffering, obstinate at times and hazardously sure of himself, Gandhi was, with all that, India's good boatman and, all through the twentieth century, a spark for consciences across the world.

Acknowledgements

ENRICHING THESE JOURNEYS with Gandhi were the companions with whom Gandhi was blessed. We realize that many were worth lingering with, and we are fortunate that several left behind notes, diaries and memoirs making possible this and the numerous other portrayals of Gandhi. If we are irredeemably in their debt, they are also capable of stirring us.

We can think of Joseph Doke, Johannesburg's Presbyterian minister and Gandhi's first biographer; Henry and Millie Polak, allies in South Africa; Gandhi's grandnephew Prabhudas who put down details of the South African years; Mahadev Desai, the secretary with a sensitive and literary mind and a pure commitment who was 25 when he joined Gandhi, served Gandhi for 25 years, and recorded much of Gandhi's cogitation from 1917 to 1942;

Pyarelal, the gifted secretary-biographer who joined Gandhi in 1919 and, among other works, bequeathed the irreplaceable *Early Phase* and *Last Phase* volumes; his sister Sushila Nayar, whose faithful portrayal of Gandhi's and Kasturba's 1942-4 detention in Pune complements the volumes she has written to fill the gaps in her brother's massive biography; Krishnadas, whose *Seven Months with Mahatma Gandhi* is an invaluable record of 1920-1;

Kaka Kalelkar, Gandhi's close associate from 1915 and the provider of many a meaningful glimpse; Gandhi's young grandniece Manu, who despite great challenges to body, mind and soul captured the details of the final 13 months of Gandhi's life; Mira Behn, the British Admiral's daughter whose correspondence with Gandhi and recollections since joining him in 1925 add to our understanding; Nirmal Kumar Bose, the professor who assisted, probed and recorded the Gandhi of 1946-7; Brij Krishna, who loved and served

Gandhi and caught many significant responses and remarks; and other companions like G.D. Birla and Ramnarayan Chaudhary preserving a record of the scenes they witnessed.

Though they did not spend time with him and perhaps did not even meet him, 'companions' like Erik Erikson, Martin Green, Judith Brown, James Hunt, Chandran Devanesen and B.R. Nanda, to mention only some of those seeking with skill and perseverance to accompany Gandhi's heart on its journeys and wrestlings, have also helped, sometimes movingly. Then there are the numerous interviewers of Gandhi — Indian and foreign, politicians and journalists, scholars and thinkers, evangelists for different causes, and others — whose notes, and in several cases books, assisted us in comprehending Gandhi. Out of a long list we can pick the names of Louis Fischer, Vincent Sheean and William Shirer.

In a special category are the functionaries of the Raj — including Viceroys, Secretaries of State, Governors and others — who kept a record of their verbal or written interactions with Gandhi, and of their continuing assessment of his mind. If his encounter with the British Empire was of vital importance in shaping Gandhi, the Empire's diarists and archivists, including non-official ones, present vivid pictures of Gandhi right from his student days in London, through his South African years and his tussle with the Empire in India, to independence and his death.

We should recognize, too, that apart from the other things they did, Gandhi's political allies like Nehru, Patel, Rajagopalachari, Prasad, Azad and Kripalani assist us in understanding him — through their agreements and disputes with Gandhi and in some cases with their books (we can think of Kripalani's valuable *Life & Thought*). In probing Gandhi's personality we are also aided by critics and adversaries like Jinnah and Ambedkar.

A goldmine has been placed on bookshelves by the compilers of *The Collected Works of Mahatma Gandhi*, among whom mention must be made of K. Swaminathan, the dedicated scholar who died in 1994. In the hundred-odd volumes in this collection we meet Gandhi in innumerable aspects and also his friends in all their variety. Their interaction with Gandhi, in the form of queries, banter, support, dissent, objections or opposition, helps reveal the man.

Then there are the anthologists — Anand Hingorani, R.K.Prabhu, U.R.Rao, Homer Jack, Martin Green, Raghavan Iyer, Nirmal Kumar Bose, and others — who provide evidence of the range of Gandhi's concerns and spark probes, not always successful, into the origins and contexts of Gandhi's remarks.

To the named and the unnamed I offer heartfelt thanks.

Glossary

angarkhun	long loose coat for men
Bhagavat	the ancient text or book of the *Bhagavat Purana*
Brahmacharya	perfect chastity
chappals	sandals
Dinabandhu	friend of the poor
goonda	bully; criminal
karmayogi	seeker or ascetic dedicated to action
Khalsa	Sikh brotherhood
Manusmriti	text containing the code of Manu
Pindari	freebooter, dacoit
Purana Qila	Old fort
rakshasa	demon
rakshasi	demoness
Ramnam	the name of Rama, God's name
Ramdhun	melody in Rama's praise
Sarpagandha	traditional medicine for high blood pressure
satyagraha	nonviolent stand or action in just cause
sowar	trooper, mounted aide
Vaishnavi	woman devoted to Vishnu

Bibliography

Ahmad, J., *Creation of Pakistan*, Publishers United, Lahore, 1976.

Ahmad, J., *Middle Phase of the Muslim Political Movement*, Publishers United, Lahore, 1969.

Ali, Chaudhari Muhammad, *The Emergence of Pakistan*, Columbia, New   York, 1967.

Allana, G.A., *Jinnah*, Ferozsons, Lahore, 1967.

Ambedkar, B.R., *Writings and Speeches*, Bombay, 1982.

————, *Thoughts on Pakistan*, Thacker, Bombay, 1941.

————, *What Congress and Gandhi have done to the Untouchables*, Thacker, Bombay, 1945.

Andrews, C.F., *Mahatma Gandhi at Work*, Allen and Unwin, London, 1931.

————, *Mahatma Gandhi : His Own Story*, Allen and Unwin, London, 1930.

Ashe, Geoffrey, *Gandhi : A Study in Revolution*, Asia, Bombay, 1968.

Bajaj, Jankidevi, *Meri Jeevanyatra*, Sasta Sahitya Mandal, New Delhi, 1965.

Bajaj, Ramkrishna (ed.), *Jamnalal Bajaj : Patravyavhar*, Sasta Sahitya Mandal, New Delhi, 1958.

Banerjee, Subrata, *The R.I.N. Strike*, People's Publishing House, New Delhi, 1958.

Bhattacharya, Bhabani, *Mahatma Gandhi,* Arnold Heinemann, New Delhi, 1977.

Birla, Ghanshyam Das, *In the Shadow of the Mahatma*, Vakils, Bombay, 1968.

————, *A Talk on Bapu*, Sangeet Kala Mandir, Calcutta, 1981.

Bondurant, Joan, *Conquest of Violence : The Gandhian Philosophy of Conflict*, Princeton, 1958.

Bose, Nirmal Kumar, *My Days with Gandhi*, Nishana, Calcutta, 1953.

————, *Lectures on Gandhism*, Navajivan, Ahmedabad, 1971.

Bose, Subhas, *The Indian Struggle*, Asia, Bombay, 1964.

Brecher, Michael, *Nehru*, OUP, London, 1959.

Brij Krishna, *Gandhiji ki Dilli Diary* (3 vols.), Delhi, 1970.

Brown, Judith, *Gandhi: Prisoner of Hope*, OUP, Delhi, 1990.

Campbell-Johnson, Alan, *Mission with Mountbatten*, Robert Hale, London, 1972.

Chagla, M.C. *Roses in December*, Bhavan, Bombay, 1973.

Chalapati Rau, *Gandhi and Nehru*, Allied, New Delhi, 1967.

Chandra, Bipan, *Communalism in Modern India*, Vikas, New Delhi, 1984.

Chatterjee, Margaret, *Gandhi's Religious Thought*, Macmillan, New Delhi, 1983.

————, *Gandhi and his Jewish Friends*, Macmillan, London, 1992.

Choudhary, Valmiki, *Dr Rajendra Prasad: Correspondence & Documents*, (20 vols.), Allied, New Delhi.

Choudhari, Manmohan, *Exploring Gandhi*, Gandhi Peace Foundation, New Delhi, 1989.

Churchill, Winston, *My African Story*, The Holland Press, London, 1962 Reprint.

Desai, Mahadev, *Day-to-day with Gandhi* (several vols.), Sarva Seva Sangh, Varanasi.

————, *The Diary of Mahadev Desai* (2 vols.), Navajivan, Ahmedabad.

Desai, Narayan, *Agnikundma Ugelun Gulab*, Ahmedabad, 1992.

————, *Bliss was it to be Young — with Gandhi*, Bhavan, Bombay, 1988.

Devanesen, Chandran, *The Making of the Mahatma*, Orient Longmans, New Delhi, 1969.

Doke, Joseph J., *An Indian Patriot in South Africa*, Publications Division, New Delhi, 1967.

Durgadas (ed.), *Sardar Patel's Correspondence* (10 vols.), Navajivan, Ahmedabad.

————, *India from Curzon to Nehru & After*, Collins, London, 1969.

Dutt, B.C., *Mutiny of the Innocents*, Sindhu, Bombay, 1971.

Edwardes, Michael, *Nehru*, Allen Lane, London, 1971.

Erikson, Erik H., *Gandhi's Truth*, Norton, New York, 1969.

Fischer, Louis, *The Life of Mahatma Gandhi*, Harper, New York, 1950.

Fisher, Frederick B., *That Strange Little Brown Man Gandhi*, Orient Longmans, New Delhi, 1970.

Gandhi, Devadas, *Ba, Bapu Aur Bhai*, Sasta Sahitya Mandal, New Delhi, 1956.

Gandhi, Kanu and Abha, *Bapu ke Sath*, Publications Division, New Delhi, 1990.

Gandhi, M.K., *My Experiments With Truth*, Navajivan, Ahmedabad.

————, *Collected Works*, (100 vols.), New Delhi.

————, *Hind Swaraj*, Navajivan, Ahmedabad.

————, *Indian States' Problem*, Navajivan, Ahmedabad, 1941.

————, *Satyagraha in South Africa*, Navajivan, Ahmedabad.

————, *Speeches & Writings*, Natesan, Madras, 1922.

————, *Unto This Last: A Paraphrase*, Navajivan, Ahmedabad, 1956 Reprint.

Gandhi, Manu, *Bapu ki Ye Baaten*, Navajivan, Ahmedabad, 1969.

————, *Biharni Komi Aagmaan*, Navajivan, Ahmedabad, 1956.

————, *Dilhimaan Gandhiji*, (2 vols.), Navajivan, Ahmedabad, 1966.

————, *Ekla Chalo Re*, Navajivan, Ahmedabad, 1957.

————, *The Lonely Pilgrim*, Navajivan, Ahmedabad, 1964.

Gandhi, Prabhudas, *Jeevan Prabhat*, Sasta Sahitya Mandal, New Delhi, 1967.

Gandhi Rajmohan, *India Wins Errors*, Radiant, New Delhi, 1989.

————, *Patel*, Navajivan, Ahmedabad, 1990.

————, *The Rajaji Story*, (2 vols.), Bhavan, Bombay, 1984.

————, *Understanding the Muslim Mind*, Penguin, Delhi, 1987.

Ghosh, Sudhir, *Gandhi's Emissary*, Rupa, Bombay, 1967.

Glendevon, John, *The Viceroy at Bay*, Collins, London, 1971.

Gopal, S., *Nehru* (3 vols.), Oxford, New Delhi.

Gore, M.S., *The Social Context of an Ideology*, Sage, New Delhi, 1993.

Goswami, K.P. (ed.), *Mahatma Gandhi: A Chronology*, Publications Division, New Delhi, 1971.

Gracie, David M. (ed.), *Gandhi and Charlie*, Cowley, Cambridge, Mass., 1989.

Green, Martin, *The Challenge of the Mahatmas*, Basic, New York, 1978.

———, *Gandhi: Voice of a New Age Revolution*, Continuum, New York, 1993.

Hasan, Mushirul (ed.), *India's Partition*, OUP, Delhi, 1993.

Hingorani, Anand (ed.), *God is Truth*, Bhavan, Bombay, 1971.

———, (ed.), *On Myself*, Bhavan, Bombay, 1972.

Hodson, H.V., *The Great Divide*, Hutchinson, London, 1969.

Hunt, James D., *Gandhi in London*, Promilla, New Delhi, 1978.

———, *Gandhi and the Nonconformists*, Promilla, New Delhi, 1986.

Huttenback, Robert A., *Gandhi in South Africa*, Cornell, Ithaca, 1971.

Iqbal, Afzal, *Mohamed Ali*, Idarah-i-Adabiyat, Delhi, 1978.

Irwin (Halifax), *Fulness of Days*, Collins, London, 1957.

Iyer, Raghavan, *The Moral and Political Thought of Mahatma Gandhi*, OUP, New Delhi, 1973.

———, *The Essential Writings of Mahatma Gandhi*, OUP, Delhi, 1991.

Jones, E. Stanley, *Gandhi*, Abingdon, Nashville, 1948.

Juneja, M.M., *The Mahatma and the Millionaire*, Modern, Hissar, 1993.

Kalarthi, Mukul, *Ba and Bapu*, Navajivan, Ahmedabad, 1962.

Kalelkar, D.B., *Bapu ki Jhankian*, Navajivan, Ahmedabad, 1948.

———, *Gandhi Charitra Kirtan*, Navajivan, Ahmedabad, 1970.

Kamath, M.V. & Kher, V.B., *The Story of Militant but Nonviolent Trade Unionism*, Navajivan, Ahmedabad, 1993.

Kapur, Sudarshan, *Raising Up a Prophet: The African-American Encounter with Gandhi*, OUP, Delhi, 1993.

Keer, Dhananjay, *Dr Ambedkar*, Popular, Bombay, 1954.

————, *Mahatma Gandhi,* Popular, Bombay, 1973.

Khaliquzzaman, Choudhary, *Pathway to Pakistan*, Pakistan Longman, Lahore, 1961.

Khosla, G.D., *A Taste of India*, Jaico, Bombay, 1970.

Kripalani, J.B., *Autobiography* (Typescript), Kripalani Papers, New Delhi.

————, *Gandhi: His Life and Thought*, Publications Division, New Delhi, 1970.

Kripalani, Krishna, *Gandhi: A Life*, NBT, New Delhi, 1968.

Krishnadas, *Seven Months with Mahatma Gandhi*, Ganesan, Madras, 1928.

Limaye, Madhu, *Prime Movers*, Radiant, New Delhi, 1985.

Lohia, Rammanohar, *Guilty Men of India's Partition*, Kitabistan, Allahabad, 1960.

Mani, P., *The Secret of Mahatma Gandhi*, Arnold, New Delhi, 1989.

Mansergh, N. and Lumby, E.W.R., (ed.), *The Transfer of Power* (12 vols.), Her Majesty's Stationery Office, London, 1970-83.

Mashruwala, K.G., *In Quest of Truth*, Shravana, Ahmedabad, 1983.

Mende, Tibor, *Conversations with Nehru*, Wilco, Bombay, 1958.

Menon, V.P., *The Transfer of Power in India*, Orient Longmans, Calcutta, 1957.

Merriam, A.H., *Gandhi vs. Jinnah,* Minerva, Calcutta, 1980.

Mira Behn, *The Spirit's Pilgrimage*, Longmans Green, London, 1960.

Mishra, D.P., *Living an Era* (2 vols.), Vikas, New Delhi, 1978.

Moon, Penderel, *Divide and Quit*, Berkeley, 1962.

————, (ed.), *Wavell: The Viceroy's Journal*, OUP, London, 1973.

————, *Gandhi and Modern India*, The English Universities Press, London, 1968.

Moore, R.J., *Escape from Empire,* Clarendon, Oxford, 1983.

————, *Endgames of Empire*, Oxford, New Delhi, 1988.

Moraes, Frank, *Witness to an Era*, Weidenfeld & Nicolson, London, 1973.

Moran, *Winston Churchill*, Constable, London, 1966.

Mujahid, Sharif Al, *Quaid-i-Azam M.A. Jinnah*, Karachi, 1981.

Munshi, K.M., *Pilgrimage to Freedom*, Bhavan, Bombay, 1967.

Namboodiripad, E.M.S., *A History of India's Freedom Struggle*, Social Scientist Press, Trivandrum.

Nanda, B.R., *Gandhi: Pan-Islamism, Imperialism and Nationalism* OUP, Delhi, 1989.

————, *Gokhale, Gandhi and the Nehrus*, Allen & Unwin, London, 1974.

Nandy, Ashis, *At the Edge of Psychology*, OUP, Delhi, 1980.

Nayar, Sushila, *Bapu ki Karavaas Kahani*, Sasta Sahitya Mandal, New Delhi, 1950.

————, *Mahatma Gandhi* (vols. 4 & 5), Navajivan, Ahmedabad, 1989 & 1994.

————, *In Gandhiji's Mirror*, OUP, Delhi, 1991.

Nehru, Jawaharlal, *The Discovery of India*, John Day, New York, 1946.

Omvedt, Gail, *Dalits & the Democratic Revolution*, Sage, New Delhi, 1994.

Padmanabhan, R.A., *V.V.S. Aiyyar*, NBT, New Delhi, 1991.

Panter-Brick, Simone, *Gandhi against Machiavellism*, Asia, Bombay, 1966.

Parekh, Bhikhu, *Colonialism, Tradition, and Reform*, Sage, New Delhi, 1989.

Parikh, Narhari, *Sardar Vallabhbhai Patel* (2 vols.), Navajivan, Ahmedabad, 1971.

Patel, C.N., *Mahatma Gandhi in his Gujarati Writings*, Sahitya Akademi, New Delhi, 1981.

Patel, Ravjibhai, *The Making of the Mahatma*, Ahmedabad, 1990.

Philips, C.H., and Wainwright, M.D., (ed.), *The Partition of India*, Allen & Unwin, London, 1970.

Pirzada, S.S., (ed.), *Quaid-i-Azam's Correspondence*, East and West, Karachi, 1977.

Prasad, Rajendra, *Autobiography*, Asia, Bombay, 1957.

Publications Division, *1921 Movement: Reminiscences*, New Delhi, 1971.

Pyarelal, *The Epic Fast*, Navajivan, Ahmedabad, 1932.

———, *The Early Phase*, Navajivan, Ahmedabad, 1965.

———, *The Last Phase* (2 vols.), Navajivan, Ahmedabad, 1956.

Ramachandran, G., *Thoughts and Talks*, Madurai, 1964.

Rao, B. Shiva, *India's Freedom Movement*, Orient Longmans, Madras, 1960.

Ravindran, T.K., *Vaikkam Satyagraha and Gandhi*, Sri Narayana Institute, Trichur, 1975.

Reddy, E.S., and Gandhi, Gopalkrishna, (ed.), *Gandhi and South Africa*, Navajivan, Ahmedabad, 1993.

Rizvi, Gowher, *Linlithgow and India*, Royal Historical Society, London, 1978.

Roy, Dilip Kumar, *Among the Great*, Jaico, Bombay, 1950.

Roy, Ramashray, *Self and Society: A Study in Gandhian Thought*, Sage, New Delhi, 1984.

Rudolph, Susanne, H. and Lloyd I., *Gandhi: The Traditional Roots of Charisma*, Orient Longman, 1987.

Rustin, Bayard, *Down the Lane*, Quadrangle, Chicago, 1971.

Saxena, S.K., *Ever Unto God*, Indian Council of Philosophical Research, New Delhi, 1988.

Seshadri, H.V., *The Tragic Story of Partition*, Bangalore, 1982.

Sharp, Gene, *Gandhi as a Political Strategist*, Extending Horizon, Boston, 1979.

———, *Gandhi Faces the Storm*, Navajivan, Ahmedabad, 1961.

———, *Gandhi Wields the Weapon of Moral Power*, Navajivan, Ahmedabad, 1960.

Sheean, Vincent, *Lead Kindly Light*, Random House, New York, 1949.

Shirer, William, L., *Gandhi: A Memoir*, Rupa, Calcutta, 1993.

Shukla, Chandrashanker, (ed.), *Incidents in Gandhiji's Life*, Vora, Bombay, 1949.

———, (ed.), *Reminiscences of Gandhiji*, Vora, Bombay, 1951.

Singh, A.I., *The Origins of the Partition of India*, Oxford, New Delhi, 1987.

Sitaramayya, Pattabhi, *The History of the Indian National Congress, 1935-47*, Padma, Bombay, 1947.

Studdert-Kennedy, Gerald, *British Christians, Indian Nationalists and the Raj*, OUP, Delhi, 1991.

Swan, Maureen, *Gandhi: The South African Experience*, Ravan, Johannesburg, 1985.

Tagore, Rabindranath, *Mahatma Gandhi*, Visva-Bharati, 1963.

Templewood, *Nine Troubled Years*, Collins, London, 1954.

Tendulkar, D.G., *Mahatma* (8 vols.), Bombay, 1951.

Tendulkar, *Abdul Ghaffar Khan*, Popular, Bombay, 1967.

Watson, Francis, and Brown, Maurice, *Talking of Gandhiji*, Orient Longmans, Calcutta, 1957.

Wolpert, Stanley, *Jinnah*, Oxford, New York, 1984.

Woodcock, George, *Gandhi,* Fontana/Collins, London, 1974.

Yagnik, Indulal, *Gandhi as I Knew Him*, Danish Mahal, New Delhi, 1943.

Ziegler, P., *Mountbatten*, Collins, London, 1985.

Notes

Introduction

1. *Collected Works*, Vol. 48, p.364.
2. See *Homage*, Publications Division, Delhi, 1949, p.27.
3. Tolstoy quoted in Green, *Gandhi*, Continuum, New York, 1993, pp.198-9; Gokhale in Karve and Ambedkar (ed.), *Speeches and Writings of G.K. Gokhale*, Asia, Bombay,1966, Vol.2, p.420.
4. In *A Commemorative Volume*, Office of Information, Central Tibetan Secretariat, Dharamsala, 1990.
5. Message of 23 June 1995, in the files of the Tibetan Office, New Delhi.

Chapter 1: *Nonviolence*

1. Devanesen, *The Making of the Mahatma*, p.221.
2. Hunt, *Gandhi in London*, p.48.
3. Green, *Gandhi*, p.247.
4. Ibid., p.14.
5. Rajendra Prasad, *Autobiography*, p.104.
6. To N.R.Malkani, as quoted by him in Shukla (ed.), *Incidents in Gandhiji's Life*, p.158.
7. Francis Watson, *Talking of Gandhiji*, p.47.
8. Raihana Tyabji in Watson, *Talking of Gandhiji*, p.48.
9. From entries in *The Diary of Mahadev Desai*, May 1932, and Narayan Desai, *Agnikundma Ugelun Gulab*, Ahmedabad, 1992.
10. See R. Gandhi, *The Rajaji Story*, vol.2, p.49; and R. Gandhi, *Patel*, p.283.

11. Ghani Khan quoted in Tendulkar, *Abdul Ghaffar Khan*, p.425.
12. Quoted in Shukla, *Incidents*, pp.107-8.
13. Tendulkar, *Mahatma*, vol.2, p.131.
14. From Robert A. Huttenback, *Gandhi in South Africa*, p.330. Huttenback cites W.K.Hancock, *Smuts*, p.345.
15. Quoted in Mira Behn, *The Spirit's Pilgrimage*, p.143.
16. Quoted in Bhabani Bhattacharya, *Mahatma Gandhi*, pp.193-4.
17. Quoted in Bhikhu Parekh, *Colonialism, Tradition and Reform*, p.167.
18. Ibid., pp.162-3.
19. Ibid., p.121.

Chapter 2: *Two Inner Voices*

1. Andrews quoted in Homer Jack, *The Gandhi Reader,* pp.389-91.
2. Mahadev Desai, *Day-to-day with Gandhi*, vol.1, pp.60-2.
3. Kalelkar, *Bapu ki Jhankian*, p.99.
4. In Shukla (ed.), *Reminiscences of Gandhi*, p.188.
5. *Congress Report on the Punjab Disorders*, p.34.
6. Quoted in Tendulkar, *Mahatma*, vol.2, p.176.
7. See Kalelkar, *Gandhi Charitra Kirtan*, p.70.
8. In Desai-Parikh Correspondence, Gandhi Sangrahalaya, New Delhi.
9. Ibid.
10. Kalelkar, *Bapu ki Jhankian*, p.22.

Chapter 3: *Violence*

1. P. Moon, *Gandhi and Modern India*, The English Universities Press, London, 1968, p.289.
2. Quoted in Watson, *Talking of Gandhiji*, p.37.
3. Ibid., p.37.
4. See Devanesen, *The Making of the Mahatma*, p.316.
5. Birla, *A Talk on Bapu*, Sangeet Kala Mandir, Calcutta, 24.12.81.

6. See Kalelkar, *Gandhi Charitra Kirtan*, p.178 and pp.188-9.
7. Bose, *Lectures on Gandhism*, p.112.
8. See Kantilal Shah, *Gandhi Jaisa Dekha Samjha Vinoba Ne*, Sarva Seva Sangh, Varanasi, 1970, p.4.
9. Quoted in Martin Green, *The Mahatmas*, p.28.
10. Churchill, *My African Journey*, The Holland Press, London, 1962 Reprint, pp.35-7.
11. In Shukla (ed.), *Incidents*, pp.41-4.
12. In Prabhudas Gandhi, *Jeevan Prabhat*, Sasta Sahitya Mandal, New Delhi, 1961, pp.197-8.
13. Letter of 21.12.17 in Desai, *Day-to-day with Gandhi*, vol.1, p.4.
14. Sushila Nayar, *Mahatma Gandhi*, vol.4, p.739.
15. Quoted in Karve and Ambedkar (ed.), *Speeches and Writings of G.K.Gokhale*, Asia, Bombay, 1966, vol.2, p.420.
16. Quoted in Khaliquzzaman, *Pathway to Pakistan*, p.33.
17. In March 1918. See Desai, *Day-to-day with Gandhi*, vol.1, pp.56-7.
18. Ibid., p.157.
19. Ibid., p.182.
20. Indulal Yagnik, *Gandhi As I Knew Him*, Danish Mahal, New Delhi, 1943, pp.9-10.
21. Desai, *Day-to-day with Gandhi*, vol.2, pp.323-6.
22. Pyarelal, *In Gandhiji's Mirror*, pp.5-7.
23. Letter of 18.2.20 in Desai, *Day-to-day with Gandhi*, vol.1, pp.54-5 fn.
24. Hore to Montagu in Iqbal, *Mohamed Ali*, p.212.
25. Ibid., p.199.
26. Quoted in Dhananjay Keer, *Mahatma Gandhi*, p.324.
27. R. Gandhi, *Understanding the Muslim Mind*, p.100.
28. Iqbal, *Mohamed Ali*, p.267.
29. Ibid., p.267.
30. Tendulkar, *Mahatma*, vol.2, p.89.
31. Iqbal, *Mohamed Ali*, p.285.
32. Narhari Parikh, *Sardar Patel*, Navajivan, Ahmedabad, vol.1, p.165.

33. Quoted in Limaye, *Prime Movers*, p.34.
34. Sitaramayya, *History of the Indian National Congress*, vol.1, pp.755-63.
35. Sayyid, *Jinnah*, p.433.
36. See Allana, *Jinnah*, p.213.
37. Lester quoted in Watson, *Talking of Gandhiji*, p.75.
38. Most London conversations including with Sheridan from ibid., pp.70-85.
39. Shukla (ed.), *Incidents*, pp.84-5.
40. Templewood, *Nine Troubled Years*, Collins, London, 1954, pp.59-60; and Pyarelal, *Mirror*, p.22.
41. Templewood, *Nine Troubled Years*, p.58.

Chapter 4: *East vs. West*

1. Entry dated 11.8.1950 in the Diary of Maniben Patel.
2. On 19.10.39. Linlithgow Papers, India Office Library, London.
3. From J. Ahmad (ed.), *Historic Documents of the Muslim Freedom Movement,* Publishers United, Lahore, p.372.
4. Linlithgow to Zetland, 18.11.39, quoted in Gopal, *Nehru*, vol.1, p.258.
5. See Birla's contribution in Shukla (ed.), *Incidents*, pp.26ff. and *Collected Works* 76:63.
6. Note dated 3.8.42 for Horace Alexander in 76:361-2.
7. On 31.8.42. See Linlithgow Papers, F125/158, India Office Library, London.
8. Birla in Shukla (ed.), *Incidents*, p.27.
9. In M.M.Juneja, *The Mahatma and the Millionaire*, Hissar,1993, pp.201-3.
10. Lord Moran, *Winston Churchill*, Constable, London, 1966, p.52.
11. Watson, *Talking of Gandhiji*, p.93.

Chapter 5: *'Hind Swaraj'*

1. Devanesen, *The Making of the Mahatma*, pp.357-63.
2. See Gandhi to Polak, 30.7.09, in 9:322.
3. Prabhudas Gandhi, *My Childhood with Gandhi*, p.90.
4. See 71:238.
5. Rajan in Shukla (ed.), *Incidents*, pp.259-61.
6. In Shukla (ed.), *Reminiscences*, p.17.
7. Preface to 1921 edition, reprinted in *Hind Swaraj*, 1938 edn., Navajivan, Ahmedabad, p.xxv.
8. See Gandhi's speech, 21.2.40, in 71:238.
9. Devanesen, *The Making of the Mahatma*, p.368.
10. Prabhudas Gandhi, *Jeevan Prabhat*, p.87.
11. A.J.Parel in *Gandhi Marg*, Oct.-Dec.1991.
12. Preface to 1921 edn. reprinted in *Hind Swaraj* (1938), p.xxxiii.
13. Vinson Brown, *Voices of Earth and Sky*, Stackpole, U.S.A.,1974, pp.176-7.

Chapter 6: *Gandhi and his God*

1. To Mott in 1938, in M.K.Gandhi, *Christian Missions*, p.186.
2. M.K.Gandhi, *My Dear Child*, Navajivan, 1956, p.106.
3. In Anand Hingorani (ed.), *God is Truth*, p.80.
4. Desai, *Day-to-day with Gandhi*, vol.1, pp.2-3.
5. 11.5.18. Ibid., p.126.
6. 13.1.17. Ibid., p.1.
7. E.S.Jones, *Gandhi*, Abingdon, Nashville, 1948, pp.33-4.
8. Pyarelal, *Last Phase*, vol.1, p.62.
9. Written on 16.3.46. In Shukla (ed.), *Incidents*, pp.99-100.
10. M.K.Gandhi, *Indian States' Problem*, Navajivan, Ahmedabad,1941, p.561.
11. Hingorani (ed.), *God is Truth*, Bombay, 1957, p.84.
12. Kalelkar, *Bapu ki Jhankian*, pp.24-5.
13. Quoted in Green, *Gandhi*, p.13.
14. Mukul Kalarthi, *Ba and Bapu*, Navajivan, 1962, pp.63-4.
15. Ibid., pp.44-5.
16. See Gandhi's letter to Father W. Lash, 5.2.33, in 53:229; and

account of conversation with E.Stanley Jones in 53:259.

17. Desai, *Day-to-day with Gandhi*, vol.2, p.217.
18. Green, *Gandhi*, p.284.
19. Ibid., p.284.
20. Ramnarayan Chaudhary, *Bapu As I Saw Him*, Navajivan, Ahmedabad, 1959, p.174.
21. Kalarthi, *Ba and Bapu*, p.108.
22. Ibid., p.49.
23. Ibid., p.118.
24. Narayan Desai, *Bliss was it to be young — with Gandhi*, Bharatiya Vidya Bhavan, Bombay, 1968, p.72.
25. Ibid., pp.73-4.
26. On 8.6.47; from Manu Gandhi's diary. See 88:105.
27. Kalarthi, *Ba and Bapu*, pp.40-2.
28. Green, *Gandhi*, p.12.
29. On 31.7.18. See Desai, *Day-to-day*, vol.1, p.201.
30. On 23.2.19. Ibid., pp.293-4.
31. On 26.11.18. Ibid., p.264.
32. Devadas Gandhi, *Ba, Bapu Aur Bhai*, Sasta Sahitya Mandal, New Delhi, 1956, p.28.
33. Sudhir Ghosh, *Gandhi's Emissary*, pp.68-9.
34. Tendulkar, *Mahatma*, vol.2, p.405.
35. Ibid., p.93.
36. Devadas Gandhi, *Ba, Bapu Aur Bhai*, p.16.
37. Ibid., p.29.
38. Birla, *A Talk on Bapu*, Calcutta.
39. In Juneja, *The Mahatma and the Millionaire*, pp.76-7.
40. N.K.Bose, *My Days with Gandhi*, Nishana, Calcutta, 1953, p.8; and N.K.Bose, *Lectures on Gandhism*, Navajivan, p.65.
41. Bose, *Lectures on Gandhism*, p.106.
42. Told to author in 1993 by L.P.Singh, witness to the scene as a Bihar Govt. officer.
43. Kalelkar, *Bapu ki Jhankian*, p.130.
44. Ibid., pp.129-30.
45. Ibid., pp.106-7 & p.116.
46. Bose, *My Days with Gandhi*, pp.60-2.

47. Quoted in Bose, *Lectures on Gandhism*, pp.61-2.
48. Khosla, *A Taste of India*, Jaico, Bombay, 1970, pp.21-2.
49. Roy, *Among the Great*, Jaico, Bombay, 1950, p.110.
50. Sheean, *Lead Kindly Light*, Random House, New York, 1949, pp.190-3.
51. Manu Gandhi, *The Lonely Pilgrim*, Navajivan, p.45 and p.93.
52. 29.3.36. See Sushila Nayar, *Mahatma Gandhi*, vol.3, p.68.
53. On 10.3.18. Desai, *Day-to-day*, vol.1, pp.60-2.
54. Roy, *Among the Great*, p.111.
55. Bose, *My Days with Gandhi*, p.191.
56. On 12.8.47. Ibid., p.261.
57. 20.12.32. See David M. Gracie (ed.), *Gandhi and Charlie*, Cowley, Cambridge, Mass., 1989, p.158.
58. C.F.Andrews, *Mahatma Gandhi: His Own Story*, Allen & Unwin, 1930, p.225.
59. Margaret Chatterjee, *Gandhi's Religious Thought*, Macmillan, New Delhi, 1983, p.69.
60. Quoted in Green, *Gandhi*, p.229.
61. Woodcock, *Gandhi*, Fontana/Collins, London, 1974, p.54.
62. To Esther Faering in Desai, *Day-to-day*, vol.1, p.78.
63. Chatterjee, *Gandhi's Religious Thought*, p.1 and p.57.
64. See Andrews, *Mahatma Gandhi At Work*, Allen and Unwin, London, 1931, p.402.
65. *Speeches and Writings of Mahatma Gandhi*, Natesan, Madras, 1922, pp.153-66.
66. *Harijan*, 24.12.38.
67. Bose, *My Days with Gandhi*, pp.149-50.
68. Desai, *The Diary of Mahadev Desai*, vol.1, p.77.
69. Letter of 24.7.32 to Kalelkar. Ibid., p.252.
70. *Bombay Chronicle*, 5.2.24.
71. Manu Gandhi, *The Lonely Pilgrim*, p.50 and pp.167-8.

Chapter 7: *The Colour Line*

1. Sushila Nayar, *Mahatma Gandhi*, vol.4, p.168.
2. Ravjibhai Patel, *The Making of the Mahatma*, Ahmedabad, 1989, pp.216-7.

3. In Maureen Swan, *Gandhi: The South African Experience*, Ravan, Johannesburg, 1985, p.133.
4. In 'Gandhi the Prisoner' by Mandela in B R Nanda (ed.), *Mahatma Gandhi — 125 Years*, Indian Council for Cultural Relations, New Delhi, 1995, p.150.
5. Prabhudas Gandhi, *Jeevan Prabhat*, p.105.
6. Gracie (ed.), *Gandhi and Charlie*, p.33.
7. James Hunt, *Gandhi and the Nonconformists*, Promilla, Delhi, 1986, p.110.
8. *Speeches and Writings of Mahatma Gandhi*, Natesan, Madras, 1922, p.175.
9. Yagnik, *Gandhi As I Knew Him*, p.303.
10. Rustin, *Down the Line*, Quadrangle, Chicago, 1971, p.103.

Chapter 8: *Castes and Outcastes*

1. Ravjibhai Patel, *The Making of the Mahatma*, p.102.
2. Quoted in Ainslee Embree, *India's Search for National Identity*, Chanakya, Delhi, 1988, p.1.
3. Tibor Mende, *Conversations with Nehru*, Wilco, Bombay, 1958, pp.24-7.
4. Gracie (ed.), *Gandhi and Charlie*, p.135.
5. T.K.Ravindran, *Vaikkam Satyagraha & Gandhi*, Sri Narayana Institute, Trichur, 1975, p.89.
6. Gail Omvedt, *Dalits & the Democratic Revolution*, Sage, New Delhi, 1994, pp.151-2.
7. Rustin, *Down the Line*, pp.292-3.
8. Watson, *Talking of Gandhiji*, p.16.
9. Desai, *The Diary of Mahadev Desai*, vol.1, p.52.
10. Shirer, *Gandhi: A Memoir*, Rupa, Calcutta, 1993, p.162.
11. Gracie (ed.), *Gandhi and Charlie*, p.155.
12. See dedication to Mahatma Jotiba Phule in Ambedkar, *Who Were The Shudras?*, Bombay.
13. Gracie (ed.), *Gandhi and Charlie*, p.178.
14. In 1936. Keer, *Dr Ambedkar*, Popular, Bombay, 1962, p.254.
15. Ibid., p.258.

16. Ibid., p.495.
17. Told to author in Bombay, 1994, by S.Ramakrishnan, who was present.
18. G. Ramachandran, *Thoughts and Talks*, Madurai, 1964, p.179.
19. Talk with Syed Mahmud, New Delhi, 26.7.47, in 88:434.
20. Khairmode quoted in M.S.Gore, *The Social Context of an Ideology,* Sage, New Delhi, 1993, pp.180-1.
21. Durgadas (ed.), *Sardar Patel's Correspondence*, vol.6, Navajivan, p.302.

Chapter 9: *Partition*

1. R. Gandhi, *Understanding the Muslim Mind*, p.25.
2. Bipan Chandra, *Communalism in Modern India*, pp.145-6.
3. Previous three quotes from ibid., p.14 and p.26.
4. Ibid., pp.244-5.
5. 5.9.39. Ibid., p.270.
6. H.V.Sesnadri, *The Tragic Story of Partition*, Bangalore, 1982, p.115.
7. Bipan Chandra, *Communalism*, pp.215-6 and p.118.
8. Ibid., p.96.
9. K.M.Munshi, *Pilgrimage to Freedom*, pp.47-8.
10. Mushirul Hasan (ed.), *India's Partition*, OUP, Delhi, 1993, pp. 401-2.
11. Quoted in R. Gandhi, *Patel,* p.262.
12. Linlithgow to Zetland, 25.9.39, in Linlithgow Papers, India Office Library, London.
13. See Gowher Rizvi, *Linlithgow and India*, Royal Historical Society, London, 1978, p.90.
14. See R. Gandhi, *India Wins Errors*, pp.22-3.
15. Rizvi, *Linlithgow and India*, p.102, citing letters from Linlithgow.
16. Ibid., p.102.
17. Hodson, *The Great Divide*, Hutchinson, London, 1969, p.89.
18. Ibid., p.83.
19. Told to author in 1974 by B.Shiva Rao of *The Hindu*, the intermediary between Sikandar and Srinivasan.

20. Linlithgow to Hope, 8.5.41, in Linlithgow Papers, India Office Library, London.

21. Contribution dated 3.2.46 by Birla in Shukla (ed.), *Incidents*, p.26.

22. A file in the National Archives in New Delhi, seen by the author, quotes an admission by a well-known Delhi journalist to an official of the Central Intelligence Department that the words were his. The file number has been mislaid.

23. Hodson, *The Great Divide*, p.103.

24. Quoted in Philips and Wainwright (ed.), *The Partition of India*, p.214.

25. Ibid., p.185.

26. Hodson, *The Great Divide*, p.106.

27. M.Yunus, *Persons, Passions & Politics*, Vikas,1980, p.15.

28. See A.H.Merriam, *Gandhi and Jinnah*, p.89.

29. R. Gandhi, *The Rajaji Story*, vol.2, p.102.

30. Jinnah quoted in the Aga Khan, *Memoirs*, Cassell, London, 1954, p.94.

31. Hodson, *The Great Divide*, p.124.

32. Message from London to Delhi quoted in A.I.Singh, *The Origins of the Partition of India*, 1987, pp.121-3.

33. Hodson, *The Great Divide*, p.125.

34. Cripps in the House of Commons, 18.7.46, quoted in Philips and Wainwright (ed.), *The Partition of India*, p.218.

35. R.Gandhi, *Understanding the Muslim Mind*, p.167.

36. Pyarelal, *The Last Phase*, vol.1, pp.238-9.

37. 23.10.46. See Hodson, *The Great Divide*, p.174.

38. Pyarelal, *The Last Phase*, vol.1, p.251.

39. Letter of 17.7.46 quoted in Munshi, *Pilgrimage*, p.446.

40. Nehru, Jinnah and Gandhi quoted in Philips and Wainwright (ed.), *The Partition of India*, p.466.

41. Campbell-Johnson, *Mission with Mountbatten*, p.57.

42. Entry of 13.4.47. Rajagopalachari Papers.

43. Stanley Wolpert, *Jinnah*, Oxford, New York, 1984, p.317.

44. Quoted in Ambedkar, *Thoughts on Pakistan*, Bombay, 1941, pp.132-3.

45. Gillian Wright in *The Book Review*, New Delhi, issue of Feb.-Mar. 1994.
46. Ambedkar, *Thoughts on Pakistan*, p.190.
47. See Collins and Lapierre, *Mountbatten and the Partition of India*, Vikas, New Delhi, 1981, vol.1, pp.68-9; and Hodson, *The Great Divide*, p.318.
48. See Asim Roy, *The High Politics of India's Partition* in M.Hasan (ed.), *India's Partition*.
49. Girilal Jain quoted by T.N.Madan in *Times of India*, New Delhi, 19.11.94.

Chapter 10: *Sons & Heirs*

1. See Munshi, *Pilgrimage*, p.53; and A.C.Guha, *India's Struggle*, 1921-46, Part 1, New Delhi, 1982, p.425.
2. As witnessed by Ramnarayan Chaudhary and recorded in his *Bapu As I Saw Him*, Navajivan, 1959, p.217.
3. 23.1.28. Quoted in Gopal, *Nehru*, vol.1, p.112.
4. Brecher, *Nehru*, OUP, London, 1959, p.137.
5. Namboodiripad, *India's Freedom Struggle*, p.388.
6. Quoted in Durgadas, *From Curzon to Nehru and After*, p.134.
7. Brecher, *Nehru*, p.142.
8. Quoted in Gopal, *Nehru*, vol.1, p.210.
9. J.B.Kripalani, *Autobiography* (Typescript), pp.390-1.
10. Namboodiripad, *India's Freedom Struggle*, p.649.
11. File 4/23, Pyarelal Papers, New Delhi.
12. From entry of 16.9.48 in the diary of Maniben Patel, Ahmedabad; Kripalani, *Gandhi*, pp.248-9; and Durgadas (ed.), *Sardar Patel's Correspondence*, vol.10, p.xxxviii.
13. Kripalani, *Autobiography* (Typescript), p.236.
14. See, e.g., Durgadas, *Curzon to Nehru*, p.134.
15. See remarks by Maniben Patel in Durgadas (ed.), *Sardar Patel's Correspondence*, vol.10, p.xxxviii; and Durgadas, *Curzon to Nehru*, p.230.
16. See R. Gandhi, *Patel*, p.371 and p.583.
17. Durgadas, *Curzon to Nehru*, p.230.

18. See Brecher, *Nehru*, p.315.
19. G.L.Mehta in Shukla (ed.), *Incidents*, p.185.
20. D.P.Mishra, *Living An Era*, vol.2, pp.185-6.
21. B.Shiva Rao, *India's Freedom Movement*, pp.69-70.
22. Brecher, *Nehru*, p.100.
23. Bose, *Lectures on Gandhism*, Navjivan, 1971, p.112.

Chapter 11: *The Last Lap*

1. Amiya Chakravarty quoted in Gene Sharp, *Gandhi Wields the Weapon of Moral Power*, Navajivan, pp.259-60.
2. See 89:124-54; and Dalton, 'Gandhi During Partition' in Philips & Wainwright (ed.), *Partition of India*, pp.259-60.
3. In 'Czech Memories' by Miloslav Krasa in B.R. Nanda (ed.), *Mahatma Gandhi: 125 Years*, ICCR, New Delhi, 1995, p.104
4. See 90:342.
5. Brij Krishna, *Gandhiji ki Dilli Diary*, vol.3, p.287; and Nehru to Patel, 27.10.48 in *Sardar Patel's Correspondence*, vol.7, p.672.
6. In Birla, *A Talk on Bapu*, Calcutta, 1981.
7. Brecher, *Nehru*, p.269.
8. Jehangir Patel and Marjorie Sykes, *Gandhi: His Gift of the Fight*, Rasvlia, 1987, p.188.
9. Ibid., p.187
10. Account of fast from 90:408-54; and Sharp, *Gandhi Wields*.
11. Account of Gandhi's last day and hours from 90:530-6; Brij Krishna, *Gandhiji ki Dilli Diary*, vol.3, pp.576-81; and Kanu and Abha Gandhi, *Bapu Ke Sath*, New Delhi, 1990, pp.50-1.

Chapter 12: *In Perspective*

1. R. Iyer (ed.), *The Essential Writings of Mahatma Gandhi*, pp.80-1.
2. See Narayan Desai, *Agnikundma Ugelun Gulab*, Ahmedabad, 1992, pp. 392-5.

3. Desai, *Day-to-day with Gandhi*, vol.1, pp.56-7.
4. See Green, *The Mahatmas*, p.26.
5. Sushila Nayar, *Bapu ki Karavaas Kahani*, p.316.
6. Millie Polak, *Mr Gandhi: The Man*, p.142
7. To author in Austria, 1978.
8. Kalelkar, *Gandhi Charitra Kirtan*, pp.52-7.
9. In Raghavan Iyer, *The Moral and Political Thought of Mahatma Gandhi*, vol.2, pp.559-60.
10. Bose, *Lectures on Gandhism*, pp.105-6.
11. Ibid., p.63.
12. Kalelkar, *Gandhi Charitra Kirtan, p.70*; Kalelkar, *Bapu ki Jhankian*, p.124; and R.Iyer, *Essential Writings of Gandl:i*, p.39 and p.242.
13. Kalelkar, *Gandhi Charitra Kirtan*, p.42 and p.133.
14. *Young India*, 6.6.29.
15. King, *Trumpet of Conscience*, Hodder and Stoughton, London, 1968, pp.68-9.
16. In 'The Making of the Mahatma' by Fatima Meer in Nanda (ed.), *Mahatma Gandhi: 125 Years*, ICCR, New Delhi, 1995, p.46
17. Kalelkar, *Gandhi Charitra Kirtan*, pp.50-1.
18. Ibid., pp.74-5.
19. In Rabindranath Tagore, *Mahatma Gandhi*, Visva-Bharati, 1963, p.62.
20. See Kalelkar, *Gandhi Charitra Kirtan*, p.68.
21. Kalelkar, *Bapu ki Jhankian*, pp.95-6.
22. Bhabani Bhattacharya, *Mahatma Gandhi*, Arnold Heinemann, New Delhi, 1977, pp.13-4.
23. Quoted in Gene Sharp, *Gandhi Wields*, p.226.

Index